Aerial 10
Lyn Hejinian

edited by
Rod Smith & Jen Hofer

Edge Books

for Leslie Scalapino

This book began its existence nearly ten years ago, as an invitation to Lyn from Luigi-Bob Drake, who was then in the process of publishing *A Wild Salience: The Writing of Rae Armantrout* on his Burning Press imprint. He asked Lyn if Burning Press might publish a volume of critical writing about her work. She agreed, with the caveat that the book could not be a festschrift, but rather should be an exploration of ideas occasioned by her work, in no way bound to a celebration of it. Lyn asked Summi Kaipa and me if we would be willing to edit such a book, and we enthusiastically agreed. Lyn, Summi and I together came up with a list of writers we wanted to ask to participate in the project; most of the texts in the present volume were generously written in response to these initial queries. Luigi-Bob and Burning Press both mysteriously disappeared some time after we began work on the "hejproj," as we called it; that mystery, coupled with some enormously educational but less-than-graceful editorial hijinx on Summi's and my part early on in the process, occasioned a rather lengthy pause which was thankfully ended by the characteristically chivalrous and tranquilly brilliant entrance on the scene of Rod Smith. By the time the hejproj had found its current and very apt home with *Aerial*, Summi (now Dr. Kaipa) had begun work toward a PhD and decided to focus her energies on her studies; I have thus had the great good fortune to work with not one but two superb partners in crime on this endeavor. I am endlessly grateful to Summi for her friendship and literary companionship, for traveling many wide roads with me over many years. I am also grateful for the trust and patience of the writers involved in this snail-paced project, whose contributions to this book have galvanized my thinking about writing process, literary ethics, and the activation of an alternate political imagination in ways I expect to reverberate in my own practice far into the future. I experience Lyn's public presence (and by "presence" here I mean both her writing and her way of being in the world) and her friendship as a challenge and an inspiration—as something to live up to, to work toward, with which to be in conversation in internal and public landscapes—and by extension, I experience the writing in the current volume similarly, as the furthering of a conversation in which I feel thankful to participate, the existence of which provides the necessary context and propulsion for my own thinking and making.

In the introduction to *The Language of Inquiry*, Lyn posits language as relation inflected by context. "Language is nothing but meanings, and meanings are nothing but a flow of contexts. Such contexts rarely coalesce into images, rarely come to terms. They are transitions, transmutations, the endless radiating of denotation into relation." (1) This book is a constellation of non-coalescing texts—repeating and open-ended attempts—that engage the ideas and formal impulses in Lyn's work. This book is contexts. It is denotation and relation, radiating spokes inciting further radiations, further relations. Relation does not hold still—it is never the same as itself from one minute, instance, context to the next. It is a mobile move in a field of mobility; what we might contain, momentarily, are moments, temporary rivets that are points of departure toward an elsewhere that glances off this surface, veering us toward that one.

Dynamic processes in chorus: to be concussive rather than conclusive

Earlier in the same introduction, Lyn affirms the "dynamic process" of poetics as carried out through the "dynamic process" of poetry; "(t)he two practices are mutually constitutive and they are reciprocally transformative. It is at least in part for this reason that poetry has its capacity for poetics, for self-reflexivity, for speaking about itself; it is by virtue of this that poetry can turn language upon itself and thus exceed its own limits." (1) It's not that Lyn's work has no limits—and these writings occasioned by her work are likewise not without limits—it's that the impulse to exceed the limitations that structure any endeavor is inherent to the work. Each text suggests and incites other texts (or other thoughtful iterations of experience in the form of conversations, meals, walks down the street, music, visits to friends, etc). Nothing is complete, other than praxis, which is completing without completion.

The texts in the present volume are poems, letters, musings, memoirs, arguments, scholarly contemplations, experiments, formulations, attempts, conversations: a range of views through and toward and spanning out from the ideas and language Lyn inhabits in her own ongoing processes of inquiry, written by poets and thinkers who have been central to Lyn's work, and for whom Lyn's work has been of central importance, over a nearly thirty-five-year trajectory. This book is in no way definitive; the table of contents could easily be double or triple what it is and still only begin to represent the poetic, philosophical and political possibilities Lyn's work proposes and encourages, or the contemporary writers who have something usefully provocative to say in relation to those possibilities. As I experience it, this volume is more than anything an invitation to extend its parameters, to expand the conversations begun here into other spaces and toward other modes of thinking and expression.

Lyn's work encourages us to do our work, whatever that may be. Lyn was originally concerned that this book not become a festschrift; the concern, I think, is entirely unnecessary. Her work is constitutionally resistant to mere celebration of itself. Rather, it suggests celebration—and lament, which can be construed as a kind of celebration—of the world and all the complexity the world entails, and all the complex interrelation of us in the world, improvising and deliberating to make our contribution to a larger and more meaningfully cacophonous chorus. The concussive reverberates, where the conclusive closes. The concussive listens as it sounds, where the conclusive resolves. This book resolves nothing. It is a place to begin.

July 2008
Los Angeles

from The Book of a Thousand Eyes

Lyn Hejinian

Walking around, posing, entering conversations, proposing
Events are staged
Carefully, artfully, tentatively, and relentlessly
Though the stage is a little one
In a theater maintained exclusively for magnificent premieres
Of consciousness
Whose adagios are long and always in the middle
While the allegros promising jollity telling lies all around feature virtuosic bits
Whose Caribbean, Basque, or Romany origins can be heard
In the striking of the clock
Past noon or almost three or midnight
Which is always five o'clock
Somewhere
The cowboy drinks
A hurricane, the horse drinks from the lake a blue
That's gray or green and may be
Reproduced by mixing Dr. Ph. Martin's radiant concentrated Slate Blue (22B)
       with his or her radiant concentrated Saddle Brown (13A)
But that's mere speculation
As I'm writing this
Pretending to be a filmmaker
Cinematically
Making things unfold
Not gradually but all at once like a letter
Folded
In thirds taken from an envelope and opened
In 2 seconds
Its message divulged: "your insurance premiums are going up" or "it's time to
       renew
Your membership in the NAACP" or "My name is Philip
And I am offering you an opportunity"
To which I will not wake

But stare
Disconsolately at the window or out
It at the blowing leaves on the light green tree
That cheers me
Up so I get up
And go
Into a room which is a robe
Left by an aerialist now on high in flesh-colored tights swinging and swaying
And swooping now back
To earth where her mask of being unmasked must be masked
Because she *still* looks naked
And feels it around the midriff and in her butt
On which she bounces back
Home again after a day at a circus—what a circus!

+++

        To explain would sever linkages, interrupt
whereby encounters come
foregrounded in storm
or music
invented strategies

        An activist's work
of doing
aloud in rounds
to distribute and also to time
creates forces and forces to allow
in phrase or flow
that public and that language
aloud in rounds of salamanders

        Figure some permeability
once
—we're there?

        Afterwards (the current one)
of irritation I feel imposed

that in the end around some picnic
table provided
with excellent food and abundant drink
the "diary" presents
Eros for frustration

      Abrogation leaps
out to make sure it's pertinent
"once I am blue"
and "painting roses"
that are not always exactly "faithful"

      One should know
who it is one loves and one should
know the tradition of love should know the erotic reference points
that are salient to one's love
and to one's beloved
lover

+++

constant change figures
the time we sense
passing on its effect
surpassing things we've known before
since memory
of many things is called
experience
but what of what
we call nature's picture
of the many things we call
since memory
we call nature's picture
surpassing things we've known before
constant change figures
experience
passing on its effect
but what of what

constant change figures
since memory
of many things is called
the time we sense
called nature's picture
but what of what
in the time we sense
surpassing things we've known before
passing on its effect
is experience

++

When we want something we have to reckon
With probabilities watching
For repetitions observing
Rocks
Causing ripples in the stream
Of consciousness
Occurring over sand
And submerged things
In the shallows
Where our best hope of finding what we want lies
To tell the truth
Where we care the least—
Hear world, see
Whorl
While saying who
We are—hardly worth mentioning—say
Chicken-Licken seizes power
If not legally then at least to the degree that her fear obliges her friends ...
Passerby: Are they pleased by it?
Farmer: Are they doing all their tasks as required?
Turkey-Lurkey: Run Goosey-Loosey—or Lucy—
Froggy-Boggy: Are you sad? Don't be sad. Why are you sad?
Toady-Roady: Jump, Snakey-Shakey
Sluggy-Wuggy keeps her cool between the long leaves of the irises growing
        along the edge of the path

Lizardy-Tardy sits on a warm gray rock in a field listening for gnats, suddenly
As an incoming missile explodes, the gray horse Shadow, the brown horse
Duke, the black horse Prince, and the sorrel horse Rondo in terror
Stampede blindly
Run, Bunny-Money, shouts Piggy-Jiggy
Run, Sheepy-Sleepy, weeps Goaty-Throaty
Because sorrow and anger are very much the same
As celebrity
Animals
We are misled
At a frantic pace
As we have a completely erroneous concept of time

+++

Yesterday has arrived and remains
Under suspicion
By the bereft of bereavement, by the adrift of generating distance
That makes description of the shore almost impossible
And of the distance too shuddering beyond the tents
Pitched like heads under hats on the sand
And chattering nonsense that we try to interpret
To our continual embarrassment—we are the idiots here
And the tents and heads and hats and sand
And the water, too, bobbing and sagging
Or nagging, finally, as people do who are sick of themselves—
But this could all have taken a different course
And maybe it will
Yet
There are more than the usual number of hummingbirds hovering
Over the morning glory strangling the fence and the sun
Is shining on pepperwood trees
That offer good shade and cover for fish
In the ripple
Area 80% gravel, 10% rubble, 5% boulder
And 5% silt
A full 100%
Of dreams occur at such times as these

When one's asleep (a term
Used to name a state, imperfectly
Understood
During which one expresses no discomposure
Except perhaps for a slight twitching of the eyelids, compression of the mouth,
        occasional grinding of the teeth, changes
In the depth and rate of inhalation and exhalation and (rarely) comprehensible
        (though mumbled) speech
Proving that insensibility is not a site of calm) and lies
On one's side, a witness to a shooting in a savings
Bank near a bank
Of steel
Safe
Deposit boxes sealed
And all much the same
To which waking has no key—we've no master
To cut from
The sky pure and simple
Or what we call sky and hope
Everyone does so too—how else could we communicate to each other
Secrets—they're so precise, intimate, and detailed but their secrecy lies
In their incommunicable atmospheric suffusion
They are flushed with something like color but instead it's their very secrecy—
        my darkest
Thoughts are fucking immaterial
And impossible for words
To hide
Paint
Though it goes by names
(Cyan, cerulean, viridian, alazarin lake, etc.)
Calls things only by those names and music
Transmits constellations
Which it can't contain—that's realism—
Which is
To say realization—hate, optimism, mourning, and pleasure wake
One from one's dreams
In which are hidden one's most dire clichés—one's eyes, one's brain, one's
        claims
And they don't respond, refuse

To answer
Even to George, Amelia, Claude, Juan, Janice, or Bob
Though Bob turns back indeed
He flips, falls
Down he goes and immediately he's up
Again, arms out—vengeance is hollow

+++

The clown cannot escape gravity; it cannot be light.

With its round paper-white baby face and enormously exaggerated facial features, the clown must appear to a child like a nightmarish caricature of the figure at which the child first smiled.

The clown is at once both newborn and a ruin. Gesticulating like a flailing infant but too big to be one, it is then the epitome of a senile being—and under its preposterous baggy pants perhaps a diapered one. We begin as small clowns and end as repulsive overgrown ones—perhaps this is the truth with which the clown frightens us.

The clown is a swollen prototypical human, its flopping inflated body a travesty of the rounded features of young creatures that we see as adorable, vulnerable, vivacious, which is to say "cute." It appears before us to taunt us for the inadequacy of our sentimentality, the limits of our generosity, and to deny us the narcissistic pleasure of nurturing the tiny beings through which life has a future.

This goofy, looming, unpredictable, garish, frantic, bouncy, nonsensical parody of the child has emerged from beyond the horizon of childish optimism; it is clear from its expression that it has come forth out of despair to reproduce its own failure.

Like an adolescent, its feet are too big for it—as if it had yet to grow into them, but it never will. The only fate left to the clown is to accept its punishment, its humiliation, and then depart.

We laugh awkwardly and perhaps too loudly, as we identify with the clown.

+++

From sleep it's getting the elements I want, those

Not harried, not unclaimed
Not steam, not moderation
They minutely vary and stay the same
From waking I know that common names for a wind are echo, engine, and
        shadow
Memory is plasticene, farming protein, forgotten, and free
I have a board from a cave, it's the one with which I roofed it, a bluish gray but
        rosy and owlish adamant board, now a walkway
So off we go
No mention of mention but much of prediction and of musical time in wake-
        fulness echoing
Musical time goes on
Sleep goes on what—on horses' buses and beetle chat

+++

Ambivalence may be hidden in any act of kindness
Or every murky show of weakness thrown
Between giving and getting to the unforgiving whom one wants
To know what one doesn't show
In one's dream diminishments
Of the fullness of life
From which one wakes with neither watch nor shoes shouting
I've been robbed
Of sleep
Of which I've had way too little since childhood
Which was so long ago it might just as well have taken place
In a dream
Or between dreams
In a gap for which there's no evidence
From 7 to 9 pm on Wednesday, August 4
We can get to know our neighbors at a block party
With local musicians and a police officer to discuss safety
Issues
There are measures
We can take
A little further
Down the beach armed

With briquets after gathering driftwood
We can warm ourselves and warn others
Through the smoke
That with the wind off the desert will be driven toward Magadan
Where many worked harder than we are doing now
And died
Worse off than we are dying
Now
But every suffering
Is incomparable and unique
To the woman knowing what the weather was wailing
Over the dead
And specific
To the prisoner
Who knows that everything's misjudged
That's paraded through the universe
Behind men
Performing the cigar smoking dance
Or the one about stalking
A panther or painter
Or women
Panting with invention
Since when one invents it is said that one's navel is attempting to leap
Off to another place
With laughter
Taking with it all the money it otherwise holds
Hidden just inside the entrance to the belly
A stunning tissue, a landscape
Of parallels, rhymes
Pairing years with tears, lizards with wizards, beauties
With cruelties, fun
Lovers with gun-runners coming forward
Off to the right
Under flattering lights—they look ten
Years younger than they are all thanks
To a cyan filter casting blue-green compensation (it might as well be money)
        toward the edge of the scene for the suffusion of pinks
That fail to warm the players for the payers
Attending the theater with its stage

Of life revealed as the curtain
That rises
Trails threads from its tattered hem
Over hams fat with layers of meaning extravagantly and elegantly but subver-
        sively and cruelly imitating
Contemporary personages
Whose self-appointed task it is to piss on every erect iris, purple violet, tripartite
        trillium, and tongue of fern growing under the ancient trees
Which, though binoculars
May flatten them, provide bouncing habitats for nesting
Shocking birds as the cumulonimbus clouds darken
Deeply overhead
Forming pockets for all who have lovingly feared the light of day

+++

Off in the distance just a minute ago we were going elsewhere
To see merchants on elephants said to be mischievous
As wind in the hay over secrets naughtily divulged
And dollars in markets soon fruitlessly spent
On wonderful books from which it's too late to learn
Anything memorable—that is, anything that *I* will remember
Facts having broken free and drifted off at will
And speedily from me though some come back
To my delight: they all look new
When they arrive—at least
I think they do surely
Something at least is out there in the dark
And light
Even if it's only bugs astride
Bucking molecules of water vapor
Rising from puddles (natural
Libations) leaping color from east to west with no promise
Of safe return—is that full
(Is that not full)
Disclosure
As when we watch the proud
Performers giving cues—a glance, a nod, a gesture

Without a break
The action changes and the twirling naked plates
Wobble like the courage of first-time lovers
And fall
With a roar from the ashen lions in a large white room leaping
Over a vase of white flowers, their petals
Now black
As laurel crowning clowns (those fast-paced characters)
Whose job it is to chatter over bones

+++

I have this to say but I do not know when to
There was a great forest that I went to
I may never return there but I want to
I have just one memory of it and I want two

An Interview with Lyn Hejinian

Rae Armantrout

DEAR LYN:

To start with the obvious, you are clearly no minimalist. Your writing, though it has changed over time, and also from book to book, has always been marked by an inclusive impulse, and by a kind of extravagance. Here are two passages, one from *My Life* and one from *A Border Comedy,* which, I could argue, manifest extravagance differently: "Losing its balance on the low horizon lay the vanishing vernal day." and "Well—*ha, ha*!/There's a pink pop, a critical pick, a joke, a skinned dog/And a little dead man now lies on the floor/ Is something funny?/Did I/you vote for a gnome and get goat legs?" The first of these passages combines a lush beauty with the implicit comedy of day taking a pratfall off the edge of the world. Part of the comedy here comes from the excessive use of alliteration and from the prominent rhyme between lay and day as well as from the high romantic tone of vanishing and vernal. This sentence seems to both manifest and ridicule a kind of stylistic lushness. In the second passage, the extravagance is more in substance than in style. That is, these lines seem to celebrate the arbitrary and the unpredictable. *Anything* can pop up next, in the mind and therefore in the poem. At least that's the sense I get. So, I guess my question is this—how do you feel about extravagance and or lushness in poetry? Are you working with or through an ambivalence here? I wonder because I know that you admire the works of poets such as George Oppen whose style is spare and whose poetics seem to require that the material of the poem be somehow happened upon. (I mean in an Oppen poem you couldn't vote for a gnome and get goat legs.) You give yourself a wider permission, I think. Do you feel it as such? I don't mean to ask you why you're not George Oppen! The passages I've quoted here have a kind of fearlessness I admire. I just hope you'll talk a bit about the ethics of the spare and the lush or of the essential and the extravagant.

DEAR RAE:

You are right that the excessive use of alliteration and the heavy-handed rhyming work to comic effect in the passages you cite, and in those cases it is largely the excessiveness of the gestures that is responsible for the comedy. But in the right contexts, alliteration and rhyme can seem comical even when not used excessively. This isn't because those or any other prosodic devices are inherently ridiculous, but because they point to something—perhaps to the ridiculous tragedy of life (or Life), the eternal return of the same. Certainly the discovery of similarities—the observation of things matching up—has a strong psychological force. At the sight of it, we often erupt in laughter—a sign that things are getting out of control. And at that, a little paradox appears—the orderliness that similarities impose is the starting point of chaos. We see the boy with the bucket of paint, we see the banana peel on the floor, we've seen them before, we'll see them again, we know just what's going to happen, the rules of physics and narration are about to coincide, and bing—man, banana peel, bucket, and paint flying in all directions. Even the most modest elements can turn excessive, or at least I attempt to sustain a degree of optimism by believing that things are not always under control.

At a lesser level (to continue for a moment before answering your question), the discovery of similarities seems to play with our deep ambivalences about our place in the world, our fear of being the same and our fear of being different. Or to put it in other terms, it toys with our inability to decide which we desire more—which is to say that fear steps on the banana peel of desire (or desire on the banana peel of fear) in a matching up that knocks whatever we're carrying out of our hands and sends us flying.

But you asked if I could say something about the reasons underlying my tendency to be more fulsome than spare in my work. There are several different but related reasons that I avoid lapidary constructions (although not, I hope, lapidary—stony—spots along the way), but you are right to suggest that, in the end, there is an ethical consideration at play here. To put it very bluntly, that comes out as a decision to foreground (and hence, implicitly, to advocate that we attend to) sociality over austerity, inter-related, cross-implicated and multiply-responsible liveliness over the isolate and spare. I take it as a given that we live worldly lives—lives in the context of the world, subject to but also agents of what's happening—and there is a lot happening, physically, historically, chemically, domestically, etc.

I don't think that the more lapidary, spare sorts of poetry deny this, by the way; I am only saying that in my work I want to emphasize it, as a source of delight and trouble.

And now that I've said all this, I've imagined a "spare" project, or a project built out of spare parts (the pun here wasn't intended—I dislike puns—but it's apt so I'll leave it). One could imagine it as analogous to a film, each lapidary poem filling a single frame and moving by quickly, yielding to the next frame, producing a sense of motion—the Japanese renga form does precisely this. The result is neither aesthetically nor intellectually more emotionally spare.

DEAR LYN:

Your description of your imagined project sounds a bit like the way I conceive of my own poems—that is, my poems are often composed of parts, "spare" parts in both senses, which, put together, can create, I hope, the (illusory) forward momentum of a movie. Your project, if you write it, though, will be on a much larger scale, I'm sure.

Anyway, I'm interested in the status of the assertion in your work. Many of your sentences seem to make a truth claim or they seem to be, in some sense, definitions. I can pick out examples at random. For instance, from p. 13 of *Slowly*, "Fate can never in a new way nor as before overcome its dependence on the present once and for all" or from *Slowly* p. 10, "Repetitive exposure to anything provokes sensations." Both of these statements *appear* to reveal their writer's opinions. Let me give you my response to them. The first one, in its basic premise, strikes me as both true and deep, but, at the same time, I don't know whether to trust my reaction. For one thing, the basic premise is conspicuously complicated by qualifying phrases such as "never in a new way," etc. The second one, "Repetitive exposure to anything provokes sensations," immediately suggests counter-arguments. Don't repeated exposures dampen sensations, I want to ask. It seems to me that you may be making a kind of deliberate counterpoint, a kind of music, out of assertions, some of which will strike the reader as true and some as false. I wonder if you could comment on that process.

DEAR RAE:

In a perverse way, by making assertions I suppose I'm tempting truth, and doubting it as I go. Or, leaving truth (though not principles—the two are different) aside, let's say I'm tempting fate, if by that we mean all that has happened, whether in reality or imagination—all that has been experienced as happening, inviting it to prove me right or wrong. Methodologically, a debt to Oppen seems clear to me in this respect; he writes heuristically, testing reality, which exists independently of him, "none of his own making" (to [mis]quote you). The assertions are meant to set new phenomenological or epistemological horizons, and, I should add, not necessarily straight ones; I'm more than happy to see them wigging and wagging.

But of course I do have opinions. It would be disingenuous of me to pretend that what you are terming "assertions" are not, and even often, expressions of opinion. To pretend otherwise would be to deny agency and shirk responsibility. I thought about the second of the two statements, for example, questioning the accuracy (or the truth, if you will) of the statement, and I came up with the very objection to it that you did—based on the point that Viktor Shklovsky, most convincingly, makes, namely that habituation (the result of "repetitive exposure") to anything dulls (rather than "provokes") our sensation of it.

Shklovsky is right, but habituation doesn't occur in all circumstances. In this case, in the context of the passage that ends with the statement in question, I am speaking of hints, whose cumulative effect is to bring an experience to one at last. I was talking about the process of experiencing, the ways in which one thinks about or remembers something not only slowly (as per the title of the little book) but in terms of other adverbs, i.e. in a multiplicity of different ways. Things come to one—I have liked that phrase, the implicit metaphor it expresses, and the independence of things from us that it announces.

And maybe announcing is what is really at play, rather than asserting. Stein does a great deal of announcing in her work. "Saints," she will say, and then there are saints. Maybe that is one of the things that poetry can do: bring things into existence by announcing them. "Along comes something."

DEAR LYN:
I like what you say about "tempting truth and doubting it, tempting fate." It reminds me of a Blanchot essay I read recently which quotes Rilke this way: "The work of art is linked to a risk … Works of art are always the products of a danger incurred." To tempt truth and/or fate sounds dangerous or at least problematic. It seems to me that many of the poets associated with "language writing" are interested in problematic assertions. This is certainly true of Barrett Watten, for instance. His poem "Complete Thought" is almost entirely composed of such statements. "Things fall down to create drama" is one example. That statement is blatantly false as regards things while being, at the same time, a very apt definition of, say, melodrama. The end of my poem, "The Creation," might be another example: "To come true/a thing must come second." I wonder if you see such declarations and/or faux-declarations as characteristic of the Language group.

That's only a warm-up question. My second question is obliquely related, I hope. I don't know how to put this without sounding hopelessly retro—but, when I read your poems, I recognize the "voice" or maybe the "speaker," though not exactly as the person I sometimes speak to on the telephone. Increasingly, I think, the speaker in your poems is a mischievous, adventurous *character*. I hear this voice clearly in the beginning of your poem, "The Distance," which was published in *Conjunctions* magazine. That poem starts, "Banned from ships as if I were fate herself, I nonetheless long hankered/after adventures." Somehow I see traces of a fictional character in these lines. Perhaps it's because the word "hankered" reminds me of the nineteenth century. So—can we talk about "voice"—or has the term been ruined by the way it's been used in writing work-shops? Do you imagine a "speaker" for your poems?

DEAR RAE:
Generally the "voicing" that occurs in my poems is far more a matter of tone than of speaker, a play of affect and energy rather than an expression of per-sonality or persona. But you are right to discern traces in "The Distance" of what in fiction gets called "character." The poem was for a while subtitled "A Sea Saga" and, though the initial situation is autobiographical (I did, as a girl, want to go to sea, or at least to go out for a day with a family friend who was a commercial fisherman, but because "women are bad luck at sea" I was never allowed to do so) I was toying also with, as you noted, 19th century (Romantic) narrative conventions—Coleridge, Poe, even (don't laugh) Longfellow. When I abandoned the project (which I seem to have done), by the way, it was largely because those conventions turned out to be stronger than I am. The poem grew ponderous and the situation it purported to come out of became heavily sym-bolic: a woman at sea, the distance, fog, a ship becalmed, etc.

And so enough of that.

Yes, I do think that among the Language writers one can discern an unusu-ally strong interest in the declarative. Sometimes, as I've said is often the case in my own work, the declarative (or assertive) sentence functions as a heuristic device. But also, to the degree that it has been inherently a Marxist and/or feminist practice, Language writing has always been interested in examining and critiquing power structures. And in wanting to challenge both bad uses of power and uses of bad powers, Language writing has generally chosen a more revolutionary than liberalist approach. I'm not engaging in self-flattery by using the term "revolutionary" here. The point is that, while liberalism's response to bad power is to try to soften it, the revolutionary's response is to counter it. When it comes to the question of who's running the economy, who's in con-trol of the media, whose wealth is increasing, who's getting away with murder, Language writing doesn't say, and doesn't want to say, "let's all just get along."

When we're talking about Language writing, we are, of course, talking about an aesthetic practice, but Language writing as such has never separated aesthetic from social practice. And it's here, in the context of the commitment to the social, that developing a sense of "speaker" (rather than "author") may be important. One's presence is a social occurrence, a presence among others; one's utterances bounce around among other utterances in (and as) a social space. It's not about self-expression but about living.

And now that I've said all that, it occurs to me to note that "the social" is not an exclusively human realm. We live among rats, leaves, and scraps of sedimentary rock, too. Indeed, according to Ovid (as good an authority on such matters as any, I suppose), each of us may on occasion turn into one or another of those, and we may just as easily have been turned out of them.

And so, to answer your question: no, I tend not to think of a "speaker" for or in or of my poems. I'm apt to think more about prepositions than about speakers. But in the course of responding to your question, I've come to think that I should do so at least some of the time.

DEAR LYN:

In *A Border Comedy* we often hear the voice of a storyteller. For instance, there is "The Tale of the Raven" in Book Two, which begins "Once there was a hillside entirely given over to a garden...." And in Book Twelve you tell a story about telling a false story about a high school principal who kept a two-headed goat. The (perhaps) mendacious storyteller seems to me to be a central trope in the book. Did *A Border Comedy* grow out of an interest in narratology?

I'm interested in the way you begin a long work like *ABC*. I know, for instance, that you often write in response to your reading. *ABC* is the only book of poetry I can think of with end notes. In the notes you tell us what you were reading at the time of composition—and it's an astonishing array of philosophers, novelists and poets. Yet the poem doesn't sound as if it's composed of found language. I don't really pick up quotes—or not many anyway. I wonder if you could talk about the relation of your reading to your writing. In this case, did you choose your reading based on its relevance to what you wanted to do in the poem? And how would you describe your poetry's relation to narrative and, specifically, storytelling? I wonder, for instance, whether you've been reading fairytales and children's books since your grandchildren were born.

DEAR RAE:

My interest in stories and, especially, in storytelling goes back so far that I don't think I can ascribe a source to it. At some very basic level, it must be that storytelling (and with it, the urge to be the one to tell the story) reflects a will to power or, to put it another way, the will to live—the will to expand and continue one's experiences, and, of course, to invent some.

It is important to me that this be a social (and, at best, a sociable—friendly—) activity.

Otherwise—well, clearly storytelling can perform a variety of functions: via one's stories, one can, for example, take on an empathic and heuristic relation to events; or, on the contrary, one can defensively harden oneself to them, shielding oneself psychologically by means of one's stories and storytelling devices; or, yet again, one can lay a proprietary claim to events of which one tells, or to knowledge about them, which is virtually the same thing. At the very least, by virtue of one's stories, one acknowledges what comes along (whether in "reality" or in one's imagination), and, better yet, one registers one's shock at not really ever knowing what it is (unless, that is, one nullifies the shock and disguises one's ignorance with interpretations or explanations).

To the degree that poems offer experiences (whether of themselves or of something else or of both) without an overlay of interpretation, they are very like stories, or at least very like stories as Walter Benjamin (an obvious influence on what I'm saying here) characterizes them—as a medium for the sharing of experience.

As for the little stories that are embedded in the larger story of *A Border Comedy*—they are of different kinds, of course. Some were influenced technically and rhetorically by traditional kinds of fairy tale. I own a number of the Dover Press *Fairy Books* (*The Violet Fairy Book*, *The Orange Fairy Book*, etc.) edited by Andrew Lang, and I like to read the tales in them from time to time. At a conceptual and strategic level, my decision to use those kinds of models was influenced by my reading of Marina Warner's *From the Beast to the Blond*. But some of the stories, or story-like elements in *A Border Comedy*, derive from my interest in anecdotes, the things people tell one about what's been going on, what they've done, what they've seen. I like knowing what's going on. I admit to only rarely understanding *why* things are going on as they are, but this failure of understanding may contribute to my pleasure in the stories themselves.

The other kinds of materials—the other reading I was doing over the period I was writing *A Border Comedy*—enter the work in a variety of ways, most of them pretty obvious (as a source of ideas, concepts that might not have occurred to me otherwise, bits of information). They are all over the work; I'm not sure I can track them for you now and I'm not sure that anything would be gained even if I could. The things I "got" or "took" from my reading were almost entirely at the level of detail. I can't very well invent detail, but I can spot it, and I can put details together in new contexts—that, I think, is what I may be good at: the detailing of contexts.

In any case, I listed the sources at the back of the *A Border Comedy* mostly for the sake of "honesty," although the list serves also as an expression of enthusiasm (enthusiasm, after all, is no fun unless it's expressed).

DEAR LYN:

I wonder if you see your poetry changing and in what ways? It seems to me, for instance, that in your newer works, such as *Slowly, Happily, The Beginner* and *A Border Comedy*, form is not as evident, as much in the foreground, as it was in, say, *My Life, Writing Is An Aid To Memory*, or *Oxota*. The newer works seem looser, more freewheeling. Do you think that's true? If so, what accounts for the change?

DEAR RAE:

I'm delighted to think that the newer works and *A Border Comedy* especially seem "freewheeling." I very much wanted *A Border Comedy* to have the kind of energy, the sense of rushing contingency and risky unpredictability and sheer hilarity, that the term "freewheeling" implies. There was, actually, a background structure to the book, however, or a structural model governing its shape. That model was Ovid's *Metamorphoses*; it contains fifteen "books," hence the fifteen books of *A Border Comedy,* and in the original, first draft of *A Border Comedy* every book contained exactly half as many lines as are in the equivalent books of the *Metamorphoses*—half since my book was written in homage to, rather than in competition with, Ovid (to compete would have been an act of hubris). In revision, the books of *A Border Comedy* got even shorter, which is to say that I didn't feel compelled to adhere very tightly to my model, and in any case it only governed the very largest structural elements and left plenty of room for play (and for playing).

The only other compositional rule was guaranteed to keep me from knowing what I was doing and where I was going. I had all fifteen books underway and never allowed myself to add more than two or three lines to a book at a sitting. Because I write slowly, this meant that there was a gap of about a week between sessions of work on any one book, with the result that I was always slightly disoriented, always alighting in territory whose conditions I'd forgotten or had never had time to learn—I was, in other words, perpetually in a border zone.

Apart from the fact that they would be written in sentence-length lines, there were no formal constraints or structural predeterminations at all governing the composition of *Happily, The Beginner*, or *Slowly*. In *Slowly*, obviously, I was interested in using an abundance of adverbs, but my doing so wasn't governed by any particular rule.

In addition to the obvious, the title of *Happily* is meant to allude to "happenstance," the "haphazard," etc.—notions which are etymologically and hence semantically bound up with the notion of happiness—so questions of contingency, chance, change, etc. are at issue in this work too, though what's at stake in *Happily* is different from what's at stake in *A Border Comedy* (and *Happily* doesn't include the kinds of physical or morphological play that run through *A Border Comedy*).

The point I'm trying to make is that the "freewheeling" quality is relevant thematically in all these recent works, but it wasn't in the earlier works, and this may explain the change you note. I'm not sure I can account for it any other way. I try not to repeat myself, and to the extent that I succeed, my books will differ from each other one way or another, but that doesn't explain why the recent work should differ from earlier work in just this way. It may be that as I get older—as I approach my "late style"—I'll write more wildly. I hope so. Beethoven did so, and so did Henry James. (It's hubris, of course, to compare myself to Beethoven or James, but there's no harm in aspiring to those heights; the harm would be in expecting to get there.)

DEAR LYN:

It seems to me that these new works share a preoccupation with time; they seem to create a sort of elaborated present that passes but doesn't end. In *Slowly* we read, "I wake to the waking shadow of the world/the waking have in common for one long visit slowly" and "Movement prolongs the finitudes a person/moving achieves which lacks finality imperceptibly." I'm struck by your use of adverbs here and in other recent work. Do you use them to create a sense of elastic time? What do you like about adverbs? Would it be fair to say that *My Life* and *Oxota* deal with a more or less definite "then and there" while the new poems focus on an indefinite here and now?

DEAR RAE:

Time has been a major preoccupation and perpetual puzzlement for me for as long as I can remember, but when I thought to open up space for adverbs in my recent work (and in *Slowly* especially), it was only partially for the sake of the temporal effect they would have, the slowing down of the processes they characterize, the impeding of the "progress" of events. I wanted that retarding effect not for its own sake but for two other reasons: first, to offer a challenge or counter to what I see as a traumatic speeding up of contemporary life; and second, to suggest that the big question for reality as for ethics is not always *what* but rather (or at least equally) *how*. The question of attitude emerges obviously in *Happily*, and then again, but as if from the opposite point in time, in *The Beginner*. To the extent that it argues for some sort of *amor fati*, an acceptance of one's life through an acknowledgment of all that's happened, *Happily* is situated in a present that's oriented toward the past. *The Beginner*, on the other hand, suggests that the present is always (and only) a site of incipience. Even in retrospective moments, one is a beginner considering beginnings; to remember is to begin the past and see what it began. *Slowly*, which is the third part of this trilogy, was meant to intensify the study a bit by holding us for longer in the present.

I've just remembered, by the way and contrary to what I said above, that I *was* working with a specific compositional device when I was writing *Happily*. Every sentence of the work was meant to express the perpetual accuracy of the sensation *this is happening*; each was meant to acknowledge that a lot happens and each was also meant itself to happen. The experiential moment is what's happening, and all that's happening is being perpetually interjected into the temporal present we call consciousness or fate. I came up with a device that I thought could represent something of this. I composed phrases that gave a sense that they might be the beginning of a sentence, and I composed phrases with a terminal tone, and in between these beginning and ends I inserted various materials. I can give you two relatively clear examples—I'll put the interpolated material between brackets: "Here I write with inexact straightness [but into a place in place immediately passing] between phrases of the imagination" (page 3); "Does it all come to a distinction [for accidental wanderings having to wait widening the view] between optimism and pessimism?" (page 38).

As for your last question—the answer is yes. I've become less concerned with noting this and that and more concerned with wondering what and how this and that are and why.

What we call time—our sensation of temporality—probably emerges from the difference between those two orders of question, between the order of recognizing what things are and questioning what they are doing.

DEAR LYN:

Do you have a favorite book (or two) among the many you've written?

DEAR RAE:

No, not really. *A Border Comedy*? Maybe. But really, all of my books are a dis-appointment. I say that without intending pathos—it's built into my project (to the degree that, like Stein's or Oppen's, it's heuristic, and to the extent that it is increasingly comedic, i.e. tragic) that everything is a disappointment.

DEAR LYN:

I've noticed how often "fate" comes up in your work. Frequently it's paired (in a paradoxical way) with freedom. Out of a number of possible examples, I've chosen two favorites. The first is from *My Life*: "Their random procedures make monuments to fate." The second is from *The Beginner*: "But it is fate that has given the spider freedom and it runs for cover, it doesn't exhaust its possibilities." I see these two sentences as being emblematic somehow, central to your project. Could you talk about your sense of fate—and of freedom?

DEAR RAE:

Things happen and relations form between them (and between them and us)—this is what forms experience. Immediately that phrase brings me up short: this is what forms experience. It can be read in two ways, depending on whether "forms" is a verb or a noun. The syntax in which I thought I was writ-ing had "forms" as a verb: the sense was that experience is formed by this. But the better answer to your question has a different syntax, one that has "forms" as a noun: forms experience this (the relations between things that happen, in-cluding all the relations that happen) and the name of that experience, which is of nearly infinite possibility and hence of freedom, is fate. (Freedom incarnated in nearly infinite possibility is fate for better or worse, by the way—many things happen that are awful.)

In the turn to language that philosophy and literature have taken (and that Language writing—now at last released from tweezers [' ']—underscores), the semantic content of grammar in itself (and of individual grammatical com-ponents) has been widely investigated, but I cannot resist pointing out the critical and conceptual importance of the so-called "little words" (pronouns and prepositions, in particular) and "secondary" elements (adverbs, but also the oft-denigrated adjective). And while I'm at it, I'd like to put in a good word for some kinds of clichés—as for example "to put in a good word" (though one usually then puts in more than one, as I'm doing here), and "as for example." Poetry, figuratively speaking, is literal.

DEAR LYN:

In "The Rejection of Closure" you wrote, "the conjunction of form with radical openness may be what can offer a version of the 'paradise' for which writing often yearns." There seems to be a sort of utopian impulse in your poetry. Can the form of writing (or other arts) illustrate a social ideal? We're living in a dark time now, under an administration bent on depredation and conquest. How can poetry respond to this? In what ways can poetry be successfully political?

DEAR RAE:

Taking an action (and to write is to do so) in response to profound negativity (such as the destructiveness of global capital we're experiencing today) produces a "constructivist moment;" this is the focus of Barrett's new book (*The Constructivist Moment: From Material Text to Cultural Poetics*). In the wonderful (and to me re-inspiring) introduction, he says, "The constructivist moment is … a confrontation of aesthetic form with social negativity" undertaken "both to disclose the nature of the system and to develop an imagined alternative." As I see it, an artistic work in our time can, and should, create a constructivist moment, in Barrett's sense of the term. That undertaking is both realistic and utopian; it addresses things head on, with the force of a corrective (and self-corrective) and the aspirations of a revolution. Whether or not it can be successful politically depends, obviously, on what we deem a success and what we mean by political.

I've come to think of the political and of political success as local, and in some senses site-specific, phenomena. My notion of the political is taken more or less whole from Hannah Arendt's discussion of the classical Greek notion of the polis, as a social space of a particular kind, a "space of appearance" in which people and ideas are allowed to come into view and be acknowledged, presenting themselves to each other reciprocally. It is also (and now I'm putting my own spin on Arendt's notion) a space in which alterity is equally distributed but never nullified. A classroom (speaking as a teacher) in which people join to puzzle over a difficult text can be such a social space. So can the meeting of a grassroots activist community to seek solutions to a dreadful situation. (The gathering of diverse grassroots groups in Seattle on the occasion of the World Trade Organization meeting gives some indication of the potential inherent in such social spaces.) Successes are often short-lived, so that struggles have to be undertaken over and over, and often we only have negative successes to celebrate: e.g., no homosexuals were arrested for sodomy in Texas today.

No poem can unseat capitalism, no matter how many impeach it. No poem can reduce Bush's approval rating, no matter how many impugn him. Struggles have to be undertaken again and again, but we learn from art (at least I hope we do) that there are no repetitions. Gertrude Stein locates the discovery of the fact that there is no repetition as the source of the will to life. Can't we say then that the will to life is inherent to poetry, even if only, as *A Border Comedy* says,

> Humanly speaking
> With fortune in it
> Curving judgment

17 Uncollected Poems, 1978–1983

Lyn Hejinian

Song 2 (also)

also that is proper to the afterthought

      often

      ordinary
afterthoughts

  gives a
air

  explanations gently as friends also
         patiently as becomes

            peculiar in kind
             show

            nevertheless, where, and as well
    in place

            remember
to introduce the noise is also under the tiles

(*Hills* 5, July 1978)

Later Grammer Rim (no. 3)
for Ron Silliman

Impression
   to language   is intricate
The   to language less, direct, stamped
   to language   full
   the   interesting thing in the open
   in
The intentional comment and the   rarely combine
   thoughtfully   the
The yearly summer   the   thoughtfully
   and almost combine with comment
      and the yearly comment ot ost   rry
   around the
         give
         add
             keep
          tin distance
          to language
The restless part comes past

(*Hills 5*, July 1978)

(for Paull)

a slide of time side or aside

teen to music reason stay up

someone lost alike

days off so to see

without exactly all right

your mind

mind you soon

to break stock
another thought
is the most complete!

(1978; published in *One Hundred Posters*, 1979)

bus stroke
        home on

                                              made up
                                              turn back

                   turn up
term it

                                  unforgettably termed

   dressed for a planned dance
brush up   song-tip
button up
               the tub will tumble
            over lower corner

(published in *One Hundred Posters*, 1979)

One Discerns One Really Knows

appearance contains welcome event
                  the big dog alone was all thanks
                  the emotions are called turning from experience
                  the maximum tenth and full of muscle
                  the memory only for the larger stick circles
an affinity is felt for likeness is reciprocity only
apron with thanks was mute pass
                  the action of the sky might be as wide
as it moves over a profound depth
            religion can go so far versus change
            the rock turtle moves apace
     to have a stone parts bare parts
ask in relieving humor for deeds of a hero
   for a letter in a balloon

(*One Hundred Posters*, 1979)

Velous Three

        thodically many not shadow copy mena
larger little bird
like a flap of liquid
        this Ida, Nell, Anna
        who states the rise

all the other sings that stifle stop
        nius could have shown press loud
around in little struck air velous
        three times four the algae weird wash who drives

(published in *One Hundred Posters*, 1979)

first I hear love stem present
how foolishly later barred not rimmed

it's awful to lose
little particulars of tall later light

some form of more admitted
regard between the feet

what I mean of what I know furthers slippage
naturally lines up others rode

off nature the elided forces drop the order
riffled if the grime makes wood

broken curves in consequence and lightness too
— grass if poor a quartered sea

(from undated manuscript; [probably 1979–80])

Moving House

desk. deck.
        so ghosts stretch
                an angle
           lodged in the medium.

(from undated manuscript; [probably 1979])

the waves
once

and diagonally
the unoccupied chair

useless
but indifferent without them

(from undated manuscript; [probably 1979–80])

Lower Row the Colors

color arms the manner lower
another gotten whose the heifer

the leaf-trimmer or
the wood-pigeon and loafers

plump on a rumpled wise
almond how mind of a kind of mirror

patch scoop foot
o melancholia

(from undated manuscript; [probably 1979–80])

Realism

What he told us was not a dream but an actual happening. Theodore Roosevelt was aggressive. The magnet attracted the iron. The tall columns stood against the sky in austere beauty. This advantageous position commands three roads. We all admire a brave boy, a beautiful picture, or a fine piece of work. Smith had the business acumen to foresee that cotton would drop in price. The building abuts on the sidewalk; the sidewalk abuts on the street; the street abuts against the railroad. The farmer can adapt the barn for use as a garage. Squirrels store up nuts against the winter. Success often attends hard work. May is an amiable girl and does not quarrel. She angled for an invitation to his party by flattering him. Teachers of business methods often try to analyze the causes of success. The authorization of policemen to arrest beggars put an end to begging on the streets. In our neighborhood most people adhere to the church of their parents. The little girl spoke to her doll in tender accents. Feeding the hungry is a kind act. The human body will not assimilate sawdust. Prosperity is a good antidote for political unrest. The pretty girl received many attentions, such as invitations to parties, candies, and flowers. She thinks lamps are only an apology for sunlight. This millionaire has three houses, a yacht, and all the other appendages of wealth. Ability to get along is an asset in business. The miser heard the beggar's story with apathy. Talk will not avail without work. Money will not avail you after you are dead. Our characters appear in our acts. The new buildings appreciated the value of the land. This well-kept garden owes more to art than to nature. Aeons passed before life existed on the earth. Wild rumors were in the air. I gave my fur coat a thorough airing. The streets were alive with people. Murder, stealing, spitting in a train, and spreading diseases are antisocial acts. The angry crowd advanced toward the building. A position as head of the department, but with no real authority, is anomalous. You can see the absurdity of wearing shoes on your head and hats on your feet. Many different races are being amalgamated in the United States. Alice does so much reading that she cannot assimilate it all. The apparent truth was really a lie. A good dictionary is an authority on the meanings of words.

(from undated manuscript; 1981)

The Wink

From trivia, magnificent square.

The first noticeable thing (two of them on a wooden bench) is the sun and a curve. Flies fly like cobwebs before the broom.

They land in traditional trade of surface for space.

Fifty two is *not* divisible by three. There is no need for it, absolutely none at all.

And no wonder (winking), keeping instinct to the fact.

Pointing out mobs to a mob (reluctantly), giving them water (crouching there), a false bottom. We hand in cocoa, potatoes, stretching the tent, building improvements. A forested hill can do it well.

These useful falsehoods (carrying the child) permanently (paying up) sentimental. Nevertheless bent straight again (crossly) we slip the dull side out and face plain painstaking reality.

Nail nail, pile pile, light light, block block, caves in, lead on. Objects bare the direct view, surround (surrendering) the primary colors of flowers (pen, pot, Lipton, cat, Kenmore, Windex).

Knot packed full. Constancy is also strong (I get tails on a two-headed coin).

I stare into the jukebox (pleasant colonnade) and pick a beauty. Printed words are furnished with the phonograph records of the song, mere interjections of pronouns (conceptually) sold.

Night hawks in a vacant lot. Consoling (but rather secret) documents, the more illegible the better.

Slight red-green color, blindness.

They begin clearing up (cheering up enormously), if you grease my palm, at what price we "get" from the kind of day we "had."

Gloating through the kitsch. Looking back (stuck) one cannot speak of a real forgetfulness (a railway line filled with trees). Blow a whistle and a trained dog (prop) runs to the window.

Darts into the light.

(Rambling) anthropomorphism contains all the fabulous animals we never possessed.

A pigeon passing the window, the face looking out in constant embarassment (erased) brooding (isolation) set off (removed) loved.

Possess the subject of the photoed object, obsessive mess without fumbling observed (counting) infinities (goes by).

Gusts (panning around) shot skyward.

The paragraph is a place, transferred from pencil to paper (paste). An episode is more likely than an event.

At niche's edge a block. Muttering nuts, sun, in the sings with a laugh (exactly) counterpart.

(*Grossteste Review*, winter 1981–82)

Vide

Grapes in a compact cluster undisturbed swamped underneath over-
    graced in beams like a child with a bunch of keys then went
    down to the street
The infant survivors are every inch athletes
Vide gabble travail
Of the commodious discourse a part is picaresque
Some I confess
A stack importunes social studies
The hut is the parent form of timber house—and the cave of
    masonry
The tongue takes to the intimacy of this connection
The story collapses in denouement
A speech is the reflex, 'ye gods!'—are your goals imagined in
    haste?

(from undated manuscript; 1982?)

Prose

The leaf is shed from my potted begonia falling
    in a forest
Sure I remember
    my name is vocabulary
Harmonies imply annihilation
It parallels the twill
The lunatic with apples, a shrill white wall
    a strain in the speech of a jay
    the weather that hasn't aged
The air is wooly as one wakens
    the crowding light
    oppressive rather than expansive
But after a series of bounces
    a big enough enough push carries
    one from the springboard
The instrument spirits a way
These various means burrs carry
'On behalf of' qualifies the display
A beautiful style representing
    the inevitability of events
    fills to detach the sky from each direction
    read with sympathy
    (physical reality consists of sympathetic units)
I lost my place in a volume of separate fascination
    recorded by everyone
    about houses who have landmarks
One sees its bedrock
The indolent psyche, the resistance on waking
    to being awake
The yard is a work of insistent description
    properly panicking for all again
Bulk brightened by collapse
So sensory data favor the likely normal face
    and diminish over the unlikely hollow face
Wind wears where air is in
    the moving inch

The residing edge extends
    from some riddle point, quote:
    "I was in a room where I watched a piece of wood"
The typing a motive assured
    by the last bit of criticism
Because just a minute ago I (the disciplinarian)
    said that about the psyche
    because it's not optional
There's a considerable amount of crossing-out in the dream
Stale air pauses vertically between scenes
Punctuation lets the light in
The skin itches at a restless nerve end
From the toe a landmark falls
The stable spires topple
A spectacle is pressed
    right up to the eye
    or a spectacle draped over the face
As if to say, I'm here, show me, show it to me
That's how I think
    of getting out of town with self-confidence
Mere dislocation put off its clay
"And from there you could
    if necessary spit on
    the heads of the speakers"
But you ruin the risk of exaggerating
Fanatics with happy endings are selfish
Fissures fill in the stain
The protean is fat
    then sockets or blanks develop
    as 'flux & solder' elated
    by all activities of trees
Then craving for knowledge might mean
    craving for noise
One syllable, 'sounds like …'
    and combines awkwardly

(1982; published in *Boxcar* 1, 1983)

places
a rain
passes

May's grass
now I guess

(undated manuscript; probabably 1983)

(for Anna)

she
after we
St. Francis

what for short hit
hold five of that

being as she does the difficult
and I have to hit ten

you've taken in
especial on I
she crosses as sounds as grace

(1983)

(for Larry)

                    waiting long enough where
            the less to say for more to appear

a little less neatly formed
a little rougher
comes from looking

for thousand late years warm
downwards
outside all the rest besides

(from undated manuscript; probably 1983)

The Orders of Interruption

(alternative title: Rough Understanding)
(First presented at the University of Michigan, March 31, 2005)

Lyn Hejinian

This essay is ambivalent in its intention and in its outcome; it resents interruption, decries the betrayal of confidence that interruption produces, and it seeks to defy interruption, by setting out to make something *of* interruption, by discovering generative, meaningful, and possibly ethical as well as aesthetic possibilities in the disorders and re-orders issued by both interruptions and interrupting.

Ambivalence, then, informs the progress of the argument, and that ambivalence is in turn a subject of ambivalence—but, let's hope that it takes the form and has the force of a dialectical self-reflexivity, such that progress does indeed occur. Grounds for belief that a dynamic of this sort is possible are ready at hand in George Oppen's early masterpiece, "Discrete Series" and in his late masterpiece, "Of Being Numerous." If we consider these two long poems as a continuum—something that Oppen himself seems to have done—then the progress of thought through them begins by erupting out of boredom into action and hence into time, and it culminates not with decision but with curiosity. In a letter written in 1970, Oppen wrote, "There are thoughts easily available to me because they have already been thought. There is an almost audible click in the brain to mark the transition between thought which is available because it has already been thought, and the thinking of the single man, the thinking of a man as if he were a single man ... 'Of Being Numerous' is constructed around that click, of course—and the poem ends with the word 'curious.' I had set myself once before to say forthrightly "We want to be here," and the long poem ends almost jokingly with 'curious.' But it is not a joke entirely. If I were asked, Why do we want to be here—I would say: it is curious—the thing is curious—Which may be referred to, briefly, as O's Affirmation." And in another letter, he elaborates further: "I ended with the word 'curious,' of which the root is *curia*: care, concern[.]"[1]

What Oppen means by "the thinking of the single man, the thinking of a man as if he were a single man" is not immediately clear, but given that it is offered in distinction to "thoughts easily available ... because they have already been thought," "the thinking of the single man" seems to speak of an Hegelian undertaking, a quest of sorts across the horizons of the common and continuous, demanding, as Oppen puts it, "very drastic revision" of his ideas and "changes in the thinking too" (*Selected Letters*, 209). His project entailed major propositional and methodological adjustments, in other words, and the poem embraces and sustains them. Oppen's will to ambivalence is heartening, though it may seem a strange or estranged form of desire.

2

Toward the end of *The Education*, Henry Adams remarks, "[A]ll opinion founded on fact must be error, because the facts can never be complete, and their relations must be always infinite".[2]

In composing that sentence, Adams was responding to a sequence of shocks occurring in and as defining moments of modernity. New technologies and the forces of industrialization were producing the shocks, but of course capitalism, with its roots in the Enlightenment, had been in development for a long time. By the end of the 19th century, as Adams saw it, human visions of unity had been crushed under the burden of multiplicity, but recording that multiplicity had been in progress since the Renaissance.[3] The result is a body of literature, or at least of writing, with a distinct style—a style bound to a theorizing of an investigative methodology and deeply informed by its fundamentally secular project, that of gathering information about reality's particulars without favoring any of them. The style attempts to present without prejudice all that there might be to present, whether of clear interest or not—the degree of interest to be determined later, as doing so on the spot would be premature and prejudicial. So, for example, we get something like the following from Gilbert White's *The Natural History of Selbourne,* "Apricots set very fast. The willows in bloom are beautiful. Men pole their hops: barley is sowing at the forest side. Several swallows, h. martins, & bank-martins play over Oakhanger ponds. The horses wade belly deep over those ponds, to crop the grass floating on the surface of the water" (a record of things observed on April 20, 1789), or the passage from the *Journals* of Lewis and Clark recording their observations of October 17, 1804 in seven sentences that take note of the weather; the terrain; its vegetation; the wind; the usage of technical equipment; sightings of animals; their habits, habitat and food; sightings of birds and reptiles; evidence of seasonal change; more on the terrain; geological formation; its mineral content and color; and finally their exact location at the end of the day:

The weather was pleasant. We passed a low ground covered with small timber on the south, and barren hills on the north which came close to the river; the wind from the northwest then became so strong that we could not move after ten o'clock until late in the afternoon, when we were forced to use the towline; we therefore made only six miles. We all went out hunting and examining the country. The goats, of which we see large flocks coming to the north bank of the river, spend the summer, says Mr. Gravelines, in the plains east of the Missouri, and at the present season are returning to the Black mountains, where they subsist on leaves and shrubbery during the winter, and resume their migrations in the spring. We also saw buffalo, elk, and deer, and a number of snakes; a beaver-house too was seen, and we caught a whip-poorwill of a small and uncommon kind. The leaves are fast falling; the river is wider than usual and full of sand-bars; on the sides of the hills are large stones, and some rock of a brownish color is in the southern bend below us. Our latitude by observation is 46° 23' 57".[4]

The penultimate sentence is exemplary for my purposes: "The leaves are fast falling; the river is wider than usual and full of sand-bars; on the sides of the hills are large stones, and some rock of a brownish color is in the southern bend below us." What we have here are juxtaposed particulars, presented paratactically and free of heuristic or narrative intent.

Ezra Pound's Imagist program is a clear derivative of the "natural philosophic" method. In a passage that will, of course, be familiar to many of you, Pound writes, "In the spring or early summer of 1912, H.D., Richard Aldington and myself decided that we were agreed upon the three principles following:

1. Direct treatment of the 'thing' whether subjective or objective.
2. To use absolutely no word that does not contribute to the presentation.
3. As regarding rhythm: to compose in the sequence of the musical phrase, not in sequence of a metronome."[5]

This last principle is intended as a declaration of independence from the dictates of conventional prosodic rules and the regularities they impose; Imagism rejects their attempt to interfere with observation, their tendency to impede perception, in favor of what George Oppen's friend and fellow poet, Louis Zukofsky, when formulating his own, Objective principles some 18 or 19 years later, termed *sincerity*. The last principle, "as regarding rhythm," also declares poetry's independence from clock time and its clocks.

In the same decade that Ezra Pound, H.D., and Richard Aldington were formulating the Imagist principles, Henry Adams, describing New York City as he observed it in 1904, wrote, "The city had an air and movement of hysteria, and the citizens were crying, in every accent of anger.... Prosperity never before imagined, power never yet wielded by man, speed never reached by anything but a meteor, had made the world irritable, nervous, querulous, unreasonable and afraid" (*Education*, 1176).

What Adams was perceiving was temporal anxiety of the same sort that we feel to be so much a part of our experience of life in the 21st century. In fact, a feeling of *temporal affliction* has been an intrinsic part of the history of modernity and of modernism.

George M. Beard, the author of *American Nervousness: Its Causes and Consequences*, a study written toward the end of the 19th century, "blamed 'clocks and watches' and the 'necessity of punctuality' for the American middle class's generally strained nerves.... The very perfection of timekeeping instruments, he claimed, 'compel[s] us to be on time, and excite[s] the habit of looking to see the exact moment.' 'A nervous man cannot take out his watch and look at it,' he argued, 'without affecting his pulse.'"[6]

With modernity, both unpredictability and plethora of content take on velocity, producing concomitant intrusions on (or invitations to) human attention and demands on human concern. Terms like measure get newly charged; a unit of writing becomes not that which is being measured out but that which is doing the measuring. Form becomes action. Ultimately, to cope with velocity of content, Imagism, already conceived as dynamically-charged, became Vorticism (at least for Ezra Pound): the times in a whirl.

3

And yet it wasn't so very much earlier—as recently as 1883—that time became standardized in the U.S. In the early 1880s in the U.S. local populaces and governmental agencies were put under considerable—one might almost say relentless—pressure from railroad and manufacturing interests to establish fixed and nationally applicable time standards; the railroads wanted to be able to regulate the comings and goings of goods-bearing trains for maximum efficiency, the factories wanted to regulate the comings and goings of goods-producing workers for precisely the same reason. To establish a national standard for time, local times (of which there were almost as many as there were locales) had to be abolished. In addition, time-selling services, of which Western Union was the largest but the Harvard Observatory, for example, was in on the game too, had all to agree to a single standard—the one being proposed by the railroads. Local populations, for a variety of reasons, felt affronted that their time—their noon, for example—was to be superseded by someone else's (and that the hour was to be based on the Greenwich [British] meridian tended to add to the affrontery). Boston, for example, was horrified to think that it would share noon with cities in the Deep South when it was so clear that Boston differed profoundly from them. Reform-minded people were concerned, too, at the corporate take-over of time. William B. White, a Congregationalist Church pastor in Boston, "rose up and denounced standard time as an immoral fraud, a lie and a 'piece of monopolistic work adverse to the workingman's interest.'"[7]

Western Union, too, was slow to come around, as a significant part of its business involved the selling of time. Beginning in 1877, Western Union had dropped a time ball from the tower of its New York headquarters every day at noon, local New York time (as determined by astronomical observation).[8] In addition to allowing immediate observers to regulate their watches and clocks, the dropping of the ball also telegraphed a signal to paying subscribers, including the principal watchmakers of the city.

The commercial interests won the day, and at twelve o'clock noon on Sunday, November 18, 1883—"the day of two noons"—the standard went into effect. People in cities "gathered at jewelry stores and near public clocks" to see what would happen. According to the account given in Michael O'Malley's *Keeping Watch: A History of American Time,* "Crowds of several hundred began forming in front of New York's Western Union building as early as 11:30 a.m., to await the time ball's drop. In Boston a similar crowd of about two hundred waited with 'a sort of scared look on their upturned faces' [*St. Louis Globe Democrat*]. The *New York Times* described two stock Irishmen, supposedly watching in puzzlement as the clock stopped, waited, then started again. 'Begorra,' remarked one in newspaper Irish, 'Divil a change at all, at all I can see.' The pair walked away in disgust."[9]

The standardization of time, along with the invention of the telephone and the spread of electric lighting, produced "in the decades after 1880, a generally heightened sense of punctuality and urgency about time and clocks, a new and widespread formality in the experience of time in everyday work and life."[10] Among other things, an ability (or lack thereof) to cope with time became a class marker; "highbrow" theatrical and musical performances started punctually, "lowbrow" entertainments kept a more casual relation to clock time. "'Unpunctuality,' a Boston newspaper claimed in … 1884 …, 'shows a relaxed morality in the musical community.' Indifference to time stigmatized the latecomer as a moral leper and a social inferior."[11]

(We might pause for a moment here to reflect on the contemporary poetry reading, with its typically relaxed or even lax relation to maintaining any correspondence between the announced and the actual beginning time of the event. Those who insist that avant-garde poetry is a "highbrow" or "elitist" undertaking should take note that poetry readings almost never begin "on time" and may commence as much as 40 minutes later than scheduled. Though perhaps not attuned to what Pound called "the sequence of the *musical* phrase," the poetry reading does proceed in harmony with the sequence of the "*social* phrase"—and things do not unfold socially according to the clock.)

4

In the wake of inscribing time with moral value, while at the same time relegating it to the status of the commodity (recognizable in metaphors of time saved, time spent, time wasted, time lost, free time, etc), *interruption* is perceived as a threat—a source of unpleasantness, a bother, or, if it occurs in the form of a so-called "welcome distraction," it becomes so nonetheless in a negative sense, as an occasion for irresponsibility, uselessness, the avoidance of *reality* (with which *work* is the exemplary mode of engagement), etc.

There are, indeed, various instances of interruption that are negative in the extreme. There are total interruptions (death is the obvious example) as well as totalizing ones: the ruination produced by war, for instance, or ecological disaster.[12] And there are wasting (which is to say, wasteful) interruptions—every instance of injustice is one of those.

Justice, properly speaking, should be uninterruptible; justice, because it must remain a dynamic condition, attendant on the ever-active particulars of situation, has to be continuous. This is the reason that the discourse of "closure" (which in recent years has become so popular with proponents of capital punishment) is incompatible with the discourse of justice.[13] Karl Marx, certainly one of the greatest theorists of time, in elaborating his own principles of justice (which were not, admittedly, principles of criminal justice but rather intended as principles guaranteeing abiding socio-economic justice), foresaw a need for them to unfold in two stages, each concomitant with the current stage of society as it progressed. To a large extent, the first principle assures what we would term, in a very strict sense, justice, and the second progresses from justice to mercy. The earlier of the principles can be stated as "From each according to his abilities, to each according to the amount of work done"—a principle that holds, according to Marx, only during the early phase of a post-revolutionary society. It is to be superseded at a later, more stable stage by the principle recast as "From each according to his abilities, to each according to his needs," reflecting a more realistic assessment of the human condition, one that acknowledges that not everyone is born with equal abilities, that society does not support everyone's abilities equally, that various dis-equalizing circumstances come into play, etc. This principle allows for equal treatment of unequal human beings with all their unequal needs. And though, to the best of my knowledge, Marx nowhere says this, inherent to this second principle of equality is the act of forgiveness—an act that Hannah Arendt, in *The Life of the Mind* and doubtless influenced by Hegel, examines at some length.

Arendt turns her attention first to the act of *forgetting*, which, quoting Nietzsche, she terms "a power of obstruction, active and, in the strictest sense of the word, positive," creating conditions that allow us "to make room again for the new."[14] The *failure of forgetting* is at the heart of ancient Greek tragedy; it is the source of the relentlessness of the tragic "fate" that pursues and ultimately overtakes the hero. But paradoxically, given that to remember is to keep something in mind, the failure to forget, like forgetting, also constitutes a failure to recognize, a failure to acknowledge. This is because the failure to forget devolves into fixity; it cannot allow for the possibility (which is also the inevitability) of something's alteration, of its becoming different. And *forgetting* misses the differences altogether.

For these reasons, forgetting is an inadequate response to injustice; forgiveness must come into play. As Julia Kristeva remarks, in her book *Hannah Arendt* (the first volume of her trilogy *Female Genius*), "Guilt, which appears to result from a breach of a prohibition or a moral precept, turns out to be deeply bound up with the very experience of temporality, that is, when temporality is coextensive with the life process. Breaking this chain requires an interruption, which in Arendt's view can no longer be forgetting but rather forgiveness"—of the person, not the act (and only, by the way, if the act was indeed carried out by a person, rather than a nonperson, for example Eichmann, ("a robotic bureaucrat").[15] Forgiveness makes room for "natality," another key concept for Arendt, the "miracle," as she puts it "that saves the world."[16]

5
The Flow of Interruption: Oppen's Boredom

Here is the first poem of George Oppen's *Discrete Series:*

The knowledge not of sorrow, you were
              saying, but of boredom
Is——aside from reading speaking
              smoking——
Of what, Maude Blessingbourne it was,
              wished to know when, having risen,
"approached the window as if to see
              what really was going on";
And saw rain falling, in the distance
              more slowly,
The road clear from her past the window-
              glass——
Of the world, weather-swept, with which
              one shares the century.[17]

Cutting away the myriad subordinate clauses so as to find the core sentence, what we have is "The knowledge not of sorrow but of boredom is of the world," a world which is one "with which one shares the century." It is also knowledge "Of what, Maude Blessingbourne it was, wished to know," and knowledge "aside from reading speaking smoking"—a trio of activities unpunctuated by commas and therefore merging into one in the open space, the void, the encompassing interruption of boredom.

The *syntax* of the poem/sentence, being subject to a flow of interruptions, is sufficiently complicated as to upset, or at least impede and therefore delay, discovery of this core sentence and then understanding of the sentence in its entirety—the poem's one sole sentence. It is, one might say, a sentence that one could expect to find in a work by Henry James, and indeed it includes part of a sentence from Henry James— about whom, by the way, Oppen curiously once said, referring to the days of the Great Depression, "James and not Hemingway was the useful model for 'proletarian' writers."[18] Oppen in his poem is quoting from James's 1902 story, "The Story in It." As the story begins, two women, a Mrs. Dyott and her houseguest, Maude Blessingbourne, are together on a rainy afternoon in England in a sitting room, where Mrs. Dyott is attending to correspondence and Maude Blessingbourne is reading a "French novel" (the equivalent nowadays to something like a Harlequin Romance).[19]

Here is the passage from which Oppen quotes: "Nothing had passed for half an hour—nothing, at least, to be exact, but that each of the companions occasionally and covertly intermitted her pursuit in such a manner as to ascertain the degree of absorption of the other without turning round. What their silence was charged with, therefore, was not only a sense of the weather, but a sense, so to speak, of its own nature. Maud Blessingbourne, when she lowered her book into her lap, closed her eyes with a conscious patience that seemed to say she waited; but it was nevertheless she who at last made the movement representing a snap of their tension. She got up and stood by the fire, into which she looked a minute; then came round and approached the window as if to see what was really going on."[20]

Boredom, which Oppen took to be a productive mood, functions as an extended discontinuity that ultimately creates time as well as, significantly, history. For James, as for Oppen, what is "really going on" is rain, but for Oppen, in addition, through the window-glass, through the rain, a century appears—a stretch of historical (i.e., commonly and consciously shared) time.[21]

The moment of rupture within the condition of boredom wherein Maud goes to the window is not unlike that in which Proust tastes the madeleine, except that where the trajectory passing through Proust's moment is retrospective, that of Oppen's is projective, "the path," as Oppen, quoting Heidegger, put it in a 1964 letter discussing this particular poem, "the [...] path, the arduous path of appearance."[22]

As Oppen later acknowledged, "The word 'boredom' is a little surprising there."[23] It was however, as Oppen to his delight discovered much later, a term that Heidegger too was developing at the time, as he prepared the speech with which he accepted the Chair of Philosophy at Freiburg in 1929, the very year in which Oppen was writing this poem. Heidegger explained it in this way: "In the end an essential distinction prevails between comprehending the whole of beings in themselves and finding oneself in the midst of beings as a whole. The former is impossible in principle. The latter happens all the time in our existence. [...] No matter how fragmented our everyday existence may appear to be [...] it always deals with beings in a unity of the 'whole,' if only in a shadowy way.[...] Profound boredom, drifting here and there in the abysses of our existence like a muffling fog, removes all things and human beings and oneself along with them into a remarkable indifference. This boredom reveals beings as a whole."[24]

Oppen's explanation is characteristically briefer, but it expresses much the same thought: "It means, in effect, that the knowledge of the mood of boredom is the knowledge of what is, 'of the world, weather-swept.'"[25]

Some 38 years later, in the 37th section of "Of Being Numerous," Oppen wrote a reprise of the poem, rethinking it in the process:

'... approached the window as if to see ...'

The boredom which disclosed
Everything——

I should have written, not the rain
Of a nineteenth century day, but the motes
In the air, the dust

Here still.

What have we argued about? what have we done?

Thickening the air?

Air so thick with myth the words *unlucky*
And *good luck*

Float in it ...

To 'see' them?

No.

Or see motes, an iron mesh, links

Of consequence

Still, at the mind's end
Relevant

Those last lines are key: "links / Of consequence / Still, at the mind's end /
Relevant." What else renders time into history—into time regained—if not
"links of consequence," consciously experienced experiences that remain "still at
mind's end relevant." Oppen decries ideology's "thickening" of the air, since it
prevents events from coming to ground and taking root as history. It is not rain
that Oppen "should have written," he says, since rain effaces what's happening
and obscures its traces; instead, he says, he should have written "the dust /
Here still"—thus bringing to view the continuing historical residue.

6
Robert Creeley's Hesitation

The "arduous path of appearance" is, in part, always a temporal one, and writing, in following it, will be affected structurally as well as semantically.

Syntax and prosody register the presence and pressure of time on semantics. That word order should establish a syntax of cognition, a grammar of coming to mind, is obvious. It should be obvious, too, that the coming to mind as well as the passage through thought may be turbulent. The more precisely encounters with reality are represented, the more likely a rough understanding will be the result, "the sentence," as Ezra Pound noted, "being the mirror of man's mind, and we having long since passed the stage when 'man sees horse' … can in simple ideographic record be said to display anything remotely resembling our subjectivity"[26] Nor does it display our objectivity.

In various ways, the following two short sequences from Robert Creeley's *Pieces*, function phenomenologically to register the impeded paths of discovery, and in doing so they have, also, an ethical thrust; the truth of the poems lies not in the detail but in the change of detail, which is to say in the syntax itself—the move from one word to the next. Just as the movement in a movie occurs, as it were, between the film frames—in the *as it were* moments that turn metonyms into metamorphoses—so the truth of Creeley's poems lies between words or phrases. Creeley's ethics is manifest at line breaks in his poetry and at points of punctuation (and in his prose especially at his commas).[27]

Having to—
what do I think
to say now.

Nothing but
comes and goes
in a moment.

*

Cup.
Bowl.
Saucer.
Full.

*

The way into the form,
the way out of the room—

The door, the hat,
the chair, the fact.

*

Sitting, waves on the beach,
or else clouds, in the sky,

a road, going by,
cars, a truck, animals, in crowds.

• • • • • •

The car
moving
the hill
down

which yellow
leaves
light forms
declare.

*

Car coughing moves with
a jerked energy forward.[28]

Creeley's *Pieces* is dedicated to Louis Zukofsky, and the writing seems exem-
plary of what Zukofsky, in his 1931 essay called "An Objective," termed *sincerity*.
"Writing occurs which is the detail, not mirage, of seeing, of thinking with
the things as they exist, and of directing them along a line of melody. Shapes
suggest themselves, and the mind senses and receives awareness."[28] Intricate
and meticulous, and because of the resistance set up by the brevity of the lines,
these poems seem to develop slowly; they are marked (and even shaped) by
punctiliousness and hesitation.

At the points of hesitation opposition occurs—not between a positive and
a negative but between two positives—or, sometimes, multiple positives. The

effect is, as I've said, cinematic, so that even while the brevity of the lines re-tards our reading, their hesitancy and even jerkiness make it impossible for hesitation to stall. The hesitations occur so as to allow for adjustment, for a shift in trajectory, a correction of attitude. The poetry's logic, and its ethics, are re-leased in interruptions and accrue possibility—dynamism—action—as a result of them.

7

Bernadette Mayer's Haste

Lived temporality is neither regular nor of a single modality, and the syntaxes that register it may, as in much of Bernadette Mayer's writing, range across multiple (and often incompatible) temporal regimens (of thought, event, action, etc.) while also registering the changes we make from regimen to regimen, as modes of attention shift, jumping from time to time. Mayer's sentences often traverse multiple temporal, sense, and event regimens. And in this respect, as in many others, they often seem dreamlike in their transmutations, as in the following, which is the opening paragraph/stanza of the prose poem "The Day Thurman Munson Died," in Mayer's book titled *The Desire of Mothers to Please Others in Letters*:

It's OK what I say in writing, nobody could ever object to that, even the moon is almost full again over my left shoulder like all learning, no ending and salt. You see this light is kind of an interim night and suddenly what we thought of as life is something different, not quiet with time to write and stuff but interrupted and also still so hot. A lot of people said, first of all, it was unfair to make the comparison, with even reference to the O'Hara poem, but since this thing isn't one, as if it's missing one, and the questions of likes and dislikes is lost anyway—the fish jumped—I guess it's ok. I always liked his name, its distortion of forgetful letters.[32]

Mayer has frequently worked at the level of the project, rather than the poem. The rigors in play are conceptual, and temporal constraints are often put in place so as to serve as conduits for the episodic and encyclopedic sequences that are characteristic of her work. The project from which I'm quoting here (*The Desire of Mothers to Please Others in Letters*) involved (or required) the composition over a period of nine months a series of letters, addressed to specific people (not named in the book) but never sent. The result is an investigation into epistolary vivacious spontaneity, tracking the contingencies that mediate friendship and love—that spark it and lark through it with vivacious velocity. The "letters" are marked by repletion in all its senses: the "Bernadette" in them takes things in to excess; the letters are filled up and even overcrowded; they seek fulfillments of desire, they yearn for satisfaction. And they can't be interrupted (though they themselves are replete with just that), which is why they weren't sent. "It's OK what I say in writing, nobody could ever object to that, even the moon is almost full again over my left shoulder like all learning, no ending and salt."

The nine-month period during which the "letters" were composed coincides with a stretch of time beginning with Mayer's discovery that she was pregnant with her third child and culminating in the writing of the last (very brief, one-sentence) "letter" ("A Few Days Later It's With Pleasure I Write") announcing the birth of the child, a son who is to be named Max. It is not surprising, then, that even as virtually every sentence is composed metonymically, phrase by phrase, their sum ultimately produces a radical metamorphosis. This move from metonymy to metamorphosis is not without a classical precedent, and one that Mayer would have been familiar with; Ovid's *Metamorphoses*, after all, is an account of change, and thus inevitably a history of time.

8
The New Sentence

"[T]he only possible remedy [for a failed politics] is to change our relationship to time." So writes Julia Kristeva in *Hannah Arendt*.[33] As we've seen, Arendt invokes the term "natality" to name the interruption with which the relationship to time makes a change—literal natality, in the first instance, but one whose character remains inherent within the realm of possibilities that constitute living life. As Arendt puts it, "the new beginning inherent in birth can make itself felt in the world [...] because the newcomer possesses the capacity of beginning something anew, that is, of acting." It is in the context of "the constant influx of newcomers who are born into the world as strangers" that we must "create the condition for remembrance, that is, for history."[34] History is not a conservative practice for Arendt then, but a turbulent and dynamic one. Natality constitutes a condition of "revolutionary temporality,"[35] it represents a radical interruption that brings into play the single most important thing we have in common, which is that we are not alike. This is our context and our context-rich condition, this is what we have to share: difference. As Arendt puts it, "Plurality is the condition of human action because we are all the same, that is, human, in such a way that nobody is ever the same as anyone else who ever lived, lives, or will live."[36]

A syntax that generates plurality, a poetry that practices alterity and heterogeneity, is of course only that—syntax and poetry. But to turn our attention to the *materiality* of language is to direct it away from mere images and, I hope, toward history—which is to say, dynamic and dynamically remembered lived time.

The negatively interrupted character of contemporary life—the intrusions and distractions that render it vulnerable and then ruptured and fruitlessly fragmentary—is a key factor in what Julia Kristeva calls "the destruction of psychic space and the annihilation of the life of the mind that has threatened the modern era."[37] Powerful features of late capitalist/postmodern temporality have brought about a dearth of, and possibly death of, dialectics in favor of endless, even relentless distractions—the sorts of event spectacles that substitute for reality and that the Situationists began decrying some 40 years ago. In such a milieu only a halting *inner* life is possible; only briefly and rarely do any encounters occur between consciousness and the unconscious, and such encounters as there are are apt to be confused and unproductive. Outer life, the *social* sphere, meanwhile, has been so thoroughly commoditized and opaquely superficialized that it is difficult to discern its underlying structures. We are bobbing in an ahistorical milieu which passes itself off as the "nature of things."

The "post" in postmodernism situates the contemporary not in a period that "follows the modern" but in relation to cultural production following "the end of history." Postmodernism names a post-historical and hence ahistorical temporality. It occurs when history ends because capital as ideology can claim to have achieved perfect stasis, having become not a means but an end in itself—whose end, as an end-all and be-all, is to declare that whatever it is is all there is; this is a lie, but one that manages to block thinking, and hence is a form of madness.

The interruptions in which I am interested are not the *distractions* of postmodernism. They are rather, the interferences that Eduardo Cadava, in his *Words of Light*, describes as "the separation and discontinuity from which history emerges;"[38] constructed around Oppen's click, they are the caesuras that produce new meaning, the interventions that generate difference.

As Giorgio Agamben remarks, "a work's material content cannot be separated from its truth content."[39] What is history if not consciousness of what's happening in context—in its context as well as our own. Interruptions bring contexts into view; they are foregroundings (and sometimes self-foregroundings) of what's being overlooked, by-passed, a means of avoiding what Guy Debord has called "the universal wrong of ... exclusion from life."[40]

Notes

1. Rachel Blau DuPlessis, ed., *Selected Letters of George Oppen* (Durham: Duke University Press, 1990), 402–03.

2. Henry Adams, "The Education of Henry Adams" in Henry Adams, *Novels, Mont Saint Michel, The Education:* edited by Ernest Samuels and Jayne N. Samuels (New York: The Library of America, 1983), 1094.

3. In seeking out the facts of the world, Renaissance naturalists and explorers were, of course, picking up where Aristotle and other great Classical philosophers or knowledge-gatherers had left off. But in important ways, Enlightenment motives (and motifs) are distinct from Classical ones.

4. Meriwether Lewis and Willam Clark, *The History of the Lewis and Clark Expedition,* Vol. 1; edited by Elliot Coues (New York: Dover Publications, Inc., reprint of 1893 edition), 170–71.

5. Ezra Pound. "A Retrospect," in *Modern Poetics*, ed. James Scully (NY: McGraw-Hill Book Company, 1965), 31.

6. Michael O'Malley, *Keeping Watch: A History of American Time* (NY: Penguin Books, 1991), 150; *American Nervousness* was first published in 1881; it was reprinted in 1972.

7. Michael O'Malley, 120. Almost the entirety of my information detailing the establishment of standard time in the U.S. comes from O'Malley's fascinating book.

8. The time ball that drops in Manhattan's Times Square at midnight on New Year's Eve is probably the last operating time ball in the U.S., but in the post-bellum 19th century a number of cities maintained one; each was keyed to local noon.

9. Ibid, 147.

10. Michael O'Malley, 123.

11. Ibid., 147.

12. Curiously (as well as dangerously) the threat of ecological catastrophe, in its most extreme form, remains, apparently, nearly impossible for humans to believe real—perhaps because ecological catastrophe belongs to a temporal realm—that of the irreversible and eternal—that the human imagination cannot contemplate without vertiginous confusion and even panic.

13. Why the concept of *closure* has replaced that of *deterrence* as the keystone to arguments in favor of the death penalty is not entirely clear to me. Certainly the fact that studies strongly suggest that the threat of capital punishment does not serve as a deterrent must be figured in. But the shift of attention from alleviating a *public, social* threat (by deterring potential murderers) to curing the *private* psyches of *individuals* (by killing the person whose actions brought on their suffering) is such a significant one that any analysis of it will have to take into account other broad trends in contemporary culture.

14. Friedrich Nietzsche, *On the Genealogy of Morals,* II; edited by Walter Kaufmann and translated by Walter Kaufmann and R.J. Hollingdale; in Friedrich Nietzsche, *On the Genealogy of Morals and Ecce Homo* (NY: Vintage Books, 1989), 57.

15. George Oppen, *New Collected Poems* (NY: New Directions, 2002), 5.

16. Julia Kristeva, *Hannah Arendt*; tanslated by Ross Guberman (NY: Columbia University Press), 233.

17. Hannah Arendt, *The Human Condition* (Chicago: University of Chicago Press, 1958), 247.

18. Ibid. 241.

19. No doubt inadvertently, in his poem Oppen added a final e to James's "Maud."

20. Henry James, *Complete Stores 1898–1910* (New York: Library of America, 1996), 403–04.

21. The dreariness that we generally associate with boredom is obvious here—the dreariness of the explicitly mentioned gray and rainy afternoon and the dreariness of the century that Oppen was experiencing when he wrote this poem in the early 1930s, in the midst of the

Great Depression and as Fascism was on the rise in Europe. Coming to an awareness of the dreariness—the depressive effects—of injustice was integral to Oppen's self-education at this time—his coming to "the window as if to see what was really going on." Immediately following publication of *Discrete Series*, Oppen abandoned poetry in favor of political activism, joining the Communist Party and devoting himself to work on behalf of labor unions and the unemployed. He didn't return to poetry for 25 years.

22. Rachel Blau DuPlessis, ed., *The Selected Letters of George Oppen* (Durham, NC: Duke University Press, 1900), 105.

23. L.S. Dembo, "Interview with George Oppen," *Contemporary Literature* 10, 2 (Spring, 1969), 169.

24. Martin Heidegger, "What Is Metaphysics?" in *Basic Writings*, ed. David Farrell Krell (San Francisco: HarperSanFrancisco, 1993), 99.

25. Dembo "Interview," 169.

26. Ezra Pound, *Pavannes and Divigations*, (NY: New Directions, 1958), 3.

27. There is also, of course a dialectical relationship underway within and between the sequences; the poems as published appear in close proximity—the first 6 lines on page 6, the others all on page 7 of the book.

28. Louis Zukofsky, *Prepositions* (Wesleyan University Press, 2000), 12

29. Julia Kristeva, *Hannah Arendt*, 164.

30. Kristeva, 165.

31. Robert Creeley, *Pieces* (NY: Charles Scribner's Sons, 1969), 6–7.

32. Bernadette Mayer, *The Desire of Mothers to Please Others in Letters* (West Stockbridge, MA: Hard Press, 1994), 98.

33. Julia Kristeva, *Melanie Klein* (New York: Columbia University Press, 2001), 15.

34. Arendt, *The Human Condition*, 8.

35. Ibid.

36. Ibid.

37. Kristeva, *Hannah Arendt*, 8.

38. Eduardo Cadava, *Words of Light: Theses on the Photography of History*, (Princeton, NJ: Princeton University Press, 1997), xx.

39. Giorgio Agamben, *The End of the Poem;* translated by Donald Nichelson-Smith (NY: Zone Books, 2004), 85.

40. Guy Debord, *The Society of the Spectacle;* translated by Donald Nichelson-Smith (NY: Zone Books, 2004), 85.

10 Letters, 1976–1994
Lyn Hejinian

This selection was made with an eye toward presenting the importance of correspondence, the activity of it—its ongoingness, and variety, within the broader context of Hejinian's work. Jen Hofer did the archival work. Mel Nichols helped with the transcription and selection. Our thanks to all at the Mandeville Special Collections Library at the University of California, San Diego, who made this work possible. We have appended a section of notes following the letters. —R.S.

Letter to Carolyn Andrews

LYN HEJINIAN
TUUMBA PRESS
P.O. BOX 1075
WILLITS, CALIFORNIA 95490

16 May 76

Dear Mom,

Thanks so much for the addresses—I'd thought of a few of those people—Florence and Stanley, for example—but the Goodins is a wonderful idea. Subscriptions are trickling in; the letters of inquiry from hopeful authors; enthusiastic participation from the writers I've solicited materials from. I'm a member of COSMEP.

The name Tuumba—well, everyone in the family has taken turns naming the family pets—cats, dog, pony, horses. When I got my horse, it was Larry's turn, and became something of a joke, until he began mumbling pseudoswahili—mumba dala raba TUUMBA. Hence, Tuumba—that's the name of the horse.

When I thought of doing the chapbook series, I spent days trying to think of names—but none of them were right, since anything that meant anything was somehow defining and therefore confining. Or else, precious, overly cerebral, etc. I wanted to avoid stating a position—to avoid stating anything.

It does sound African, though, doesn't it. Well, it's a nice name, I think.

The Tuumba series is taking up a prodigious amount of time and energy, but there seems more of both the more I spend. At least, I feel very busy, but satisfactorily so. We enlarged the garden and it's thriving—the plants already huge. I also made an herb garden around the house, and a stone wall to keep the dogs out (neighbor's dogs, of course). And the fruit trees are growing—thanks to a secret trip to the nursery for some rather inorganic fertilizer. It's almost organic, though, the young lady told me.

Young lady—lordy, I wonder if I'll ever feel like a grownup. I don't yet—and I'll be 35 tomorrow. I stayed up through the wee hours last night with some friends, talking about getting old—at what point did we stop feeling unique; did we think we were meant for something special in life, or something else (one friend said that she had always assumed that what she was doing was temporary, that this wasn't her real life, and had just, in the last months, come to realize that in fact today was her life); and at what point did we realize that we, too, were vulnerable to the hardships and tragedies of life (I always thought that our family was invulnerable, until Daddy got sick).

Larry Woiwode's book contributes to this train of thought, of course. Those burdened lives. And I've been reading Joyce Carol Oates stories, which are no lighthearted affairs, either.

I suppose there is no other news. The 'fugitive' turned himself in. Anna is teaching Snowy to shake hands. Paull just outgrew all his pants, and hasn't taken off the shirt you gave him (except on Thursdays, which is laundry day).

Love to Ken. And to you,

from

Me

Letter to Clark Coolidge

November 14, [1982]

Dear Clark,

I think Steve Benson is the only writer I know who leaves in as much as Stein did—the yawning, and the poking in and under (testing for the right word, seeing what it reveals), and the turning back or around without erasing tracks, even those that give evidence of clumsy bumbling. Of course, sometimes Stein leaves in altogether too much—but possibly clogged corresponds to her perception of the world. Did she see the world clogged?

I've been thinking about, nearly meditating on, gaps, myself. What is there, in the so-called 'new sentence,' which tends to be complete (a statement, the case)— what is there that might move one to the next sentence? what presses forward, from within? where is the gravity—or, rather, how does one shift the gravitational pull from the center of the sentence to the end, so that rather than sagging it goes to the next sentence? how does one prevent the writing from becoming complete at every point? This again is me addressing the fight against closure. Perhaps in the paragraph one can discover the relationship between sentences.

Writing *My Life* I learned how to write sentences, or complete thoughts, which is the dictionary definition of the sentence, and now find that enormously problematic. Periods turn into blockades. Every sentence isolates itself and seems to deny contingency—a smug stasis. The isolation that human beings feel is different from the isolation of sentences—so it's no good saying that such writing is like life. Larry says that Stockhausen and the 'pointillist' composers tried to make each musical note self-sufficient and independent, worthy of total attention, isolable, and that it didn't work. However, neither words nor musical notes are objects—nor are poems or musical compositions.

I always loved that the Action Painters were denying the object status of the painting—at least that's how I interpreted much of what their work was about. The gesture wasn't even about the psychology of the gesture—I never really got much from the idea of Expressionism vis a vis their work. Hmm—just thinking about them now I feel a great urge to see, right now, a giant show of deKooning's work, then another of Kline's, then Pollock, and Motherwell—maybe end with the deKooning, for the color.

I'm having fantasies. You say that your response to the Fifties was that you 'didn't hope to think that you really could do anything like what you were reading or seeing or hearing.' I think my response was the opposite—I not only hoped to think that I could—I was sure I could, and would. I couldn't of course—but the opening doors were certainly ones I was walking through, entirely by instinct, according to my nature. No decisions were being made.

I didn't understand that there was something to be against; I wasn't angry initially, nor for years, and then I had to struggle against whatever it was that had socialized me into a 'nice,' 'kind,' and 'understanding' person. Perhaps at this point I am still going through the transition from pacifist to terrorist.

Would I plant bombs in Bernadette's Utopia?

The idea appeals to my comic sense, in any case. I read the section of her Utopia work that just came out in United Artists. I actually enjoyed it; there are some wonderful grammatical twists that made me assume 'twistedness' in general. I mean, the whole thing was so ridiculous—it reads like a description of a hippie commune in the Santa Cruz Mountains written by someone with a selective memory who has forgotten that the chickens ate each other, the pig succumbed to tape worm, the kids drowned the kittens in the hot tub, and an ax murderer disemboweled the pet dog on Thanksgiving. The electric typewriters were short-circuted in the lentil soup. All of which is to say, Utopia is a comedy.

Larry is still away, though he gets home in six days, which seems soon after six weeks. The tour is over, but there's a possibility that Black Saint will do a record and he decided to accept their invitation to come to Milan to talk about that. Also we have friends in Italy, people who have entrepreneured previous Rova trips and who have visited us here. It is a good time for Larry to unwind—become a person again, he says, before he gets home and I try to have conversations with him. It is impossible to mean anything, I am sure, when one is as exhausted and stunned by social, artistic, and geographical encounters as Larry must be after six weeks of touring.

I've been reading Freud—I probably was last time I wrote you, too. The Interpretation of Dreams and The Psychopathology of Everyday Life. The latter makes me question the meaning of my typos. The former makes me wonder why I dream of police.

I may dream of police because I've been reading mystery novels, too. When I work until it is late and I'm exhausted it is hard to sleep and hard to think. I don't try to solve the mysteries. I like to follow the procedures. I seldom care who did it and I seldom remember. In that vein, I read Blood on the Dining Room Floor, by the way. I mean, late at night. It is very funny. Then I read the 'true' story, Stein's other rendering of it, which involves Francis Rose and the servants and so forth, which seemed actually very mysterious—but I just went to see if I could find where I had read that and I can't seem to find it—maybe in The Autobiography of Alice B. Toklas which I can't find either.

I can't seem to read Laura Riding, either, nor HD, though for entirely different reasons. I share your irritation with Laura Riding's inflated difficulties; I'm suspicious of their genuineness and her protestations seem coy. In any case, I feel as if the writing itself is behind blockades and not arresting.

There has been, and continues to be, lots of literary activity around town. Every year about this time everything happens at once. Alan Davies was here for a week, to give a Talk at 80 Langton Street and a reading at S.F. State with Carla; the reading was one of the really great ones, from both Alan and Carla. Alan's talk was extremely provocative and clear—I disagreed from the heart, as it were, as did others, but usefully, and the discussion that night and for the rest of the week was extremely good. Poets Theater is doing two new plays—performing for three weekends, of which this one is the second. I've been twice, the first time preferring Eileen Corder's play, the second time preferring Alan Bernheimer's. Both are really wonderful. Ron Padgett begins a four days residency at Langton Street. Ron Silliman is giving a series of Monday Talks on prose and Bob Grenier a series of Friday Talks on here. And then there are the two on-going reading series and another series of Talks that has just started. I miss a lot of all of this, intentionally or not. By being selective I've been pretty consistently pleased. I am leaving the fanaticism, proof of devotion, to the younger generation of writers—and feeling grateful that there is one.

Must go hang out the laundry in what remains of the sun in winter, which in drifting south leaves the backyard and laundry line, which are on the north, in a slipping chill shadow. I love the fireplace. I've been listening to a lot of music in front of it.

Love,

Lyn

Letter to Rae Armantrout

January 5, 1984

Thursday, Berkeley

Dear Rae,

The way Frank O'Hara and later Ted Berrigan began their poems—it is 9:39 p.m. and my back is to the night—say (only that is my beginning—or my in medias res)—it's a wonderful utensil, because from there you can continue anywhere. So—it is 9:41 p. m. (you see how long I think between sentences); Paull is back at Harvard; Anna is writing term papers and bored, because she will soon be back at college (Wesleyan); Larry is playing music with Greg Goodman; and I am home, cheerfully—very happily—having worked all day at my desk and feeling wedded to it now. And so, completely tired, I thought—should I read (I couldn't concentrate); should I sleep (I couldn't dream); should I ... vacuum, launder, scrub etc etc (I couldn't stand it). But I do feel like answering your letter—only you have to be patient. I've been working on my translation, for the next Poetics Journal, of the Francoise de Laroque article, all day long and I think it may be quite insane. Carla agrees—that gives me confidence that I'm not.

Your letter arrived just before Christmas. You sounded pretty cheerful, although the thing with Dalton's sounded pretty weird—perhaps more weird to tell than to witness. (Is it spelled weird—yeah.) I won't tell anyone, but truly you shouldn't be embarrassed. It is probably to your credit, and to their discredit, that you aren't working there anymore.

But the bigger issue, of self-confidence, that I do think about seriously. I think about it in various ways, in terms of myself, in terms of women, in terms of poets (in our culture which makes of poetry such comedy, an unremunerative comedy), in terms of humans. At an early stage I thought writing might be compensation of sorts—maybe a way of explaining my inadequacies. Even now, when I am really angry at Larry, I write to him—being convinced he'll take that more seriously. Maybe because the page is an incontrovertible fact. More likely because my hysteria doesn't have to participate in his encounter with my ideas.

Stephen Rodefer told me that when Barry visited his class at S.F. State (in November, I suppose), Barry said Language School Poetry was dead.

Whether he said it or not (he probably did) the statement fills me with an exhilarating sense of possibility. ("Now we are grownups and the work begins.")

As you know, for me the conflict (or should I say "dialectic") between solitude and community is always painful. But maybe there is a natural pulse, a time for one, a time for the other, and I don't have to feel so anxious. In any case, I haven't been indulging in that, and I've been getting some writing done.

And visiting with family—first Paull home from college, not altogether unlike himself but emotionally bigger; and my mother who has grown very dear to me; and Larry's sister Jacki who is wonderful. She went to Russia with us, and so we can sit and gossip and analyze impressions, and figure out what's between the lines of the letters we've received. Letters arrive a) through the post office b) through couriers (people who conduct tours in the USSR or are tourists there) and c) via friends living elsewhere who carry letters out. Different kinds of letters say different things—that is, the medium influences the content (i.e. McLuhan). But not as much as one would think.

As for local writing—I agree with you about Carla's book. In fact, I think it is the most exciting writing to come out of here in a long time. I bought a lot of copies to give for Christmas presents, and I've read the book several times myself. The forward momentum keeps covering new ground while still embracing itself—it kind of literally covers the field—and then, still, you want to know where you'll end up, in an excited curious sort of way. One reads it eagerly.
For me, it seems like a prototype for a style of aesthetic thinking that is both creative and—well, not thorough, but encompassing, or embracing.

Susan Howe's essay reached me safely, I have hardly looked at it but I will— we are publishing the first part in PJ and I like that very much.

And I like "Fiction" too. I have two picky comments: The 10th sentence— "The new television ..."—I would prefer "on" to "upon"—the latter seems stilted and uptight, prissy. And in the next sentence ("A ballerina") it should be "fluttered on point" rather than "fluttered on toe." At least, that's ballet lingo, and it is good in the context.
Over all the writing in this (as usual) is brilliant—but the piece seemed incredibly bleak. It is ironic, given the title, that I should feel reservations about the narrative content—but, anyway, for what it's worth, I felt that there was a narrative content, that it wasn't very enlightening, and that it was depressing. I mean the "ours" (if you wanted one) would be to add more material between the lines, but then, I admit, that's my whole mode of composition—full of contradiction, too.

Now Anna wants me to "go over" her editorial for the newspaper (school—on "competing with the Eastern prep schools").

Sorry for the fragmentary letter. And happy new year. And love,

Lyn

Letter to Clark and Susan Coolidge

Lyn Hejinian
2639 Russell St.
Berkeley, CA 94705
September 19, 1984
Wednesday night

Dear Clark and Susan,

I left your house and drove to New Hampshire without any misshaps, feeling very grateful to you both for the visit, and happy, and continuing to follow strands of our conversation.

Writing while driving is somewhat similar to carrying a lollipop in one's mouth while running. I had the same good luck as most children, and didn't run into anything that would drive my pen anywhere lethal. I did take the precaution of switching to the far right lane when suddenly inspired, but there one finds oneself between a semi (George Carleno, Truckers) and another semi (Filene's), whose drivers tend to conceive of space as something to squeeze.

I passed under several groups of people gathered on overpasses to wave at oncoming traffic. Why do they do this?

People seem to carry on a flirtation with movement—at Niagara Falls there are guards who patrol the guardrail at the vistas, lest eagerly transfixed tourists decide to participate radically and permanently in the great flow.

Are people restless and attracted to anything that moves? (water, shadows, traffic). Does the eye more easily watch movement than stillness and so find looking at traffic relaxing? Beyond abstract video and MTV, is the Mass. Pike in motion aesthetically complete? Is there a cargo cult located in Billerica, Natick, or Framingham?

I tried very hard to think about "the good" and poetry, since that seemed the most difficult subject to imagine—I mean, one wonders if one is being lazy for a reason. First I tried to imagine what Bernadette might want, and then what the masses might want—all of these, including Bernadette, being entirely hypothetical. Finally I tried to think about what I might want—which, of course, is an old subject.

That poetry is good is self-evident, but perhaps it is good in a way that does no good.

Or, perhaps, Bernadette (and me too, for that matter) needs solutions to problems that are not poetical—but, in that case, poetry, in our personal history and in the history of our culture more generally, has shaped the sensitivity and sensibility that makes us care (about hunger, poor schools, people's frustrations, etc.).

It seems to me that worrying about poetry is similar to worrying about being "nice."

I think I resolved my own personal crisis over poetry and politics from inside the poem, somehow—at some point, the poem (in the abstract sense) began to radiate confidence and purpose from within. That assumes an intuited faith in large reaches of time, and therefore it can be interpreted as a privileged position. But I don't at all mean to disregard the urgent time that is the context of suffering.

I guess there is the sea and there is the storm, and the poet regards the sea while the coast guard regards the storm.

I've been reading Chekov's Letters—he wrote without guilt about good and bad guys the way they are, and used the proceeds from his writings to build a hospital and two public schools in his provincial neighborhood. That seems entirely appropriate.

But I don't think there is any doubt at all as to there being an ethical element (and therefore ethical responsibility) in art. Maybe disco is (was) unethical—I remember mouthing off at it as "fascist" and so forth, Larry and I forming a sort of chorus of the insulted—but who knows. I usually am embarrassed to remember adamant positions I have taken—either because I was showing off or because I was uncontrollably curious and so wanted to provoke "more" of whatever it might be.

Anna has written us four long letters from Wesleyan already. She is taking Alvin Lucier's course on contemporary music: "Today we began John Cage; we learned all about his piece for amplified toy pianos and then listened to part of it. Mr. Lucier made us all comment on it. Alot of people were appalled by it, saying it was "haunting," "superficial," "random." I said that it made you think more than Bach, for example, because less of it is out in the open." She is taking Philosophy of Art: "Tolstoy dismissed Shakespeare, Manet, Monet, etc etc etc for being unclear. He especially loathed King Lear and Beethoven's Ninth. I can't believe anyone would be so dense, especially someone like Tolstoy." She is also taking advanced calculus and the Moral Basis of Politics.

Meanwhile Paull went back to Harvard last Friday.

I had anticipated feeling sad, but I've been surprised at how really terrible I feel. I guess it's a form of terror. Anyway, it makes me feel stupid and angry and pathetic, and so I've been reading a lot, and making meticulous translations of letters from Russia. And thinking about the limitations of the literary scene, and bugging Larry.

Feeling depressed is somewhat like having a birthday—one sort of wants someone to know about it, but one doesn't want them to say anything.

I had such a good time at your house.

When I got to my mother and stepfather's house in New Hampshire, my sister and her two children were there, and my 5 year old nephew immediately proposed: "Lynnie, take me out in the canoe." It was perfect—"Well, Anthony," said I, "do you think the space between our canoe and that tree is empty or full?" "There's a bunch of water in it."

If I were Chekov I would end this letter with "God grant you the best of everything, and, principally, good health." Or, better, "I wish you all the blessings of heaven and earth, and thank you with all my heart."

Whenever I travel, I mostly have to remember to eat and breathe. I never can write anything or anyone—I seemed consumed with absorbing. So don't feel you have to write from Italy unless you feel like it. Have a wonderful time.

Thanks again, and love,

Lyn

Letter to Alice Notley

Lyn Hejinian
2639 Russell Street
Berkeley, California 94705

December 4, 1985

Dear Alice,

I bought a copy of Margaret & Dusty when it came out and stayed up late one night reading it and in the end wrote a poem and at the bottom put "for Alice Notley" although, really, I almost never dedicate poems to people. In this case I wasn't talking to you nor writing because of your book, but I was feeling the most intense admiration for the book and also thinking personally about you and wondering how you are. And it seemed that this gave me some burst of creative energy and I wrote the poem.

That was in September.

Now Tom Savage wrote me a note (inviting me to send some work to Gandhabba) and sent me a copy of his magazine and I read your poems there and found myself all over again full of admiration and wondering how you are. And so it seemed time to write you. First, here is the poem:

Poem

The adamant, and happy
The mud begins to stand out for the cloud
Innocuous with smoke—who's on the phone?
All waters fall

A city creased
by someone with a voice
for the uneven midnight smells
Whenever I correct, I count

and look for the sound-alike
The concentration gets chipped
And thus? invite all structures
Weirdness—assemble everything you thought

But not in the form of a diary—
the very word "diary" depresses me

9/17/85
for Alice Notley

I don't know why I announced such a harsh opinion of diaries, since in truth I find other writers' literary diaries fascinating and valuable. My own attempts to keep diaries have come from the very worst impulses and resulted in the worst possible writing, in part, perhaps, because of the problem of audience. It is a strange dis-communicative gesture (unless one is imagining oneself as later famous and so fascinating as to compel an audience of eavesdroppers).

But they say that traditionally women have been writers of letters and diaries (because they weren't taken seriously enough for anything else, I guess). I love letters—both to write them and to receive them; but I have destroyed all my diaries and journals and I am beginning to destroy notebooks.

Maybe I feel suspicious of the sincerity of the diary-keeper—as if he or she wanted to make a display of being private. It resembles sulking. Or a histrionic gesture: "I'm not going to tell anyone what I think" (while writing it for every-one to see).

But, as you can tell, this is all leftover adolescence. And therefore forgotten.

As always, literary life in the Bay Area is lively and full of contention. I've been much more than usually withdrawn, at first because all the controversies and mean-spiritedness of some of the attacks on various writers (while neglect-ing to address their writing) depressed me. But while it depressed me, it also gave me an occasion for thinking about my commitment to poetry and to a specific kind of poetry and I figured out the nature and rationale for that com-mitment (at least temporarily) and got fired up with enthusiasm. And stayed withdrawn in order to write—and even to think.

Both my children are away at college now so there is time to think. I mean all the way to the end of a train of thought.

Meanwhile, it is strange having the children away. It was horrible at first—I felt old, useless, finished, ugly, etc. Then I luckily got a chance to go to Russia again (for a month) and then joined Larry in Europe, where he was on tour for four months with Rova Saxophone Quartet. We spent a month in Paris, which was rejuvenating—mostly because it isn't dominated by a youth culture such as we have here in the U.S.

It was wonderful being somewhere where women are more admired than girls.

As for the subject of women—there is much feminist discussion going on, and I listen and even join in, and yet I find much that is disturbingly out of touch with my own experience of myself and being a poet. I find, in these discussions, that my intellect doesn't agree with my emotions—that is, I can grasp the idea and even the possible truth of the notion that women have been deprived of language, that the symbolic order is authoritarian and male (phallic)—and yet in my heart I don't feel a loss of language or a desire for a penis.

Beverly Dahlen (whom I admire very much) gave a trio of Talks ostensibly about Emily Dickinson but actually about feminism and poetry, and I found them immensely disturbing and even disturbed. I think that Bev truly thinks that to be born a woman is a catastrophic event, that all of a woman's life is led in a state of absence and loss, that women are literally and in every metaphorical way castrated.

She has been able to make art out of her radical negativity. But that doesn't prove her position. Meanwhile a number of people in the audience (mostly women but some men, too) were nodding and applauding in agreement with her. That made me feel terrible, somehow.

Then the other night some man fan called me to tell me how he loved The Guard because it was very womanly and it was womanly because I included the kitchen in it. !

And how are you? Write me sometime if you have a moment.

Love.

Lyn

Letter to Kit Robinson

November 16, 1986

Dear Kit,

The Postmodernism issue is developing all by itself without interference from Barry or me. Hence very slowly. Barry has been preoccupied with innumerable other things, so that PJ matters have been displaced, or misplaced. I was eager to work on PJ last summer, but now I am content to wait for Barry to get interested again—which will be fairly soon, I think; he is beginning to attend to the articles we have already received.

There are a couple that went to him and that I haven't seen, but those that I have seen are quite good. Ron sent us one that is wonderful—exemplary. When I read it I wasn't sure anything more needed to be said on the subject.

Lots can be said in the context of the subject, however. Almost anything. At least (and this may come from teaching various manifestations of "poetics"), there ought to be a real thrill informing and resonating from any theoretical formulation, and that thrill takes the form of activity. I find myself inclining toward the least conventional contributions to this issue.

I won't go on about this. The truth is that I have repeatedly to renegotiate my own relationship to theory—mostly to the various possible forms theoretical writing can take. It is because I haven't yet found myself a form, a writing design, in which to put my ideas, that I write so little theory—or criticism.

I think I am writing so happily and easily to you (the poems) because the form was established—one can come up with designs endlessly.

This reminds me of my conversation with a psychic reader. I had never gone to one, nor "tried" anything remotely similar. But two years ago I felt the necessity of stepping entirely out of character, since I felt very miserable in character (this was around the time when both Paull and Anna had left, and when our poetry scene seemed to inspire dread and anxiety). I asked the psychic about literary form—I was writing "The Person" and was (and still am) entirely perplexed at the apparent formlessness of the work (or works—I still don't know whether it will be one long work or a group of poems). Eyes closed, leaning back on the ochre sofa, she said that my poems were "life projects" and must have a form that was very large but clear and in which many variations were possible—"It has to be like the sea, which has tides, but also waves, and small ripples."

Have you ever read Melville's <u>White Jacket</u>?

In your 16th poem, to (or from) which my 20th responds, you mention "a book by the bed." I had just been reading Clark's "Book of During" section in the new <u>Sulfur</u> and in that context thought of pornography. Meanwhile, I had used the word "slit" (as a noun) in translating one of Arkadii Dragomoshchenko's poems (it is coincidentally a 12-poem sequence, and I began my #21 with a line from each poem, though in the end I didn't follow that rule very strictly; a variation of the line with the slit is included in the poem); a slit for me has sexual connotations. I don't know why I was thinking about stars—but I "heard" or "said" in my mind something about stars as slits in the sky. Hence the first line of my 20th poem.

I wonder if I am right that eroticism is stirred by incongruities in scale. The vast emotion in the minute moment. Or the huge body in a tiny house. Or can the incongruous exist without comparison? I wonder if eroticism always requires more than one thing—but now I'm confusing the erotic with desire, which is different.

<u>A Day Off</u> is very beautiful. I read it aloud and it sounded elegiac, even when I was laughing. An elegy usually is addressed to (experienced, rather than anticipated) mortality (time) and significance (single existences)—and your poems are, too. But in your poems time is some kind of loose (maybe even baggy) structure with an enormous capacity, and there is a lot of busy, mortal activity in it. The activity is somewhat fabulously ludicrous (comical) and the tone is somewhat fatalistic (I suppose that might be a problem although it derives from some essential kindness). "Archangel" is a great poem. The whole book is great. It makes me want to be a publisher again.

I guess we should get together before the reading to decide how to read our poems. Maybe we could think of some way to construct the entire reading as a whole—obviously you will want to read <u>A Day Off</u> and maybe I will get together sections of "The Person" so we have three works altogether?

But, are you willing to go on writing 12's back and forth? I would like to.

Love,

Lyn

Letter to Charles Bernstein

December 6, 1986

Dear Charles,

Your long and wonderful letter from weeks ago has been sitting beside me on my desk all this time—it seemed worth such a long and detailed answer that I have continually postponed answering it until I had time. But when the times came, my tongue had been wagging (in my mind, if not my mouth) already for hours, so that I had used up all available words and felt dumb. I won't bore you with an account of all that I've been doing—only to say that teaching has turned out to be compulsively fascinating in the loose and divagating atmosphere of the Poetics Program at New College (which is, however, leaving New College); that translating resembles an endless battle between unlikely lovers; that thanks to a suggestion from Kit, and working parallel to Kit, in October I began a long work or work-series that has finally provided me with a form that accommodates the method I have always been proposing. I'm not sure the new poems read much different from my other writing, but the moment of composition feels different—feels great, to tell you the truth. I confess that I have been writing poems whenever I felt articulate and alert—and my correspondence has fallen behind.

I did receive, both from Donald Wesling and from Rodefer, copies of the Archive Newsletter with Wesling's review of Redo. This whole business of "Language School" —it is getting quite hilarious, actually (at a meeting at New College the Chairpersons of the Law School and of the Humanities Dept. questioned the Poetics Faculty (me, Michael Palmer, Louis Patler, David Meltzer) about Language writing because they had been told that the Poetics Program was a podium for L-S ideology, at which David Meltzer turned purple and appeared close to apoplexy, Louis Paler flailed and emphatically said he didn't understand a word Ron Silliman writes, and somewhere Robert Duncan wrote out a Curse to be mailed by a Muse, Michael Palmer spoke circuitously about postmodernism, and I said, "Give me a break!"). A recent many-paged article in the very local Berkeley Monthly attacked L-S writing for its theory—for having a theory. The author liked the poetry but not the theory.

There was a more interesting criticism, one to which I intend to reply if I have time before we leave—Larry and I and Paull are going to Rome for Christmas! to meet up with Anna who will fly there from Nairobi!— The author characterized us (who remained for the most part nameless; although he said there were

50 L-poets in the Bay Area, he named only Ron, Barrett, and Bob P, which means there are 47 more Cold Negatives out there looking much like normal people while constituting a danger to Singers and Song)—but he characterized us as Avant Gardists with the traditional avant garde desire to shock the philistines, to knock the top hats from the heads of the bourgeoisie (there are no women in any of this). In other words, and here I am quite serious in my sense of rage, he misses altogether the context in which we are working. Of course we don't care about philistines, and who can possibly be outraged at the bourgeoisie when there is nothing else. He fails to see that we are angry—furious—at real criminals, who seek to overthrow the legitimate government of Nicaragua, who dump dioxin in rivers, who legitimize and sanctify a system of greed, murder, destruction—etc. If any single poem of mine could wreak revenge for these things, I would set it lose, I think.

With regard to Donald Wesling's review, when he says that I am not a Language Poet I want to say, realistically, I am I am. And at the same time, for different reasons, I can say truthfully that I'm not, there is no such thing. Bob Perelman is quoted in the Berkeley Monthly as saying that it used to be possible to open a magazine and recognize a Language Poem but not any more. And I think he is completely right. (I was interviewed by a student of David Bromige's a week or so ago, who referred consistently to me as a "Language Realist." I thought that was quite interesting and regaled her with my own thoughts on the term and your correctives.)

When your letter arrived about "realism," I was reaching many of the same points in my own train of thought about the topic—and, for example, separating out the topic from the term. If I am very fortunate next year, I will teach a year-long course called "The Language of Inquiry," and try to approach my sense of the relationship of the poem to the real (as of and in the real, perhaps) via 17th and 18th century scientific writing, in particular the descriptive writing that bore witness to the voyages of discovery. There is a remarkable book by a Bishop Spratt that influenced the devices (rhetoric) of that writing—arguments over the use and misuse of simile and metaphor, for example. Can a tropical shoreline or a turning iceberg ever usefully be said to be "like" anything? Poetics for awhile embraced science, then turned against it, then seems to have aspired to the scientific again (or at least has been inspired by it). A poetry of cognition? I think that is what I write—that is, the writing is itself the act, process, and moment of cognition.

It isn't a very interesting word, "cognition."

But it implies that there is a real world out there; in fact, it assumes so. A world that is, as you put it, untouched by being perceived. You think there is no such independent reality—but I do. It is fundamental to my scepticism. I like Freud's little quote, in The Future of an Illusion,

"The town of Constance lies on the Bodensee;
if you don't believe it, you can go and see"

I don't think language, even as perception, is magical in the way that, for example, Robert Duncan, HD, and probably Susan Howe do. There is a bird on the tree. I will tell you about it without my doing so in any way effecting the bird. I will be altered perhaps by having told you and you, if you listen, may be altered. But not the bird or the tree.

My use of the word "accuracy," however, has been consistently a mistake, I think. "Sincerity" is closer to what I mean. In this area, of course, I am trying to get at the ethical motives (and motifs) that underlie my own personal commitment to poetry—to writing it, publishing it, theorizing about it, attending readings of it, distributing it, propagandizing for it, teaching an enthusiasm for it, etc.

When I think of the world, I don't think of an "outside" in the Spicer/Blaser sense—I should add that.

In the end, all of my pronouncements on this subject (and I am sure I will continue to make them for years and years) reflect my perplexity—about the real, real language, real death.

I say "real death" as one says, "Hey, this isn't a movie, it's real life." I spent some days with a friend—I think perhaps my friendship with her goes back farther than any other non-familial relationship—in June. She has cancer and died on June 21, and the memorial gathering for her was a few days later in our backyard, which is what her two children, who are exactly Paull and Anna's age, wanted. As my friend was dying, and of course afterwards, it seemed that her death was real in the sense that it wasn't a blank, a negative, non-existent. I learned a lot, sitting beside her—she was mostly sleeping and I was mostly looking out the window at a somewhat stunted tree and some unmown grass. Oddly enough, I found myself thinking about discontinuity and the poetic line; I didn't come up with any revelations that way.

The program from the "Three Saints" was nice. I've been reading the new biography of Langston Hughes; in fact, trying to make up for never having learned much at all about the Harlem Renaissance and the American poetry of that tradition. In my white education, that tradition didn't exist—although my mother and father used to read Langston Hughes aloud to me sometimes, along with Stephen Vincent Benet and … is it John Masefield who wrote "The Highwayman" (came riding, riding, riding, etc.—I probably liked it because of the horse!)

As for your visit to the Bay Area on the weekend of the 25th—you certainly are invited to stay with us. Anna's room, large and sunny, will be available, and

Larry and I are beginning now to recover from 3 months (!) of houseguests, from mid-July to mid-October—a week at a time with never more than 3 days off, which was just long enough to change the sheets; I felt like a hospitality factory. Or a hospitality factotum.

I don't know anyone with a crib. Offhand, that is—the topic of beds, in general or specifically for children, seldom comes up in the course of my conversations. But tonight I am going to Bob and Francie's where poets are gathering to celebrate Bob's birthday, and I will try to remember to ask Alan and Melissa, for example, and Nick and Eileen, if they are there, about cribs or other possible sleeping rigs. Could Emma sleep on a futon on the floor? Because two of our chairs make into futons. We have 3 cats—is anyone allergic?

I hope that you like teaching as much as it turns out that I do—it is completely thrilling to me. I haven't worked so hard for years. The students love poetry, and so I love them.

And love to you too, and Susan, and Emma,

Lyn

P.S. Perhaps you should telephone me in mid-January about your visit; if you decide to stay with Tom or George that is of course fine, also.

Letter to Susan Howe

November 21, 1987

Dear Susan,

You are right, it has been a long time since we've written to each other, and I think about you nonetheless, as you say you do about me.

All the days seem crowded and busy, unless I become apathetic and unable to make them so. For awhile in September and early October things were just as I would want them to be—I was writing seriously and had a sense that the days were perfectly long. Or rather, that the days had more of space and less of time in them. I don't like time. And it's not because I'm getting old.

I hated being 45, but I like being 46—it seems a somewhat comical age, remarkably old and yet insignificantly so. The point, I guess, is that it isn't a "landmark" year. I won't like being 50 but I expect it will be fine to be 51—those in-between, post-significant years allow one to maintain one's ageless dignity.

I'm going to write a third version of My Life when I'm 60. I won't be twice as old then as I am now, but the book will be almost twice as long. I absolutely can't figure out why.

But meanwhile, I'm very happy that you like the new (45 year old) book.

Your writing me about it reminded me that I hadn't written you about your Awede book, although I've read it a couple of times and I've bought extra copies of it, one to send to Russia and one to give to a composer (Charles Boone) who asked me to suggest work that he might set to music. The title completely amazed him—his great interest is in the relationship of music to architecture and architectural form. I heard him give a lecture on the topic in a "Meet the Composer" series in San Francisco. Larry had met him a few times and thought I would like him—it turns out that I do; he is very formal, kind, and demanding. Actually, Larry says that Charles reminds him of Barrett Watten, and perhaps there is something to that.

In any case, probably nothing will come of my desire to hear Articulation of Sound Forms in Time with chamber orchestra. I'm going to meet with Charles in a couple of weeks.

I really don't know what effect our being women has, either on our correspondence or our writing. It is a big question but it lacks big answers. The political and social issues are very clear to me, but the aesthetic issues are not—that is, I know that my position vis a vis the power structure is conditioned and even determined by my being a woman and I know how and why that is so—I can watch it be so. But I don't know what there is in my imagination or my syntax or my literary or linguistic impulses that is specifically determined by my being a woman. Do you? about yourself, I mean?

And should we care? There's something narrowly essentialist about the question, and essentialism seems potentially dangerous.

What we need to know is what kinds of thinking and writing and knowing are being suppressed—and then to do, or help others do, that thinking, writing, and knowing. A giant task. I'm glad there are lots of women to help with it.

You have Maureen and I have Carla Harryman. Carla has been working for Rova Saxophone Quartet for the last 14 or 15 months as the quartet's administrator. The Rova office, hence her office, is in our house—which means we see each other pretty constantly. And so we talk a lot, about general and about specific things. We talk often about feminism and writers-as-women. We seem often to come up with a strong moral sense—a moral agenda for writing and for our role in our own literary community here. It is tricky trying to pinpoint what I mean.

My teaching situation collapsed, just before the classes I thought I was teaching were to begin. Antioch-San Francisco, which had expressed enthusiastic acceptance of our poetics program, never even listed the poetics courses in their catalogue—so their support was fraudulent and my many months of preparation went for nothing.

But of course, it did go for something. I don't know about the Eunuch Ho, but I know something about exploration and the language of description that it generated beginning approximately 200 years later. Also I know a little about Antarctica.

I was almost elated when my course was canceled, because I was getting deeper and deeper into my material with a less and less clear idea of what it was about and why I was wallowing in it. I was terrified to invite students to jump in beside me. Which is to say that I understand perfectly your trepidation about teaching at Buffalo. I also know that you'll do a magnificent and exemplary job, just as you did at Vancouver and at New College. The combination of scholarship, independence, and insistence is very important—I mean, it's important for students to know that it is possible to think in those ways.

As for my family—everyone is fine. Larry is busy with both Rova and his other group, a trio called Room. Touring, recording, commissioning pieces—Larry is one of those people around whom (and because of whom) things happen. My going to Russia, for example. Currently there is a lot happening around him.

Paull is living in London, working for a Labour Party Member of Parliament and trying to discover a way to continue living abroad. The job with the MP is sponsored by a Grant from Harvard and only lasts for a year. He sounds very happy there—his office is in Westminster Abbey and he has found a spacious inexpensive flat through the son of a musician friend of ours, which he shares with a man who is a gourmet chef.

Anna is finishing her last year at Wesleyan, depressed over the state of the world, unable to imagine how to change things, and thinking about going to medical school or public health school before returning to Africa.

It is sad news about George Butterick; I have never met him, but even so I was (and am) stunned. Out here more and more, one hears of or knows people who have contracted AIDS. People don't seem to talk about the disease so much now, but we just know it is all around us. Anna says that in East Africa, where she was, many many people are sick and dying of AIDS but everyone denies that it exists.

Out here, literary life continues much as always. Barry and Carla are coming to dinner here tonight. Michael Davidson and Lori Chamberlain have moved to Berkeley while Lori goes to law school. Bob Perelman is perpetually boyish and perpetually absorbed by his studies—or, I should say, he is perpetually absorbing them. I see Steve Benson quite often and am trying to write an articulate blurb for his next book. I talk to Jean Day on the phone at least every 10 days. Kit Robinson and I have been working on parallel collections of poems for the last year—independent works but accruing through a correspondence. So we write to each other once or twice a week, although we live within ten blocks of each other. Ron Silliman has learned to drive a car and made his first solo expedition last Tuesday night to a Poetics Journal benefit, allowing 30 minutes for parallel parking. And everyone else—according to an attack in a Berkeley tabloid there are 50 Language poets skulking around the Bay Area, all of them holding Theories—everyone else is probably busy and fine, too.

And now the sun is out and the floors are dirty.
I should respond appropriately to one or the other of these two facts.
But first—thank you for your letter. Please give my love to Maureen.

Let's write more often to each other.

Love,

Lyn

Letter to Fanny Howe

Lyn Hejinian
2639 Russell St.
Berkeley, CA. 94705

January 8, 1993

Dear Fanny,

I've been drinking too much coffee this morning, and it has had the effect of making me feel overconfident, i.e. drunk.

Or maybe stoned (which reminds me to tell you that I'm having dinner with Bob Grenier Sunday—I haven't seen him in ages but he sounded fine when we talked on the phone).

Anyway, my thoughts have been flying, and they flew into incredibly heretical realms, which I could describe only to you. Besides, your wonderful letter is here on my desk, and I wanted to write to you anyway. So here I am, heretical and in high spirits.

You have begun teaching, I know—the dreadful "Craft of Poetry" course among other things-—but I still have two weeks of aimless interim, and so this morning I've been writing. I've been working on my Sleeps project, which oscillates between being about memory and about universals—those kinds of abstractions—whatever can be deduced from "everything." I think for the first time, actually, I am being influenced by Arkadii's writing. I've been spending several hours every afternoon working on my translation of his Phosphor manuscript, and the last several afternoons on one long, logical, but almost (and appropriately) incomprehensible sentence about Nothing. The essential notion of this sentence about Nothing is that everything changes, therefore everything is boundless, each thing becoming another thing, therefore all things are the same, any thing is every thing, and both anything and everything are infinite and eternal.

But maybe not in imitation of Arkadii but because of the nature of Sleeps, I've been thinking about dream life, with respect to memory (the stuff of dreams) and oblivion (the stuff of sleep, but the stuff of waking to the extent that the dreams are mostly, at least consciously, forgotten). And death seems to have a place in this landscape—or maybe I find myself thinking about it for other reasons (recent friends claimed by death, a sense of my own aging).

Meanwhile I talked on the phone with my sister-in-law about this and that and then about our kids, about worry, and she said she no longer worries about her son (who used to get in some frightening scrapes with mortality), since "if God wants to take him there is nothing I can do about it."

That comment seemed to pass me by—God doesn't usually enter into my concept of the scheme of things (though I know, of course, that he must for you)—but as if somewhere behind me (Larry says one's own death is always standing behind one—I wonder if that's a Jewish superstition) the notion of Death and God was taking shape. Death, by the way, is not an evil for me. Not a good, either, I should add. Just a presence, unknowable, and inevitable. Could that be God?

There's my heretical thought.

Or maybe it's just semantics.

But no, unfortunately—one couldn't pray (at least not easily) to Death for a safe journey (I'm thinking of Patsy's quick prayer as we turned onto Bonair on our way to Berkeley last spring.)

Those days in San Diego don't really seem so long ago. I can picture the salad bar at the Price Center, the oddly dark cavernous area in front of it, the rattle of the air conditioning in the ceiling of my office—and my incredible exhaustion when the quarter was done. I wonder how Barry is fitting in. Are you teaching anything other than the Craft of Poetry thing? Will Misha Iossel be coming there at some point? Are you going to continue commuting from Los Angeles? Most of all, have you heard yet about the London position?

All these questions don't require answers—that is, I'm not demanding that you write me back immediately.

Your holidays sound very nice. Ours were mostly childless—Anna went with her Thomas to Germany to visit his family (where she had a better time than he did, since she isn't German and isn't so rawly vulnerable and angst-ridden and fatally guilty when evidence of neo-nazisms and ancient racisms turn up), and Paull was with his Lottie in Minnesota with her mother and sisters. But we spent time with all the local family—my brother, sister-in-law, nephew, nephew's wife, nephew's wife's mother—and with friends who are family equivalents, and then on Dec. 29 Larry went to Europe for a month of Rova touring and I went to Minnesota to spend New Years with Paull and Lottie.

Lottie's mother is terrific, and we had a wonderful and hilarious time. The temperature stood at minus 16 degrees—heaven, perfect for your film about snow—except the camera would freeze.

Larry saw George Lewis during the fall at the Memorial Service for the musician Gerald Oshita. George delivered one of the eulogies, and Larry said it was magnificent. I gather George talked about the hardships of the artist's life, and the gloriousness of such a life as lived by an artist committed to it—Gerald being such a person. As Larry described the eulogy it sounded rousing and delicate.

Well—I guess I'll return to my poetical writing. Will you forgive this crazy letter?—I began it spontaneously and suddenly, wanting to talk about death and feeling Love, and I wanted to talk to you.

All love,

Lyn

Letter to Jack Collom

Lyn Hejinian
2639 Russell St.
Berkeley, Calif. 94705

Oct 7, 1994

Dear Jack,

It's evening—sometime after 7, with the last iridescent blue glow of a warm (too warm for my taste) day still clinging to the sky and the sounds of city wanderers coming in from the street. Larry has gone to the corner cafe to get something to eat—we are on somewhat different schedules today, and rather than impose DINNER (as some ideal meal) on ourselves, as if it were part of a martial regimen, I'm at my desk (a glass of wine to my right) recovering from 5 1/2 hours of teaching (3 hours in class, 2 1/2 more leading a study group—a sort of continuation of the class but geared to answering questions) and Larry is picking up a sandwich in anticipation of going to hear Clark Coolidge, David Meltzer, and Tina Meltzer do their poetry and jazz thing at 8.

My class today was on Marxist theory. But last week my friend Jalal Toufic (I think I've mentioned him before; he's a writer who teaches film theory at S.F.State—father Iraqi, mother Palestinian, grew up in Lebanon—a multiply exiled leftist)—he's sitting in on my class, and last week he brought up Nietzsche's "master-slave" narrative to make a point, and I could see that the Black students in the class were uptight and the White students embarrassed. So I thought I should explain the master-slave narrative so that the students didn't think he was propounding a racist paradigm. And, since we were talking about Marxism, I decide to throw in Hegel's version of the same narrative (it's odd that they both use a master-slave model, since the import of it is so different in each case). This in addition to the other material I'd planned to discuss made for a lot of lecturing.

But now it's evening. Glass of wine (I guess I should drink a little of it)—glass of wine, the blue light now, Larry at the corner …

And I'm at home.

Cooling out, as they say.

I wish it would get really cold.

But the teaching is going well.

I did tell Adam Cornford my fantasy/desire of teaching full time for half the year—he nodded ponderously but didn't shriek or weep. I think it may work out—I am telling myself that it will—indeed, I will make sure that it does.

The only thing lacking now is titles for the two works I've begun and will return to when there's time.

I got a letter from dear Tom Raworth today, who seems better and in moderately good spirits.

And a note from Max Regan answering my questions about the class I'm to teach during the week I'm at Naropa this summer (I wanted to know if it met once, twice, thrice. etc.).

Eleni Sikelianos is sitting in on my New College class.

Hoa has been accepted as a member of WritersCorp (part of the Clinton administration's AmeriCorp (is that what it's called?) project)—she looks tired and she's way behind on papers, but in terms of the big picture, opportunities seem to be opening up for her; I see her a lot because she's taking my class and also an Independent Study with me. As you know, I like her immensely.

I can't think what else to tell you.

O yes—tales from the cradle.

The first tale is a ghost story.

We lived in a house on Filbert Street in San Francisco. My grandfather bought the house for my parents in 1942, a few months after I was born (May 1941) and a few months after Pearl Harbor and after my father enlisted in the Navy (Intelligence—he spent the war in Hawaii reading soldiers' mail home, a terrifically hard time for him). Life in this house was normal except that at night I (18 months) couldn't sleep—I'd cry instead of sleep, or sleep and wake up crying.

One night my mother was awakened by sounds downstairs—the frontdoor closing, and then footsteps on the wooden floor—not normal footsteps but halting, as of someone limping, and with one step sounding different than the other—like slap, clump, slap, clump. The sound moved from the door to the stairs. The stairs were carpeted; the sound ceased. My mother got out of bed. She heard something just at the top of the stairs. The silence. Then I began to cry.

She ran to my room. No one was there.

A night or two later she was at a small party and spoke about this. A man was at the party and he said he had been the architect of the house—he had designed it for a man who had lost his leg in World War I and who had killed himself in the house—in the "small bedroom."

Next letter: The little people in the rock wall.

Or perhaps: A horseback ride to the virgin forest with the deaf man who could suddenly hear.

Or: I dance with Earl Warren and get lost in the vineyard.

Or: High Spot—his contract with my grandfather, we go to Fall Creek, Mrs. Feather's property, and …

Red Sinnott rides High Spot to hell.

Much love,

Lyn

Notes

To Carolyn Andrews, 5/17/76
"Tuumba Press"—Tuumba Press was founded by Lyn Hejinian in 1976, and between then and 1984 Hejinian produced 50 handset letterpress chapbooks. A bibliography of the press is included in this volume.

To Clark Coolidge, 1/5/84
"previous Rova trips"—The San Francisco–based Rova Saxophone Quartet, founded in 1977 by John Raskin, Larry Ochs, Andrew Voigt, and Bruce Ackley. Voigt left and was replaced by Steve Adams. Influenced by free jazz, 20th-century Western experimental music, and numerous world musics, the group has released over two dozen live and studio recordings.

"80 Langton Street"—Also known as New Langton Arts. A nonprofit arts organization founded in 1975. Part of the first wave of alternative art spaces in the U.S., New Langton Arts was a leader in exhibiting new media forms in art, and involving artists in the decision-making process.

To Rae Armantrout, 1/5/84
"As for local writing—I agree with you about Carla's book."—Carla Harryman, *The Middle*, Gaz Press, San Francisco, 1983.

"Susan Howe's essay"—An early version of the opening of what became Howe's seminal critical study *My Emily Dickinson*, "My Emily Dickinson Part One" appeared in *Poetics Journal 4: Women & Language*, 1985.

"And I like 'Fiction' too."—Rae Armantrout's poem "Fiction" in *Precedence*, pg. 27, Burning Deck, 1985.

To Alice Notley, 12/4/85
"The Guard"—Lyn Hejinian, *The Guard*, Tuumba, 1984.

To Kit Robinson, 11/16/86
"The Postmodernism issue"—*Poetics Journal 7, Postmodern?*, ed. Hejinian and Barrett Watten, 1987.

"I think I am writing so happily and easily to you (the poems)"—See Robinson's essay in this volume.

"Clark's 'Book of During' section in the new Sulfur"—Clark Coolidge, "from The Book of During, III," *Sulfur 17*, ed. Clayton Eshleman, 1986.

"A Day Off is very beautiful."—Kit Robinson, *A Day Off*, State One, 1985.

To Charles Bernstein, 12/6/86
"copies of the Archive Newsletter with Wesling's review"—Donald Wesling review of *Redo* by Lyn Hejinian, *Archive Newsletter* [Mandeville Department of Special Collections, University of California, San Diego], Fall 1986, 23.

"Redo"—*Redo*, Hejinian, Salt-Works Press, 1984.

"Language School"—A group of widely influential writers influenced by radical modernists such as Gertrude Stein and Louis Zukofsky who began publishing in the 1970s. The name of the group emerged largely as a moniker used by critics of the work, but it aptly foregrounds the writers' close attention to semantic and syntactic structures of meaning. A useful single-volume representation of the group is the anthology *In the American Tree*, edited by Ron Silliman, National Poetry Foundation, 1986; second edition, 2001.

"He named only Ron, Barrett, and Bob P"—Poets Ron Silliman, Barrett Watten, and Bob Perelman.

"I will teach a year-long course called 'The Language of Inquiry'"—Hejinian was a member of the Core Faculty of the Poetics Program at New College of California at the time. In the event, she taught a half-year version of the course, titling it "Language and 'Paradise.'" *The Language of Inquiry* became the title of the collection of her essays; University of California Press, 2000.

"a remarkable book by Bishop Spratt"—Bishop Thomas Sprat, *The History of the Royal-Society of London, for the Improving of Natural Knowledge;* London: The Royal Society, 1667.

"The program from the 'Three Saints'"—Actually "Four Saints": the program from the November 1986 performances of Gertrude Stein's *Four Saints in Three Acts* by the Opera Ensemble of New York at the Lillie Blake School Theatre in New York City; sent to her by Bernstein.

"new biography of Langston Hughes"—Arnold Rampersand's two-volume *The Life of Langston Hughes* (Oxford University Press, 1986 and 1988).

To Susan Howe, 11/21/87
"I'm very happy that you like the new (45 year old) book"—Hejinian, *My Life*, Sun & Moon Press, 1987.

"your Awede book"—Susan Howe, *Articulation of Sound Forms in Time*, Awede, 1987.

"you have Maureen"—Maureen Owen.

"the Eunuch Ho"—Zheng He (1371–1433), formerly romanized as Cheng Ho, was a Ming Dynasty diplomat and explorer.

To Fanny Howe, 1/8/93
"I've been working on my Sleeps project"—The collection of works that became *The Book of a Thousand Eyes* (Richmond, CA: Omnidawn, 2012).

"influenced by Arkaadi's writing"—The Russian poet Arkaadi Dragoshchenko (1946–2012). Hejinian translated his first two collections in English, *Description* (1990) and *Xenia* (1994), both published by Sun & Moon Press.

"George Lewis"—Trombone virtuoso, recording and installation artist, scholar, and founding member of the AACM (Association for the Advancement of Creative Musicians).

"Gerald Oshita"—San Francisco–based musician and composer. Specializing in unusual wind instruments, he frequently worked with Roscoe Mitchell and Thomas Buckner.

To Jack Collom, 10/7/94

"Hoa has been accepted as a member of WritersCorp"—Poet Hoa Nguyen.

Lyn Hejinian's Poetics of the Middle
Carla Billitteri

Readers of Lyn Hejinian's *The Language of Inquiry* may be puzzled at the abstract resoluteness of the author's introductory remarks on poetry. I want to take up these remarks as emblematic of an internal conflict in the speculative design of Hejinian's poetics.

> Poetry comes to know that things are. But this is not knowledge in the strictest sense; it is, rather, acknowledgment—and that constitutes a sort of unknowing. To know *that* things are is not to know *what* they are, and to know *that* without *what* is to know otherness (i.e. the unknown and perhaps unknowable). Poetry undertakes acknowledgement as a preservation of otherness—a notion that can be offered in a political, as well as an epistemological, context. This acknowledgement is a process, not a definitive act; it is an inquiry, a thinking on. And it is a process in and of language … the language of poetry is the language of inquiry, not the language of a genre. It is that language in which a writer (or a reader) both perceives and is conscious of the perception. Poetry, therefore, takes as its premises that language is a medium for experiencing experience.[1]

I will return to these initial remarks throughout my text. Let me say, for the moment, that what is laid out here is the fundamental divide between two poetics, oppositional in nature: a poetic of "that-ness"—of ostensivity—and a poetics of "what-ness," which is, by contrast, contextual, relational, mediational. This second is what I will subsequently call a poetics of the middle. The epistemological conflict at the basis of this divide derives from the fact that ostensivity is non-relational, and non-contextual, it also calls forth certainty, the undeniable certainty of knowing that things are, subsisting in their obtuse "that-ness," entirely independent from any attribution of "what-ness."

The poetics of what-ness reflects Hejinian's life long interest in William James' radical empiricism, structured around the assumption that our "[k]nowledge of sensible realities … comes to life inside the tissue of experience. It is made; and made by relations that unroll themselves in time."[2] Filtering James' influence through the rethinking of the political impact of poetry, a gesture which characterized the aesthetic avant-garde of the 1970s, Hejinian approaches the practice of poetry writing as a continuous inquiry into the structured and structuring influence of the "sensible realities" constituting our experience as a web of "permanent [linguistic] constructed-ness," that is at once social, cultural, poetic and political.[3] "Poetic language," writes Hejinian, "must address both the material character of the political and the political character of the material ... heighten the sensibility of realities and add to knowledge of them."[4] As a result of this valuable confluence of aesthetic and philosophical legacies, Hejinian's speculative interest predominantly unfolds as the careful scrutiny of the specific determination of sensible realities, or the "what-ness-es," of her objects of study. This scrutiny involves on the one hand the close observation of the shifting, unstable relations of words, things, ideas, and definitions, and on the other, an acute sensibility for the epistemic condition of uncertainty that derives from such scrutiny. As Hejinian writes, her interest lies with "the unstable existence and recurrent or persistent experiences" of being "drawn into the world in and by perception, implicated by language, moving around in life, and unwilling to give up attempts at description ... exploration, discovery, and communication."[5]

The poetics of what-ness reflects these concerns, and should be comprehended as a post-foundational phenomenological poetics, or, in other words, a contextual and historical poetics that describes the moveable grounds of our being in between states of temporarily defined determinations. As any other post-foundational poetics, "what-ness" uncovers and multiplies epistemic uncertainty, for it calls into question the apparent simplicity of our perceptions of reality. Yet, as we read in Hejinian's introductory statement to *The Language of Inquiry*, this relational poetics of "what-ness" is also an ostensive poetics of "that-ness," relying on the perception that "things are." This immediate and certain recognition of existence is only problematized by the immediately following reflection that acts of perception are only acts of "acknowledgement," which, for Hejinian, constitutes a sort of "unknowing." Though it begins in the certainty "that things are," the act of perceiving furthers an undoing of certainty.

This puzzling combination of ostensivity and non-ostensivity, certainty and uncertainty, has coexisted in Hejinian's thought since the early 1970s in a mute symbiosis. Thus, in *My Life*, to cite one of many examples, Hejinian recalls her adolescent interest in science as "a basis for descriptive sincerity" and her consequent "thinking aloud of ... [her] affinity for the separate fragments under scrutiny."[6] At this early stage, Hejinian found that "only fragments are accurate" and writing was an exercise in "breaking up language into single words."[7] This "descriptive sincerity," preparatory in its inquiring scope to the ostensive acknowledgement "that things are," is later rejected when Hejinian, "despite an analytic or investigatory impulse" became "keenly aware of the non-isolability of objects and events in the world, our experience of them, and our experience of that experience."[8] It would then seem, at a first look, that the ostensive functioned as a prior intellectual inclination, superceded by the non-ostensive, more complex form of thinking, a transition strongly influenced by her reading of William James.

Let me return to the initial quote, to clarify the role of knowledge, certainty, and uncertainty in this conflict between early inclinations and later cognitive schemata.

It is noteworthy that in this passage Hejinian's accent falls on the unnarrated (unspoken, but nonetheless present, as warrant of her claim), element of certainty in her rather unusual equation of "acknowledgment" to "unknowing." This ostensive claim that the *certainty* of acknowledgment corresponds to a condition of "unknowing" echoes the philosophical contrast between G. E. Moore and Ludwig Wittgenstein on the question of knowledge and certainty. Hejinian's position parallels Wittgenstein's, but as we will see, this parallel points out the unsolved fracture between a poetics of "what-ness" and one of "that-ness."

The contrast between Moore and Wittgenstein is formulated, a posteriori, by Wittgenstein in *On Certainty*, written as a polemical response to G. E. Moore's 1939 influential paper "Proof of the External World," a summation of his earlier "Defence of Common Sense" (1925). In his paper, Moore used a most definitive (and immediate) ostensive argument: "here is one hand" (indicating his own hand on the desk) to prove the indisputable certainty of empirical knowledge and, in fact, to equate certainty to knowledge. Ostensivity, however, did not sit well with Wittgenstein, who attacked Moore's position in his counter-ostensive study *On Certainty* (1950–1951) a manuscript left unpublished at the time of his death and edited and published by G. E. M. Anscombe and G. H. Wright in 1969.

Wittgenstein's argument, a relentless and often humorous demolition of Moore's foundational philosophy of presence, bestowing full authenticity and authority to empirical experience, opens with the daring words: "If you do know that *here is one hand*, we'll grant you all the rest"—but there is nothing left to "rest" upon after the very foundations of certainty have been destabilized by Wittgenstein's anti-foundational, descriptive approach to knowledge and philosophy as discursive events based on agreed-upon rules, or, in other words, agreed-upon language games.[9] In his analysis of certainty, Wittgenstein claims that knowledge is but a form of system recognition, and therefore, not knowledge at all. He writes: "when we say 'We are quite sure of it' … [we do] not mean just that every single person is certain of it, but that we belong to a community which is bound together by science and education."[10] Certainty, then, is not knowledge but the *acknowledgment* of the operative rules of a determinate language game (to use Wittgenstein's definition) or the operative constraints of any given epistemological construct. Thus, Wittgenstein argues, when we say "I know," we actually mean "I am familiar with it as a certainty."[11] By extension, we can say that certainty (acknowledgment) is not knowing, or (to recall Hejinian's term) "unknowing." Wittgenstein compares the "unknowing" of certainty to a comfortable state of intellectual familiarity, a somewhat fashionable or recognizable *attitude*, an attitude, we should add, of no epistemological value. He remarks: "[I]t's not that on some points men know the truth with perfect certainty. No: perfect certainty is only a matter of their attitude."[12] Because all "knowledge is in the end based on acknowledgment," uncertainty occurs whenever the language game is punctured or disturbed, whenever, as Wittgenstein writes, "Certain events ... put [us] ... in a position in which ... [we] could not go on with the old language-game any further. In which ... [we are] torn away from the *sureness* of the game."[13]

Even though there is no open reference to this particular text of Wittgenstein in the corpus of Hejinian's work, she does discuss the certainty of knowledge as a form of acknowledgement, that is, as an automatic, familiar response to what is perceived. Thus, for instance, in "The Green," Hejinian notes that "one's attention intersects with recognition, because awareness includes the urge to get a likeness."[14] And in a manner parallel to Wittgenstein's coupling of certainty with cozy familiarity, Hejinian in *My Life* presents what she explicitly terms a "a poetry of certainty" as a warm medium that dispels difficulties and arrives at a point of rest. She does this by presenting the image of the poet "as a person seated on an iceberg and melting through it" that is, arriving at the "bottom" of knowledge where presumably he or she can say with certainty, as G. E. Moore did, "here is one hand."[15] In contrast to this poetry of certainty, Hejinian stages her epistemic search for uncertainty in the inhospitable *cold* of poetry, a notion reminiscent of Laura Riding's definition of poetry as a "fifth season" of snow.[16] In the inhospitable "cold of poetry," Hejinian writes, "particulars are related, but particulars are related to uncertainty. // The experience of experience ... [lies] in shifts ... in rivers ... in gaps."[17] In this, as in the many other occurrences—both in her critical essays and in her poetry—the experience of uncertainty is presented as an indispensable medium (and/or condition) of cognition, and Hejinian articulates the poetics of "what-ness" as a poetic of uncertainty *and* a poetic of the middle.

Hejinian's most compelling discussion on certainty and uncertainty occurs in her essay "La Faustienne," where she discusses the epistemological implications of the myth of Faust, a myth central to Western culture and thought. This exploration culminates with an allegorical fable on knowledge dedicated to Carla Harryman, and the promise, made to Carla Harryman, that one day "Various women writers will take up the philosophical quest for uncertainty."[18] Central to this essay is Hejinian's discriminating differentiation between the certainty of knowledge and the uncertainty of "knowing." The certainty of knowledge, a certainty that motivates Faust's desire to know "all," is a falsely reassuring narrative of mastery, instrumental, as Hejinian argues, to the functioning of patriarchal ideology. By contrast, the uncertainty of "knowing," modeled after Faust's counterpart, la Faustienne Scheherazade and exemplified by Scheherazade's interlocked, and always unfinished tales, offers a relational and processual form of cognition that functions as a "destabilizing process, a process of transformation" of the reader as well as the writer.[19] In Hejinian's view, the collective effort of Faustienne women writers is both a radical departure from the patriarchal ideology of knowledge as mastery and an open challenge to the reassuring certainties of its language games. Like Scheherazade, Faustienne women writers are invested in "knowing," as a form of "making," of creating a new—and an affirmative—feminist pragmatic cognitive poetics, a poetics of uncertainty. This poetics is participatory and "heuristic" in so far as the reader is supposed to (and invited to) participate in the meaning-formation of the text—indeed, to "discover" (*HEURISKEIN*, to discover by experience) the meaning of the text by "trial and error," by intelligent guesswork.

In *A Border Comedy*, Hejinian muses about the possibility of a poetry that unfolds as a *"narrative of heuristic suspension."*[20] This *narrative* poetics, as I would describe it, develops from Hejinian's interest in exploring realist description as a means of inquiry into the fabric of experience as well as of language itself, a *heuristic* means that "raises scrutiny to consciousness."[21] This narrative poetics, of description (a description that "makes" knowledge) is presented as the challenging ground of certainty, for the act of describing reconstructs the real outside given categories of knowledge. Description, Hejinian writes, "is apprehension. The term *apprehension* is meant to name both a motivating anticipatory anxiety and what *Webster's Dictionary* calls 'the act or power of perceiving or comprehending.' Apprehension, then, is expectant knowledge."[22]

The dedication to Carla Harryman is not accidental, for although, as I have mentioned, the question of uncertainty began as a speculative interest in Hejinian's early writing, when, as Hejinian says, "uncertainty seemed to open up infinite varieties of meaningfulness,"[23] It was only after the publication of Carla Harryman's *The Middle* that Hejinian arrived at a comprehensive elaboration of uncertainty within the relational poetics of the middle, based on the rhetoric of description. Hejinian welcomes "Harryman's *The Middle* as a "signal work … an organizationally radiant critique … of conventional (patriarchal) power structures" and she adds: "In *The Middle* the power of authority gives way to the power of invention, with its plenitude of focus, and to the power of performance. The subject position is in the middle—an uncontainable presence making meaning."[24]

Driven by the epistemic engine of uncertainty, the poetics of the middle has a powerful centripetal force in Hejinian's thought. In it, everything converges, to it, everything returns. Writing begins in the middle—as in "Language and 'Paradise'" Hejinian explicitly affirms: "I begin in the middle—of my own writing and of the larger project which writing represents. It is only after the beginning and before the end that things and thinking about them can begin anew."[25] Likewise, the concept of "person" as lyrical agency inhabiting writing, resides ("exists") in the middle: "The idea of the person enters poetics where art and reality, or intentionality and circumstance, meet. It is on the improvised boundary between art and reality, between construction and experience, that the person (or my person) in writing exists."[26]

The middle is a poetic praxis punctuated by specific and recurrent tropes: enjambment, ellipses, metonym. The enjambment, Hejinian explains, insists on the "contingency, and contiguity" between things, an unstable condition "always susceptible to change."[27] Ellipses are active agents of the middle—in Hejinian's analysis, they are "nonterminal, interstitial" gaps that cause the poem to "stagger, impeded by temporal and cognitive discontinuities." The uncertain pace ellipses force on the act of reading is a punctual description of "the discontinuity of consciousness interwoven through the continuity of reality."[28] Metonym, lastly, is the principal trope of middle, or, as Hejinian precisely writes, "a cognitive entity, with immediate ties to the logic of perception," which "maintains the intactness and discreteness of particulars, [while at the same time] its paratactic perspective gives it multiple vanishing points."[29]

As already evident in the analysis of these rhetorical tropes, the poetics of the middle reflects Hejinian's cognitive dimension of reality. Reality, Hejinian writes, following William James's thought, "is that which is, or can be, shared with other human beings, and it is to be found in spaces of appearance, places where things happen, where things do their thinging." In this particular context the middle should not be seen as a liminal space separating semantic events, but as a inherent and inherently porous border, a productive (if barely perceived) site of cultural change. In Hejinian's words, the middle is not "a circumscribing margin but … the intermediary, even interstitial zone that lies between one culture and another, and between one thing and another."[30] Taken as inherent border, the middle is "a zone of alteration, transmutation, a zone of forced forgetting, of confusion, where laws and languages clash, where currency changes value and value changes currency, and ... everyone is a foreigner."[31] This inspired conceptualization of the middle as border, causing a sudden, and evenly distributed, existential and epistemic condition of foreign-ness, well expresses the emotional impact of Wittgenstein's notation on uncertainty as a feeling of being "torn away from the sureness of the game." Just as a foreigner is torn away from the certainty of her language games, Hejinian's poetics of the middle tears her readers away from familiar epistemological certainties.

In its condition of provoking agent of foreign-ness and epistemic uncertainty, the middle marks an overlap of the cognitive, aesthetic, and, most importantly, the ethical dimensions of poetry. The poetics of the middle makes explicit the cognitive process of "knowing" as an open form of transformative mediation between the subject and the world. This kind of mediation, as discussed by Isobel Armstrong in *The Radical Aesthetic*, "transforms categories and remakes language" and is, emphatically, "a social, not a private act." Hejinian's poetry is precisely meant to create and implement a space of uncertainty through and *in* mediation, a "space where linguistic experiments change meaning by questioning categories ... [and by] redefining what knowing is."[32]

This understanding of poetic language as mediation and as a transformative conjunction of cognitive and esthetic functions (an essential constituent of Hejinian's poetics of what-ness) descends from Hegel's *Encyclopaedia Logic*, where the middle is described as "a point of change and transition ... a vital moment of conceptualization" and, more importantly, a "structuring *activity* ... a relational movement."[33] Mediation, in Hegel, is a "kind of three-dimensional thinking ... [that] reconfigures experience and temporalities ... [a] problematization which produces a new interpretation ... [and] a transformation." Mediation is a "thinking over," a processual cognitive moment that, like art, unsettles the given certainty of knowledge, thus uniting epistemé and emotions. In fact, as Armstrong writes, if on the one hand "[i]t is only through the mediation of alteration that the central aspects of an object come to consciousness ... [and therefore] [t]hings cannot be understood unless they are altered," on the other hand "this 'thinking-over' is not set in motion without discomfort, a frustrated awareness of the non-correspondence of consciousness and the world."[34]

Hejinian consciously forefronts this emotive discomfort as "foreign-ness" as a potentially positive cognitive tactic, and makes it the center of poetry's ethical commitment to the real and the stronghold of a new political praxis for the poet. Poetry, Hejinian insists, "has ... the obligation to enter those specific zones" that define the middle, zones of border between different ideas, meanings, people, values.[35] Upon their entrance in this space of mediation, poets "must assume a barbarian position, taking a creative, analytical, and often oppositional stance, occupying (and being occupied by) foreignness—by the barbarism of strangeness."[36] This, for Hejinian, is the ethical obligation of poetry, and indeed, in a time of heightened xenophobia and nationalism, of religious and ethnic profiling, and homeland security measures, nothing can be more pertinent and more profoundly ethical than a poetry that invites its readers as well as its makers to identify themselves with the *barbaros*, [Latin for "stranger"] or more accurately, as Hejinian argues, with the *xenos*, [Greek for "stranger" as "guest" *and* "host"]—a poetry that invites us to explore the ambivalence and multi-valence of our existential and epistemological conditions—outside the static certainty of the so-called state of knowledge.

Let me now return again, for one last time, to the initial quote, and focus on the passage concerning the scope of the ostensive moment of "that-ness." Here the ethical mandate of poetry is explicitly given to the recognition of otherness that follows the ostensive recognition of "that-ness." To elevate "that-ness" to the status of conceptual warrant of poetry's ethical mandatum seems a rather problematic move, for "that-ness" by definition indicates existence, but does not differentiate, does not distinguish, and thus, ultimately, cannot and does not partake of the epistemological destabilization caused by the scrutiny of "what-ness." It is "what-ness" that is, in fact, the necessary, preliminary step that allows us to perceive (and therefore challenge, transform) our differences, our quiddities. As Hejinian accurately says:

> [W]e can only know things and indeed can only perceive them as things, distinct from one another, by virtue of their differences, and hence on the basis of their details. Quiddity—thingness or thingitude—consists of the detailed differences that make one thing *what it is* and not what another thing is.… It is only when differences emerge, making differentiation possible, that perception, observation, and making sense can occur. A world in the state of chaos is one that remains closed to us. Chaos, the state of undifferentiated everything, is a state of sameness. It is eventless.… It's only by virtue of differences, that anything can occur at all.[37]

Knowledge as "knowing" is based on the understanding (a perceiving, and an observing) of differences or "quiddities"—that is to say: differences in (and of) relational positionality—or, more simply, "what-ness-es." Anything else outside "quiddity" (and that would necessarily include "that-ness") does not differentiate and brings forth the unknowing (or "chaos") of sameness. What-ness consists of difference, gives us "difference." That-ness, on the other hand, predicates sameness—the unknowing of sameness, for in that-ness things appear, but their differences and determinations are "closed to us." Not surprisingly, then, the ethical mandate of the poetics of the middle can only come from (and can only be fulfilled by) what-ness.

Since the differential value of uncertainty (tested, as if, in the interstitial reality of the poetics of the middle) is only meaningful in so far as we understand the what-ness of each thing or object in the first place—how can then the undifferentiated unknowing of the ostensive "that-ness" become, in the introductory remarks to *The Language of Inquiry,* the vehicle of recognition of differences? Is this an opaque turn of events in Hejinian's otherwise unfailingly lucid thinking—or a provisional tactical move?

In what can only be defined as a provisional conclusion of my thoughts, I am inclined to choose this last option—and to consider the ostensive as a form of provisional certainty. This seems to be what Hejinian suggests when she says that "the acknowledgement of "that-ness" is a process, not a definitive act; it is an inquiry, a thinking on."[38] The ostensivity of "that-ness" in this case, under this specific provision, is as uncertain and provisional as the poetics of "what-ness," for the certainty of the acknowledgement is weakened, as if, from the inside, by the radical shifting of the epistemic focus, from the teleological to the processual. Hejinian recuperates the ostensive by folding it back into the folds of discourse, in this case: description, analysis, scrutiny. "That-ness" gives us certainty—but that certainty that is quickly weakened from the inside, by the workings of "what-ness," the workings of inquiry. This recuperation, however, demonstrates that the division between "that-ness" and "what-ness" is false. The poetics of "that-ness" does not precede "what-ness" but is in fact a discursive game within the poetics of "what-ness"—or, in other terms, the specific "what-ness" of culture produces the "that-ness" of experience as its ostensive metaphysics, and not the other way around. This is, in Hejinian's phrasing, a game of "occurrence" in any structured series of events.[39]

In her essay "Language and 'Paradise," Hejinian shows a lucid awareness of this problem. She writes: "[W]herever there is a fragility of sequence, the particular character of diverse individual things becomes prominent; their heterogeneity increases the palpability of things. This palpability has both metaphysical and aesthetic force, which is to say these particulars are not isolated, but to understand their relations under conditions in which sequential logic is in disarray, one must examine other connections."[40] The "fragility of sequence," another rhetorical trope of the poetics of the middle, allows Hejinian to arrive at the "that-ness" of things (their occurrence as "palpability") but only as an after-effect of the examination of their "what-ness," in this case of their determination and positionality in the "sequential logic" of discourse. What-ness opens the possibility of conceiving or even just experiencing that-ness—and reframes the familiar metaphysical certainty /palpability/ of "that-ness" as a discursive possibility of what-ness. Here the ostensive becomes a tactical move in the overall strategy of uncertainty—perhaps the most daring of all, if we consider the alluring temptation to fall into a state of stupor, silence, sheer "astonishment," a temptation that accompanies the ostensive, as Hejinian presents it, in her commentary on Gertrude Stein's *Stanzas in Meditation*.

At the epistemological center of *Stanzas*, Hejinian individuates a primordial moment of "that-ness" in the "wonder at mere existence" experienced by Gertrude Stein, as well as by any writer. This sense of wonder is prior to "consideration of whether the things that happen are good or bad"—prior, therefore, to the "what-ness" of things.[41] This sense of wonder is transmitted to the reader, to the extent of paralyzing her critical faculties. Thus, Hejinian writes:

> It is impossible to 'explain" *Stanzas in Meditation*. This is not because meaning is absent from or irrelevant to the commonplace but, on the contrary, it is precisely because it is inherent to it—identical with it … and it is this that is ordinary, commonplace, since this does not involve analysis … cognizance and apprehension of a thing take place *prior* to analysis.[42]

This astonishment of being (astonishment *at* being) Hejinian registers in *Stanzas in Meditation* throws into relief the implicit dangers of the poetics of "that-ness": a poetics of immediacy that merges language (meaning) and thing and cancels inquiry and analysis—the exact opposite of the epistemological mandate of a poetics of the middle. In the astonishment at the ostensive we are back in G. E. Moore's hands—back in the comfort zone of certainty. An illusory comfort, for the disappearance of analysis in the immediate apprehension of ostensivity, (the foundational Cratylist moment of ostensivity where linguistic meaning and things are fused), naturalizes the ideological matter of knowing—a naturalization so extreme it cancels out the discourse of knowing altogether. The ostensive poetics of "that-ness" is indeed a <u>silencing</u> poetics of the limit.

The "fragility of sequence," by contrast, is an open invitation to consider poetry as the "middle" of the on-going discourse on knowing. In this respect, Hejinian's poetics is akin to Gianni Vattimo's and Pier Aldo Rovatti's conceptualization of the post-modern condition as "weak thought" (*pensiero debole*): anti-foundational, open-ended, and dilemmatic.[43] But there is no thinking, no dilemmatic "thinking-in-the-middle" outside the radical epistemé of "what-ness," the most profoundly innovative force of Hejinian's thought, what makes her capable of going beyond the limits of the familiar metaphysical certainty of "that-ness."

Notes

1. Lyn Hejinian, "Introduction," *The Language of Inquiry*, (Berkeley: University of California Press, 2000), 3–4.

2. William James, quoted in Hejinian, "Strangeness," *The Language of Inquiry*, 136.

3. Hejinian, *My Life* (1980, 1987) (Los Angeles: Green Integer, 2002),134. See also Hejinian's reflections on the "what-ness" of language and identity construction in her interview with Manuel Brito: "The book [*My Life*] is about the formative impact of language, and at the same time it is a critique of that language—suggesting that one can construct alternative views. *My Life* is both determined and constructed. My life, too." "Comments for Manuel Brito," *The Language of Inquiry*, 187.

4. Hejinian, introduction, "Strangeness," *The Language of Inquiry*, 137.

5. Hejinian, "The Person and Description," *The Language of Inquiry*, 203–4.

6. Hejinian, *My Life*, 71.

7. Hejinian, *My Life*, 75.

8. Hejinian, "Language and 'Paradise,'" *The Language of Inquiry*, 67.

9. Ludwig Wittgenstein, *On Certainty* (New York: Harper & Row, 1969), #1, 2e.

10. Wittgenstein, *On Certainty*, #298, 38e.

11. Wittgenstein, *On Certainty*, #272, 35e.

12. Wittgenstein, *On Certainty*, #404, 52e.

13. Wittgenstein, *On Certainty*, #378, 49e, and #617, 82e.

14. Hejinian, "The Green," *The Cold of Poetry* (Los Angeles: Sun & Moon, 1994), 137–8.

15. Hejinian, *My Life*, 103–4.

16. See Laura Riding, "Goat and Amalthea," *The Poems of Laura (Riding) Jackson* (New York: Persea, 1980), 47. As in Riding, the cold of poetry is in the first place, the cold of thinking. Thus Hejinian: "But all week I've felt my mind, how cold its thoughts are, how reluctantly they leave my head." *My Life*, 130.

17. Hejinian, "The Quest for Knowledge," *The Language of Inquiry*, 224.

18. Hejinian, "La Faustienne," *The Language of Inquiry*, 261.

19. Hejinian, "The Quest for Knowledge," *The Language of Inquiry*, 222.

20. Hejinian, *A Border Comedy* (New York: Granary Books, 2001), …, my emphasis.

21. Hejinian, "Roughly Stapled," 8.

22. Hejinian, "Strangeness," *The Language of Inquiry*, 139. As "expectant knowledge," description *may* unsettle familiar assumptions, as Hejinian affirms, quoting Wittgenstein, it is an attempt to "let the fly out of the bottle" (137). But precisely because this poetics is geared toward the real and aims at a reconstitution of reality, one wonders if description may run the risk of assuaging given epistemological certainties—rather than challenging them. For any act of uncertainty and destabilization can always be re-absorbed and re-inscribed as "knowledge." Thus the problem of creating uncertainty (of the real as what is given/framed) from within a realist desire for certainty seems problematic —and so presents problematic moments in Hejinian's work. Indeed, it's a Faustian challenge, in its own right, for it is primarily a form of desire, destined to remain unfulfilled, destined to repeat itself in a form of iteration a la Stein, iteration that in and of itself creates more uncertainties. Hejinian is of course aware of the paradoxical nature of her poetic project, and one must note the difference of register here. Faust ends up high and dry, for the category of unfulfilled desire is a negative limit in his epistemological universe. The Ür-Faustienne Scheherazade, instead, thrives on the multiplication of unfulfilled desire. Interestingly, though, her desire is fulfilled in the end (her life is spared) and, even more interestingly, her desire is fulfilled in the middle—in this case, quite literally, in the middle of her stories, for as Hejinian points out, between stories the night brings fulfilling erotic pleasure

for both Scheherazade and her companion/audience. The Faustian mold is not really overturned or broken, then—but transformed (modified) from the inside.

23. Hejinian, "Materials for Dubravka Djuric," *The Language of Inquiry*, 164. See also the following passage from Hejinian's "Redo":

> Discontinuity in my experience
> to me means radical coverage. With garrulous scanning
> —as the cobweb that humiliates the space that waves
> —constantly distracted, the vulnerability
> not of the fragile but of the fake—
> those whom it assimilates with anticipation.
>
> (The Cold of Poetry, 102)

24. Hejinian, introduction, "The Rejection of Closure," *The Language of Inquiry*, 40.

25. Hejinian, "Language and 'Paradise,'" *The Language of Inquiry*, 65.

26. Hejinian, "The Person and Description," *The Language of Inquiry*, 207.

27. Hejinian, introduction, "A Thought Is the Bride of What Thinking," *The Language of Inquiry*, 8.

28. Hejinian, "Language and 'Paradise,'" *The Language of Inquiry*, 76–7.

29. Hejinian, "Strangeness," *The Language of Inquiry*, 151, 148.

30. Hejinian, "Continuing Against Closure." *Jacket* #14, July 2001.

31. Hejinian, "Continuing Against Closure."

32. Isobel Armstrong, *The Radical Aesthetic*. (London: Blackwell, 2000): 60.

33. Armstrong, *Radical Aesthetic*, 67, 68. Armstrong points out that mediation is perhaps one of the most underestimated or overlooked Hegelian concepts. She also emphatically argues that Hegel's *Encyclopedia Logic* is "implicitly a poetics" (65). A reading of Hejinian's poetics of uncertainty as a poetics of the middle proves Armstrong right.

34. Armstrong, *Radical Aesthetic*, 68, 69.

35. Hejinian, "Barbarism," *The Language of Inquiry*, 326.

36. Hejinian, "Barbarism," *The Language of Inquiry*, 326. This ethical obligation is flanked by the pedagogical responsibility of educating the audience to the new barbarism of poetry, a question that has been part of Hejinian's concerns since the appearance of the "audience stasis" in *My Life* and the problem of being an avant-garde writer. see Hejinian, *My Life*, 32.

37. Hejinian, "Continuing Against Closure," my emphasis.

38. Hejinian, "Introduction," *The Language of Inquiry*, 3.

39. On "occurrence," see Hejinian, "Three Lives," *The Language of Inquiry*, 289.

40. Hejinian, "Language and 'Paradise,'" *The Language of Inquiry*, 67–8.

41. Hejinian, "A Common Sense," *The Language of Inquiry*, 362.

42. Hejinian. "A Common Sense," *The Language of Inquiry*, 364.

43. Gianni Vattimo e Pier Aldo Rovatti, eds., *Il Pensiero Debole* (Milano: Feltrinelli; 1988). Hejinian in fact discusses poetic thinking as dilemmatic in "Reason," *The Language of Inquiry*, 337–354.

Numerousness and Its Discontents: George Oppen and Lyn Hejinian

Peter Nicholls

A striking feature of Lyn Hejinian's recent work has been her development of a series of terms which permeates both her poetic and critical writings: words such as "incipience," "border," "reason," "dilemma," "context," "aporia," and "occurrence" are deployed to create a terminological matrix in which ideas from theorists such as Hannah Arendt, Jean-François Lyotard and Jacques Derrida are loosely interwoven. In long poetic works such as *A Border Comedy* and in essays that include "Reason" and "Barbarism" (both collected in *The Language of Inquiry*), Hejinian has been exploring the possibilities of what might be called a phenomenology of the social. I want to suggest in this essay that in addition to the major theorists I've named, George Oppen has had a particular importance to this project as a poet who explored many of the problems that currently interest Hejinian.

In proposing this association I am in part merely tracing out connections that the poet herself has acknowledged. Objectivism, of course, has always been a key point of reference for her, and in an unpublished draft of her 1994 George Oppen Memorial Lecture, she goes so far as to speak of herself as "a poet influenced more by the Objectivists than by any other group of writers."[1] In her notes for the lecture, Hejinian dates her interest in Oppen back to 1968, and it's clear from this material that she returned to a concentrated study of his work in the early nineties.[2] The lecture, called originally "O's Affirmation" and subsequently retitled "The Numerous," remains unpublished, but in 1998 Hejinian produced two other essays, "Barbarism" and "Reason," which also take Oppen as a major point of reference for her own meditations on philosophical and phenomenological conceptions of community or "numerousness," to use Oppen's term.[3] His work continues to act as a primary touchstone for Hejinian, as was clear at the 2002 Modernist Studies Association conference in Madison when she gave a paper titled "George Oppen and the Space of Appearance."

In recent years, Hejinian's fascination with Oppen's work has focussed increasingly on his long serial poem "Of Being Numerous" (she gave a whole course at the University of Iowa based around this text in 1997). This was the title poem of the volume which brought Oppen the Pulitzer prize in 1969 and it remains, for most readers, his best known work. "Of Being Numerous," which builds upon an earlier poem called "A Language of New York," has many inter-related concerns: in forty short sections it ranges over life in the contemporary metropolis, it considers the possibilities of the new "urban art," and it also recalls Oppen's wartime experience in Alsace, powerfully connecting this to the current horrors of the Vietnam war—"the news / Is war // As always," he writes.[4] This is, then, a poem with strong political themes, though the extent to which it can be satisfactorily read through any conventional political frame remains questionable. Indeed, Oppen once observed that "Of Being Numerous" was "An account of being in the world, to stick to H[eidegger],"[5] one remark among several which suggests in fact that the poem situates its concerns some-where at the interface or border between the political and the philosophical.

I want to emphasise the importance to both Oppen and Hejinian of this idea of a "border," an intermediary zone, where a clash of opposing concepts cannot be resolved but is supplanted by a lived experience of what Hejinian calls after Derrida "impasse" or "aporia." In her Oppen Lecture, Hejinian glosses section 9 of "Of Being Numerous" with a series of observations spon-sored by Derrida's *Aporias*. The "experience of the aporia," she says, "is "a *passage*, both an impossible and a necessary passage," which is to say it is both a passage and an impasse, and it is so in being an experience simultaneously of border as limit and of border as limitlessness."[6] The contradictory nature of the "border" in this sense situates it in the realm of experience rather than in that of the con-cept; glossing section 23 of the poem, Hejinian speaks of "an aporia, which will allow us to go beyond the limits of any one viewpoint and remain there."[7]

In the thirties, Oppen had resolved the conflict between politics and poetry by a single-minded commitment to social action, but when he returned to poetry at the end of the fifties after almost a decade of enforced political silence it was partly at the instigation of Jacques Maritain's *Creative Intuition in Art and Poetry*, a work which evoked an existential world in which the boundaries between politics, philosophy and poetics seemed to acquire a new permeability.[8] It is quite wrong, I think, to argue that "When Oppen put pen to paper again, it was ... as an existentialist, not as a socialist."[9] For Oppen, as for Jean-Paul Sartre, the insights of Marxism and existentialism came to be regarded not as incompatible but as complementary, not least because, as Fredric Jameson notes in his account of Sartre, each called in question the priority of thought over being ("existentialism with the principle that existence precedes essence, Marxism with the determination of consciousness by social reality"[10]); in this sense, as Sartre would argue in *Search for a Method* (1960); English translation 1963), existentialism was a necessary supplement to a post-War Marxism which had grown mechanical and economistic. In Oppen's case, his involvement with the Left since the thirties had made him similarly aware of a tendency in Marxist practice to privilege ideology over experience, and it is clear that during the period in Mexico the Oppens suffered a growing disenchantment with the communist world, both in terms of Party practice and the policies of the Soviet Union. Their experience demonstrated that political thought had become remote from Maritain's "existential world" of being and making, that it had degenerated into a universalising form of knowledge whose idiom was increasingly that of conspiracy and surveillance.[11] As Burton Hatlen correctly notes, Oppen never repudiated his Communist past,[12] though he was inevitably critical of Party manoeuvering: "Communism and our communism—the 15 years or more: many lies, absurdities, cruelties, self deception—and yet were we wrong even for ourselves?"[13]

Maritain's claim that "poetry has its source in the pre-conceptual life of the intellect" offered what must have seemed a highly attractive alternative to the degraded knowledge that was now "politics,"[14] but most importantly for Oppen it opened a way back to politics grasped as experience rather than as "ideas." This would also be the main point of Sartre's *Search for a Method* which aims

> to engender within the framework of Marxism a veritable *comprehensive knowing* which will rediscover man in the social world and which will follow him in his *praxis*—or, if you prefer, in the project which throws him toward the social possibles in terms of a defined situation. Existentialism will appear therefore as a fragment of the system, which has fallen outside of Knowledge.[15]

In their different ways, Sartre and Oppen were each looking for a means of articulating together forms of interiority and exteriority so as to avoid the "idealist" dichotomy of subject and object and to recover instead "the *unsurpassable opaqueness* of the lived experience."[16] Sartre, for example, would name as the "crucial discovery" of dialectics that "man is "mediated" by things to the same extent as things are "mediated" by man"[17]; Oppen hit on Maritain's similar if more poetic formulation that "creative subjectivity awakens to itself only by simultaneously awakening to Things."[18] In each case, this way of *situating* the subject emphasised the irreducibility of experience to knowledge and, for Oppen, made poetry as its privileged embodiment the source of a kind of generative opacity within political thinking.[19] In that sense, Oppen seems to have associated poetry with the acknowledgment of a certain indeterminacy and resistance that might save politics from ideology and mere "argument." It is in this context that we should understand his earlier refusal, as he put it in 1959, "to write communist verse. That is, to any statement already determined before the verse. Poetry has to be protean; the meaning must begin there. With the perception."[20] This is a poetry in which "the thinking occurs at the moment of the poem, within the poem," a poetry in which "the image is encountered, not found."[21]

The alternative to the "statement already determined" seems to to be a new "clarity" generated by the poem, as we learn in section 22 of "Of Being Numerous" where Oppen writes:

Clarity

In the sense of *transparence*,
I don't mean that much can be explained.

Clarity in the sense of silence. (*NCP*, 175)

This paradoxical "clarity" is not the measure of intelligibility (as it is for the Thomist Maritain) but rather the illumination produced by what Oppen calls elsewhere "the absolute glare of the real."[22] The function of the poem, then, is not to impose meaning but to allow the world, as it were, to "shine" through it; Oppen writes in one of his notebooks, "The poem replaces the thing, the poem destroys its meaning—I would like the poem to be nothing, to be transparent, to be inaudible, not to be—"[23] Yet if absolute transparency is impossible, these lines do suggest some limit to expression, a "silence" chosen by the poet as a defence against the cacophony produced by (as he puts it in section 13) "shoppers/ Choosers, judges.... They develop/ Argument in order to speak" (170).

So we are invited to weigh the political implications of "numerousness" without descending into "argument" and "explanation." This aim, which of course accords with Oppen's earlier claims in "The Mind's Own Place" for a poetry lacking in deliberate ideological purpose, may account for readers' very different understandings of "Of Being Numerous."[24] Burton Hatlen, for example, in one of the best readings of the poem, views it as an extended meditation on what he calls "the ontology of the human collectivity":

at bottom, Oppen's vision of the world remains stubbornly political rather than philosophical, in one key respect: "truth" for him exists, if it exists at all, neither in "nature" nor in the splendid solitude of the reflective mind, but only in the collective, ongoing life of the people "*en masse*" (as

Whitman liked to say), as they collectively make through their labor the only world we can know.[25]

Compare now Marjorie Perloff's contention that "what is projected in the poem is less the wish to transform the social order than an acute distaste for people. 'We have chosen,' says Oppen bravely, 'the meaning / Of being numerous,' but it is not a 'meaning' he can bring himself to accept."[26] Where Hatlen finds a celebration of "the people *en masse*,'" Perloff reads the sequence as what she calls a calculated "withdrawal from human contact." The disagreement is striking, and certainly exceeds the difference between these critics' respective political orientations. There is, we must conclude, something at work in the poem which doesn't merely obscure the issue but which actually calls in question the very terms of the disagreement. The idea of "numerousness" is, in fact, loaded with such ambivalence for Oppen that it triggers a kind of indeterminacy in the writing, a studied uncertainty of tone and inflection which does indeed make "clarity" the index of a kind of "silence" or reserve.

We may detect this indeterminacy even in the much earlier *Discrete Series*, where the poem called "Party on Shipboard" broaches the basic conceptual problem of "numerousness" but does so in a characteristically oblique way:

> Wave in the round of the port-hole
> Springs, passing,—arm waved,
> Shrieks, unbalanced by the motion —
> Like the sea incapable of contact
> Save in incidents (the sea is not
>   water)
> Homogenously automatic—a green capped
>   white is momentarily a half mile
>   out —
> The shallow surface of the sea, this,
> Numerously—the first drinks —
> The sea is a constant weight
> In its bed. They pass, however, the sea
> Freely tumultuous. (*NCP* 15)

The poem enacts a "tumultuous" motion in which the only pronoun—"They" in the penultimate line—refers with equal plausibility to the passengers and the waves. Their conjunction, however, occurs only "in incidents" and the emphasis here on contingency and unpredictability suggests a certain skepticism about collective identification which is underscored by the spectatorial distancing in the last two lines, the people and waves seen at some remove as "They pass." That the concerns broached in this early poem were ones to which Oppen would return in "Of Being Numerous" is clear from some unpublished comments written soon after the completion of the later poem in which he observes that "I think I'll be a long time starting again. I've come to the end of what was attempted in Discrete Series.... Put the seeds of all of it in Discrete."[27] He then refers to "Party on Shipboard" where, as he puts it in another unpublished note, "like the waves, the people appearing as individual, are accidents of the single mass, a single body."[28] In 1965, he again recalls the earlier poem in which, he says, "I try to get again to humanity as a single thing, as something like a sea which is a constant weight in its bed...."[29]

This attempt to see humanity as "single" runs through Oppen's poems before "Of Being Numerous," acquiring a certain Heideggerian pathos, for like Being, "humanity" as a collective entity seems constantly to elude articulation and to "withdraw" into individual beings. "Of Being Numerous," he says in one interview, "asks the question whether or not we can deal with humanity as something which actually does exist."[30] Tellingly, the poem does not use the word "humanity," preferring instead "populace" and "people(s)" which with their root connection to an idea of "commonness" seem to offer an alternative to what Oppen calls elsewhere "the metaphysical concept of humanity," "a single figure, A monster."[31] Yet against this particular "singleness" which offers a false ideal of a social unity without division there is the equally problematic notion of "singularity." While numerousness leaves us, as he puts it in the poem, "pressed, pressed on each other" (165), it is also a condition we seem to have chosen for ourselves:

> Obsessed, bewildered
>
> By the shipwreck
> Of the singular
>
> We have chosen the meaning
> Of being numerous (166)

The motif of shipwreck, linked here to the tale of Robinson Crusoe, runs through the poem and section 26 seems to allude also to *Moby-Dick* with its talk of "Behemoth, white whale" (179).[32] On the face of it, Oppen's meaning is clear enough: as he says in section 6, the fact that we speak of Crusoe as having been "Rescued" shows that "We have chosen the meaning / Of being numerous" (166). In his various comments on this part of the poem, Oppen speaks of "a dead end, the shipwreck of the singular,"[33] and of "the concepts evolved from the fact of being numerous, without which we are marooned, shipwrecked."[34]

This theme had appeared in some of his earlier poems: in "From Disaster," for example, the shipwreck was associated with the social "disaster" of the thirties (*NCP*, 50), while in "Myself I Sing" a man marooned sits down near a sand dune and "finds himself by two" (*NCP*, 56), meaning, as Oppen noted elsewhere of the poem that "we find ourselves, conceive ourselves by reaction to some other existence."[35] Only if such singularity is imagined to have "unearthly bonds," as he puts it in section 9, only if individualism acquires some false metaphysical sanction, can "the shipwrecked singular and his distance from them, the people" appear in anything but a negative light.[36] And curiously enough, such "light" gives more than merely metaphorical illumination, for Oppen now speaks of "the bright light of shipwreck" (167,173) and toward the end of the sequence of "The narrow, frightening light / Before a sunrise" (181). The illumination is, to say the least, ambiguous, at once "frightening" and apocalyptic, while also promising a certain enlightenment.

That positive sense of the image comes across strongly in an unpublished poem which begins "beautiful as the sea / and the islands' clear light // of shipwreck," a light that here "prove[s] us part / of the world not fallen / from it" and that embodies what Oppen calls "conviction forceful / as light" (*NCP*, 301).[37] The implication is that shipwreck, as in the tale of Crusoe, must prove to us that value resides ultimately in numerousness. But there is a further twist to this logic which Oppen confirms in a letter of 1973:

> "The shipwreck of the singular" I wrote. We *cannot* live without the concept of humanity, the end of one's own life is by no means equivalent to the end of the world, we would not bother to live out our own lives if it were - - - -
>
> and yet we cannot escape this: that we *are* single. And face, therefore, shipwreck.
>
> And yet this, this tragic fact, is the brilliance of one's life, it is "the bright light of shipwreck" which discloses - - - - - - "all."[38]

Here "humanity" is apparently rehabilitated, but only, we note, as a "concept" or horizon which we need to live out our individual lives. As in the passage cited earlier from "The Mind's Own Place" (see note 24), the syntax is elliptical and tentative—"and yet ... and yet"—and suggests the impossibility of establishing "humanity" as a collective, material presence. For the fundamental truth remains that "we *are* single" and this recognition roots the aporetic relation of individual to society in the very condition of human finitude. Both singularity *and* numerousness, it turns out, are sustained by fantasies of oneness and separation. There may be echoes here of a contemporary concern with American individualism and conformism voiced in classic works of the time such as David Riesman's *The Lonely Crowd* (1950); but more specifically this line of thought may have been triggered by one of William Bronk's poems, "Not My Loneliness But Ours," which, said Oppen, expressed "The loneliness not of the individual, but of the group."[39] Part of the poem reads: "The human loneliness / is the endless oneness of man. Man is one; / man is alone in his world. We are the one...."[40] Bronk's poem reminds us too that the ironies of such social "oneness" were very much a matter of debate at the time Oppen was writing "Of Being Numerous." Saul Bellow in his 1964 novel *Herzog*, for example, has his hero negotiate a subway turnstile:

> He dropped his fare in the slot where he saw a whole series of tokens lighted from within and magnified by the glass. Innumerable millions of passengers had polished the wood of the turnstile with their hips. From this arose a feeling of communion—brotherhood in one of its cheapest forms."[41]

Oppen notes similarly in "Of Being Numerous" that "The shuffling of a crowd is nothing—well, nothing, but the many that we are, but nothing" (*NCP* 168). In other words, we must resist the ersatz feeling of oneness—what Bellow calls "potato love"—while at the same time eschewing a compensatory fetishism of the other oneness that is our singularity. And that, perhaps, is the meaning of the passage in Oppen's 1973 letter where he says that "'the bright light of shipwreck' ... discloses—'all,'" for it is only in the harsher light of our mortality—in our living-toward-death—that we may grasp the concept of "humanity" in its authentic form, as the sum of those who live on after us. This is, indeed, to arrive at "the *meaning* of being numerous" and it perhaps explains why the strongest affirmation of numerousness in the poem stresses proximity to others rather than identification with them:

> For us
> Also each
> Man or woman
> Near is knowledge
> Tho it may be of the noon's
> Own vacuity (*NCP*, 185)

These lines may echo section 4 of Whitman's "Crossing Brooklyn Ferry"—"The men and women I saw were all near to me; / Others the same—others who look back on me, because I look'd forward to them" (196)—but Oppen's end in equivocation, the syntax deliberately eschewing Whitman's easy assurance and making of "nearness" a borderline space which resists precise designation.

Oppen's tentative and elliptical comments in these lines and in the 1973 letter remind us that such thoughts are caught up in what Sartre calls "the opaqueness of experience" and must remain difficult to think if the poet is to avoid mere attitudinising.[42] Accordingly, "Of Being Numerous" stakes out a shifting, liminal space where a constant oscillation between numerousness and singularity is enacted in the very grammar of the poem. Such movements are especially clear in the handling of pronouns which constantly propose distinct identities only to show them becoming permeable with others. Even the idea that "we" reckon with "our" mortality, as I put it in the previous paragraph, might be seen to unravel in light of Heidegger's insistence that "by its essence, death is in every case mine, in so far as it "is" at all."[43] And this statement itself reveals an aporia, as Derrida observes:

If death … names the very irreplaceability of absolute singularity (no one can die in my place or in the place of the other), then all the *examples* in the world can precisely illustrate this singularity. Everyone's death, the death of all those who can say "my death," is irreplaceable.[44]

Numerous *and* singular, again, and this "and" marks the border or aporia which is not the condition of a blocked "argument" but rather of the experience of *living between* these two possibilities (much as, for Heidegger, death is not a final event but "a way to be"[45]). So Derrida asks, in a passage which Hejinian quotes as a gloss to section 9 of Oppen's poem: "Can one speak—and if so, in what sense—of an *experience of the aporia*? An experience *of the aporia as such*? Or vice versa: Is an experience possible that would not be an experience of the aporia?"[46] Numerousness and singularity begin to come into existential relation once we grasp the inherence of death in existence, for, like Heidegger, Oppen regards the acceptance of death as some sort of opening to the future, though unlike Heidegger he seeks to define that opening in terms of a numerousness ("humanity") that will survive the individual.[47]

If "Of Being Numerous" neither celebrates some ideal collectivity nor seeks to withdraw from human contact, as Hatlen and Perloff respectively propose, it's because in a curious way the acceptance of some ultimate singularity makes the individual *supernumerary*. I draw this idea from a suggestive passage in Eric Santner's *On the Psychotheology of Everyday Life*:

To "count" as singular one has to be, as it were, *supernumerary*, to persist beyond the logic of parts and wholes, beyond cultural systems of exchange, distinguished not by this or that trait but rather by *being left over*, by *remaining* once all particularities have been accounted for. It is death that first endows existence with this kind of singular density....[48]

The singular, then, "persist[s] beyond the logic of parts and wholes," most obviously, perhaps, in the survival of shipwreck, but also, as Hans Blumenberg reminds us in his study of the metaphorics of shipwreck, as a *spectator* of the disaster. Like the party on shipboard, Oppen's "bright light of shipwreck" is something seen from afar, the very emblem of, as Blumenberg puts it, "the insoluble dilemma of theoretical distance versus living engagement."[49] This separateness marks an acceptance of finitude which may lead either to a defeated sense of what Oppen calls "the closed self,"[50] or, more positively, to the initiation of what section 26 of the poem defines as "the metaphysical sense of the future":

> They have lost the metaphysical sense
> Of the future, they feel themselves
> The end of a chain
>
> Of lives, single lives
> And we know that lives
> Are single
>
> And cannot defend
> The metaphysic
> On which rest
>
> The boundaries
> Of our distances
> We want to say
>
> "Common sense"
> And cannot. We stand on
>
> That denial
> Of death that paved the cities ... (*NCP*, 177–8)

A culture which "stands on" a "denial of death" while casually meting it out to others, as in section 18's "A plume of smoke, visible at a distance / In which people burn" (*NCP*, 173), such a culture is "without issue, a dead end":

> Unable to begin
> At the beginning, the fortunate
> Find everything already here. They are shoppers,
> Choosers, judges; … And here the brutal
> Is without issue, a dead end.
>   They develop
> Argument in order to speak, they become
> unreal, unreal, life loses
> solidity, loses extent, baseball's their game…. (*NCP*, 170)

The emphatically distanced "they" of both passages recalls the "they" of *Being and Time* where Heidegger speaks of "an impassioned freedom toward death— a freedom which has been released from the illusions of the "they", and which is factical, certain of itself, and anxious."[51] Oppen's shoppers, choosers and judges, however, are still caught up in the unreality of the "they," where everything is "already here," the social interpellations already in place and the possibilities of power withdrawn.

The "dead end" which Oppen signals in these lines might recall Claude Lefort's famous account of the "empty place" within democracy:

> The legitimacy of power is based on the people; but the image of popular sover-eignty is linked to the image of an empty place, impossible to occupy, such that those who exercise public authority can never claim to appropriate it. Democracy combines these two apparently contradictory principles: on the one hand, power emanates from the people; on the other, it is the power of nobody.[52]

Lefort highlights the tendency in democratic and in totalitarian systems to "dissolve the subject, wherever it can express itself, into an "us,"" to constitute numerousness, we might say, in a fiction of what he calls "the People-as-One."[53] Such is the primary discontent of numerousness, a discontent which plays itself out in Oppen's struggle to "test" the pronouns which circulate throughout his poem. So, for example, the false experience of the "they" in section 13 draws the conclusion that "one may honourably keep/ His distance/ If he can" (170–1), and the slippage here from generic ("one") to singular ("he") leads to a personal recollection of Oppen's wartime experience:

I cannot even now
Altogether disengage myself
From those men (*NCP*, 171)

Such experiences suggest some way of giving substance to the otherwise
empty pronouns of collective identity. So it is through "The baffling hierarchies/
Of father and child" (182) and "the beauty of women" (183) that the "we" finds
a voice "Which is ours, which is ourselves,/ This is our jubilation/ Exalted
and as old as that truthfulness/ Which illumines speech" (183–4). Yet it is the
achievement of Oppen's poem to see such "jubilation" against a background
which shows up the very fragility of this sense of "ourselves." As the starkly
moving section 38 reminds us, human finitude must ultimately compel the in-
clusive pronouns of authentic numerousness toward objectification and division:

You are the last
Who will know him
Nurse.

Not know him,
He is an old man,
A patient,
How could one know him?

You are the last
Who will see him
Or touch him,
Nurse. (187)

The reiterated "him" is the final condition of singularity, the patient no longer
a person to be known, but just "an old man" who can only be seen and touched.
But the very "transparency" of the diction here and the studied impersonality
of its pronouns also affirm "'the bright light of shipwreck' … discloses—'all,'" a
disclosure which, paradoxically, makes this absolute singularity the unsentimen-
tal ground of what is truly held in common.

Oppen's attempt to negotiate some middle way between monolithic con-
structions of self and community is surprisingly close to the work of recent
post-Heideggerian theorists who have sought at the interface of politics and
philosophy a way of talking about sociality while acknowledging division and
singularity.[54] I have suggested elsewhere that Jean-Luc Nancy's attempt to think

what he calls "being-in-common as distinct from community" might provide some kind of analogy with Oppen's thinking and with the sense they both have of Being as at once divided and shared.[55] It may be, too, that Nancy's idea of "The retreat of the political [as] the uncovering, the laying bare of being-with" echoes the Heideggerian cast of "being" in "Of Being Numerous."[56] At the same time, though, Nancy's *Being Singular Plural* from which these quotations are drawn also exhibits a level of rhetorical abstraction that reminds us that, for the poet, such formulations must, as Oppen had put it in "The Mind's Own Place," "substantiate themselves in the concrete materials of the poem." Here the closing lines of a poem called "World, World—" written a little before "Of Being Numerous," give us a preliminary sense of what that might involve:

The self is no mystery, the mystery is
That there is something for us to stand on.

We want to be here.

The act of being, the act of being
More than oneself. (159)

The radical simplification of the idiom in these lines along with the emphasis attaching to the deictic "here" make the principal object of reference— "being"—coincide with the poem's own occasion. To put it another way, thought embodies itself in the spatio-temporal "hereness" of the poem, with its phonic echoes and silences, its syntactical shape and typographical layout. Says Oppen, "I do not mean to prescribe an opinion or an idea, but to record the experience of thinking it."[57] Far from the act of "Find[ing] everything already here," what is sought in the poem is what Oppen calls "a new cadence of disclosure,"[58] a phrase which quite deliberately recalls Heidegger's way of contrasting the Greek sense of the "unconcealedness" of truth (*aletheia*) with the modern logos as "something-already-there.... something handy that one handles in order to gain and secure the truth as correctness."[59] Oppen's emphasis on disclosure is designed to counter any reification of either numerousness or singularity, making the poem instead an opening of a world which situates man not as a distanced observer, but as one being amidst others and in that sense "more than oneself," in the words of the poem.[60] The idea of having "something to stand on" may allude to and qualify a passage in one of Pound's late Cantos where he complains that "the lot of 'em, Yeats, Possum and Wyndham / had no ground beneath 'em // Orage had."[61] The "ground" referred to here, of course, signifies economic understanding, but in contrast Oppen's lines emphasise once again that it is not concepts that are at stake, but rather the contradictory experience of being between numerousness and singularity, an experience which alone can materialise the collective pronoun "we" in the powerfully stressed "here."

Lyn Hejinian has remarked that "Like George Oppen, I am aware that poets work in the context of "being numerous,""[62] and her recent work might be read in terms of an engagement with just this set of questions. Of especial interest here is the way in which Hejinian incorporates Oppen's poetics of disclosure into the particular "phenomenology" she developed in her early work from Gertrude Stein and Merleau-Ponty. As I've suggested elsewhere, the importance of Stein to Hejinian is not that her skepticism about knowledge and memory produces a simply autonomous poetic language, but rather that her result-ing rejection of an instrumental language of means and ends makes possible a new kind of encounter with, and address to, a world that exceeds the self.[63] The "phenomenology" Hejinian evolves from Stein thus exhibits a number of features that resonate with Oppen's poetics as I have described them so far: there is Hejinian's recurring emphasis on perception rather than on knowl-edge, on evaluation and "testing" rather than on the pursuit of "truth," on the idea of "description" as phenomenal rather than taxonomic, on an openness to contingency and unpredictability, and, finally, on what she calls a pervasive "doubt" which, in formal terms, "hovers" so that words, as she puts it in the early poem *The Guard*, achieve "the inability to finish // what they say."[64] Just as we have seen Oppen resisting the tendency to "Find everything already here," so Hejinian attempts to reformulate the concept of "reason" (in the essay of that name) as the measure of an encounter in which something new occurs which cannot simply be inserted into a pre-existing frame of reference: "Something which wasn't here before is here now; it appears and it appeared to us, and it is acknowledged by the sensation *this is happening.*"[65]

The terms of this argument are indebted to Lyotard's *The Differend*, but leav-ing aside that connection, suggestive as it is, we can see how close in principle this also is to Oppen's association of an open poetic form with ideas of "encoun-ter" and social connection. In her MSA talk, Hejinian observes that

This is not a poetry of single moments, however—Oppen's singularities may be impenetrable but they are not transcendent, they can't be removed from their own history nor from the fact that they share it with other singularities. Oppen's is a poetry of combination, a poetry with little interest in universality and enormous interest in heterogeneity.[66]

Hejinian's position here endorses Oppen's refusal of any simply binary relation of numerousness to singularity. Like Oppen, she has attempted in a sequence of works to expand a phenomenology of perceptual experience to one of collective relationality. She too understands phenomenology by way of Heidegger, as directed toward a conception of politics as something lying beyond specific institutions and as grounded instead in a being-in-common, to use Nancy's phrase, which moves ceaselessly *between* an experience of sameness and difference, of numerousness and singularity, without ever rigidifying into the false oneness claimed by either term in isolation. Hejinian in her MSA talk catches precisely this movement in "Of Being Numerous":

Oppen proceeds from the initial vantage point of his individual singularity to an encounter with similarity and thence numerousness, and suddenly he and we are no longer in the terrain of sameness but in that of difference, which invites (one hopes) interest, tolerance, a sense of self and singularity open to alternatives and correctives and readiness for yet another horizon shift."[67]

What, arguably, this account doesn't acknowledge is the importance attaching to death and human finitude in Oppen's poem, though in her gloss on Section 39 she writes (after Lyotard):

To sense the antiquity of the realization that *this is happening* alerts one to the perennial presence of the immediate, an immediate in which one has always participated in the anticipation of death. It is in the phrase *this is happening* that the presence of death is acknowledged.[68]

At the same time, Hejinian's response is strongly shaped by her reading of Hannah Arendt's *The Human Condition*, and Arendt, of course, substitutes for Heidegger's philosophy of mortality a philosophy of what she calls "natality," a philosophy of birth and beginning. "Men, though they must die," writes Arendt, "are not born in order to die but in order to begin."[69] Rudiger Safranski, Heidegger's most recent biographer, notes that Arendt's philosophy "knows the mood of anxiety, yet it also knows the jubilation of arrival in the world,"[70] and it is this "jubilation," the "happiness" of Hejinian's recent volume *Happily*, that is the condition most frequently sought in her current work.[71] Arrival," beginning, "incipience": these are some of the words Hejinian now uses to define a poetics of "appearance," and "appearance" in exactly the sense of Heidegger's formulation "Appearing is the very essence of being."[72] In other words, "appearance" is not what is traditionally set over against the real, but the event in which being is disclosed. Oppen observes similarly in one of his notebooks that "Reality is *apparent*: to appear is fundamental to its reality," and his third collection of poems, *This In Which*, takes as one of its epigraphs Heidegger's reference to "the arduous path of appearance" in his *Introduction to Metaphysics*.[73]

For Hejinian, Gertrude Stein's writing, with its commitment to "beginning again and again,"[74] embodies the same recognition: Stein, she says, "invented a mode of iteration to indicate not recurrence but phenomenological *occurrence*, the perpetual coming into being through accumulated instances of the person that is."[75] "Occurrence," of course, is one of Oppen's key words, providing the title for two poems (*NCP* 144, 212) and figuring in a series of terms disclosive of "being" which include "event," "marvel," "miracle," and "adventure."[76] In the draft of her Oppen lecture, Hejinian also glosses Section 39 with several passages from Lyotard's *The Differend*, including his penultimate proposal that "there is not "language' and "Being", but occurrences," the latter word elsewhere said to be synonymous with "the event, the marvel, the anticipation of a community of feelings."[77]

It's clear from her recent essays that Hejinian's principal aim is now to find in poetic form a means by which to articulate that "coming into being" that she has also discerned in Oppen's concept of "disclosure." The ambition is to grasp this concept as a means of seeing numerousness not just as, in Oppen's phrase, "the mere number of us" (*NCP*, 157), but, as Nancy puts it, "a singular-plural constitution or configuration that is neither the 'community' nor the 'individual.'"[78] It is here that Hejinian's reading of Arendt's *The Human Condition* seems to offer some linkage between a poetics of "disclosure" and a conception of the political which is here traced back to the Greek *polis*: "The *polis*, properly speaking, is not the city-state in its physical location; it is the organization of the people as it arises out of acting and speaking together, and its true space lies between people living together for this purpose, no matter where they happen to be."[79] This space, which is, crucially for Hejinian, named by Arendt as "the space of appearance" is "the space where I appear to others as others appear to me, where men exist not merely like other living or inanimate beings but make their appearance explicitly."[80]

In her MSA paper, Hejinian speaks of Oppen's "Of Being Numerous" as "a space of appearance" in just this sense, and in another recent piece called "Continuing Against Closure" she explains the implication of Arendt's concept for her own writing:

What has come to be of increasing interest to me over the past few years is not so much consciousness itself but the sites of consciousness. And by sites of consciousness I do not mean heads or brains but places in the world, spaces in which an awakening of consciousness occurs, the spaces in which a self discovers itself as an object among others (and thus, by the way, achieves subjectivity). My notion of these sites of consciousness, these zones of encounter, derives much from Hannah Arendt's elaboration of what she termed "the space of appearance," where human and world come into being for and with each other.[81]

But what might be the result of splicing together Arendt's concept of the "space of appearance" as the public realm of thought and action with the poetics of Stein and Oppen? Arendt's book is, of course, neither playful in Stein's manner nor brooding in Oppen's; and Hejinian has remarked too that *The Human Condition* has no place for dreams and art, whereas she "would argue that one of the functions of art is to bring dreams and other works of the imagination into the space of appearance."[82] For Hejinian, as for her friend Kit Robinson, whose essay on dreams is named as one of the sources for Book 1 of *A Border Comedy*, the dreamwork offers a particularly vivid instance of "appearance" and one that suggests a "grammar" that exceeds merely semantic interpretations of dreams. As Robinson puts it, "The possibility of a grammar of dreams leads away from the consideration of the dream as a code for the analysis of the individual psyche toward a more general view of dreams as problems in perception and description, that is, as problems for writing."[83] Hejinian's "space of appearance" is, then, less Arendt's arena of public action than it is the text itself which, like the dream, is a medium of ceaseless and unexpected change. Another of Hejinian's "sources" for Book 1 of *A Border Comedy*, Osip Mandelstam, speaks of Dante's work as "a continuous transformation of the substratum of poetic material" which demonstrates "a peculiarity of poetic material which I propose to call its convertibility or transmutability."[84] Like the condensation and displacement of the dreamwork, the open form of the poem allows thought to be grasped as something "happening," as an unpredictable event which constitutes a "zone of encounter" because it interpellates "us" as co-present (compare Lyotard's "anticipation of a community of feelings"). Hejinian's recent work thus strives to grasp numerousness as a condition of "comedy" because "laughter always implies ... confu-/ sion—a process of joining, a desire for sharing."[85] "Joining" and "sharing," then, but always with the proviso that poetry, like comedy, makes its real capital out of difference and hetereogeneity. As Hejinian puts it in *Happily*:

Perhaps there were three things, no one of which made sense
  of the other two

A sandwich, a wallet, and a giraffe
Logic tends to force similarities but that's not what we mean
   By "sharing existence"[86]

"Happiness" is thus allied with contingency and difference, linked etymologically to "hap," "happenstance," "haphazard" and, perhaps most importantly, to "happen"[87] —happiness is things happening, then, things beginning rather than repeating themselves;[88] or as Hejinian puts it in her essay "A Common Sense," "Happiness is a complication, as it were, of the ordinary, a folding in of the happenstantial."[89] And happiness, unlike *un*happiness, which is tied to loss and privation, is "complete unto itself; it is atelic, goal-free, aimless."

If we seem to have moved a long way from the philosophy of action in the public realm that Arendt derives from Greek thought, that is because (so Hejinian argues in this essay) Arendt's conception of the "space of appearance" undervalues the everyday, household sphere. Yet it is here, with the commonplace, that for Hejinian the political ultimately has to "appear." The commonplace, as she puts it, "is the totality of our commonality; it is meaningful as that, as the place where we know each other and know we are together."[90] For Hejinian, as for Oppen, it is within the poem as "a space of appearance" that this knowledge is tested and the grammar of numerousness compelled to disclose its ambiguities.

Notes

I am grateful to Linda Oppen for permission to quote from published and unpublished material by George Oppen and to Lyn Hejinian for permission to quote from her unpublished work. I would also like to thank the Leverhulme Trust for the award of a Research Fellowship to support my work on a book-length study of Oppen, of which this essay is part. I am indebted to Richard Godden and Peter Middleton for their helpful comments on earlier drafts of this essay. This essay was first published in *Humanities Review*, 9.1 (Spring 2011).

1. Quoted from the collection of Lyn Hejinian's papers held at the Mandeville Special Collections, University of California at San Diego Library, MSS 74, Box 44, Folder 35. The note continues by attributing to the Objectivists "[t]he sense of scientific method; discontinuities; experiential and empirical attention. More than any other poets, involved with ethics, but neither dogmatic nor moralistic nor instructional. To a large extent, they were unable to solve the ethical dilemmas they witnessed—for historical rather than for artistic reasons."

2. Hejinian also engaged in periods of intensive study of Zukofsky's work in the seventies and eighties—see Kate Fagan, "'Constantly I Write This Happily': Encountering Lyn Hejinian," unpublished DPhil dissertation (University of Sydney, 2002), 115.

3. *The Language of Inquiry* (Berkeley, Los Angeles, London: University of California Press, 2000), 318–54.

4. *George Oppen: New Collected Poems*, ed. Michael Davidson (New York: New Directions,

2002), 168, 174 (hereafter cited as *NCP*).

5. *The Selected Letters of George Oppen*, ed., Rachel Blau DuPlessis (Durham and London: Duke University Press, 1990), 177 (hereafter cited as *SL*).

6. "The Numerous," UCSD 74, 44, 35 (the inset quotation is from Derrida's *Aporias*). Cf. "Barbarism," *The Language of Inquiry*, 327: "The border is not an edge along the fringe of society and experience but rather their very middle—their between; it names the condition of doubt and encounter which being foreign to a situation (which may be life itself) provokes—a condition which is simultaneously an impasse and a passage, limbo and transit zone, with checkpoints and bureaus of exchange, a meeting place and a realm of confusion."

7. Ibid.

8. For a detailed discussion of Oppen's time in Mexico and of his reading of Maritain, see my "George Oppen in Exile: Mexico and Maritain," *Journal of American Studies* (April, 39.1, 1–18 2005).

9. L. S. Dembo, *The Monological Jew: A Literary Study* (Madison, WI: University of Wisconsin Press, 1988), 137.

10. Fredric Jameson, *Marxism and Form: Twentieth-Century Dialectical Theories of Literature* (Princeton, NJ: Princeton University Press, 1971), 206.

11. Jacques Maritain, *Creative Intuition in Art and Poetry* (New York: Meridian Books, 1955), 159–60, and 316 n.14: "... in the field of art, the mind does not have to know, but to *make*" (his emphasis).

12. Burton Hatlen, "Not Altogether Lone in a Lone Universe: George Oppen's *The Materials*," in Hatlen, ed. and introd. *George Oppen: Man and Poet* (Orono, ME: National Poetry Foundation, Inc., 1981), 331 (hereafter cited as *GOMP*).

13. Oppen papers in the Mandeville Special Collections, University of San Diego (referred to by collection number [16], followed by box and file numbers),UCSD 16, 17, 9. This note seems to have been written in the early seventies.

14. Maritain, *Creative Intuition*, 3.

15. Sartre, *Search for a Method*, trans. Hazel Barnes (1963; New York: Vintage Books, 1968),181. Cf. Sartre, *Critique of Dialectical Reason*, trans. Alan Sheridan-Smith, ed. Jonathan Ree (London: NLB, 1976), 40: "Our extremely slight dissociation of ourselves from the letter of Marxist doctrine (which I indicated in *The Problem of Method*) enables us to see the meaning of this question as the disquiet of the genuine experience which refuses to collapse into non-truth."

16 *Search for a Method*, 9 n.6.

17. *Critique of Dialectical Reason*, 79.

18. Maritain, *Creative Intuition*, 159. Oppen's version of the phrase provides the epigraph for *The Materials* (1962): "We awake in the same moment to ourselves and to things." See also Oppen's 1962 essay "The Mind's Own Place," reprinted in Robert Creeley, ed., *George Oppen: Selected Poems* (New York: New Directions, 2003), 175 on modernism and "the sense of the poet's self among things."

19. See, for example, UCSD 16, 18, 1: "in everything that is real there is an irreducible element" of an hallucination, the irreducible element is that you experienced it." I have not traced the source of Oppen's quotation.

20. *SL*, 22.

21. "The Anthropologist of Myself: A Selection from Working Papers," ed. Rachel Blau DuPlessis, *Sulfur*, 26 (Spring 1990), 160; "The Mind's Own Place', 175.

22. UCSD 16, 17, 7. Cf. 16, 18, 1 on "the courage of clarity, but NOT the "clarity" of argument."

23. USCD 16, 14, 5.

24. "The Mind's Own Place," 176: "It is possible to say anything in abstract prose, but a great

many things one believes or would like to believe or thinks he believes will not substantiate themselves in the concrete materials of the poem." Note Oppen's deliberately equivocal presentation of "belief" here.

25. *GOMP*, 331.

26. Perloff, "The Shipwreck of the Singular: George Oppen's "Of Being Numerous","*Ironwood 26* (1985), 199.

27. UCSD 16, 19, 12.

28. UCSD 16, 19, 13.

29. *SL*, 111.

30. L. S. Dembo, "The 'Objectivist' Poet: Four Interviews," *Contemporary Poetry*, 10. 2 (Spring 1969), 8.

31. Oppen, "The Philosophy of the Astonished": Selections from the Working Papers," ed. Rachel Blau DuPlessis, *Sulfur*, 27 (Fall 1990), 214; *SL*, 190. Cf. UCSD 16, 22, 58: "The word/ Populace, not humanity/ Which cannot be given meaning. But the sense/ Of populace/ Necessary."

32. An early draft of section 12 (UCSD 16, 22, 58) incorporates a quotation from Owen Chase's *The Shipwreck of the Whaleship Essex*, Melville's principal source, suggesting that Oppen may at one time have intended to expand this set of allusions.

33. *SL*, 116.

34. *SL*, 121.

35. UCSD 16, 17, 12.. Cf. the reference in "The Speech at Soli" to "Friday's footprint" (*NCP*, 239).

36. UCSD 16, 14, 6.

37. Cf. "Two Romance Poems" (*NCP*, 261): "bright light of shipwreck beautiful as the sea."

38. *SL*, 263 (Oppen's emphasis).

39. *SL*, 77: "The purport of the poems, of course, is the solipsist position…. I don't think I have ever before heard the statement in Not My Loneliness But Ours: once said, as it is here said, it seems inescapable. The loneliness not of the individual, but of the group." The poem appeared in Bronk's *The World, the Worldless* (1964) which Oppen had been reading in manuscript in 1963, the year of this letter.

40. William Bronk, *Life Supports: New and Collected Poems* (Jersey City, NJ: Talisman House, 1997), 44.

41. Saul Bellow, *Herzog* (1964; Harmondsworth: Penguin Books, 1965), 183.

42. Compare the rather lame expression of a similar idea in William E. Connolly, *Identity/ Difference: Democratic Negotiations of Political Paradox* (Minneapolis and London: University of Minnesota Press, 2002), 19: "connectedness to a future that stretches beyond my life and our lives provides me with pride in the present and consoles me somehow about the end that awaits me." The uncertainty here ("somehow") seems purely rhetorical.

43. Heidegger, *Being and Time*, trans. John Macquarrie and Edward Robinson (Oxford: Blackwell, 1962), 284.

44. Derrida, *Aporias,* trans. Thomas Dutoit (Stanford, CA: Stanford University Press, 1993), 22.

45. Heidegger, *Being and Time*, 289.

46. Derrida, *Aporias*, 15.

47. Cf. James M. Demke, *Being, Man, and Death: A Key to Heidegger* (Lexington, Ky: Kentucky University Press, 1970), 3: "Death leaves man "open", or necessarily pointing to something beyond himself, ultimately to being itself."

48. Eric L. Santner, *On the Psychotheology of Everyday Life* (Chicago: University of Chicago Press, 2001), 72 (his emphasis).

49. Hans Blumenberg, *Shipwreck with Spectator: Paradigm of a Metaphor for Existence* (Cambridge, MA: MIT Press, 1997), 67.

50. Letter to June Oppen Degnan, *Ironwood 26* (Fall 1985), 223.

51. Heidegger, *Being and Time*, 311.

52. Claude Lefort, *The Political Forms of Modern Society: Bureaucracy, Democracy, Totalitarianism*, ed. John B. Thompson (Cambridge, MA: MIT Press, 1986), 279.

53. ibid, 290.

54. See, for example, Jean-Luc Nancy, *The Inoperative Community*, trans. Peter Connor (Minneapolis and Oxford: University of Minnesota Press, 1991) and *Being Singular Plural*, trans. Robert D. Richardson and Anne E. O'Byrne (Stanford, CA: Stanford University Press, 2000); Philippe Lacoue-Labarthe, *Heidegger, Art and Politics: The Fiction of the Political*, trans. Chris Turner (Oxford: Basil Blackwell, 1990); Jacques Derrida, *Politics of Friendship*, trans. George Collins (London: Verso, 1997); Maurice Blanchot, *The Unavowable Community*, trans. Pierre Joris (New York: Station Hill Press, 1988); Giorgio Agamben, *The Coming Community*, trans. Michael Hardt (Minneapolis and London: University of Minnesota Press, 1991); Jacques Rancière, *Disagreement: Politics and Philosophy*, trans. Julie Rose (Minneapolis: University of Minnesota Press, 1999); Alain Badiou, *L'Etre et l'événement* (Paris: Seuil, 1988).

55. See my "Of Being Ethical: Reflections on George Oppen," in Rachel Blau DuPlessis and Peter Quartermain, ed., *The Objectivist Nexus: Essays in Cultural Poetics* (Tuscaloosa and London: University of Alabama Press, 1999), 240–53.

56. The quotations from Nancy are from *Being Singular Plural*, 24, 37. Nancy remarks of "being-with" that "This coessence puts essence itself in the hyphenation—"being-singular-plural"—which is a mark of union and also a mark of division, a mark of sharing that effaces itself, leaving each term to its isolation *and* its being-with-the-others"(37).

57. UCSD 16, 19, 4.

58. *SL*, 97: "A new syntax is a new cadence of disclosure, a new cadence of logic, a new musical cadence. A new "structure of space"...." Cf. UCSD 16, 14, 3: "Prosody: the pulse of thought, of consciousness, therefore in Heidegger's word, of human *Dasein*, human "being there"."

59. Heidegger, *An Introduction to Metaphysics*, trans. Ralph Manheim (New Haven and London,: Yale University Press, 1959), 189.

60. Cf. Joan Brandt, *Geopoetics: The Politics of Mimesis in Poststructuralist French Poetry and Theory* (Stanford, CA: Stanford University Press, 1997), 228 on Nancy: "As the relational ground out of which being emerges, community cannot be thought in terms of political ends or origins, nor can it be seen as a common substance or being; it should be thought instead as the means by which being is made manifest, as a network or interweaving of singularities that brings being into existence by placing it in relation both to itself and to others in the movement of its "ex-posure" to the outside world." Nancy's thinking is, of course, deeply coloured by his reading of Heidegger. Oppen's acquaintance with *Being and Time* would have made him familiar with similar propositions, as, for example, when Heidegger argues that (152) "a bare subject without the world never "is" proximally, nor is it ever given. And so in the end an isolated 'I' without Others is just as far from being proximally given."

61. Ezra Pound, *The Cantos* (London: Faber and Faber, 1999), 685.

62. *The Language of Inquiry*, 4.

63. See my "Phenomenal Poetics: Reading Lyn Hejinian," in Michel Delville and Christine Pagnoulle, eds., *The Mechanics of the Mirage: Postward American Poetry* (Liège: University of Liège, 2000), 241–52. The essay considers Hejinian's reading of Lyotard in some detail.

64. *The Cold of Poetry* (Los Angeles: Sun & Moon Press, 1994), 20.

65. *The Language of Inquiry*, 343. On the relation of Hejinian's "*this is happening*" to Lyotard's "*is it happening?*" in *The Differend*, see my "Phenomenal Poetics," 248–9.

66. "George Oppen and the Space of Appearance," typescript of unpublished paper given at the Modernist Studies Conference, Madison, Wisconsin, October 2002, 3. I am grateful to Lyn Hejinian for providing me with a copy of this paper and for allowing me to quote from it.

67. ibid, 5.

68. UCSD 74, 44, 35, p.89. Cf. Lyotard, *The Differend*, xv on "the question: *Is it happening?*"

69. Hannah Arendt, *The Human* Condition, 2nd edition (Chicago: University of Chicago Press, 1998), 246.

70. Rudiger Safranski, *Martin Heidegger: Between Good and Evil* (Cambridge MA: Harvard University Press, 1998), 383.

71. "Jubilation," as Hejinian notes in her Oppen lecture, also marks the recovery of an authentic plural in Oppen's poem: "Which is ours, which is ourselves, / This is our jubilation" (*NCP* 183).

72. *An Introduction to Metaphysics*, 101.

73. UCSD 16, 19, 7; *NCP*, 92.

74. *The Language of Inquiry*, 102.

75. Ibid., 289.

76. See *SL* 419 n.52 and *SL*, 259. Compare the following unpublished comment (UCSD 16, 13, 17): " 'the world' we think of the world as that which makes it possible for things to be (the 'place' of occurrence, the 'place' of being)."

77. Lyotard, *The Differend: Phrases In Dispute*, trans. Georges Van Den Abbeele (Manchester: Manchester University Press, 1988), 181,178.

78. Nancy, *Being Singular Plural*, 74.

79. Arendt, *The Human Condition*, 198.

80. Ibid, 198–9.

81. Hejinian, "Continuing Against Closure," *Jacket*, 14 (July 2001): e-journal available at <http://jacketmagazine.com/14/hejinian.html>

82. ibid, 3.

83. Kit Robinson, "Time & Materials: The Workplace, Dreams, and Writing," *Poetics Journal*, 9 (June 1991), 32–3. Robinson argues that Freud's method of interpretation is limited because "by concentrating on the semantic dimension it leaves out the syntactic, horizontal dimension" (32). For the essay as one of Hejinian's avowed "sources," see *A Border Comedy* (New York: Granary Books, 2001), 213.

84. Osip Mandelstam, "Conversation about Dante," in *The Complete Critical Prose and Letters*, ed. Jane Gary Harris, trans. Jane Gary Harris and Constance Link (Ann Arbor, MI: Ardis, 1979), 414. The essay is listed as "a source" in *A Border Comedy*, 213.

85. *A Border Comedy*, 61 (my ellipsis).

86. *Happily* (Sausalito, CA: The Post-Apollo Press, 2000), 15.

87. See Marjorie Perloff's lively account of these word plays in her "Happy World: What Lyn Hejinian's Poetry Tells Us About Chance, Fortune and Pleasure," *Boston Review* (February/March 2000), available at http://epc.buffalo.edu/authors/perloff/articles/hejinian.html>.

88. See *The Language of Inquiry*, 361 where Hejinian quotes a long passage from Stein on "the beginning of knowing what there was that made there be no repetition" and adds: "And it is what here I am going to risk calling happiness."

89. *The Language of Inquiry*, 370.

90. Ibid, 365.

Writing Is an
Aid to Memory
Laura Moriarty

"A bedroom is cut where I went." ("Preface")

I take the book with me to visit my lover. Conveniently, he lives just down the hill in a North Beach alley. I carry a paper umbrella from Chinatown and wear a 40s dress of flowered rayon. The book and my notebooks are in my straw bag as they always are when I go to the café often for coffee and writing. But not today. Later in bed reading from the book to my companion, who, though not a writer, has an almost infinite sense of verbal curiosity, I try to convey, through the general hilarity that obtains in that luxurious moment of explication, what I believe is happening in the text. I speak of surprising and engaging the reader by promising one thing but then doing another that is, while different from the expected thing, still an interesting or convincing gesture. I cite examples. He reads. I read. I demonstrate. I focus on the turn in the middle of the sentence or phrase, "more in the grip way gets to it" (#32). The text flows easily for us now. We get it. We get to it.

"that I wish to make you do so for joy" (#26.)

   That first edition of *Writing Is an Aid to Memory*, published by The Figures in 1978, is a yellow book whose black and white cover graphics, by John Woodall, suggest antennae connectors or possibly synapses in the brain. There is a sense of connectivity. The theme of writing appears graphically in the elegant two page frontispiece by the same artist. There are thick black endpapers. It is a beautiful book. As a young writer, I would have been in my late twenties when I first bought it, I was intrigued by the work and was very happy to be reading a book by a woman whose work was so gratifyingly nonlinear and so uncomplainingly celebratory of thought. Put off by the post Beat diction of the local scene, I was reading Stein and writing single word line portraits of my friends in the wind on my roof. I was having a biography but didn't really want to write about it. *Writing Is An Aid to Memory* presented a model for writing in relation to attention.

"no soggy gossip chapter here" (#9)

There is a sense in the book of the beauty of observation, "scription" (#2) rather than description of experience, of the experience of being in thought. There is a creation and exposition of beauty. The word "beauty" appears 12 times in the 44 unpaginated sections, all to noticeable effect. "[B]eauty is only a symptom"(#25) Here it is a symptom of arrangement, of order "meanwhile extends a roll of beauty" (#21). This beauty is not associated with "sentimental tickle" but with "mental might"(#18)—the "trot of taught beauty"(#19) here is a light, measured tread.

There is in the text a lightness also of wit and externality, a dailiness in its address that seems, when I first read it, both strange and familiar. I admire what seems to me the anti-sense, non goal-oriented quality (the atelos) of the Preface: "Though we keep company with cats and dogs, all thoughtful people are impatient, with a restlessness made inevitable by language." Restlessly, I write an imitation, send it off and get an immediate reply from Lyn, polite but not hugely enthusiastic. Undeterred, and still restless, I put together the information in her work with that of other writers whose poetics are perhaps unrelated, as young writers are wont to do. The fact of utilizing a received form and communicating with it in what seems to me an accurate and intuitive manner, as in the Preface, contributes to my thinking about traditional forms like the rondeau. I perceive, accurately or not, that the use of such forms does not seem to be an approved part of the poetics of this intriguing, new (to me) group of writers and determine to do the resistant thing by using them. I note that any sort of mystical claptrap is anathema and write (in *Persia*) of tarot cards. The sense of attention and openness remains an excellent permission and, in the event, resistance turns out to be engaging and provocative to various potential readers, rather than, as it sometimes is, futile. "beautiful songs are the thing intended" (23).

Back with the book, we pay attention to time. We read intensely, experiencing the miraculous quality of real time as it occurs next. We are aware of the beauty and we are simultaneously beautiful. "a sol double perfection of beauty" (#21). We are perfect. We are perfect readers. The calm arrangement of the beautiful unfolds around us. Time becomes elastic as the reading proceeds, line after line, spread out on the page, jumping around, frolicking really, in the freedom of its arrangement.

Finally we arrive at the last page. A long day has existed in these few hours spent with the text. About the book we remember nothing but the experience of the writing. "a rhythm or obscure and joyous life" (#34). There is no catchy tune, no hook, no revelations or epiphanies but those occurring in our own perception and in the physicality and grace of the words. "a little grace familiar with simple limbs and the sudden/ reverse" (#1) Time to go home.

"I do remember that the momentum of the cadence, with its departures and arrivals within departures, was intended to push time in both directions, "backward toward memory and also forward toward 'writing,' which is always (for me) indicative of future unforeseen meanings and events. Writing gives one something to remember."*

Reading the reprint a thousand years (or at least a few decades) later there is a quiet satisfaction in noting that the 1996 Sun & Moon version retains the exact page layouts of the Figures book, even including the prose "linebreaks" of the Preface. Memory is preserved intact, "chapter amber," (#26), in the golden light of the yellow covers common to the two editions. Both use the theme of writing, handwriting, as a visual cue to the writerly experience of reading the text. John Woodall's inky drawing has been replaced by the penmanship of Adolph Wölfli. The hatted 1920s girl on the second *Writing* cover, collaged into Wolfe's intricate design, gazes thoughtfully into a maritime distance that is redolent of the choppy but meditative quality of the writing, its sharp divides, its record of thinking as it leaves itself behind "I can picture the marked page/ poke beauty/ sunset like a pack of dogs/ swaying with daylight/ it is later afternoon and I hurry/ my fault of comfort/ the streets of traffic are a great success" (#28).

*Hejinian, Lyn, *The Language of Inquiry,* "Comments for Manual Brito," University of California Press, p. 192.

Hejinian, Lyn, *Writing Is an Aid to Memory,* The Figures, Berkeley, 1978.

Hejinian, Lyn, *Writing Is an Aid to Memory,* Sun & Moon, Los Angeles, 1996.

Rules and Restraints in Women's Experimental Writing
Carla Harryman

Constraint

In the article, "Rule and Constraint," from *Oulipo: A Primer of Potential Literature,*[1] Marcel Benabou lambastes those who claim a privileged status for literary inspiration insofar as "inspiration" is taken to be a phenomenon of nature. To Benabou, the devotees of inspiration simply confuse conventional rules with a mistaken notion of natural language. The "inspired" text's properties, he writes, are conventionally thought of as "natural fact;" whereas the use of other "rules," e.g. eccentric, numeric, or unique devices, are from a conventional perspective, "perceived as shameful artifice."

In the context of contemporary women's experimental writing, the use of constraint is not particularly controversial; and in the United States, what might irritate traditionalists more than the use of eccentric devices is the literary author's use of "non-literary" vocabularies drawn from the sciences, philosophy, politics, and sociology. There is sometimes a sense that when such languages enter a literary work, the work is contaminated. In any case, I can assume that the majority of the readers of this essay will not view writers' deliberate use of constraints negatively. Yet, there are also other kinds of rules governing the experimental text. I think of these rules as the ideas that control, motivate, and limit the writer's project.

In *Writing Is an Aid to Memory*, Lyn Hejinian employs a numeric constraint based on alphabetization to spatially organize her poem, but Hejinian's interrogation of memory is less dependent on the device than on its thematic concept. In her essay, "Bodies of Work," Kathy Acker discusses the device of repetition in bodybuilding as a metaphor for confrontation with failure, but Acker's use of repetition is contingent on her a priori critique of western attitudes toward death. In my play "There is Nothing Better Than a Theory," I used a constraint by which each line of the play had to act as either a grammatical, semantic, or rhetorical hinge for the next line, but without its reliance on the a priori concept that language itself is the site of performance, the text would not offer itself as a challenge to the way that plays get made. I would argue then that, in the case of these texts, there are concepts or questions related to pre-existing concepts that motivate the text and create the need for constraint, "a commodious way of passing from language to writing." [2]

In my use of it, the rule is the rule of thought, not of literary convention. This rule of thought is the convention on which the experimental work relies and what the experimental work cannot question without destroying itself. This rule of thought or intellectual position is then what allows the difficult text to come into being at all, and it is what limits its own complexity.

In each of the works under discussion here, the text is directed toward communal knowledge or practice—as it questions conventions of communal practice; the use of writing to aid memory, the use of repetition to create change, the use of text to invent localized as opposed to normative performance. These works also inscribe the regulatory mechanisms and desire of compelling ideas, imply their own limits, create as well as make use of resistance.

The writing that follows is divided into three sections that are meant to variously characterize the "resistant" values of each writer's works. In addition, I take a different approach to my discussion of each writer. I do this to emphasize the difference among each of us.

The Recalcitrant Text

"Walking Backwards with the Maintains" was a site specific "talk," which I "performed" in the San Francisco live-in loft of Bob Perelman and Francie Shaw in 1977. In the performance, I gave people domestic tasks to do while I read Clark Coolidge's long poem, The Maintains, walking backwards. No documentation of the performance remains, although I did videotape the piece for purposes of later discussion with my interdisciplinary art seminar run by movement artist Susanne Helmuth. At the time, the videotaping of the piece was a rather uncomfortable issue for me; I wasn't going to be able to convince many artists to go to a literary event, but I also knew that "the writers" were not going to respond very analytically to the art event. So I did the performance for writers and discussed it with artists. In addition, I felt ambivalent about the trend toward documenting every act of performance art; it went against the grain of my disruptive impulses. I was flirting with a kind of now-you-see-it-now-you-don't aesthetic. I also didn't like the use of the video camera to magnify the self-conscious position of the audience, since it would additionally exploit that position later as the documentation became commodified artifact. This is why I destroyed the tape. It is also why, given that I did choose to use the video camera, I tried to make my use of it obvious. The video camera became an extension of my own tyrannical role in the performance as I commanded others to do my bidding and floated around reading "sacred" text in the wrong direction.

I now think of "Walking Backwards with the Maintains" (1977) as a precursor to "There is Nothing Better Than a Theory" (1982), a piece for the stage in which theoretical language, abstract language, language derived from domestic situations, and language of public culture are put into play. I suspect that when I performed "Walking Backwards," the wish had been, in part, that I had written The Maintains: even if it wasn't exactly what I would desire to write. The event was as if a performance of something I would someday, and did, write.

In the performance of "Walking Backwards," I thought of myself as an androgynous figure. I was performing the relationship between abstract art and domesticity; enacting the abstract (male power) work conceptually (backwards) while the audience (subjugated and feminized) did my bidding/my chores. Some of the men later told me that they liked being told what to do and others wouldn't talk to me. The performance, then, was a critique with a lot of twists: nothing was settled precisely in a familiar place. And I was also satirizing the role of the author by enacting a tyrannical (unraveling, whimsical, and arbitrary) authority over Coolidge's text and the audience/performers at the same time. This was also a source of discomfort, partly because Coolidge's abstract work was still in the process of being recognized as a "breakthrough" text. Why be so irreverent? These were questions I imagined, or imagine, the silent unquestioning audience participants would have asked, had they chosen to speak. But I wanted to step into and reverse the man's shoes. This was even to myself somewhat off-putting.

Yet, this performance would disappear, was even intended to disappear while Coolidge's text remained. In the context of the performance, the text was recalcitrant. And even though I performed the text in the wrong way, choosing words in the wrong order, nothing actually changed the text. This concept of a recalcitrant text, within the situation of performance, has been the basis of much if not all of my writing for theater. The text for theater in my oeuvre is not meant as an unequivocal medium for performance. The text is meant to perform its own object status as linked to and separate from the live performance of its language.

Perhaps the recalcitrant text, or that of the text resistant to easily lending itself to a performed interpretation, restrains one from being able to know it in the way one would know a person. It cannot be transgressed, because the performers will go off and do something else, but, like the indestructible personae in a farce, its words will bounce back up and resume their unruly organization. This fractious order, which is neither opaque nor narrative nor fully definable, resists restagings that bear any relationship to each other. It is highly unlikely that any director or group of collaborators would create even a similar play based on the same text in a restaging of the work. The textual language, because of its freedom from context, suggests to performers open interpretations and open orders, but one pretty much has to reinvent the performance from scratch for every "new" occasion. Such performative writing practice encourages a certain energetic community-based interpretive activity, but it also resists continuity of interpretation: what the text reflects then is an assumed lack of continuity of stable meaning and an assumed loss of continuity within performance community. "There is Nothing Better Than a Theory" speaks for itself, also in this regard:

Oh, theory
Yes
There is nothing better
Than a theory
But confess
What?
We will eat anything.
Anything?
The book
The idea
Or the product
I would prefer that the painting resemble something a little less dry
This has nothing to do with technique
It is all in the sequence
The sequins?
Are on the table
They are not
Looking for a place to stay?[3]

The Selected Text

What are the rules, what restrains the text or the reader of the text? A positivist way to think about resistance is through a method of selection. William James, in his *Principles of Psychology*, is interested in the question of selection in thought. If consciousness is a stream, much of it passes by unnoted. When consciousness selects anything or commits itself to any particular thing, it is not choosing many other things. James also questions the normative basis on which selections are made, especially, I think, to defeat moralisms about what passes as legitimate knowledge. Such questions influenced the writings of Gertrude Stein, and certainly they affect the writings of Lyn Hejinian, who has been reading James since 1961. In his essay, "Thought is in Constant Change," James suggests that we use "conventions" of feeling in respect to language consciousness. We gravitate toward particular uses of language related to our subjective feelings for things or our evaluation of what our psychic states are "about." According to James, "So inveterate has our habit become of recognizing the substantive parts that language almost refuses to lend itself to any other use."[4] Yet, James suggests, "we ought to say a feeling of *and*, a feeling of *if*, a feeling of *but*, a feeling of *by*, quite as readily as we say a feeling of *cold* or a feeling of *blue*."[5] Like James, Hejinian is interested in the question of the subjective mental fact, not as only that which is defining, definable, or principled but also as an event that is fuzzy, vague, not fully explicable. In a Steinian manner, Hejinian transports James's ideas about the psychological dimension of language to the question of aesthetic practice: why ought poetry to draw from consciousness only that which is easy to objectify, clear, and discernable, when the "subjective stream" offers so many instances of unclarity—even impossibility and unrepresentabilty—relevant to thought? James writes

> From the cognitive point of view, all mental facts are intellections. From the subjective point of view all are feelings. Once admit that the passing and evanescent are as real parts of the stream (of consciousness) as the distinct and comparatively abiding; once allow that fringes and halos, inarticulate perceptions, whereof the objects are as yet unnamed, mere nascencies of cognition, premonitions, awarenesses of direction are thought *sui generis*, as much as articulate imaginings and propositions are; once restore, I say the *vague* to its psychological rights, and the matter presents no further difficulty. And then we see that the current opposition of Feeling to Knowledge is quite a false issue.[6]

One might describe *Writing Is an Aid to Memory* as a work that deals precisely with such mental facts. In some sense, it is as if Hejinian had designed to produce an artwork that would serve as an example of a Jamesian consciousness. Hejinian interestingly, given the debates in the '70s about the splitting of feeling and knowledge in feminist discourse, assumes that the opposition of "feeling to knowledge" is a priori a false issue. What the poet then would want to know is what does the co-presentation of evanescence along with distinctness of language look like? What does it do? *Writing Is an Aid to Memory* begins with the following lines:

apple is shot nod
    ness seen know it around saying
        think for a hundred years
but and perhaps utter errors direct the point to a meadow[7]

The line, "apple is shot not" could be described as definite, even as its declarative comic metaphor complicates its decidability. The line "ness seen know it around saying" could be described as evanescent. The line "think for a hundred years" is definite, and the fourth line, "but and perhaps utter errors direct the point to a meadow" indicates without precisely identifying them, a relationship between the indefinite, mistakes, and direction. In addition, the use of the word-particle "ness" could be thought to represent a fringe of a word or preceding phrase, while the line "ness seen know it around saying" creates a halo effect through the variations and repetitions of vowel sounds. The poem is certainly as replete as "fits that finally riddle an infinite nature" with what one might call nascencies of cognition such as "purely outward by the time so churches of" or "do edge the so dark." While articulate propositions such as "memory is a trick of coincidence," or "much intention is retrospective/where as much extension is prospective" are everywhere in evidence. Vagueness, then, "new like little with those filling loops," is restored to poetry without overriding other conventional devices of poetic language: rhythm, alliteration, and repetition.

Because of the poem's numeric constraint, and in this work it is an arbitrary device to support temporal fluidity with spatial pattern, I am hyper-aware of Hejinian's method of selecting details from the otherwise unassimilable flow. The fact of the deliberately varied indentations, arranged according to the first letter of a line's place in the alphabet, underscores other features of the writing, including the poet's playing on notions of "selected" memory in her selection of James's work as an influence on her own.

In doing this, Hejinian proposes, I think, a kind of "personness," which is very far from the self-obsessed autobiographical subject but present everywhere in the text. This, this, and this, all of these things were selected by a person. Some of them came from books which are recollected, some of them came from personal recollections of two years, or two minutes. Recollection could be in relationship to anything that the person has selected.

Underpinning Hejinian's poem is the immanently selectable aesthetic category of beauty. Hejinian wanted to make a beautiful poem in order to recuperate, after her move from the country to Berkeley, a relationship to the beauty of rural life;[8] so the stream itself is not natural, it is guided by cultural impulses of the highest order. Yet this categorical beauty is part of the flow, and the poem points to the paradoxes of beauty as a transcendent category. For beauty is a material of consciousness that the poet can select. The poem calls attention to its use of beauty as material as it showcases the command or instruction, "poke beauty," but of course this featuring of beauty's plasticity is again instantly assimilated into the flow.

Yet Hejinian does "poke beauty" by combining erudite pronouncements, vague language and references to unlovely, banal, and domestic events that resist conventional notions of beauty in art. Her "arbitrary" use of constraint also restrains conventional notions of beauty as it constantly calls attention to the temporality and work of making the poem. The way that Hejinian achieves the beauty she aims to make is in the movement of selection that becomes an imitation of the concept of "the stream."

What the poem can't poke at for more than the briefest of pauses is its own positive motion. The writing, which clearly resists dwelling on memory (or memories), produces a language of memory bounded to the process of selection within the domain of the flow. If the writing paused to assess the contexts it depends on to create its own momentum, the motion would stop and its fabric would tear.

Repetition

Both Hejinian and Kathy Acker are interested in the mechanics or physicality of a process of selection. If I am hyper-conscious of Hejinian's hands having done the repetitive work to place the lines of her long poem in their varied positions, I am also hyper-conscious of Acker's presencing of mental effort through the device of repetition—as if the mind is continuously trying to break down the wall of its own limits and the limitations of its culture as represented in others' texts. The mind of Acker is related directly to the social body and the psychosomatic body. The mind is as if viscerally part of the social and physical body. The social body and the physical body are both idea and thing. In her work, Acker consistently searches for ways to dissolve the mind/body split as a means toward individual and social liberation. In writing her novel *Pussy, King of the Pirates*, Acker repeatedly practices masturbating to produce language for the novel. But in this situation, the mind has to struggle to join the ego to the libido, to write and come at the same time. At some point the writing always trails off. The process results in revelation, banality, and impossibility. The text is produced through a retention of this limit of the knowable.

What Hejinian's text resists, the contemplation of its own potential negativity or limits, is exactly what Acker's 1993 essay, "Against Ordinary Language: the

Language of the Body," tries to understand. Acker is looking at the "antago-nism between the body and the verbal language" through the joined practice of bodybuilding and writing. Acker's exploration of negation is paradoxically what allows her to speak of it at all. She locates her understanding of the antagonism in the concept of "failure."

> Having failed time and again, upon being offered the opportunity to write this essay, I made the following plan: I would attend the gym as usual. Immediately after each workout, I would describe all I had just experienced, thought, and done. Such diary descriptions would provide the raw material.
> After each workout, I forgot to write. Repeatedly. I shall begin by analyzing this rejection of ordinary or verbal language.[9]

When Acker recognizes the relationship of repetition to failure, both in writ-ing and bodybuilding, she is able to approach the "speechless language." The speechless language has produced the language of the text through the trope of committed failure: "Bodybuilding," she writes, "can be seen to be about nothing but *failure*." For Acker, bodybuilding connects the literal and the metaphorical significations of writing with the material and spiritual practice of breaking down and reforming the body.

The failure in bodybuilding and in writing brings the body builder/writer to the brink of death and to chaos. At the same time 'the language of the body' is not arbitrary. When a body builder is counting, he or she is counting her own breath. The language of the body is, like a Wittgensteinian language game, "reduced to a minimal, even a closed, set of nouns and to numerical repeti-tion."[10] For Acker, the "language game" is a vehicle to enter, through a route of indirection, a realm of negativity, which seems to both connect her to others and compel her fascination of epistemological possibility and impossibility. A symbol of this "language game" for Acker are Canetti's beggars of Marrakesh who "repeat the name of God."

> In ordinary language, meaning is contextual. Whereas the cry of the beggar means nothing other than what it is; in the city of the beggar, the im-possible (as the Wittgenstein of the *Tractatus* and Heidegger see it) occurs in that meaning and breath become one. [11]

Like Hejinian, Acker, who counts her own breath, finally places the value of writing within a construction of consciousness. Yet, unlike that of Hejinian, Acker's construction is not located in the motion of temporal flow, which is in

Hejinian the source of subjectivity, but in an intensity of focus applied through repetitive processes to the body and its architecture. She reduces "verbal language to minimal meaning, to repetition, [to] close the body's outer windows."[12] The trope of bodybuilding then is used as a kind of umbilicus of consciousness that leads Acker in her essay to disclose a labyrinthine structure of references and language games. The interior, "labyrinth," and the exterior, "language game," together "mirror" the unspeakability of the somatic interior and the textual and material reality of the exterior world as symbolized in Canetti's beggars.

In connecting her somatic quest with her writing practice, Acker seems to be casting a spell on the destructive impulses that she identifies with Western systems of dualism: she deploys her own practice of inevitable *failure* against the successful ideology of duality in Western thought. Acker's critique is that the limitations of the body can't really be known, but because it is already defined subjectively and as object, it is subject to and productive of cruelty.

> In our culture, we simultaneously fetishize and disdain the athlete, a work in the body. For we still live under the sign of Descartes. This sign is also the sign of patriarchy. As long as we continue to regard the body, that which is subject to change, chance, and death, as disgusting and inimical, so long shall we continue to regard our own selves as dangerous others.[13]

And what has motivated me in this writing to say something about the resistances and the limits of "our" works is related to what I see sometimes as a disconnection between the celebration of the woman experimentalist's project and a confrontation with its underlying values. Acker always questioned the underlying values of others' and her own writing.

Notes

1. Marcel Benabou, "Rule and Constraint," *Oulipo: A Primer of Poetntial Literature*, trans. and ed. Warren F. Motte Jr. (Nebraska, 1986), 40–41.
2. Ibid., 41.
3. Carla Harryman, "There Is Nothing Better Than a Theory," in *Animal Instincts* (Berkeley, CA: This Press, 1989), 94–95.
4. William James, "The Principles of Psychology," *William James: the Essential Writings*, ed. Bruce W. Wilshire (New York, 1984), 57.
5. Ibid., 57.
6. Ibid., 117.
7. Lyn Hejinian, *Writing Is an Aid to Memory* (Berkeley, CA: The Figures, 1989), n.p.
8. Lyn Hejinian, personal correspondence with the author, August 1999.

9. Kathy Acker, "Against Ordinary Language: The Language of the Body," *Kathy Acker: Bodies of Work* (London, England: Serpent's Tail Press, 1997), 150.

10. Acker writes in a footnote, "here and throughout the rest of this article, whenever I use the phrase 'language game,' I am referring to Ludwig Wittgenstein's discussion of language games in *The Brown Book* (151). Acker's references to Wittgenstein are of interest to me both in respect to a larger consideration of her work as systems of "simpler language[s] than ours" (Wittgenstein, *The Brown Book*) and in respect to Wittgenstein's obvious considerations of the writings of William James, which would bear on further consideration of Acker's and Hejinian's projects.

11. Ibid., 148.

12. Ibid., 150.

13. Ibid., 150.

Without Rift: Re/Vision in Lyn Hejinian's *My Life*

Ron Silliman

Lyn Hejinian has offered the readers of *My Life* a unique look into the composi-
tional strategies of her work by publishing different booklength versions of this
breakthrough text. The first, published in an edition of 1,000 by Burning Deck
in 1980, includes 37 paragraphs of 37 sentences each. A second, first published
by Sun & Moon in 1987, offers 45 paragraphs of 45 sentences each. Thus, in
addition to adding eight new paragraphs, one for each of the intervening years
of the project, Hejinian also added eight sentences to each of the existing para-
graphs of the first version. Hejinian also appears to have made small additions
to at least one existing sentence within each paragraph. Here is the seventh
paragraph of the 1987 version, known by its epigram "Like plump birds along
the shore," with material new to this version printed in boldface:

> Summers were spent in a fog that rains. **They were mirages, no different
> from those that camelback riders approach in the factual accounts of voy-
> ages in which I persistently imagined myself, and those mirages on the
> highway were for me both impalpable souvenirs and unmistakable evi-
> dence of my own adventures, now slightly less vicarious than before. The
> person too has flared ears, like an infant's reddened with batting.** I had
> claimed the radio nights for my own. There were more storytellers than there
> were stories, so that everyone in the family had a version of history and it was
> impossible to get close to the original, or to know "what really happened." The
> pair of ancient, stunted apricot trees yield ancient, stunted apricots. What was
> the meaning hung from that depend. The sweet aftertaste of artichokes. **The
> lobes of autobiography.** Even a minor misadventure, a bumped fender or a
> newsstand without newspapers, can "ruin the entire day," but a child cries and
> laughs **without rift. The sky droops straight down. I lapse, hypnotized
> by the flux and reflux of the waves.** They had ruined the Danish pastry by
> frosting it with whipped butter. It was simply a tunnel, a very short one. Now
> I remember worrying about lockjaw. The cattle were beginning to move across
> the field pulled by the sun, which proved them to be milk cows. There is so
> little public beauty. I found myself dependent on a pause, a rose, something on

paper. It is a way of saying, I want you, too, to have this experience, so that we are more alike, so that we are closer, bound together, sharing a point of view— so that we are "coming from the same place." It is possible to be homesick in one's own neighborhood. Afraid of the bears. A string of eucalyptus pods was hung by the window to discourage flies. So much of "the way things were" was the same from one day to the next, or from one occasion (Christmas, for example, or July 4th) to the next, that I can speak now of how we "always" had dinner, all of us sitting at our usual places in front of the placemats of woven straw, eating the salad first, with cottage cheese, which my father always re-ferred to as "cottage fromage," that being one of many little jokes with which he expressed his happiness at home. Twice he broke his baby toe, stubbing it at night. As for we who "love to be astonished," my heartbeats shook the bed. In any case, I wanted to be both the farmer and his horse when I was a child, and I tossed my head and stamped with one foot as if I were pawing the ground before a long gallop. Across the school playground, an outing, a field trip, passes in ragged order over the lines which mark the hopscotch patch. It made for a sort of family mythology. The heroes kept clean, chasing dusty rustlers, tonguing the air. They spent the afternoon building a dam across the gutter. There was too much carpeting in the house, but the windows upstairs were left open except on the very coldest or wettest of days. It was there that she met the astonishing figure of herself when young. **Are we likely to find ourselves later pondering such suchness amid all the bourgeois memorabilia.** Wherever I might find them, however unsuitable, I made them useful by a simple shift. The obvious analogy is with music. Did you mean gutter or guitar. Like cab-bage or collage. The book was a sort of protection because it had a better plot. If any can be spared from the garden. They hoped it would rain before some-body parked beside that section of the curb. The fuchsia is a plant much like a person, happy in the out-of-doors in the same sun and breeze that is most com-fortable to a person sitting nearby. We had to wash the windows in order to see them. Supper was a different meal from dinner. **Small fork-stemmed boats propelled by wooden spoons wound in rubber bands cruised the trough. Losing its balance on the low horizon lay the vanishing vernal day.**

The first thing one notices is that there is a remarkable continuity of style, rhythm and pacing, between the "original" material and that which is added later. Indeed, the cohesion of what might also be read as "first draft" and "revi-sion" is so strong it can almost be expressed mathematically. The earlier version contains 566 words in its 37 sentences, an average of 15.3 words per sentence. The later version contains 689 words over 45 sentences, increasing the average per sentence by only 0.01 words. The eight new sentences are in fact ever so slightly shorter on average—15.13 words per sentence—than those in the first version, but Hejinian also uses the occasion to add one final phrase—"without rift"—to her "original" sixth sentence. Coming as it does in material that has been supplemented—and Hejinian is well enough read in her post-structuralism to understand the implications of that—*without rift* can be read as, among other things, an elegant little tweak at the form of the work itself.

I know of no other poet of my generation—& perhaps only Jennifer Moxley from among younger writers—who would even dare phrases such as "without rift" or "vanishing vernal day." These are just two of dozens of small, almost intimate details in this paragraph alone that render this text instantly recognizable as Hejinian's writing, & which in the aggregate account for the passionate advocacy her poetry so often inspires.[1]

What interests me most, though, is the absence of any formal system for the incorporation of new material into the piece, given precisely how formal the structure of the book itself is. Six of the eight new sentences in this particular section are introduced in pairs. In the book's first paragraph, there is just one pair of inserted sentences, plus another cluster of three, while in the eighth paragraph, all new sentences appear by themselves, singletons of new data & context. Of course, after the 37th paragraph, all additional material contains only new writing.

Here in the seventh paragraph, the new material transforms the section's beginning & end, but makes relatively modest interventions in the main body of the text. The most significant is a sentence (plus two words) positioned between two sentences that were built around uses of the word "ruin." Where in 1980, the text made a sharp turn precisely at the point of the two meanings that can be wrung from "ruin," in 1987 these meanings function far more softly, echoing their common moment.

Three sentences in this paragraph can be read as alluding to the phenomena of heat-based mirages rising up of the pavement:

- The explicit new second sentence of the paragraph, which sets up the structure for the image schema—the length & detail of this sentence are necessary if the paragraph is to intelligibly re-invoke this construct later with shorter, briefer sentences.

- A sentence one-quarter of the way through the paragraph that reverses the point-of-view, focusing instead on how the narrator is "hypnotized" by the waves of the mirage.

- The paragraph's final sentence, a moment of closure radically different from the 1980 homily.

A fourth sentence is also plausible if one incorporates "The sky droops straight down" into this same image schema. Thus a point of reference that was not even hinted at in the 1980 version of the paragraph becomes the controlling image schema for its 1987 incarnation. This transformation is not insignificant. The nature of this paragraph has not been "updated," but completely re-imagined by the process. The implicit frame of late '40s radio dramas—the radio nights that then model the role given over to family stories in the 1980 version of the poem—is no longer the master paradigm for the paragraph, displaced as it were by a mirage.[2] While radio's juxtaposition to family narratives has not changed in the slightest, its position within the revised paragraph recalibrates its meaning.

There are, of course, several other things going on here, more or less all at the same time. Two of the eight new sentences—"lobes of autobiography" & the question "Are we likely to find ourselves"—function as metacommentary on the process of *My Life* itself, as does "without rift." The sentence concerning "small fork-stemmed boats" can be read—although I'm suspicious of this as the scale strikes me as wrong[3]—as related to the narrative of childhood engineering, damming the gutters, that is constructed via several sentences of the 1980 version of this paragraph.

The two word add-on, "without rift," can I think be read as contributing relatively little to what has already been written in that sentence. But it is also possible, or at least was in 1980 when the radio nights/storytelling schema dominated, to find in the image of a child that "cries and laughs" the twin masks of theater—comedy & tragedy. Here again, Hejinian's intervention mutes the earlier reading—it's a different text in 1987, with connotations distributed accordingly.

It's worth contrasting the seventh paragraph with its quantitatively modest—but transforming—revisions with one that contains only new writing, such as the 45th and final paragraph, which carries its epigram in quotes, "Altruism / in poetry":

> In the afternoon until five I sat in the room reading theory while eating a dish of carrots. Two), power. Now, overstimulated, but in depth, and not I artificially (so not "overamped"), I have laid out my papers and secured the evening, intending even to exceed the immediacy that seems for the moment like foresight (so full of plans am I).

Dogs in the fog. Someone is dying and approaches the abstract—"we can no longer ignore ideology, it has become an important lyrical language." I had heard this piece of music (it was *Shoot Pop*) in several cities, and now hearing it again a shaft of stairs and a narrow doorway opened into the revolving, lateral, humid light of Mechnikov Prospekt and its dazzling translucent dust, and I felt again the complex happiness of my own fulfilled arrogance and bemused femininity as it was aroused by the differently infinite cathedral at Amiens (my mother's mother had married her cousin, thus keeping her maiden name, and she asserted that "Ruskin" was a corruption of her "Erskine," and that he was one of the relatives), but though I could say the music brought these places "home" to me, the composition itself grew increasingly strange as I listened again, less recognizable, in the dark, as when one repeats a word or phrase over and over in order to disintegrate its associations, to defamiliarize it, and the man playing it amazed me with his assertion. Days die. You fold back the black covers and the binder opens like a snapdragon. Preliminaries consist of such eternity, rewriting in an unstable text. The voice of the saxophone, as they say, is very humanlike, yet an object of envy. It is boring to lack questions when they talk. And another thing: devious, and cotton, but with sweetly analytical hacking and hilarity (I have said, and meant, that I want people to "get" this, and yet, with expansive sensations, I hate to "lighten up"). The actuality sets (flutters) new standards of proclivity. The pattern of the linoleum tiles organizes my mopping of them, and when I have to cross clean floor in order to rinse the mop, I spread a towel and step on it, though then that makes more laundry. The reduction of expression to experience. What is the meaning hung from that depend, the impatience of the made. Language R is parallel to language E, perhaps they cannot touch, so we fall into a translation (description) trance. A person is a bit of space that has gotten itself in moments. Now with the neighbors on the left, whom we hear talking above the sound of cooking through the open windows in summer, we share a lawnmower and a fence. Bees buzz flower bound. Overhead a small plane drags a banner, it is summer, its engines revving and whining—for years I suffered nightmares in which just such a plane would lose control and plunge spinning through the roof of the schoolroom, blazing the cobalt, red, green, and yellow of the *Hammond World Atlas*. I in my chronic ideas return. Stalin medallions dangle at the windshield in trucks throughout the republics—why do they do this. The language of inquiry, pedagogy of poetry. One doesn't want to be seduced by the sheer wonder of it all, whereby everything is transformed by beauty. There is a bulging lake and sunlight juts from it like a rock, as laughter for its practitioners. Past midnight, exhausted, fainting, and very old, the gray ice—Halley's beaver—was swimming in the sky toward the deep forest on the distant ridge, its tail partially submerged. The flow of thoughts—impossible! A word to guard continents of fruits and organs, a drone in the corresponding sky. The throat singing of the Eskimo in katajak, revolving. So great is the fear of dissipating a single opportunity. For that word you must take the car, which stands in front of the dusty shingled house for two days by pale hairs and then in front of an acrid but also sweetly musty yellow hillside in shadows a mile away for another two without ever having been any place between. Take symmetry. Red mother, red father, many red and rosy children, most of them women of stability. That word. It is not imperfect to have died, it is ever a matter of remembering the right thing at the right moment. The present is a member. A peopled stone springs out of the ground at the kissing sun. Undropping ardor. I've been a blind camera all day in preparation for this dream. The wayward induction from home (to produce evidence that what I've heard was interesting) of some revolution. How long is that ball—of sound. I confess candidly that I was adequately happy until I was asked if I was … we are filled with scruples about individualism and … a disturbance on the lapping-happiness is worthless, my grandfather assured me when he was very old, he had never sought it for himself or for my father, it had nothing to do with whether or not a life is good. The fear of death is residue, its infinity overness, equivalence—an absolute. Reluctance such that it can't be filled.

The length of this extraordinary finishing flourish is somewhat illusory—subtract the 158 words of the sixth sentence and the remaining 44 average just 16.11 words each, just five percent higher than the 1980 version of the seventh paragraph. Subtract the three other sentences with over 50 words each in them and the average drops to just 13.27—these four sentences contain nearly 40 percent of the words in this 45 sentence paragraph. Another way to state this is that Hejinian arrives at her prose rhythms in good part through the judicious use of a few very long sentences combined with many shorter ones, including some that your high-school English teacher would claim are mere fragments.

Still, as a test of the general complexity of Hejinian's sentences between 1980 and 1987, the 45th paragraph shows a notable increase. Whereas the 1980 version of the 7th paragraph scores, using the Flesch-Kincaid Grade Level scale, a standard instrument for gauging readability,[4] at 7.4—a text that would not be difficult for most seventh graders—the 45th paragraph, written seven years later, scores at 10.4. (Even without the sixth sentence, the paragraph scores at 9.2.) Minus the two-word fragment, "without rift," the 1987 insertions into the seventh paragraph score 10.3, virtually identical to the final paragraph.

The sixth sentence is worth looking at more closely, though, because more than any other, it's the variable that skews the numbers upward, adding more than a grade level to the overall score. At 158 words, it's nearly three times the length of any other sentence in its paragraph (the 43rd sentence has 64 words) and longer than some short stories by Kafka. The length is a sign not of verbosity on Hejinian's part, but rather an index of her writing strategies. Functionally, this long & winding sentence—with a parenthetical statement about naming that seems at first entirely unrelated to the sentence into which it is embedded—operates as a last long pause—it's almost the textual equivalent of a deep breath—before the final sweep to the end of the book. The sentence is an exposition of narrativity (which is also the level at which the parenthetical insertion makes total sense), comparing itself with the Gothic cathedral at Amiens; contrasting itself with the most repetitive versions of pop music—that song's actual title is *Pop Shoot Pop*[5]—moving itself through several cities (Mechnikov Prospekt presumably refers to the medical school in St. Petersburg), defamiliarizing itself as we read it not through reiteration but its labyrinthine syntax. It is hardly the only sentence here that takes us on such a round-about hunt for the closure of its predicate. Try parsing the sentence concerning the car and the word. Nor is it ever clear which word, a category that is left deliberately indeterminate in more than one sentence here.

In both the 1980 & '87 versions, the final paragraph contains numerous elements that can be read as bringing the book to a close without in any sense bringing the work to one as well. The next-to-last sentence reads as though lifted from the machine translation of another language. The final sentence avoids any of the typical moves one might expect from that curious subgenre of final sentences. Hejinian herself at one point took the project of *My Life* up again, adding new sentences and paragraphs, but then apparently set it aside.

The original version of *My Life* is now 36 years old, its revision—the more widely distributed Sun & Moon edition—now 28 years behind us. Some of the changes between the two versions—sentence length & complexity, for example—might be attributed to the "simple" development of the individual over time. Others, such as the transformation of focus in the seventh paragraph of the 1987 versions, clearly are editorial. I don't think that you can develop either a narrative of "the growth of a poet's mind" between the two editions, or, conversely, any narrative of decline. I may have a personal bias toward the earlier book—reading it for the first time was one of the most intense intellectual experiences of my own life—but I think this tells you more about me than it might Hejinian.

Notes

1. Which is to say that, for many, precisely what renders Hejinian so special is a feature of her work that appears not in large identifiable constructs—Acker's assault on character might be a point of comparison, or the genre subversion of Charles Bernstein's shtick—but rather something that occurs throughout Hejinian's writing.

2. The shift from the (undescribed) aural narratives of radio to the visual chimera of mirages can hardly be accidental.

3. I grew up within a few miles & years of Hejinian & anything larger than a shrimp fork—had we known such things even existed—would have required a damning not just of the gutters but a significant portion of the street itself.

4. Flesch-Kincaid Grade Level is calculated as (.39 x average sentence length in number of words) + (11.8 x average syllables per word)—15.59.

5. Cf. Johannes Ullmaier's *Pop Shoot Pop: Über Historisierung und Kanonbildung in der Popmusik* (Ruesselsheim, Germany: Hoffman, 1995).

Lights That Were Visible
Gerhard Schultz

The pilot of the little airplane had forgotten to notify the airport of his approach, so that when the lights of the plane in the night were first spotted, the air raid sirens went off, and the entire city on that coast went dark. He was taking a drink of water and the light was growing dim. My mother stood at the window watching the only lights that were visible, circling over the darkened city in search of the hidden airport.

—Lyn Hejinian, *My Life*

Informational mining has been a method of music-making for centuries or more: forming musical data out of texts or shapes, among other things, and filtering the raw materials into a range of desirable outcomes. Once up and running, the process can act like a wind chime, automating sound, or it can leave listeners with an imprint from the source.

The now-classic work *Manifestos,* in which Charles Gaines transforms four revolutionary texts into music for string quartet, finds a way for both possibilities to work in tandem. His is an airtight filter where every letter becomes part of a very listenable situation, and still, it's a sound world where the differences between each text are somehow kept alive. One imagines that were he to slip in a driver's manual or a utility bill, these would have their own unique characteristics as well. Such a straightforward process creates a scenario in which what goes up must come down, but the chances of landing are also left unembellished. The materials respond with dimmed readability.

I saw the image of a plane circling over a darkened city as symbolic of the passage between concepts and music or philosophy and politics. The book it comes from, by Lyn Hejinian, was the source material for the following piano pieces. What began as a translation from words to notes soon left me with such an excess of musical information, I ended up sifting through and picking out the gems. Sometimes I folded one chapter over another and isolated what felt like momentary dialogues: not unlike my first encounters with the book. When reading through her memories, I so often wound up in my own that I took her title as quiet validation of the confusion.

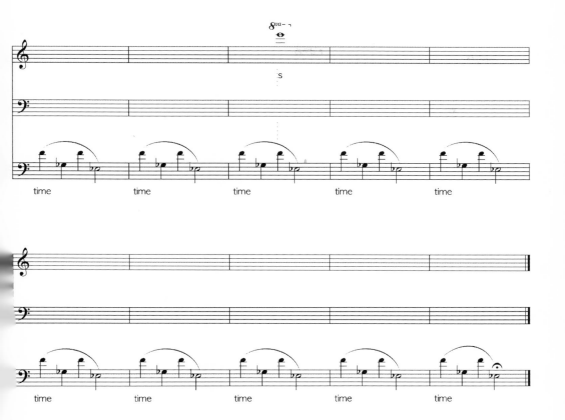

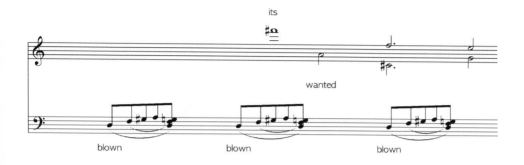

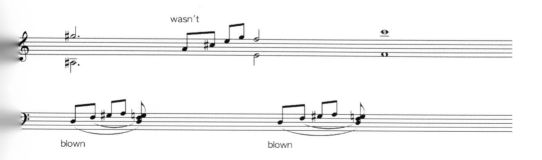

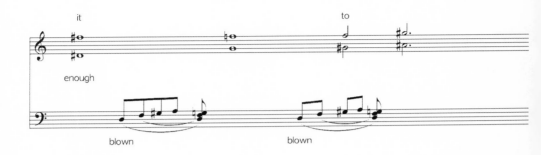

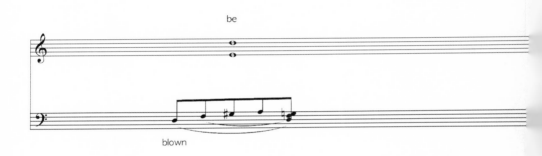

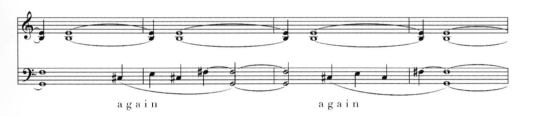

again   again   again

again   again

again   again

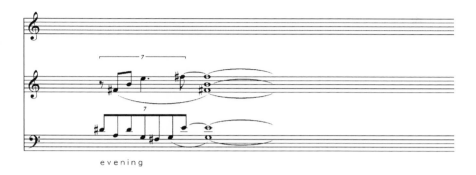

evening

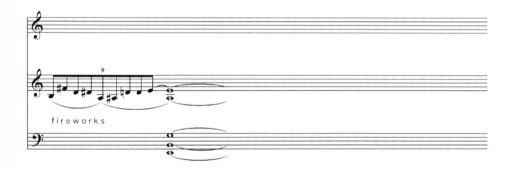

fireworks

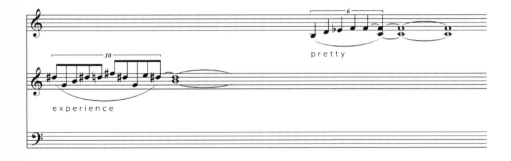

pretty

experience

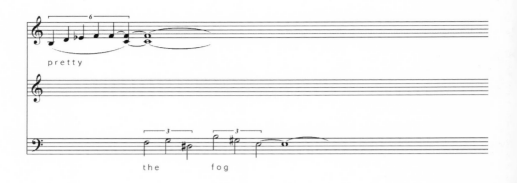

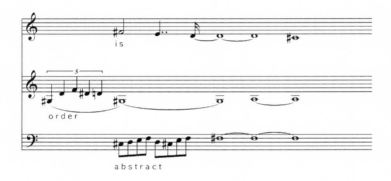

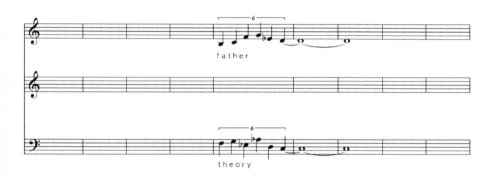

The Beginning of the Making of "The Cell"
Kit Robinson

In the fall of 1986 Lyn Hejinian told me she was having trouble writing. The problem had to do with the relationship between thinking and writing; for Lyn, thinking seemed to be inhibiting writing. I suggested we start a correspondence, writing short poems that we would exchange in the mail. The idea was to write quickly and without revision, and to use one another's poems as referent material for generating new ones.

On October 11, 1986, I received this letter from Lyn:

"Dear Kit, Here are my first three, written before I read the two poems you sent, so that it is purely coincidental that questions of vision and grass appear in both. Coincidental but timely …. I still can't stop thinking, and think more than I should, which slows me down …. Nonetheless, these were written relatively quickly …. I just reread them—I hardly recognize them."

Our correspondence continued for two years. According to my records, I sent Lyn 88 poems, ending in February 1988. Lyn's poem number 102 was dated May 1988, but she continued on her own through January 1989, and went on to revise the entire sequence, which was published by Sun & Moon Press in 1992 as *The Cell*. Lyn's first three poems became the first three poems in *The Cell*. An edition of 12 poems by each of us from the first three months of the correspondence was also published as *Individuals* by Chax Press in 1988. An additional set of mine appears as "Up Early" in *Ice Cubes* (Roof Books, 1987). The title "Up Early" refers to the life context in which my poems were written: between 7:30 and 8:00 a.m. each morning before my commute.

Repetition is a form of friction
I get mortally warmed up when I write
the cold of poetry
against the rock in the ground

LH 11/27/86

The coincidence of referents and themes Lyn referred to in her letter was strik-ing, especially in the early days of our correspondence. On one hand, each of us freely borrowed terms from the other, so that we began to weave a common vocabulary, moving shared elements into differing contexts and perspectives. At the same time, poems with identical or related contents often crossed in the mail. It felt at times as if we were generating a psychic continuum with a life of its own, a landscape with unpredictable rises and dips, intersections, curves, and cul de sacs.

We started writing 12-line poems, but Lyn soon began to diverge from this form. In February she wrote, "Here is one too long and one too short. Not legs, love, Lyn."

The ghost is only the
        poor attempt of nature to
        present herself as me in
        the language of inquiry

The Cell, January 16, 1987

Elements of unconscious play occur in both our poems. In Lyn's they're often dreams subjected to a process of evaluation by an inquiring mind. In mine, they're more often whole lines, verbal products of the unconscious, as in Breton's automatic writing, or dreams in the forms of words. These are typically used to touch off other more consciously framed lines, by way of association, sound, or inference. There is less effort in the tone of address to come to terms with the ele-ments of the unconscious in an interpretive manner. They are rather left to just sit there leaning up against one another like idiots in a post-modern frieze.

Like Stein, a Harvard-educated Californian, Lyn combines Jamesian Yankee pragmatism and pioneering spirit. A speculative naturalist, her method is to ob-serve, record, and compare. The object of inquiry is the psyche moving around in the world. Said another way, it is the daily making of the world, its composi-tion. Thus, a phenomenology of mind expressed in lines—lines whose contours are inimitable as a day.

Here is a typical exchange:

Extraordinary popular ferocity, nature

as hypotenuse—I feel
as if I've told a dream
The penitent form of leaves
in their description
Proper—
But centrifugal in modern cities
under accidental foot of the tree
Even if I got it right
I couldn't keep it right
the old codicil of the walk
I, who can't keep a joke

LH 10/23/86

unable to keep a joke
because I can't do the accent
even if I got it right
the accidental tree of modern cities
I keep safe from
would cut the parrot's tongue
coming off in the hand
I, who is trying to understand
spy thing itself through shade of
blinds, leaves
eludes my grasp

KR 11/1/86

Lyn's poem of 10/23/86 was later revised to appear in *The Cell* as follows:

With extraordinary populist ferocity (with
        nature as hypotenuse) I've told
        a dream
Both doors are flimsy
Two women from the hotel
        staff are trying to devise
        a way of jamming the
        door by leaning a pyrex

baking pan against the door
I suggest a different baking
pan—it is obvious that
none of this will work
The penitent front of leaves
spin in description
It's proper
Silver
Poplar
Tiny golden nails come in
the package with picture hooks
But the situation is centripetal
in these modern cities so
I'm worried that the police
will figure out that I
helped the prisoners escape in
time over the accidental foot
of the tree
Even if I got it
right I couldn't keep it
right
I'm carrying a white curtain
(a door substitute) on a
rod—I who can't keep
a joke
Everyone knows I'm in love
The din is incredible (because
of my present concern for
feminist issues) "like leaves"

The Cell, October 23, 1986

I never did agree with Lyn's decision in *The Cell* to break the lines into five-word units, and I still don't. It gives the look of writing in a small notebook and disguises the true expansive generosity and exuberance of the great long lines, which are Whitmanian in their spontaneous daring.

Convicted musicians in the evening between
the movie and the street

Zukofsky says, "Emphasize detail
130 times over—or there will be no poetic …"
(gives, droops, drags with the elasticity of place)
Crickets
They govern by ear
the nation of sound
Invisible physically frequent retreating unarranged lush and
unnearving
— flossy corymbose crouch
But by then gradually decisive

LH 26 & 28 October 1986

how strange to hear crickets in November
tell innocent musicians to repeat certain notes
until an entire nation is unnerved
a movie
a physical withdrawal from place
a street but a street in a song stuck in the head
then back to the frequency of
change our city
government affects
as mustard has
or cherry
making the year a round

KR 11/3/86

Government is dizzy without capitals
to name
More and more, connection takes space
and correction
Every place the imagination
occurs replace it with the word "language'
which works
It doesn't drone with anarchy
To change the city we must dictate predictions

Entire nerves
What do you suspect
The imagination congests the sex

LH 7/November/86

Quickly though, our vocabularies began to diverge. On November 11, Lyn
wrote:

"If you weren't noting the relationship of your poems to mine in letters, I am not
sure if I would have been certain of the connection. And I have been writing from
yours as they have arrived, although you say you don't notice the correspondence."

"I always liked (aesthetically) and appreciated Eigner's habit of indicating
background information along the margin of his poems. But for me—I hope it
is the same for you—this project is getting so intense that I am not sure I would
know how to annotate it."

PACIFIC INCINERATOR

all things being equal
rusted door on cracked concrete pagoda oven
I may already have taken everything inside
California back yard
the whole person a casing of outside
sun through leaves' yellow
regular, normal, daily, particular metabolism
flexes like a sweat
Cartesian screen door
and my whole calendar is filled with them
there is no such thing as a day

KR 11/9/86

Elegy   After Kit's of 11/9

Charles Olson had an articulate organ
which he called a lung

The blunt November summer
Red and yellow language coming with the tongue
the whole rusted calendar
with spunky redundancy
makes the year so long
it's blown
There's no such thing as yesterday
which rolls remote
and holds its information forward
for too long

LH 13 November 1989

I meet myself rarely to
          experience the coincidence of my
          objectivity with my subjectivity
This incongruence is independent of
          the possibility that a person
          had an articulate organ which
          he called a lung
The blunt November summer—I
          could have only said so
Red and yellow language coming
          with the tongue
A big one
The year is thick and
          long and thrust
The label sticks up from
          the collar but the hair
          hides it
The place warm
The space bar worn
There's no such thing as
          yesterday which rolls under and
          holds its information up and
          forward for long
The information is like a balmy palpitation
I like everything at a level below its name

The Cell, November 13, 1986

Here Hejinian uses the initial draft as if it were a set of chord changes, and lays a stunning, intricate solo over them.

Lyn's letters contain keys to some of the references in her poems. These include the music of Giancinto Scelsi, roofers replacing the roof of her house, a street person who has moved into her backyard, her translation of the poet Arkadii Dragomoshchenko, pornography, drawings by Jacob Lawrence based on poems by Langston Hughes, dream journals, Zukofsky, Ma Rainey, the dictionary, radio advertising, William James, Ovid, Ornette Coleman on Spike Jones, Coleridge, Ernest Schackleton's expeditions to Antarctica, a glider trip over Mt. St. Helena, chaos theory, Foucault's *History of Sexuality*, Pasternak's *Safe Conduct*, Beckett's *The Unnameable*, Schreber's *History of Mental Illness*, Gogol's story "Vivy," Eikhenbaum's *Russian Prose*, Bataille, Kafka, conversations with friends, and her persistent investigation into poetic activity.

"… I feel as if my poems are somewhat clumsy and at points inept or blurred by superfluities, but that I am finally doing in poetry what I have thought I should do—it's all exploration and inquisition at this point for me. The product-orientation has diminished and I have thought for a long time that it was becoming a problem."

LH 11/1/86

Do you patrol? outside the
        self? around a body and
        the follicle in which it
        stands
Or cell?
Request?
Have you reverted?
All memory of having looked
        is loose
It is so cold parallels
        wobble in the chamber shoes
        grain drifts
A sign on the fire

door says silence
A sign on the floor
       says come in
Patrol (but there are no
       opposites) is narrowing
But I was not moving
       anywhere on my feet
Within such fear of death
       if it is a thrill
       to cease
But in the succeeding request
       I ask decease to be
       stable, not diffused or decreased
The cell of description of
       anything (and virtually interrupted)
Her death in a beginning
It is in a prolonged,
       ruthless, unguarded kinesis
The cell in shifts
Cells in drifts
So we're feeling a loss
       but not a conclusion
The smallest unite of imagination
       in time, a retrospection
A unit of space so
       small it seems to be
       going backwards

The Cell, January 14, 1987

what is early, what late
if I start now, will I finish before the beginning?
have we been here all along?
can we say what's happened? is there time?
the children are gone, but they write
from the perfect playground of coincidence
we're like survivors, thinking of starting a business
you saw what happened last time

and the air quenches our thirst for answers
with a mental finding
either you're going to get up and go
or I don't know what

KR 8/6/87

The phrase "a mental finding" came from current events. During the Iran-Contra hearings, Oliver North's attorney's claimed that while President Reagan had not officially ordered the secret war in Nicauragua, he had issued a "mental finding," approving certain operations.

67.   (after Kit's 6/8)

One thing that I think about melody is the ordinary
        coincidence
Anything that repeats must be a childhood to affect you
The squall is resting on the polar, quenching
Perhaps there's not enough change in civilization
        or proportion
It gives you the feeling that the thing you love is not as
        important to you as it is to someone else
The coincidence (lots of sound sounds very much like water)
A water involutes
It unwound the last time
Life after sleep—there too we have genitals and mental
        findings
The sound in a childhood until it coruscates
The air is stalled in the emotion
The proportion

August 15, 1987

"I've been making small idiotic diagrams to depict to myself the relationships of your #72 to my #76. But the poems are exceeding the bounding sides of the figures I draw. They (the figures) are bulging triangles with oscillating sides, built shakily on the three points *language* (words, grammar, syntax), *things* (objects, events, systems [like "government"], etc.), and *mind* (thought, perception, consciousness—person).

"I think I am predisposed to triangles because of the rhyme with 'triangulation'—implicating an explorer and his or her measuring apparatus."

LH 10/1/87

Space is the place, as Sun Ra has pointed out, in which we can make discovery. But other seeming imperatives tended to remove space from our consideration.

"The other day Larry defined 'reality' as 'the world that won't go away.'"

LH 5/20/88

I don't have copies of my letters to Lyn. The computer disks are somewhere, the software obsolete. She thinks the print copies may be in her archive at UCSD. As I remember, they began as energetic, discursive commentary on the content of the exchange and over the course of the two-plus-year correspondence trailed off into a series of brief and increasingly grumpy notes. I was exhausted, my job left me little time or energy to write, I envied Lyn's ability to read, think, write, travel, with these and other complaints I went from suave liberator to crabby fussbudget. I had given Lyn permission to write freely and spontaneously and now she was burying me—I couldn't keep up. Recently we laughed about this. "I've created a monster! Stop!"

Writing this article has given me occasion to look back at the poems I wrote with Lyn, most of them unpublished, with new eyes. I am struck by their seeming autonomy, even from their author. They flaunt the possession of deep meaning, but refuse to give it up. By contrast Lyn's read as increasingly open, with the amendments of *The Cell* and interceding time adding new levels of access.

I think the opacity of my "Up Early" and subsequent efforts ("Later That Day") are partly accountable to the intimacy of my poetic dialog with Lyn, where everything was permitted. Haste and a sense of urgency—it was always almost time for work—were other contributing factors. I wrote carelessly in respect to thought, falling over consistently on the side of language.

Lyn and I had become professionals, she as a teacher and I as a writer and manager in the information technology industry. Our more frequent contact through social and poetry scenes had given way to other practicalities. Living in the same town and exchanging letters and poems in the mail felt oddly 19th century, but under the circumstances, necessary.

Lyn Hejinian— Intention, Selection, and Fantastic Philosophy
Patrick F. Durgin

... the noun must be replaced not by inner balance but by the thing in itself and that will eventually lead to everything.
> — Gertrude Stein, "Poetry & Grammar"

... the thing itself exercises curiosity ...
> — Lyn Hejinian, "Reason"

... one remembers the necessity of a sacrifice—the 'practicality' of a sacrifice—is as definite as—say—the sacrifice of a soldier who undertakes a suicidal mission ... Because we cannot exist ... without a sense of depth in the past and expectation in the future ...
> — George Oppen, letter to Ethel Schwabacher (1962)

Fate ... the accumulation of all that happens.
> — Lyn Hejinian, "George Oppen and the Space of Appearance"

I. Intention

If it is routine to mark the split in post-war USAmerican poetic camps by means of the claims made in the historicizing of Modernist poetic practice, the above sequence of epigraphs dramatizes a circuit of influence still rich enough to yield fresh insights into the so-called "turn to language in the 1960s."[1] Stein's total rejection of the theory of *le mot juste* can be interpreted, among other ways, as a rejection of the linguistic category, familiar to readers of Roman Jakobson's signal works, of selection. Any word selected, as such, becomes a kind of "noun" (even and especially verbs), a thing standing in relief against the store of terms negated in that movement, uniquely problematizing the representation of what is contemporary to it. And although the supposed immanence of Stein's "continuous present" promises "eventually [to] lead to everything," this everything is not just anything. According to Hejinian, it is the event of leading, of trajectory, that is operative in "the thing itself." Oppen's view of the relation of necessity to existence is typical of Objectivism's adjudication of the latent warrants of radical modernist poetics, c.f. the more gnomic pronouncements of Stein or Ezra Pound. If selection is the obverse of negation, it is a kind of suicide, an utterly disambiguating force clutched to a desire—thankfully impossible to effect—to impeach the present by reference to the past and/or future it is made to represent. This warrant makes Hejinian's statement legible. If fate exists, it does not exist for us. Our destination remains inaccessible so long as we are destined *for* it.

"Context is a past with a future," writes Hejinian, echoing Oppen's attempt to clarify the sacrificial basis of being atelic—one could say atelic being.[2] But what exists after, what persists and even subsists this sacrifice? Hejinian, in nearly the same breath, insists that history qua context is that feature of experience that "gives us a sense of *reason.*"[3] We might as well come at the question from the side of the recipient, then, rather than the offering of this gift: from the perspective of *us.* What is sacrificed when the utterance of "this is happening" becomes the object of experience, when language leads incipience? First, to go is "determinate commonality."[4] Tropes of contiguity—sitting, waiting, drifting, misprision—become figures of critical consciousness, in turn rendering sacrifice a critical mode of intentionality. The motive is, as the intentional fallacy would have it, unavailable, yet it gives onto the momentum of intentionality, the desire to make sense, to confer value. Is this peculiar intention the experience of *poiesis* in thought? Something like this irreducible ambiguity is what is meant by the literary critical trope "indeterminacy." And yet the great *variety* of work studied under this sign can hardly be done justice by it. One reason Hejinian is a crucial poet in this regard is that her sustained scrutiny of fundamental critical rubrics is also a peculiar one, suggesting a practical plurality of indeterminacies, and hence a more accurate hermeneutic vocabulary.

Unfortunately, Hejinian's 1983 talk/essay "The Rejection of Closure" has become a ubiquitous exemplar of the poetics of indeterminacy. This is unfortunate not because it is impossible to extrapolate from the "open text" a generalized sense of purposive inconclusiveness that is characteristic of certain moments and modes in poetic practice, but because the dialectic between closure and indeterminacy has no fixed motive. Oddly, the essay itself seems to caution against all but the desire for fixed purposes. A specific moment in the essay draws upon Luce Irigaray's notion of "desire" as that which, were it fulfilled, would resemble a need, something that can and must be fulfilled to maintain oppressive hierarchies.[5] But rather than offering an exegesis of this antecedent (she will critique[6] the scope of Irigaray's notion later), Hejinian situates it with a subtle distinction between motivation and intention. The "structural devices" that serve to open a text and "relinquish total control" to the participation of readers depend, she argues, "by all means on the intention of the writer."[7] It is not surprising perhaps that a tautology appears—"by all means" means the devices that form the means of so opening the text, yet the control seems totalized in the decisive apportioning of authority that resides with the poet. But in that very movement, something *else* occurs. "The writer relinquishes total control and challenges authority as a principle *and* control as a motive" (italics mine).[8] The device itself appears to issue from both reader and writer, first as what is done and then as what one does with it. The interplay of desire is the only possible motive when, as she claims, "for the moment, for the writer, the poem *is* a mind."[9] The "inherent paradox" of the succession of moments described here as a sort of shared thought process has come in for scrutiny, at least on the level of the rhetorical contraptions hoisted in its honor, in the name of indeterminacy as a critical value; Jacob Edmond, for instance, observes the way the open text suffers undue "closures" when one takes for granted the "reader accepting the authority of the claim to reader freedom."[10] "Completeness" as "perfect openness," he demonstrates, "turn[s] the open text into a form of closure."[11] But the question of form remains, of "structural devices" left to their own, which no one seems to, in fact, own. I want to argue that the matter gains traction and specificity, like the term "indeterminacy," only when openness is returned to intentionality and closure to motive. That openness is motivated is paradoxical but not, as Edmond argues, contradictory. It's the *doxa*, the doctrinaire status of "indeterminacy" that troubles Hejinian's critics. So be it. The para- of the paradox describes the fact that motive and intention move alongside one another; they are distinct but mutually dependent moments of writing (to conceive and to execute the poem). To mark this as contra-, to claim a contradiction, is hypocritical, and only arises when motive and intention are thought synonymously, something Hejinian's take on linguistic desire disallows. The hypo-thetics of the hypocritical slippage here is telling. We would never say hypotaxis and parataxis are synonyms. Neither do they have to be opposites. I would argue, similarly, that the paracritical condition of a poem's substance, for Hejinian, constitutes what she would later call a "pre-poetics" of criticism that not only relies upon discerning intentionality as the active afterlife of a particular motive but also illustrates a particular kind: critical intention.

Hejinian's work of a certain period rethinks intention. Like "indeterminacy," "intention" is a plural category. A practical distinction between "motive" and "intention," as an initial account of that plurality, illuminates several things. Of immediate interest to me here are the survival and critique of New Critical tenets in contemporary, language-oriented literary discourse[12]; language writing's unusual circuits of influence running from Stein and the Objectivists through the emergence and reification of intermedia and conceptual writing, art, and performance; and most specifically and crucially, Hejinian's peculiar approach to the problem of "selection." Intention's value resides, for many, in determining the relation of evaluation to interpretation: does a text "succeed" in doing what it set out to do. Indeed, it was evaluation that was at the heart of the New Critical canon now extended to the farthest reaches of our interpretative regimes. The fundamental challenges twentieth century artists and writers put to intention, as a subset of "agency," mirrored the burgeoning backlash against the liberal humanist tradition, a tradition that girds both William Empson's "ambiguities" and Wimsatt and Beardsley's "intentional fallacy." Hejinian was among the major figures here, and she emerged with a liberating and transvaluative, rather than evaluative, relation to thought I call, using her terms, "fantastic philosophy." Though I deal with her particular contributions here, they are indicative of a certain orientation to this rethinking of literary purpose and action. Especially in the 1980s and '90s, the *language* of intention becomes interesting again on at least two fronts. Marjorie Perloff's *The Poetics of Indeterminacy* and Matei Calinescu's *The Five Faces of Modernity* interpret postmodernist ambiguity as high modernist "undecidability," revising the narrative of "radical modernism" while foreclosing discussions of radical indeterminacy at the interface of procedural and processural poetics, form and content, aesthetic effect and, to cite Louis Zukofsky's Objectivist manifesto, "predatory intent." Meanwhile, language writers' own discussions of their intentions and motives become more visible and even, to some extent, accessible (i.e., university press publications of their "poetics" statements, which continue into the present time). Widening the implications of language acts as far as they did, implicating themselves in a repoliticized "sincerity," language writers understandably came back to the problem of intention as a revision of what it could mean to mobilize a politics and an ethics in the aftermath of 1968's various clampdowns on participatory democracy.

In 1985, *Line* published a selection from Steve McCaffery's 1976–1977 correspondence with Ron Silliman and Charles Bernstein. In it, Silliman presents "a rough, preliminary definition of the poem" as

$$p = \frac{vr}{i}$$

where "a poem, p, is a vocabulary, v, with a set of rules, r, by which to process it, limited or extended variously by intention(s), i."[13] Despite the algebraic template, this is not a response to the Deleuzian imperative to "quantify writing."[14] As Silliman explains, it is qualitative, not quantitative.

> the equation makes possible the inclusion of such works as Antin's talking pieces or the journals of Hannah Weiner in the same universe of the poem as Creeley or Turner Cassity even while separating out work which, while it may possess many of the surface features of a poem, lacks some essential, such as the songs of Bob Dylan or certain magazine advertisements, which lack intention. It is, insofar as is possible in the rough and social domain of language, a pure state. ... the very presence of the text or performance indicates, to me, an intention that there be a poem. both procedure & process, as i understand them, are conditions of i. it is not, as i see it, outside the schema.[15]

Mac Low's work is an index in the ensuing conversation about intention because, as McCaffery is careful to point out vis-à-vis "non-intentional" text generation, "procedure, i say, *is* vocabulary."[16] But this, as he says, presupposes that "the whole point in ... procedural work" is the self-generation of texts, which are merely summary vocabularies, the only vocabulary available to the reader vis-à-vis "text."[17] But as they go on to widen the social field of intention as a motivation on the part of an author toward an audience, the original limiting of this field to the intentional as "some essential" merely begs the question the equation sought to mobilize. Silliman's reduction of the category of intention to motivation thereby not only echoes the New Critical treatment of the problem but carries unnamed qualitative criteria that the New Critics, I imagine, would hardly disagree with—some "essential" lacking in popular mass culture. We can presume, knowing Silliman's work, that his specific criteria have to do with a critique of capitalism at the level of language acts[18], but it is not explicitly stated here, nor even integrally implied so much as it is, for instance, in Dylan's early work itself. The irony here points to the survival of New Critical tenets in this early articulation of language writing's take on intentionality—reclaiming the "agency" that "i" infers in no way deconstructs Wimsatt and Beardsley's conception of intention as the (tacitly or patently) expressed motives of not just an author but an authority. The irony is compounded by the fact that the formula is designed to account for the innovations of intermedia artists like Mac Low or Weiner. Moreover, it is Silliman who is so often critically responsible to, not for, the pernicious author-function of the lyric "I."

Hejinian's language of intention is more nuanced. Here is the first paragraph of Hejinian's jacket blurb for Leslie Scalapino's 1989 collection *How Phenomena Appear to Unfold*.

Where critics used to debate, as if it were a real thing, a difference between form and content, so now they would separate "theory" from "practice," and thus divide a poet from his or her own intentions and poetry from its motives. But in fact poetic language might be precisely a thinking about thinking, a form of introspection and inspection within the unarrested momentum of experience, that makes the polarization of theory and practice as irrelevant as that of form and content, mentality and physicality, art and reality.[19]

The separation, by "critics," of "theory" from "practice" is likely a reference to the tenor of the critical reception of language writing in the 1980s (see Byrd, Davidson and Weinberger, Perelman). Importantly, however, a basic claim is made for intention as belonging to a singular authorial project, intrinsically determined per "poet" as her/his "own" language act. What would a "motive" intrinsic to "poetry" be in this case? One answer might be suggested by Hejinian's 1991 admission that "[a] major component of my poetics, or let's say of my poetic impulse, is a result of [the Vietnam] war and the meaning of its never being named."[20] In her dialogue with Tyrus Miller in 1988, published in *Paper Air*, Hejinian offers this commonality between her work and that of other language writers: "maybe all of us are working toward an efficacy not of Poetry but of a radically conscious language use of which poetry has historically been exemplary."[21] So, while she appears to claim that divisions such as I'll be making between the use of terms like intention and motivation ultimately obscure the values these terms proffer, she simultaneously points to the dialogic work of motivation and intention in the use of self-consciously "literary" exchange. For such a dialogue to be made legible as a politics, intention cannot remain reducible to motivation. After all, policy is sociality motivated to acquire the future it imagines. This forward trajectory, at least, deserves the traditional appellation: avant-garde.

Hejinian goes on to express to Miller a common differential:

As writers we are not, as you point out, like-minded, but I think we are, in certain fundamental senses, like-motivated.

Even to conceive of writing as motivated, as an appropriate medium of intentionality (historical and psychological intentionality)—as a medium of consciousness and a ground for intellectual and emotional effectiveness—is, as far as I can tell, not common to many other American poetries right now, but it is something I have in common with other language poets. And, in a sense, it assumes an element of collectivity as well as a large amount of collaboration.[22]

In *what* "fundamental" sense does a conception of motivation as *a* (not *the*) "medium of intentionality" assume "collaboration"? As in the correspondence with Miller, when Hejinian addresses the "history of my collaborations" in her first entry in the collaboratively-written *Leningrad: American Writers in the Soviet Union*, she refers to correspondences with Barrett Watten and Silliman, as well as "responses to the war in Vietnam" among other New American contexts.

> And I myself, for example, had a fantastic rather than a comprehensive relationship with the works of someone like Velimir Khlebnikov, partially because his work had been only randomly translated and published in the 1970s, but more significantly because I had no Russian context for understanding the scale and intentions (and hence the meaning) of his work.[23]

The fundaments of intention seem to be sited, located, not in a reaction to a meaning (the meaning of its not being named) but in an active making (*poesis*) of meaning with spatio-temporal loci irreducible to the separation of agent and agency, so that "intention" is irreducible to the authorial "subject" (a lesson proposed on another level by the "psychological and historical" intermediality of collaboration). Logically, Miller's response to Hejinian's mention of such issues is to ask Hejinian about "the subjects" of her work, insofar as they "never seem wholly present to their languages, nor does language always have the grounding of a subject's intention."[24] The language of Hejinian's response is telling.

> [My work] is not personal in intentions, I don't write to discover, define, describe, disclose my Self, whatever that is, nor to share my epiphanous experiences of small, intimate, everyday moments. To be honest, I'm scornful of writing that aims at anything like that ... But being a person is not at all the same thing as being personal. I think that being a person is a compelling literary problem, because personhood (social, subjective, cognitive) is so closely and diversely bound up with language ... It is unclear whether it's the person or the language that is the agent of the person's life—but in my poetry it is the language. The words it uses determines, or better discovers, where the "life" (intellectual and emotional) will go and what might be known about it.[25]

"Aims" (motives) are to "life" as "intentions" are to "uses" which "determine"— with this difference, "poetry's" legislative criterion is "language." Language "discovers" intention as a "Self" discovers "the 'life.'" Poetry serves to discover two things: "where the 'life' ... will go and what might be known about it."

"Personal ... aims" are subservient to the ongoing vicissitudes of the person's linguistic construction.

Hejinian seems to work in threes. A recent project, *The Fatalist*, comprises the third in a trilogy beginning with *Slowly* and continuing from *The Beginner*. My focus is the previous triad: beginning in 1986 with *The Cell*, continuing through the early 90's with *Oxota: A Short Russian Novel* and 1994–1997's *A Border Comedy*. In this period, related writings such as "The Person," "The Composition of The Cell," and several of the essays collected in *The Language of Inquiry* contextualize a shift in Hejinian's epistemological concerns. Whereas she describes *The Cell* as the last book wherein "the consciousness of consciousness was what was at stake" (what might be known), her brief essay "Continuing Against Closure," published coterminously with *A Border Comedy*, announces a focus on "sites of consciousness" (where the life will go). It's notable how the dialogue with Miller foreshadows this move to a cognitive geography, even as it suggests that the synonymy between motivation and intention is misleading. I would argue that we disallow this synonymy altogether by virtue of the development charted in the poems. First, we must account further, beyond that whose conditions Hejinian could to some extent *choose*, for the context in which this hermeneutic shift took place.

Gertrude Anscombe's treatise *Intention* read in tandem with Frank Cioffi's rebuttal to Wimsatt and Beardsley's "Intentional Fallacy" suggests that we may think of intention's seemingly absolute relativity as neither algorithmic purity nor accidental epiphany. Anscombe is "very glad" to be a philosopher and not an ethicist or literary critic, since it is the question of an agent's "motives" instead of an agent's "intention" that is the proper one, she claims, for these disciplines.[26] Motives, she explains, "interpret" actions, but they needn't "determine" or "cause" them.[27] But she misses a crucial implication of a signal she provides from Wittgenstein, of whom she is the primary English translator, namely that the object of an effect (such as fear) needn't be the cause of it.[28] Cioffi reminds us how malleable this causal "object" or "thing" is—he relativizes the concept of "the text itself" and points to a concept of lyric becoming wherein causation is only an accident of retrospect, a limit case or critical event horizon of the artwork. Literary criticism endeavors to interpret texts (objects of effect), not acts. But revise the object of interpretation and the plot thickens. In fact, we find ourselves in territory more akin to Wolfgang Iser's work on "indeterminacies" in prose fiction than Perloff's "poetics of indeterminacy." According to Iser and most other proponents of reader-response theories of literary meaning, there is something vaguely prophetic in aesthetic experience, since textual production is a shared endeavor of selection. Authors select points of indeterminacy, "sites" of another "consciousness" whose ambiguity will be eliminated by the interpretative estimations or judgments of the reader (i.e., that "other" consciousness). Granted these movements are always more or less motivated, *we can call motives estimates of the future, hence projections of the past*. Motives hold actions to account, while they hold them at a legislative, juridical, and retrospective distance. Intention might then mean something like the mobilization language writing continued in so many compelling ways, the mobilization of the present "time in the composition," a Steinian conceit which, properly understood, has no need to "make it new."[29] *Intention is what is happening for us*. It is not necessary and probably impossible that motives and intentions will match; time itself will tell. Atelos, not surprisingly the name of Hejinian and Travis Ortiz's publishing project (and what is publishing but administering a legacy?), is not a deferred imperative stuttering along a chain of non-sequitur. The notion of necessity that grounds the figure of temporal sacrifice (of the past for the future) is transvaluative. Motives are static, they are what's at stake. Intentionality is the unfolding of acts relative to a field one's motives vainly fix that time, because of its unstinting, capillary transience, always exceeds. Because the failure is inscribed in the initiation of the literary act, one begins with a sacrificial gesture, a sacrifice of authority. Some do it more self-consciously than others, but it has to be done.

Understanding *what is happening for us* in light of the above epigraphs demands an account of the "event" in Stein's eventuality. And as much as Hejinian reminds us, for instance, of Roman Jakobson's bedrock historicism—that "The history of literature should be written from the standpoint of change, since change is the essence of literature"—we do well to maintain that "change" itself is subject to the connotations history provides.[30] The third work of the series, *A Border Comedy*, hits upon a compositional method that harnesses the act of reading, describes it, and thereby dooms every punchline to its own inevitability—causality ceases to relieve the tension our comic should so carefully plot.

That's why I've kept this writing of fifteen books unfinished
Fifteen underway
I move from one to the next
In the course of many days adding every day
A few lines to a book
Each of which takes a long time and considerable thought
And that passage of time facilitates forgetting
Then forgetting makes what's been written unfamiliar
As if some other writer had been writing

And each of my returns to each of the books is prompted
To immediates in a sudden present
Only pastness, which provides forgetting, can provide it[31]

So, Stein's eventuality is operative here, but in a peculiar way.

Of course, senses have objects—everything provides evidence of this
The objects make themselves available and laugh
Suddenly you're one of them[32]

Add to this the peculiar take on Oppen's fatalism, a sort of "future anterior" and hence "an act of redistribution, imitating / nothing, completely original."[33] And what is happening for us becomes nothing like that index of our desire for those we force to reflect our best intentions. Every mission motivated is a suicide mission.

II. Selection

The comic and the capacity for laughter are situated in the laugher and by no means in the object of his mirth. The man who trips would be the last to laugh at his own fall, unless he happened to be a philosopher, one who had acquired by habit a power of rapid self-division and thus of assisting as a disinterested spectator at the phenomena of his own ego. But such cases are rare.
— Charles Baudelaire, "On the Essence of Laughter"

... as Aristotle insists ... the poet is preeminently the maker of the plot—the framework, not necessarily of everything that takes place within that framework ... The poet does not wish to be a dictator but a loyal co-initiator ...
— Jackson Mac Low, "Statement 1965," *The Pronouns*

The influence of conceptual art, writing and performance on language writing, what Dick Higgins famously referred to as "the intermedial," is not unsubstantial. An important artist in the shift from the New American Poetry through conceptual art to contemporary conceptual writing is Jackson Mac Low, whose notion of "eventual verse" can be read as a pithy thinking-through of the relationship between intention and selection, hence informative for a reading of the way Hejinian furthers such an inquiry.[34] In the decade beginning in the mid 1980s, Hejinian moves from a concern with the "consciousness of consciousness" to "sites of consciousness." In the process, selection is redefined as something more akin to *election*, and these sites become an *elective* geography rather than a given, inevitable terrain amounting to the interminable fate of that which "exercises curiosity." Ultimately, election allows intention a motivelessness or immanence, which is radicalized in the *temporal* register of fate—Hejinian accordingly redefines "fate."

The intentional continuum Mac Low's oeuvre establishes provides a limit-case of our interpretive and evaluative categories. Louis Cabri's account of this continuum from non- to quasi- to "freely" intentional authorship situates the issue's literary expressions within the context of political action. Of course, such acts are highly motivated, if potentially less egoic: the quasi-intentional Stein poems are littered with such statements as "Never revise her accidentally."[35] In his later series, which mostly favor quasi-intentional methods, Mac Low combines procedural and processural techniques. This produced an occasion to articulate and revise his original thinking surrounding the problem of intention. In his last major statement of poetics, "A Talk on My Writingways," he suggests that his "liminally" composed works (such as the *Twenties* and *Forties*, as well as the earlier "environmental" *Asymmetries*) form a sort of conceptual arc directly connecting the oscillation between the non-intentional and "freely-composed" works. Mac Low aptly cites Hume's theory of the imagination, reduced simply to "compounding, transposing, augmenting, or diminishing the materials afforded us by the senses and experience."[36] Coincidentally Deleuzian, the point here is to provide a phenomenologically inflected ontology of the work, the latter being elided with the subject as duly constructed, a habit-forming activity! The point of liminal composition is to free the event from predetermined structures. Ensuing at and tracing the borders of a person, the event guarantees: everything fate elects to get in gets in.

Preparing his first major collection, 1971's *Stanzas for Iris Lezak*, Mac Low presents his earliest and supposedly non-intentional works as examples of an "eventual" verse form. Not to be confused with *gradual*, the qualifier *eventual* refers to a closed form with "events" as the poetic measure. His widely-known chance-operations held the "stanzas" in check according to procedural limits; the performance of the output did not, as with traditional prosodic concepts such as "beat" or "accent," recommend the "event" as a measure. Having read over 400 pages of "chance-generated stanzaic-acrostic eventual verse" in the *Stanzas*, the reader comes to the endnote and can hardly fail to concur with the author's closing points.

> In the largest sense, of course, most verse is "eventual" in that a certain
> number of events of one kind or another (syllables, accented syllables, or
> "feet" of one kind or another, whether "quantitative," as in ancient Greek &

Latin verse, or accentual-syllabic, as in most traditional English verse, or otherwise) occurs in each line of a poem or in corresponding lines of stanzaic poems in which the number of syllables, feet, &tc., changes from line to line within stanzas. What is distinctive about the verse of the STANZAS & my other chance poems is that events are not primarily phonological. Whether it is proper to call the events "lexical" (negatively lexical in the case of the silences), "syntactical" (in the case of the word-string events), or even (in both cases) "semantic" is a question whose solution I will leave to the linguists & the poeticists.[37]

Here the form/content binary Hejinian refers to above is as irrelevant as possible, with performance being a kind of lyric index. But it is an absolutely relative event—the epistemological categories of evaluation and interpretation are entirely symmetrical in the event of selection. The quantification Deleuze and Guattari call for can be seen in Mac Low's reply to the "so-called Problem of the Subject"—that it is, in Silliman's words, "a mere sum of the writing."[38] Chance operations, so intimately implicated in the development of eventual verse, are summations based on "the only way the one belongs to the multiple: always subtracted," "subtracting in each instance the value of the constant."[39] Whether that constant is the "ego," and whether or not the ethical imperative to avoid the ego is valid, the ramifications for intention and selection are complicit and irreversible, like temporal events themselves.

The period of Hejinian's work in question includes her most axiomatic statement regarding quantitative approaches to writing, in "Comments for Manuel Brito": "Quantities are change, not categories … It has been years since I read Hegel, and when I read his work I did so very fantastically. That is, I had reasons for reading Hegel that Hegel would not have anticipated nor approved."[40] But when she reads Oppen's sense of polis fantastically, so that one "could say that 'the thing itself exercises curiosity'," she qualifies it by admitting the "interpretation may push Oppen's intended sense, but not, I believe, with a result he would dislike."[41] Here she reads the continuation of his motivation through the work of her own intention. This is not exactly a "selective" interpretation—"the attempt to describe a dream raises a challenge to selection"—and this challenge, professed years earlier, leads to her own distinction between "lines of causation … [T]he most readily described motivate the events that we dream."[42] Hence, she performs a reading of her own dreams in articulating her poetics at the historical "poles" of the move—a decade long—from "consciousness" to "sites" thereof.

We shouldn't discount the influence of the more conceptualist route through the New American Poetry, the "deep image" poetics that made

an antithetical use of the relationship between intension—affective preda-
tion—and "intention" in the gaudiest sense of satisfying personal motivations.
Robert Bly is the most extensive proponent of deep image poetics. As Kevin
Bushnell has shown, Bly's concern with achieving a consciousness of *un*con-
sciousness in the reader builds on a methodological impasse situated in the
lyric attributes of gestalt imagery which, like Mac Low's "event," is, though
ultimately prosodic, not primarily phonological.

> [T]he reliance on the deep image as a device [is] designed to affect the reader's
> unconscious within a medium which necessarily operates on the level of
> consciousness. There is no way around the gap separating the intelligibility
> of language and Bly's desire for a poetry of the unconscious. The deep image
> attempts to vault this gap, although one has the impression that the attempt
> often falls short.[43]

If psychoanalysis is correct in basing the machinations of the unconscious on
a proto-structuralist concept of language, Bly's images function as props, where
Hejinian's function rather as propositions. In electing a percept as a prompt
for writing, they become what we might call *negative* deep images[44]. Hejinian's
turn from metaphor to metonymy coincides with this negativity—it is a rejec-
tion of the universality of the deep image and the humanist imperatives of the
unconscious as determinate yet sumptuously obscure agent of the events of ex-
perience: "I have no experience of being except in position."[45]

Despite that *The Cell*, a series of 150 short lyric poems, "at every point start[s]
… with the smallest percept," it is not incongruous that the vaunted and rou-
tinely abstract genre of elegy lies at its heart.[46] Elegy serves as a generic obverse
of the third in this trio of works, *A Border Comedy*. Moreover, from a position
of consciousness, there is no access to fate. And so it is not surprising to find the
elegy foreshadowed by the final sentence of the first book's opening poem: "It is
not imperfect to / have died".[47] If death is not the imperfection with which we
index fate, it is not a perfect image of negativity, that which the confluence of
purposiveness and arbitration we know as the unconscious may be. Instead, this
negativity is thematized as selection in Hejinian's work of the period.

Here I translate my thought
into language — to double fate

But fate imposes its very interesting exercise:
    select[48]

Blueness holds the sky and
    the sea is bound
Discontinuity without certainty of end
This is society, not science
Where are your polarities, your
    transitions
Only gerunds, during a seduction,
    it being a selection[49]

Any copy of the poem
    is guaranteed to be identical
What are the objects in
    this poem on selection
A bird within its range,
    within its relativity
A neighborhood wobbling within rain[50]

Through the negative deep image, Hejinian moves between the terms of intention and election as though they were identical—identity or equivalence *per se* is a theme, especially near the end of *The Cell* and throughout the previous volume of this series, *Oxota: A Short Russian Novel*: "… a false opposition … reality divides … And there is only reality."[51] If the negative deep image is a condition of bewildering plenitude, of "not imperfect" immanence—in short, if everything available to experience presents itself as paradox—the question, with no subtle nod to grammatology, becomes: *What* is the reality of thought? I think the question needs warranting by reference to another Objectivist concept, Lorine Niedecker's notion of "inference." Concise perhaps to a fault, Niedecker's notion is almost solely developed in a brief, untitled, lyric poem, which I will cite in its entirety.

You see here
the influence
of inference
Moon in rippled
stream

'Except as
and unless'[52]

The efflorescing ("rippled" and "wobbling") contiguity ("neighborhood") in-volves the self-same demarcation of the "stream" ("within rain"). Combining her rendition of surrealism with Zukofsky's Objectivism, Niedecker conceives poetry as building "folktales of the mind … creating our own remember-ing … the Self association of nervous vocables coloured by the rhythm of the moment."[53]. Likewise, when Hejinian posits, "it is not surrealism to compare apples to oranges," in a list of language writing's formative tenets, even with the caveat that "none [are] primary in relation to the others," it is to emphasize that the image as inference does not leave the thing itself (this orange, this apple) in a state, in Zukofsky's words, of "rested totality."[54] Rather than imposing, inference proposes. And while Niedecker's lyric address dismantles the formal, haiku-like hermetics of the second stanza of "You see here," the cited but unat-tributed (copied and identical) imperative to "Except as / and unless" suggests that selection goes both ways—it augments the composition while it deletes the potential of the terms selected *out* of the composition.[55] The immanence of Niedecker's image invalidates the metaphorical logic of substitution, "as" and "unless." This is the very immanence that represents a kind of spontaneous assent to the negativity subsequently celebrated in *The Cell*.

Write worldwide—with the muscular
    power of uncertainty—and approve
    the world[56]

Prove the world
The separate, profiled bulb
Broad sun, it is the
    greatest document
No head for fallibility!
I don't know of cells
    without full world[57]

One cannot select everything that is the case, adapting Wittgenstein's famous phrase about "worldwide" reference. In the first passage, we have the routine definite article describing plenitude and immanence. But the "power of uncer-tainty" then becomes, in the second, simple omission of any article. Or maybe we should say elision instead of omission, since selection tacitly omits other pos-sibilities and thus feigns certainty: decides. "[F]ull world" is exactly that which cannot be quantified, even indefinitely—*a* full world seems poorly suited, even nonsensical, in the sparse and immanently imperative texture of the second stanza. The key terms here are "document," "head," and "know[ledge]." The negative image of a world is done "without" so that one decides to know no part beyond "full world" as universal constituency: "cells" as epistemological singularities. The decision is to elect the entirety, not to favor any part.

The difference disallows the work of negation in the causal circuit Roman Jakobson devises along phonological lines. "Poetic language," writes Jakobson, "reveals two effective causes in sound texture—the selection and constellation of phonemes and their components … The poetic function projects the principle of equivalence from the axis of selection into the axis of combination."[58] Election, instead, invests lyricality with both a poetic and a metalingual function.[59] Poet-critic Lytle Shaw has memorably argued that generic and/or selective "coexistence" might "open spaces for thought" through the deleterious work of Jakobsonian poetics.[60] He makes the point, in fact, with reference to Hejinian's use of fairy tale and picaresque structures (in *The Traveler and the Hill and the Hill*). Such generic structures do retain transvaluative functions, and Shaw's reading of the increasingly allusive and citational qualities of Hejinian's poetry is important and illuminating. However, I believe a larger sense of coexistence warrants the terminological distinctions of motive from intention, and selection from election, a sense that suggests the poetics of indeterminacy have, in fact, roots in rather more domestic sites of consciousness. Ralph Waldo Emerson: "When we speak of nature … we mean the integrity of impression made by manifold natural objects. It is this which distinguishes the stick of timber of the wood-cutter, from the tree of the poet."[61] Note the epistemological mischievousness of Hejinian as she ventures into Emerson's pastoral territory, importing the gothic sensibility of Baudelaire.

> The real appears before us every second
> But to be recognized
> by a nice green tree is inefficient
> So I correct myself
>
> making constant adjustments
> Perfect life, if only this one and that one
> are real—then the world is relevant
> as the medium of recognition[62]
>
> What no one knows is that I've inserted razor blades into the fingertips
> of my gloves
> I don't even know it myself

Though embedded
Not everything is known
For example, suppose I drop a stone
Then I hit the surface I've scored with a paddle
Blood fills the shallow incisions
The message becomes legible
And the pleasure of seeing intentionality everywhere is incredible
It makes everything in the universe mental[63]

III. Fantastic Philosophy

Good and bad are only the products of an active and temporary
selection which must be renewed.
— Deleuze & Guattari, *A Thousand Plateaus*

It's the principle of connection not that of causality which
saves us from a bad infinity
— Lyn Hejinian, *Oxota: A Short Russian Novel*

If negative deep images distinguish between the motivated caprice of inten-
tion and motivation itself, Hejinian's work of this period can be read as a test
of reciprocity between agency and its world. But as a test of poetry, it will also
entail a methodological difference for critical reading practices: a hermeneutics,
what Hejinian calls a "pre-poetics." In more than one sense, this difference is
embodied in a play on genre: the novel-cum-sonnet in *Oxota*, the intermedial
fable in *A Border Comedy*, and the tabular form of "The Composition of The
Cell," to name only the most obvious instances. As a "pre-poetics" of criticism,
Hejinian's work of this period clarifies the limits, the "reason" (presumably
something more than purpose, aim, or motive), and the stakes involved in po-
tentially any critical enterprise.[64]

In what sounds like an echo of Niedecker's notion of "folktales of the mind,"
Hejinian has been heard to say, "poets have a fantastic relationship to philoso-
phy." I heard her say so in a discussion of Oppen's relationship to the writings
of Heidegger and Hegel. In response to my query regarding this "fantastic rela-
tionship," Hejinian had this to say:

[T]he relationship of foreground to background differs for the poet and the
philosopher. Fantasy worlds ... are almost entirely lacking in background. All
the essential elements (and fantasies contain only essential elements) are in

the foreground ... Poets (or, to be specific, I) build fantasy worlds out of the materials of philosophy ... whereas philosophical arguments proceed from cause to effect, cause to effect, in a chain, all of whose links except the most recent are in the background, poetry consists solely either of causes or effects, each of which remains in the foreground. Nothing is prior to anything else.[65]

At the time, I took this definition of "fantasy" to be synonymous with her definition of "pre-poetics." In turn, an equation is made with "reason" as an ethical "dilemma"; in her prefatory note to "Reason" added for its reprint in *The Language of Inquiry*, the eponymous term comes in for dual duty, as "both method and ... object" hence also "philosophy's fundamental concern."[66] From a methodological perspective, a play on the polysemous "object" (as motive and contiguous extant or "world") illustrates how, in Hejinian's poetics of indeterminacy, a determinant is required—a pre-poetics—to set things adrift. The discovery and identification of "determining principles or events" is of secondary interest to how the ethos of "determining"—its rendering this causal triad "final"—marks the determining "current," "how reason reasons its reasons—how it discovers, identifies, and acts on them."[67] The guiding principle of these distinctions, supposedly crucial to the bearing of poetics on ethical dilemmas, in Hejinian's words are "both perfect and efficient, or proximate," as well as final causation: a triad of axiomatic categories in the disciplinary context she clearly wishes to evoke. But to move from the question of *what* is *there* to serve as a dilemma, we should read "reason[1] reasons[2] its reasons[3]" as first and second method (discovery and identification), third being at last the object of effect. Pre-poetics is procreative, it seems, a stream of consciousness where ethics and authority generate an *ethos* of *critos*.

An indeterminacy is explicitly proposed by Hejinian's development of these tenets in her reading of Oppen and Hannah Arendt, deriving from the latter the axiom: "Authority over being is thus dispersed, not *because of* boundlessness but *in* the boundlessness."[68] This is why indeterminacy as such is bound to critical action (intention) in proportion to its ongoing distance from its originary purpose and telos (motive). The relationship is entropic, not static. As it reads in the essay itself, there is a logical slippage of the relative values of motive and intention. And it will be decisive, thus "fantastic." The dilemma of "reason" is mediated by what in dreams is prone to description. But again, the language exhibits agency, exerts itself; dream or fantasy constitutes a situation in which efficient cause and final cause "are completely unconnected."[69] The connection is displaced onto the latter when Hejinian defines it doubly as "*reason to* ... or *telos*."[70] The definition encompasses both motive and result, insofar as the "necessary" condition of pre-poetics marks a destination as a result of having arrived rather than predation or design. When Hejinian writes, "there are situations in which the two lines of causation are completely unconnected, of which the most readily described motivate the events that we dream," "motivate" becomes a third term *between* motive and intention. She means intention but wants to complicate it and so won't equate intention with efficient cause. Still, its ethical thrust issues from the affirmation of that very efficiency. What happens for us is a reciprocal cascade of effects that create themselves as objects by virtue of their self-same inference. Fantasy, as her initial anecdote describes, is a chance convergence of sites of consciousness—dream and waking reality—each necessary to the other.

Concerned by Hejinian's use of the term "fantasy" in such close proximity to work she figures as ethical, not to mention the vast measure or even master narrative insinuated by the notion of toying with "worlds," I suggested that this would make poetry the fantasy life of philosophy. She replied, "I might say that philosophy is the fantasy life of poetry. I think poetry can (though few poets care to attempt this) do philosophy in the Wittgensteinian sense."[71] Our correspondence has since turned up as source material for *The Fatalist* (compare the passage above to the stanza comprising page 67 of that book). When I initially found it there, the plotted unfolding of our conversation replaced by oddly appropriate puns—appropriation is a resounding of etiological and teleological scripting effects as a matter of theme. In fact, the distinction made between poetic and philosophical modes of argumentation amply describes the act of reading the sustained ruminations which inhabit all of Hejinian's poems; there is no back story or plot. Yet the distinction, insofar as it is discussed in addition to being demonstrated in the poems, disassembles the extreme disciplinary duality described above (poetry vs. philosophy). A border condition defines the limit-case of either discipline. The a priori condition is, however, not the border itself, but "fantasy." As she elaborates in *The Fatalist*, the fantastic is where "every element / is answerable to every other element"; fantasy subtends the temporal vehicle of intention (or event) and the "reason" (agential immanence) of election, where the real of thought becomes the ready world to which any poem will be considered accurate, or not (an *ethos* of *critos*).[72]

In *Oxota*, the writing is preoccupied with, as Hejinian says in "Continuing Against Closure," "the middle ... a zone of alteration, transmutation, a zone of forced forgetting ... languages clash, where currency changes value and value changes currency."[73] The border, especially between languages, forms the transvaluative "zone," which is the central conceit of the book.

Sergei asked about nigger music
You mean, I said—Black
And I see you're pink, he raged then—yes, is that your
       color?—and maybe yellow too—it disgusts me—it's
       like chicken fat
He was pleased with that
Sergei says you're a racist, Mitya told me later—he heard you
       calling niggers black
Niggers?
As Faulkner says—it's a literary word, respectful, yes?[74]

After all, between languages "Aretha Franklin *is* a man of the people."[75] No exclusively "literary" value will save the stranger to a language. ("A comedian is a foreigner at border," announces "Book Six" of *A Border Comedy*.) Such miscommunications season the metonymic ruminations of *Oxota*, often characterized by delay or temporal myopia.

We paused on the Palace Embankment
There are always monstrous prepositions, colors, murky
       juxtapositions, and flux more vast than distractions, more
       lasting than the past, in the Neva[76]

"I float forever in my paper boat ... Description of it is a form of waiting."[77] To sit and wait is a common activity of border crossings. In *Oxota*, the sites of consciousness are "between the breasts," "between profiles," "between housing blocks," even "between our legs."[78] Meanwhile, "Waiting depends on the thickness of thought" and "Patience is passion."[79] Borders introduce temporal discontinuity, but "there is only reality"—and "its author must sit on it," the "current" is "where I waited," rendering "discontinuity ... self-contained."[80] Such divided continuities, or "self-contained" discontinuities do not constitute an irreducible ambiguity so much as a *good* infinity, rendering the "negative" work of the images less deleterious than elective, exercising the curiosity the reader performs.

This brings the sexual question—broached in terms of Hejinian and Miller's discussion of personhood and gender—into the question of an elective geography. *A Border Comedy* is replete with sex toys and truly kinky thinking. In fantasies, there are "only essential elements," only intention. Citing Bataille's linking of where "poetry leads" as a sexual "fusion," Hejinian tells Miller, "I can also regard poetry as highly eroticized, in all its relationships, especially with regard to power … [A]t the moment women are capable of creating an entirely new opportunity for exploring the erotic, including uses of power (withholding power, deferring power, letting power slip away)," calling poetry an "appropriate locus" or "logical site for the moebius-stripping of male-female distinctions."[81] *A Border Comedy* links the comic to "Putting what's known into what's told in a tale that seeks its pole."[82] The phallic pun on "pole" recalls the "nice green tree" upon which the narrator of *A Border Comedy*'s blood was earlier spilt.

> People meet and they don't like each other, they fight, they devour each other
> And weep
> Their happiness erupting in *amor fati*
> Sensually expressed
> For they are fated, and the fated love
> To celebrate the fate they can never entirely receive
> Of course not
> Fate is never entirely given
> Sure, a person passes on the street and then turns—coils, even
> Right on top
> The novelist proclaims the person in love, the philosopher foolish
> It's as Nietzsche says
> A married philosopher belongs in a comedy
> Fate is funny[83]

Studded with "informative fables" and other fragmentary interludes, the book is however no more fantastic than when sexual, philosophical, and literary fantasies meld, invariably in moments when identities shift in blatant disregard of distinctions between animate and inanimate. Personification of phenomenological states is the text's pervasive effect.

> There is an intrinsic connection between the meaning of this and where you
>   find it
> But the concert was about to begin, leaving only a moment for conversation
> SINGER: In the sound?
> SOUND: Yes, then sense follows
> AUTHOR *(unable to restrain itself)*: There's far more to this than sound
> APHORISM: In the sound of a word are many logics of one kind combined,
>   [but in
>   the move from that word to the next are logics of many kinds
> COMIC: Aphorisms are as catchy as cans (pause for line break) / can be cornered

According to culture's canny (pause) accountants (laughter comes through line
    break) an opinion is compressed
Into a perception[84]

When Jakobson's axis of selection collapses: slapstick. The canny extension
seeps from the motivation of signs, formal-cum-lexical signs such as the "line /
break" make us giddy with elective offerings from intention's real-time event.
The "conversation" is "intrinsic" to the "concert." This send up of the integrity
of the real suggests that perhaps "curiosity" *will* "eventually lead to everything."
If so, Hejinian's work of this period becomes an object lesson in a much needed
"pre-poetics" of criticism.

Notes

1. Barrett Watten, "The Turn to Language and the 1960s," *Critical Inquiry* 29, no. 1 (Fall 2002).
2. Lyn Hejinian, *The Language of Inquiry* (Berkeley, CA: University of California Press, 2002), 347.
3. Ibid.
4. Ibid.
5. Ibid., 43.
6. This critique is conspicuously culled from the excerpt of "The Rejection of Closure" that
appears in Norton's anthology of feminist theory and criticism (Gilbert and Gubar, 2007), an
instance of editorial motive trumping authorial intention, dovetailing with the ubiquity of "the
open text" standing for "indeterminacy" as a critical value.
7. Ibid.
8. Ibid.
9. Ibid., 44.
10. Jacob Edmon, "The Closures of the Open Text: Lyn Hejinian's 'Paradise Found,'"
Contemporary Literature 50, no. 2 (2009): 244.
11. Ibid., 245.
12. Jennifer Ashton's recent work has critiqued the literary-historical use of the term in part
because "indeterminacy" as a set of features modulates the structure of thought that constitutes
history per se. The literary features of openness Perloff claims are, to Ashton, impertinent to
positivist excesses in modernists such as Stein and Laura Riding-Jackson. Language writing, she
argues, unwittingly extended both these excesses and the reactionary correctives of the New
Criticism, leaving us to "get over it"; it may be that she and her primary precedent, art critic
Michael Fried, mistake the motive of radical modernism for a desire to render meaning "literal."
It may be that without a practical plurality of indeterminacies, a useful rapprochement is beyond
the scope of the debate. For reasons of both space and relevance, I must defer this discussion
for now. It may mean that we need a temporal relation to the names of history evoked in the
very moment in Stein that stands for Ashton as a form of ultimate closure, perfect referentiality,
caressing the noun. That is, to cite Jacques Rancière, literary history itself would need to take
on "the production of the hidden ... a poetic operation" acknowledging the absence of agents
in the very agency of the "words" left to posterity, "an absence that literature, according to the
use of its powers, exposes or dissimulates." Jennifer Ashton, *From Modernism to Postmodernism:*

American Poetry and Theory in the Twentieth Century (Cambridge: Cambridge University Press, 2005), 1–11, 176. Jacques Rancière, *The Names of History: on the Poetics of Knowledge*, trans. Hassan Melehy (Minneapolis: University of Minnesota Press, 1994), 52.

13. Steve McCaffery, Ron Silliman, and Charles Bernstein, "Correspondence: May 1976 December 1977." *Line* 5 (1985): 60.

14. Gilles Deleuze and Félix Guattari, *A Thousand Plateaus: Capitalism and Schizophrenia*, trans. Brian Massumi (Minneapolis: University of Minnesota Press, 1987), 4, 88.

15. McCaffery et. al. 60, 62.

16. Ibid., 63

17. Ibid.

18. Silliman's critique of literary transparency links the "dream of an art with no medium" to "the commodity fetish," a link first exposed and fledglingly overcome by "novelists of serious intent," such as Stein. It is in this literary-historical tradition, he argues, that poetry becomes, "the philosophy of practice in language," to paraphrase Marx's famous pronouncement, with which he concludes his remarks, drawing the poetry of the present from the future. Ron Silliman, "Disappearance of the Word, Appearance of the World," *The New Sentence* (New York: Roof Books, 1987), 14, 17–18.

19. Leslie Scalapino, *How Phenomena Appear to Unfold* (Elmwood: Potes & Poets, 1989).

20. Hejinian, *The Language of Inquiry*, 188.

21. Lyn Hejinian and Tyrus Miller, "An Exchange of Letters." *Paper Air* 4, no. 2 (1989): 34.

22. Ibid.

23. Michael Davidson, Lyn Hejinian, Ron Silliman, and Barrett Watten, *Leningrad: American Writers in the Soviet Union* (San Francisco: Mercury House, 1991), 2–3.

24. Hejinian and Miller, 34.

25. Hejinian and Miller, 35.

26. Anscombe, G. E. M. Anscombe, *Intention* (Cambridge: Harvard UP, 2000),19.

27. Ibid.

28. Ibid., 16.

29. Charles Bernstein, "Professing Stein / Stein Professing," *A Poetics* (Cambridge: Harvard University Press, 1992).

30. Lyn Hejinian, *A Border Comedy* (New York: Granary, 2001), 33.

31. Ibid., 151.

32. Ibid., 58.

33. Lyn Hejinian, *The Fatalist* (Richmond, CA: Omnidawn, 2003), 59.

34. Charles Altieri evokes Mac Low's "formal and aleatory models of invention which make structure the creative ground rather than the result of immediate poetic thinking" as squarely within the "objectivist tradition," in which he later reads Hejinian's *The Cell*. For Altieri, Hejinian's poem dramatizes "psychological processes" as linguistic ones, or at least structured as linguistic ones: "the personal has to surrender dominance: it consists only in what becomes exhibited as and through one's concepts." I try to flesh out Mac Low's "models of invention" here to substantiate the psychological models of intention that, in part, may underpin this tradition. Readers interested in the relationship of Mac Low's poetics to conceptual art and contemporary conceptual writing should read Liz Kotz's comparative reading of his and John Ashbery's "Poetics of Chance and Collage." Charles Altieri, "The Objectivist Tradition" and "Transformations of Objectivism," *The Objectivist Nexus: Essays in Cultural Poetics*, eds. Rachel Blau DuPlessis and Peter Quartermain (Tuscaloosa: University of Alabama Press, 1999), 33, 306–7. Liz Kotz, *Language to Be Looked At* (Cambridge: M.I.T. Press, 2007).

35. Jackson Mac Low, "He Cannot Have Been Pleased Today to Hear That," *Kenning* 7 (2000):15–18.

36. David Hume, *An Inquiry Concerning Human Understanding*, ed. Tom L. Beauchamp (Oxford: Oxford University Press, 1999), 97.

37. Jackson Mac Low, *Stanzas for Iris Lezak* (New York: Something Else Press, 1972), 424.

38 Ron Silliman, "While Some Are Being Flies, Others Are Having Examples," *Paper Air* 2, no 3: 40.

39. Deleuze and Guattari, 6, 99.

40. Hejinian, *Language of Inquiry*, 182–3.

41. Ibid., 350.

42. Ibid., 139, 341.

43. Kevin Bushnell, "Leaping into the Unknown: The Poetics of Robert Bly's Deep Image," *Modern American Poetry*, accessed March 15, 2003, http://www.english.uiuc.edu/maps/poets/a_f/bly/bushell.html

44. In a brilliant reading of the ethical preoccupations of *The Cell* published in the meantime between conceiving and publishing the present essay, G. Matthew Jenkins views the "negative totality" of "the cell turned inside out" as a model of ethics according to Emmanual Levinas' philosophy of turning toward or facing the Other. I read his very impressive work as a necessary supplement to my own notion adjoining the question of openness/closure, intentionality/motivation, and the continuum of imagery between the poles of metonymy and metaphor. As he puts it, "Hejinian attempts a metonymy of the infinite, even as she is invoking notions of totality." Jenkins, G. Matthew Jenkins, *Poetic Obligation: Ethics in Experimental American Poetry after 1945* (Iowa City: University of Iowa Press, 2008), 184, 193.

45. Hejinian, *The Language of Inquiry*, 202.

46. Hejinian, interview by Charles Bernstein, *LINEbreak*, 1996, http://writing.upenn.edu/pennsound/x/LINEbreak.html

47. Lyn Hejinian, *The Cell* (Los Angeles: Sun and Moon, 1992), 92–3, 7.

48. Lyn Hejinian, "The Person," *The Cold of Poetry* (Los Angeles: Sun and Moon, 1994), 177.

49. Hejinian, *The Cell*, 119.

50. Ibid., 159.

51. Lyn Hejinian, *Oxota: A Short Russian Novel* (Great Barrington, MA: The Figures, 1991), 20, 71, 74.

52. Lorine Niedecker, *Collected Works*, ed. Jenny Penberthy (Berkeley: University of California Press, 2002), 228.

53. Lorine Niedecker, "Letter to Mary Hoard / Local Letters," *Lorine Niedecker: Woman and Poet*, ed. Jenny Penberthy (Orono: National Poetry Foundation, 1996), 87–88.

54. The Language of Inquiry, 322–3.

55. Joshua Clover suggests we attribute this imperative to William James, also a primary source for Hejinian's thought throughout this period. In any event, the decision to foreground the absence of the source is what's crucial here, allowing us to read the entire poem and the notion of inference as "the meaning of its never being named." Joshua Clover, "Reply to Patrick Durgin: The New Phrase," *Circulars*, http://www.arras.net/circulars/archives/000160.html#000160

56. Hejinian, *The Cell*, 60.

57. Ibid., 178.

58. Roman Jakobson, *Language in Literature*, eds. Krystyna Pomorska and Stephen Rudy (Cambridge, MA: Belknap University Press, 1987), 71.

59. The breath-based poetics of Charles Olson, whose legacy, in my estimation, lives on in Bly's work more than any practitioner of language writing, is an important point of contrast here. Olson's "corollary, that *right* form, in any given poem, is the only and exclusively possible extension of content under hand" transforms a usefully ambiguous dictum into a question of right, which, not incidentally, presumes that the difference between motive and intention is only

a question of degree. Although it is certain language poets and not Black Mountain poets who are routinely affiliated with Russian Formalist and Prague School literary and linguistic theories, in the contrast between the phonological and visual, Jakobsonian poetics seem more pertinent to "Projective Verse" than "The Rejection of Closure."

60. Lytle Shaw, "An Open Letter: Jackobson's Metalanguage," *Notes to Poetry:* 49, November, 2001, www.arras.net.

61. Ralph Waldo Emerson, *Emerson's Prose and Poetry*, ed. Joel Porte and Saundra Morris (New York: Norton, 2001), 28.

62. Hejinian, "The Person," 168.

63. Hejinian, *A Border Comedy*, 170.

64. Hejinian, *The Language of Inquiry*, 340.

65. Hejinian, letter to author, January 22, 2002.

66. Hejinian, *The Language of Inquiry*, 337.

67. Ibid.

68. Ibid., 352.

69. Ibid., 340–1.

70. Ibid.

71. Hejinian, letter to the author.

72. Hejinian, *The Fatalist*, 67.

73. Lyn Hejinian, "Continuing Against Closure," *Jacket* 14 (2001), accessed March 15, 2003, http://jacketmagazine.com/14/hejinian.html

74. Hejinian, *Oxota*, 34.

75. Ibid., 143, italics mine.

76. Ibid., 147.

77. Ibid., 73.

78. Ibid., 14, 97, 122, 126.

79. Ibid., 154, 200.

80. Ibid., 26, 187, 150, 204.

81. Hejinian and Miller, 39.

82. Hejinian, *A Border Comedy*, 35–6.

83. Ibid., 194.

84. Ibid., 74.

Strange Borders, Double Vision: *Oxota* as a Work of Trans-iteration

Kate Fagan

Arkadii says that the first sentence of my Russian novel should be "All things happen so often that there is no sense in speaking about them." Or this should be the epigraph, with attribution to Immanuel Kant. "Start please with the third chapter," he says.

— Lyn Hejinian, "Soviet Diary"[1]

I elaborated on the beginning of the novel, which never existed, and I said that I found myself a perpetual participant of the middle.

— Lyn Hejinian, "Language and 'Paradise'"[2]

Where does *Oxota: A Short Russian Novel* begin?

Toward the end of 1984, Lyn Hejinian received a copy of *A Hunter's Sketches* by post from Leningrad. It was the year before Mikhael Gorbachev's election as General Secretary of the Soviet Union Communist Party in March 1985, to be followed soon after by the Russian government's twin advocacy of glasnost and perestroika. It was one year before the first Superpowers Summit in Moscow, at which Mikhael Gorbachev and Ronald Reagan met to discuss international military and economic issues including the nuclear arms 'race,' the ongoing conflict in Afghanistan, and the technical and rhetorical dismantling of the Cold War. It was two years after Lyn Hejinian and poet Barrett Watten published the first edition of *Poetics Journal* in hand-printed foolscap format, stapled rather than bound; and a year after Hejinian's first trip to Leningrad in May 1983. "Improvisation begins at the moment when something has just happened," writes Hejinian, "which is to say, it doesn't begin at the beginning. Nonetheless, it is always involved with the process of beginning—that is, of setting things in motion."[3]

Writing to her mother Carolyn Andrews on 20th November 1984, Hejinian describes *A Hunter's Sketches* (*Zapiski Okhotnika*), a work by the Ukrainian-born nineteenth-century Russian novelist and poet Ivan Turgenev, as "ironic, but so tenderly ironic that one wants to weep. It is wonderful." The Turgenev edition was in English and had been published in Moscow by *Progress Publishers* as one of a series of "Russian classics in translation." It was both "gorgeously illustrated" and readily available—or at least, officially sanctioned—in Soviet literary-cultural life.[4] Hejinian's letter of November 1984 also tellingly refers to "the Reaganoid years" that she and her American friends are experiencing with critical vehemence and certain trepidation.

Turgenev's *Zapiski Okhotnika* (1852) is a cycle of short stories and was a gift to Lyn Hejinian from Leningrad poet Arkadii Dragomoschenko. He posted the book together with a volume of stories by Ivan Bunin, a Russian writer whose classically influenced poetry, novels and plays gained him a Nobel prize for literature in 1933. Bunin was born in the same region as Turgenev; Oryol in the Ukraine, not far from where Dragomoschenko also spent much of his childhood, in Vinnitsa. One of Ivan Bunin's best-known works makes a signature appearance in Chapter 116 of Hejinian's *Oxota: A Short Russian Novel* in lines that refer to an 'actual' exchange between Hejinian and Dragomoschenko:

> Arkadii, I said
> What in your opinion is the quintessential Russian novel?
> *The Life of Arseniev*
> But we can't decide anything (131)

With more than a little irony, Hejinian names this chapter of *Oxota* "Aesthetic Gratification" and concludes it with the line: "We did not fulfill our obligations." Nothing can be decided. Things are incomplete or arrested, and the borders of (textual) obligation are blurring. Chapter 117 of *Oxota* ("The Destinies of Observation") continues Hejinian's metadiscourse about the instabilities and cultural expectations of genre boundaries and nomenclatures. "A Russian novel should be called *The Adherent*," it begins. "It is obsequious / It holds / It is opportune." Hejinian concludes: "With such a phrase one can imagine another world." (132) Describing *The Life of Arseniev* (1927–1933) in comparably recondite terms, the Russian writer Konstantin Paustovski once characterized Ivan Bunin's text as "neither a short novel, nor a novel, nor a long short story, but of a genre yet unknown."[5]

Ivan Bunin left St. Petersburg for Paris after the Bolshevik revolution of October 1917. An entire chapter of *Zhizn Arsen'eva: U Istoka Dhej* (*The Life of Arseniev: The Well of Days*)—Bunin's "quintessentially Russian novel"—is devoted to an encomium for the legacy of nineteenth-century Russian novelist and poet Alexander Pushkin. "How many emotions he evoked in me!" writes Bunin. "And how often my own emotions and everything amidst which and by which I lived found a companion in him!"[6] Fifty years earlier in June 1880, in a speech that opened a new Pushkin monument in Moscow, Ivan Turgenev (*A Hunter's Sketches*) praised the poet in similarly elevated rhetoric:

> And finally, it was [Pushkin's] mighty hand which was the first to raise high the banner of poetry on Russian soil; and if the dust of battle which was raised after his death clouded this radiant banner for a while, then it is now, as the dust is beginning to settle, that we see this victorious standard shining once more on high…. Let us also hope that in the not too distant future the descendents of the Russian common people, who today do not read Pushkin, will understand what the name Pushkin means.[7]

Turgenev is reputed to once have commented, with hyperbolic deference, that he would "give both his little fingers for a single line of *Evgeny Onegin*."[8] Russian novelist Fyodor Dostoevsky also spoke at Moscow's Pushkin celebrations in 1880. He extolled the verse novel *Evgeny Onegin* as Pushkin's finest work: "*Evgeny Onegin* [is] a poem which is not fantastic but which has a tangible realism, in which the reality of Russian life is embodied so fully and with such creative force that its like has not been seen before or since."[9] *Evgeny Onegin* is a work in fourteen-line rhymed stanzas that begins beside the "grey waters of the Neva" in St. Petersburg (known as Leningrad from 1924 to 1992).[10] It develops as its core narrative conceit a love relationship between Evgeny Onegin and a singular, literate, romance-reading heroine called Tatyana. The Russian Formalist Viktor Shklovsky once held that Pushkin meant not to prioritize the novel's romance theme, but wanted rather to play an intricate textual "game with this story."[11]

Hejinian's *Oxota: A Short Russian Novel* was written one and a half centuries after Pushkin's *grande oeuvre* and is set comparably, though somewhat hazily, in Leningrad "against the outstretched water in the Neva."[12] Turning to the back cover, readers encounter an explanatory sentence that is both attractive and reductive: "Composed of 270 free sonnets inspired by Pushkin's *Evgeny Onegin*, *Oxota: A Short Russian Novel* is a stunning edifice in language that proposes and enacts an intimate and restive portrait of life in Russia today." Hejinian has offered an important qualification to the curious appellation "free sonnets": "I wasn't thinking at all of sonnets but of the fourteen-line stanzas of Pushkin's *Evgeny Onegin*. To think of the 'chapters' as sonnets is very misleading…. The formal structure I ended up using was largely influenced by Pushkin. His *Evgeny Onegin* is commonly known as 'the first Russian novel.'"[13] *Evgeny Onegin*'s methods, along with Pushkin's almost comically iconic Russian national status, were never far from Hejinian's mind during *Oxota*'s devising. Pushkin's verse epic contains eight chapters of individually numbered stanzas. *Oxota* follows suit with eight 'books' arranged in cumulatively numbered 'chapters,' two hundred and seventy in all. Hejinian also adds an eleven-line Coda, a ninth 'book'—an echo perhaps of the additional book that Pushkin omitted during initial publication of *Evgeny Onegin*, after re-casting the ninth chapter as the eighth.[14]

Between 1983 and 1991, Lyn Hejinian visited the former Soviet Union at least seven times and spent long periods in Leningrad-St. Petersburg, where she lived and worked alongside innovative poet Arkadii Dragomoschenko. Hejinian first travelled to the U.S.S.R. and Poland with the ROVA saxophone quartet, an experimental jazz-influenced group from San Francisco with underground followings in Moscow and Leningrad. Hejinian's husband Larry Ochs is a member of the quartet. Following a successful and thus potentially destabilizing ROVA concert in Moscow, officials cancelled the band's Leningrad gig, and Dragomoschenko made arrangements for an illicit performance. He later took Hejinian and Ochs to a meeting of Club 81, a 'non-official' group of Leningrad poets and writers who had begun meeting in 1981 as a necessary alternative to the state-sanctioned and heavily monitored Soviet Writers' Union.[15] Dragomoschenko was a founding member of Club 81. Its writers shared no common aesthetic programme but felt compelled rather to "deal with a number of common problems, not poetical but societal—regulatory with respect to poetry-writing."[16] Without official authorization, writers could not publish in Soviet Russia, and thus had to devise alternative means of securing readership and a kind of legitimacy and life for their poetry. Although Dragomoschenko wrote many books during the 1980s, his first complete work in Russian—*Nebo Sootvetstvii* (*Sky of Conformity*)—was not published in Russia until 1990.[17] His poems had appeared during the 1970s and early 1980s in various Russian *samizdat* journals, 'illegal' street-circulated publications often made in limited-run carbon copy. In 1986, Club 81 published a dissident anthology entitled *Krug* (*Circle*) that contained the first of Dragomoschenko's poems to be included in a Russian book. This publication scenario was shared by most of the anthology's participants.[18]

Assisted by an interpreter upon meeting in 1983, Hejinian and Dragomoschenko recognized a joint fascination with epistemologies of poetic language and constructive links between description and perception. They began planning a cultural trade that would take several San Francisco poets to Russia, to be reciprocated in U.S. visits by Leningrad poets. The crossings could not begin until 1988 when Dragomoschenko was finally given a

U.S.S.R. government visa.[19] The two poets did begin extensive translations of one another's poetry, however, that prolonged and were facilitated by a rich epistolary exchange. In December 1983 Hejinian wrote to Clark Coolidge: "My correspondence—or the world created by my correspondence—with the Russian writers (but, in particular, with Arkadii Dragomoschenko) … has put letter-writing into a new and major place in my literary life, and it is there that I have begun to be able to articulate (and even to discover) what might begin to be my own 'poetics.'"[20] Hejinian taught herself Russian in order to translate Dragomoschenko's "vivid, charming, beautiful and eccentric letters,"[21] and in 1985 was recognized by Soviet officials as an authorized translator of specific Russian texts—still a necessary formality at that time. Describing her encounters with Russian language to Fanny Howe in April 1984, she wrote: "It is absurdly difficult … . My sense is that it is close to a practical application of poetic language, based in metaphor and wildly, extravagantly resonant."[22] Hejinian's assessments of the collaborative qualities of translation are revealing. Rendering Dragomoschenko's writings into English, Hejinian feels she is generating entirely new works by creating a band of second, parallel texts. "I am not a translator," she wrote to Coolidge in 1989.[23]

During a lengthy stay with Arkadii Dragomoschenko and his wife Zina Dragomoschenko in February-March of 1989, Lyn Hejinian wrote a fascinating series of daily and exquisitely-detailed notes entitled "Soviet Diary" that are now in the Hejinian Papers of the Mandeville Special Collections Library at the University of California in San Diego.[24] Hejinian's 'diary' collates dozens of pages of remarks and descriptions that were incorporated later, often verbatim, into *Oxota*. Early in "Soviet Diary," Hejinian writes: "Talk of a Russian novel. *Komnata [Komhata]: a Short Russian Novel*?" And ten pages later: "How to begin a Russian novel? One begins a Russian novel with some confusion among the characters. If the novel is about artists or intellectuals, the confusion is less formal than that among bureaucrats or generals." Two-thirds through her diarized notes, Hejinian writes: "A novel in verse—the model of *Evgeny Onegin*." The third last line simply reads: "*Oxota: A Short Russian Novel*."[25] Hejinian's poem had at least three different 'formal' beginnings:

> I began and failed and began and failed. I am certain that I had
> told Arkadii that I wanted to write a "Russian novel"; he and our
> friends found the thought terrifically amusing. Arkadii did say all
> that I attribute to him in Chapter 89, and he said it before I had
> begun. Others also made suggestions.… I carried a notebook with
> me and wrote down everything that people told me to put into my

novel. My initial (failed) attempts at beginning were in prose. It was only when it occurred to me to use Pushkin's *Evgeny Onegin* "novel in verse" form with its 14-line stanzas (which should not be considered "sonnets") that I was able to go forward.[26]

Chapter 89 of *Oxota* is largely ascribed to Dragomoschenko, and offers a wry and insightful catalogue of archetypal tropes and methods of nineteenth-century Russian novels: "Misha should be a major character in the Russian novel / Sasha, too, and Nadia / You will start with the third chapter, Arkadii said … / There must be a sentence which claims a chapter for itself." (101) Throughout *Oxota*, "Arkadii" appears as a central character who often gives vicarious authorization to the poem's observations. Although that relationship is never straightforward: "Here, said Arkadii—a letter from Chekov / One must always suspect the beginning and end, since it's / there that the writer puts his lies." (141)

Hejinian's oblique "failed attempts at beginning [*Oxota*] in prose" and her disavowal of key formal categories prompt a brief reconsideration of *Oxota*'s back cover descriptors, in which an elegant problem is made of poetic genre. *Oxota* is a "proposition," an "enactment," a "literature brimming with signification," a "restive portrait." The book seems to be a noun-in-process rather than a tangible object. It is "a stunning edifice in language," a splendid construction of syntax, rather than a serial poem or "novel in verse." In Chapter 193 Hejinian describes her figurative exemplar—the "first Russian novel"—via an assemblage of phrases that are drawn implicitly from Russian friends, and that further complicate *Oxota*'s status:

> *Evgeny Onegin* is a novel of manners (Belinsky called it
>   encyclopedic), a family saga, an autobiography, an aimless
>   plot with the symmetry of time, an impression of
>   philosophy … (211)

The ambiguity is deepened several lines later: "conflict is resolved / into vertigoes and spun on perpendiculars." (211) Aimless plots. Symmetrical time. An impression of philosophy. Categorical classification might provide a moment of compelling (and fictive) closure for readers of *Oxota*. But when balanced against the disciplined and supple constancy of stylistic shifts propelling the poem, it is more likely to "resolve into vertigoes," adrift within its own contradictory logic. An extraordinary array of proper names, places, generic temporal cues, Russian-novelistic 'stock' characters, and narrative riffs and developments appear across *Oxota*; but the book is certainly not a 'novel.' Rather, Hejinian's use of that designation works to complicate broader issues of taxonomy and nomenclature, provoking readers into giving close and skeptical attention to naming, plots, authorial propinquity and narrativity within the poem. What sorts of specific weight might attach to the word *novel* in Russian literary-cultural and popular-cultural contexts—let alone a *novel in verse*? How does Hejinian engage with the highly invested cultural regard and artistic standing that have been afforded, historically, to novelists and poets in Russia?[27] What kind of miscegenated work or hybrid is an American serialized poem that frequently quotes and collages fragments of 'Russian' texts, and calls itself a short novel? And what sorts of relations do we observe when considering poetic genre and formal choices alongside questions of cross-cultural exchange, 'appropriate' or contextually-specific poetical methodologies, and cultural 'appropriation'? Evidently, to begin with genre—a favourite starting point in almost all existent critical material about *Oxota*—is as unstable, improvisational and generative a beginning as any.

It seems fitting when tracing the origins of *Oxota* to evoke a prolific array of firsts and foundations without coming fully to rest at any of them, and to make abundant sculptures of detail, none of which are irrelevant. Each character enters fleetingly—Turgenev, Shklovsky and Russian Formalism, the Dragomoschenko family, Pushkin—before melting into another. *Say a name and someone appears, someone without the same name.*[28] Prompted by encounters with numerous kinds of alterity, *Oxota* reflects a practical turning-out of Lyn Hejinian's local writing situation, the San Franciscan Language poetry scene of the mid-1980s, toward a different, stranger experience. A literal rejection of closure seems to be taking place. "I cannot quote, I cannot get context," declares Hejinian. (185) The poem's parameters, including those we might demarcate by genre, remain mobile and permeable. Put differently, *Oxota* is calculatedly self-reflexive about its own status as an object and about circumstances, including anticipated future audiences, that might shift to renew its meanings. Perception is scrutinized as one means by which "things" gain borders: "We are among things on which reality has been slowly settling / and is then dusted away." (22) *Oxota*'s cover image embodies this motility. Its two figures cast paradoxical shadows, possibly from two different suns.[29] A temporal clue in the poem's last pages—"December 18, 1989 to February 18, 1991"—is a Brechtian gesture whose formal symmetry merely alerts readers to the presence of a constructive authorial hand. "Objects always flicker," writes Hejinian.[30] So too do genres, which gives a lie to their volatile borders. Hejinian riffs on these concepts throughout *Oxota*: "If there can be socialist realism then there can surely be / bourgeois lyricism" (15); "The exact novel genre—satirical or resonant." (165) From its enigmatic cover art to its opaque back cover descriptors, *Oxota* is "a ceaseless consequence," (164) a poem without fixed beginnings and endings.

Genre commotions within *Oxota* suggest phenomenological and illustrative problems driving the poem as a whole: how to describe matter that appears to dematerialize constantly under the combined pressures of light, language and intrinsic difference? What does it mean, after this essay's epigraph, to be "a perpetual participant of the middle," and what might this say about authorial subjectivity? Hejinian seriously doubts her ability (and right) to impact upon scenes and places that she surveys: "I didn't change it." (165) Throughout *Oxota* she continually stresses her *own* otherness in relation to Russian cultural and linguistic landscapes, hoping to turn her narrative away from "exoticization" or romanticizing of cultural difference while reflecting upon her own strangeness in a Russian context: "I meant to exoticize myself."[31]

Whether *Oxota* succeeds in its professed task of "the complete realization of one's self-unimportance" (94) is a compelling and vexed question. In 1991, Hejinian and three other American Language poets collaboratively wrote *Leningrad: American Writers in the Soviet Union* after attending the first conference on philosophy and poetics to be held in Russia since the 1920s. Hejinian's observations in that text help to illuminate *Oxota*'s study of genre, language, object-apprehension and subjective disintegration:

> But it was dizzying trying to think of the context for meaning, and therefore the context for knowledge (and I'm convinced that poetry participates in the process of knowing), among people who are simultaneously Eastern and Western without resolution, without boundaries, at least not as I feel them. The given that is a poem would be embodied formally, not thematically.... .
>
> An array of images without corresponding objects, without correlatives, wasn't alienating, although I was sad, as if grieving. The images were saturated. And my own ego was disintegrating.[32]

In situations characterized by ongoing alterity, where might a person locate the boundaries of objectivity and subjectivity; and how useful is that dualism when comprehending place-specific linkages and separations? Is *Oxota*'s poetic of "saturated" description and desire "without corresponding objects" a successful attempt to find respectful ways of *knowing* and *saying* in difficult, cross-cultural terrain?

Images without corresponding objects

Oxota teems with figures for impeded and ambiguous sight. Objects are "shattered" by brightness or relegated to "peripheral vision," producing intensified "myopia":

> And now the sun is so bright on the street that it seems to
> shatter everything—the shops in the neighborhood are
> in splinters, fragments of cars fly by, arms and legs flail
> along the sidewalk, shards of coloured stucco catapult past
> my face, blue rags flutter in my peripheral vision—my
> myopia has increased and the wind blows my hair in my
> eyes (53)

Sight is an obvious figure for perception. It implies a threshold of transaction between subject and object, cognition and space. Troubled vision is Lyn Hejinian's marker for indeterminate affiliations between language and consciousness, and a sign of authorial hesitancy in formulating links between syntax and substance: "There was no describing horizon." (185) More importantly perhaps, *Oxota*'s raft of soluble objects exhibits Hejinian's inability to steady her own constituting subject. "I was a mere observer at my vanishing post," she writes (199); and "Slowly facing and then dissolving the subjectivity with which we / think we've always been precise." (250)

Oxota's many references to hindered sight also imply allegories of cultural and textual translation. Chapter 73 concludes: "Stains of splattered cherries in the stairwell—throat / Rain—the window shut / It all originates in a mistaken sighting." (84) Readers who move between *Oxota* (1991) and Arkadii Dragomoschenko's *Description* (1990), a collection of poems translated by Hejinian while writing *Oxota*, will recognize this last line as a playful variant of a key phrase in Dragomoschenko's "Accidia." That poem is dedicated to Hejinian and carries an exegetical note taken from one of Dragomoschenko's letters to her:

> "Everything begins as an error of vision ..." Just imagine, I somehow read
> this in I don't remember which of your letters, transmuting a simple phrase
> into a ridiculous one.[33]

Hejinian's original epistolary line transforms again within the poem "Accidia" to become "first an error of vision."[34] Quixotic and self-actualizing, the phrase begins in an English letter, transmutes into Russian, returns to Hejinian in a letter she must translate, and moves back into a Russian poem that she translates again. A "simple phrase" is literally handed back and forth, born across (*trans-latus*) in numerous incarnations—English to Russian and back to English. As a result, it begins to embody not only the animating and skewed spirits of translation (language-to-language) and transliteration (Cyrillic-to-Latinate alphabets), but of difference itself. With Hejinian's inclusion of this well-travelled phrase in *Oxota*, its sources are confused further. What was the original utterance, and who can possibly remember it?

"It is a negative dialectics," writes Hejinian of translation, "since between the original and the translation the tension remains unresolved.... . The original, "the work disposed in front of 'you,'" will always demand another translation. 'No matter. Try again. Fail again. Fail better.'"[35] All translations are "mistranslations" by Hejinian's account, "tantamount to invention."[36] They are destined to miss their subject *and* object. Rather than fashioning one-to-one correspondences or finding exact solutions for antecedent texts, translations produce an assemblage of slippages—"It's not about solving anything."[37] Their "negative dialectics" are richly generative:

> I think it is important that Arkadii and I often misunderstood each other, but in ways that furthered our respective ideas. That is, I sometimes understood Arkadii to say something "better" than what he had actually said, something he liked better and took as what he had indeed said. I did the same with things he had thought I had said but which I only wished I had said after he said them.[38]

Dragomoschenko's "a sheep thriller" appears as an example in *Oxota* (183), along with the evocative "this time we are both," which begins the poem (11), reappears transformed midway through (93), and concludes the final chapter (290). That phrase was Dragomoschenko's "mistranslation" of the title of several paintings by his son Ostap (including *Oxota*'s cover image). Hejinian writes: "The proper translation should have been 'Now We Are Twins.'"[39]

For each thing Hejinian observes in a Leningrad context, there are at least two words—Russian and English—a conundrum of representation that also embraces different alphabets. "The excitation of the same experience by two grammars—it's / not impossible," *Oxota* advises. (63) Transliteration provides a further spin, since direct conveyance between languages cannot possibly preserve the sense of Russian expressions and experiences: "Do you know what we say of a clever girl? / She has her own butter in her head." (218) How to develop "a theory of a language of the description of knowledge,"[40] as Hejinian writes, if the language of inquiry is multiply capricious?

If consciousness can be experienced doubly across two languages—*this time we are both*—then the same might be said of subjectivity, via apprehension and description of phenomena:

The object of contemplation is between profiles
I remember being so
The walls multiply
The skies slide (97)

Both Hejinian and Dragomoschenko have articulated their mutual encounter with linguistic-cultural difference as a kind of vanishing that prompts re-emergence in a space "between profiles." "We have been very diligent explorers of disappearance," offered Dragomoschenko to Hejinian in a letter. "It is the task of the translator," Hejinian responded in a later essay, "to preserve this disappearance, and she must do so by sustaining the visibility of the poem—or at least of *a* poem, since a too casual reference to '*the* poem' begs the question, 'what *is* the poem?' And to answer that we must know where is it—in Russian (let's say) or in English? Can it be in both places? Is 'the poem' an immaterial entity that can be in two places at once?"[41]

What and *where* is the poem, asks Hejinian; in other words, where are its borders? Where does *Oxota: A Short Russian Novel* begin, and can it exist in two places at once? The answer is yes, *da*, in origination and translation. This time Hejinian is both: a poet who acknowledges phenomena as they appear to happen, and a person who describes, in meticulous detail, something of her own disappearance across transcultural borders. I propose the term 'trans-iteration' for the linguistic and perceptual doublings that occur throughout *Oxota*: an attempt to synthesize the local impossibilities of translation and sensible transliteration, while stressing both the mobility (*transit*) of the poem and its objects, and Hejinian's willing inability to describe (*iterate*) without generative interference at many levels. Trans-iteration also implies the collaborative *mise en scène* situating *Oxota*—prior texts, translations, epistolary exchanges, intimate friendships.

During the early 1980s, Hejinian argued for an epistemological recuperation of the terms of "literary realism." She distinguished a lively and language-oriented poetic of actual occurrences that was grounded in perceptual activity from a "realist" and representative aesthetic in which perception is "calcified" and meanings foreclosed.[42] Hejinian now prefers the terms *worldly* and *phenomenological* to *literary realism*, as subsequent essays show:

The writings of Gertrude Stein have provided me with a demonstration of the fundamentally phenomenological, and thereby mobile, character of perceptual, articulable reality. The entirety of what's available to the senses is phenomenological in character. Everything that is happening is happening phenomenologically, as something appearing, that we appear to experience; something that we sense, coming to be sensed. This by its nature involves motion. Something's happening, something's taking place, something's taking time.[43]

English critic Michael Molnar, who has lived for many years in Leningrad, observes similar preoccupations at the heart of Arkadii Dragomoschenko's poetry. He evaluates Dragomoschenko's densely phenomenological work alongside Hejinian's "Language School [rejection of] psychology in favour of perception through language," arguing that both writers "disrupt a certain type of unified discourse on which, for many, our social order seems to be founded."[44] By focusing on a perceiving subject's active *constitution* of consciousness via apprehensions of matter, objects and occurrences—"all there is," as Hejinian says, or phenomenal "reality"—such poetry implies "a new basis for subjectivity" that is at once mobile and contextually-anchored.[45]

"This is a poetry of relationships not essences," writes Molnar of Dragomoschenko's work. "The objects sketched into the schematic landscapes are mathematical symbols defined by the way they counterbalance other figures on the page, not self-sufficient concepts." (84) While forever surveying actual or 'real' perceptions and worldly encounters, Dragomoschenko refuses to organise subjective experience into finite narratives about knowledge and its attainments. Translated into English by Hejinian and Elena Balashova, a Russian-born Berkeley resident, Dragomoschenko's *Xenia* (1994) shimmers with allusions and deferrals that are set alongside precipitous links with descriptive exactitude:

> ... once again in the rippling wooden eyes
>   an accumulation of space, like air in the lungs,
>   or thought (not yet through the throat),
>   will pass through increments of consciousness,
>   azure and arched,
>   imperceptibly joined in a free spark
>   swimming on the retina in the trace of a trace,
>   in the tender ochre of heat. "You" and "I"
>   —in hollow honeycombs
>   of words,
> in one sentence—[46]

Like Hejinian, Dragomoschenko is writing about the *perceiving of perception itself*, and the ontological and linguistic frames by which we interpret experience—"you" and "I," those "hollow honeycombs of words." Things are "imperceptibly joined" in "accumulations of space," within "azure and arched" intervals of the poet's consciousness.[47] "Such an idea as 'the true nature of the world' is either unknowable or irrelevant here," observes Molnar of Dragomoschenko's poetic; "what is in question is the nature of perception, whether of language or any other phenomenon." (87)

We might fruitfully compare this with Peter Nicholls's evaluations of Lyn Hejinian's "phenomenal poetics," which are weighted similarly toward linkage and contextual inquiry rather than a *telos* of causality and completion. Reading Hejinian beside the North American objectivist poet George Oppen, Nicholls notes their comparable use of "an open syntax which constantly proposes relationships and shared experiences without formulating them absolutely." Such syntax articulates its diffidence "through ambiguity and apposition—through devices which evoke relationship without reducing it to two terms, to a subject-object dualism."[48] *Oxota: A Short Russian Novel* is perhaps Hejinian's most accomplished study of a phenomenal poetics in which relationships—between subject and object, person and culture, poem and world—are anticipated constantly without finding resolution:

> Someone tells a long anecdote binding some condition
> Its irrelevance is as inevitable as a fog at noon
> The competence of pink shadows, ungeneralized and
>   ungeneralizing—the old pause
> The city is spread by nature, fits in light
> It's light that waits, the reserves of dispersal (282)

Through vertiginous object-apprehension, subjective perception is kept in ambiguous motion or a state of "local strangeness."[49] Stemming from "a sort of unknowing,"[50] in Hejinian's terms, such a poetic of correlations and dispersals is radically different from one in which totalizing ideational schemata are sought or subjective 'authority' goes unquestioned.

Oxota turns back to the difficult subject at every juncture, as Hejinian allows her apprehension of objects to recurrently contest the borders of subjectivity and make them strange. After Louis Zukofsky, we might relate this to a mode of poetic objectification or objectivism, in which a poem formally and thematically emphasizes its own status as a "context based on a world" and an "object in process"[51] and thus inexorably calls attention to trans-active limits between a world of phenomenal happenings and a perceiving subject. This manoeuvre is performed repeatedly in *Oxota*:

> Subjects separate into themselves and then come out again
> Four padded apertures round a sour air
> The canals cannot tower
> Subjects (that is, all of us—and we speak for ourselves) have
>   the thirst of our finitude and we hoard unsatiated
>   elaborations why ...
> A man on the roof points toward a gap in the tower at the
>   corner of the inactive church
> Optical reality and uncertainty around (102)

By emphasizing the movement and separability of subjects in relation to a world of objects, Hejinian foregrounds the object status of *subjectivity* itself and bids readers to direct intense scrutiny toward its (descriptive) constitution. "Optical reality" and "uncertainty" about objectification become tropes for "apertures" in subjectivity, despite "the thirst of our finitude."

Oxota's many plays with beginnings and object-perception also suggest a poetics in which temporality is a phenomenological function of place and spatiality. The poem studies "time as it takes place in a landscape," an observation Lyn Hejinian has made of Gertrude Stein's dramatic landscapes and their temporal organization.[52] In "The Guard," a poem identified by Hejinian as her first "Russian-influenced" work, she puts it differently: "The landscape is a moment of time / that has gotten in position."[53] Hejinian argues that Stein's compositions of the "synchronous present" explore an "existential density in which present relationships and differentiations ... are the essential activity."[54] She typifies Steinian grammar as an unsolvable dialogue between spatial and temporal elements: "What occurs as time and what occurs as space, the movement, have grammatical value and can be understood as such at least incompletely— by which I mean that it is likely that the understanding remains unfinished."[55] *How could we ever finish what we never started*, asks *Oxota*. (94)

If we make a descriptive riddle of beginnings we scrutinize, most obviously, our notions of temporality. We witness time *in* and *as* its inhabitation of space and language: as a discrete series of local, spatialized events, rather than a chrono-logical progression. Across *Oxota* the perceivable borders of things and materials are Hejinian's plane of chronic significance. The poem provides an important clue: "By thing I mean object, subject, event, scene, situation, or even milieu, like the numbers 202 or 17." (220) Time is indicated principally in *Oxota* by spatial movement and change. We observe things in difference or transformation—at beginnings or edges—and thus gain a sense of *spatialized time*, or *time passing in place*:

> Not the one with not the other in the very place around the
>   stairwell or onion
> Not waiting
> The thousand tints for difference
> Hints
> Milks
> Pinks
> Procrastinations will gleam, yearning for keeping
> The arrival of disappearance—awake, in sight
> Everything was before—returning our famous *glasnost*
>   metaphor
> The light ground, what's seen in its grains
> The old grannies were out, conspiring over space (272)

"Arrivals" are flagged by the presence and absence of objects, which become cognitive negotiations of language and space. *Telos* is without teleology; hence Hejinian's recurrent use of "suspension" and "procrastination" as terms of experience. Time resides, rather, in "conspiracies of space"—a fold of linkages *between* everyday things and events: milk, light, the grannies. "A thousand" differences and links are acknowledged and embodied in words. "Tints" become "hints," then "milks," then "pinks." These progressions are spatial rather than temporal, and exemplify Jacques Derrida's formative notion of *différance*, where each sign gains meaning in a relational chain of infinite and transforming variations.[56] Borders between consciousness and substance (including poetic language itself) are prioritized as *Oxota*'s temporal markers: "No form at all— it's impossible to imagine its being seen from above / Nor sense of time." (12)

Writing about her poem "The Guard," Hejinian observes that it "throws time into space"—and this could also serve as a tidy description of *Oxota*. "In thinking about time and space," she continues, "I'm thinking about the non-isolability of objects and events in the world, our experience of them, and our experience of that experience."[57] Hejinian's frequent use of repetition in *Oxota* stresses the "non-isolability" of matter while preventing readers' appraisals of "objects and events" from stabilizing. Snatches of conversation, scatterings of cultural and political history, narrative hooks and the Leningrad equivalent of urban myths repeat in somewhat aleatory patterns, always with different spatial horizons: the city, the colonel, Misha, Gavronsky, the saturated light. True to her critique of genre, Hejinian subverts a temporal scheme of conventional novels in which things 'progress'—including and especially the novel's diverse subjects. While we recognize each character or figure of *Oxota* as it re-enters, we don't necessarily gain a coherent sense of plot. As Brian McHale notes, a "proliferation of 'minor' narrative forms" works across *Oxota* to "inoculate against master-narratives."[58] We might think of Cartesian time, or chronolinear time, as one of these disrupted major narratives.

Perhaps we could argue that Hejinian is trying to *objectify* a subject's perceptual grasp of time. She withholds 'the subject' from linear development while simultaneously placing it in a spatial carousel of local objects, influences and effects. Chapter Two offers a fine example:

> No form at all—it's impossible to imagine its being seen from
>   above
> Nor sense of time because work is only done discontinuously
> I had no sense of making an impression
> The blue shadows of footprints and a diffuse pink or green
>   light between them on the saturated park were soaking
>   the snow
> A reflection of the violent word MIR painted green was
>   mirrored warped on a stretch of deserted ice
> All my memories then as Leningrad lay like the shallow streets
>   of water banked by rubble and melting snow which
>   covered the field in a northern housing district of the city
>   across which we were often walking toward the housing
>   blocks in winter, its surface wildly broken by the light
> Something impossible to freeze, or the very lack of thing
> Dusk as it continued to be
> In the evenings particularly we made notes and took dictation
>   in anticipation of writing a short Russian novel, something
>   neither invented nor constructed but moving through
>   that time as I experienced it unable to take part
>   personally in the hunting
> Taking patience and suddenness—even sleeping in
>   preparedness, in sadness
> No paper for books
> I had lost all sense of forming expressions
> No paper at all in the south, and the butcher stuffs pieces of

greasy black beef into the women's purses
Other links exist, on other levels, between our affairs (12)

Chronos is observed as a series of repeating, situated events: nightfall, a stroll toward the housing blocks in winter, a city field "across which we were often walking." Duration becomes a medium of linkage that works "between affairs." Although living is felt to be "discontinuous," it is clear that something phenomenological, ongoing and actual ("neither invented nor constructed") is occurring: "dusk as it continued to be," for example, or the peculiar "something impossible to freeze." Things are not steady, however. Objects are "wildly broken by light" or simply absent: "the very lack of thing / … No paper at all in the south." Despite witnessing an elaborate series of related and actual occurrences, Hejinian's authorial subject struggles for integrity. *I had no sense of making an impression, I had lost all sense of forming expressions.* Juxtaposed against this continual melt is Hejinian's contradictory hunt for graphic precision: "The blue shadows of footprints and a diffuse pink or green / light between them on the saturated park were soaking / the snow." Familiar description is calibrated against strange dissolution—and both require each other to generate differential borders of apprehension. Despite avowed disintegration of authorial stability, Hejinian keeps a very careful record of matter in constant change as she takes readers on a series of flâneur-esque perambulations down streets of water, past banks of rubble, through liquefying snow. She leaves a gate open, however, on the epistemological finity of such objects and moments.

Meeting strangeness

For Lyn Hejinian, relinquishing perceptual and subjective authority in the face of Leningrad life is both an aesthetic refusal and a poetic and ethical necessity. How to say what cannot be known? Amidst "the constant change of detail," Hejinian returns often to a "complete realization of … self-unimportance," and experiences object-apprehension in Russia as "strange work" that engenders "present incorporeality."[59] Although she casts Russian scenes with uncanny acuity in *Oxota*, she simultaneously questions her acculturated (Western) interpretations of the epistemic order of things:

I didn't change it …
It is fascinating to be afraid and not to possess it …
I could only move, even naming in place …
Nobody's business, nobody's narration[60]

Hejinian is determined, even while naming in place, not to portray her Russian encounters through an anthropologizing or appropriative lens. She instead somewhat anxiously stages her own objectification and incapacity to fully comprehend or translate her engagements: "The idea of *in Russia* was dispersed into rain." (134) Such cultural strategies are not trouble-free, however, as evinced perhaps by a university discussion of *Oxota* that Hejinian facilitated in the early 1990s. "One [student] was himself a Russian émigré, and fairly recently," relates Hejinian. "He didn't like the book at all. He thought that I was exoticizing Russia. So I came back and I said that was something I very particularly wanted to avoid doing. And my attempt was to exoticize my own self at the same time, if we're going to use the word 'exoticize.' Everything ended up being strange. I didn't even know my own self, and had a very strong sense of an almost pathological disintegration of personality. I had no idea what I did, or what I wore, how I spoke. I was gone."[61]

Within *Oxota*, dis-integration and estrangement are not about the object as such. Rather, they perform a drama of impeded cognition in response to Hejinian's *own* sense of otherness. The poem's descriptive strategies are weighted toward this dilemma—as implied in "Strangeness," an essay written by Hejinian in concurrence with *Oxota* and indelibly shaped by her time in Russia as both translator and visiting guest:

> Ultimately, conditions are incomprehensible without the use of analytical conceptual structures, but an initial, essential recognition of difference—of *strangeness*—develops only with attention to single objects, while others are temporarily held in abeyance.[62]

Oxota's metonymic calibrations of exacting lyricism and cinematic dissolve embody this requirement of strangeness. Is Russia "exoticized" in the process? The question cannot be answered simply. Hejinian deftly places her own authority and authorship on trial, and foregrounds the contradictory nature of romantic-cultural intentions, by repeatedly storying her own differences in a Leningrad context: "I have my experience but do I give it / It requires a high level of consciousness along with loss of self / The authority of waking is lost." (168) Every dislocation in *Oxota*, however, is counterbalanced by a linkage or precise moment of facing that conjoins dissimilarities over a common spacing of time: "We sat in the common abstraction / Hulls of two halves of a Cuban grapefruit lay on one white plate / What does it mean? / Changing rice / ... Lifting dishes / The future—we agreed absolutely."[63]

Here we arrive at one of *Oxota*'s most appealing gambits, in which Hejinian achieves an informed evolution of two strands of modernist thinking about *poiesis* that remain greatly influential upon her poetics, while giving the poem's phenomenological milieu a distinctly post-modernist leaning. In a canny inversion of Stein's technique of a "continuous present," *Oxota* uses the machineries of descriptive repetition to estrange the borders of familiar authorial subjectivity, and to suggest a kind of continuous absence.[64] Hejinian is developing Russian Formalist Viktor Shklovsky's directives toward *defamiliarization*— "making strange the familiar" or *ostranenie*—in which things are put "out of their normal context" via poetic methods such as disordered language and odd juxtaposition, to remove them "from the automatism of perception" and thus revitalize perceptual processes themselves.[65] Simultaneously, *Oxota* casts Hejinian's experiences in Russia as the strange-made-incompletely-familial. As both disintegrating subject *and* repeatedly reconstituted object, Hejinian is continuously present *and* absent, a somewhat boundless character-in-becoming within her "short Russian novel." She is a familiar stranger among her host of players, including Arkadii Dragomoschenko and his wife Zina Dragomoschenko—whose foreign or 'strange' domestic life expands in part to accommodate Hejinian, and to whom *Oxota* is dedicated: "we sat in the common abstraction."[66]

Perhaps *Oxota*'s strange borders are not messengers of alienation but navigations of productive shocks of encounter, where differences might become sites of acknowledged commonality. In "Some Notes toward a Poetics," Hejinian suggests something akin to this:

> At points of linkage, the possibility of a figure of contradiction arises: a figure we might call by a Greek name, *xenos*. *Xenos* means "stranger" or "foreigner," but more importantly, from *xenos* two English words with what seem like opposite meanings are derived: they are *guest* and *host*.
>
> A guest/host relationship comes into existence solely in and as an occurrence, that of their meeting, an encounter, a mutual and reciprocal contextualization. The host is no host until she has met her guest, the guest is no guest until she meets her host. In Russian the word for "occurrence" captures the dynamic character of this encounter. The word for event in Russian is *sobytie*; *so* (with or co-) and *bytie* (being), "being with" or "with being" or "co-existence."[67]

Arkadii Dragomoschenko describes this ontological state as *xenia*: a similarity experienced between radically dissimilar parts, such that estrangements are not resolved or easily disciplined but allowed to remain active and mobile.[68] "Meeting balances wandering," accords Julia Kristeva. "A crossroad of two othernesses, it welcomes the foreigner without tying him down, opening the host to his visitor without committing him. A mutual recognition, the meeting owes its success to its temporary nature."[69] *Oxota* explores a series of transitory encounters with Russian language and culture under the lasting auspice of a guest/host poetic, in which recognition of shared otherness becomes an event of "being with." Returning to the poem's opening lines, we identify such reciprocal facing as a guiding premise: "But here is a small piece of the truth—I am glad to greet you." (11)

This critical *oxota*, a hunt for desired meanings, began with the question of beginnings; and more especially, the stormy question of where *Oxota* itself begins.[70] Perhaps we are closer to a reply. *Oxota: A Short Russian Novel* begins with "an initial, essential recognition of difference."[71] It employs *xenia*, the scrutinized experience of mutual strangeness, as a key formal, perceptual and narrative trope. Jean-Luc Nancy puts it this way:

> The like is not the same. I do not rediscover *myself*, nor do I recognize *myself* in the other: I experience the other's alterity, or I experience alterity in the other together with the alteration that "in me" sets my singularity outside me and infinitely delimits it. Community is that singular ontological order in which the other and the same are alike: that is to say, in the sharing of identity. The passion that is unleashed is nothing other than the passion of and for community.[72]

To begin in *otherness* permits a kind of witness or *withness*, as Lyn Hejinian discovers in *Oxota*: this time we are both. Our shared and divergent beginnings and endings might illuminate a new commonality, a love story of kinds, experienced in and as the crossing passions of pleasurable incongruity.

Notes

1. Lyn Hejinian, "Soviet Diary," 37 page unpublished manuscript, Lyn Hejinian Papers, Mandeville Special Collections Library (Archive for New Poetry), University of California, San Diego [74, 14(U), "Soviet Diary 1989"]. Citation from page 27 of manuscript. See also Lyn Hejinian, *Oxota: A Short Russian Novel* (Great Barrington, Massachusetts: The Figures, 1991), 101. Note: "(U)" in all relevant citations from the Lyn Hejinian Papers refers to a previous and now redundant distinction between "Processed" and "Unprocessed" materials in the collection. Time and distance have prevented updates to my referencing system.

2. Lyn Hejinian, "Language and 'Paradise,'" *Line: A Journal of Contemporary Writing and its Modernist Sources* 6 (Fall 1985): 88. Although the essay appears also in Hejinian's recent essay collection *The Language of Inquiry*, Hejinian omitted this sentence when revising for that text. See Lyn Hejinian, "Language and 'Paradise,'" *The Language of Inquiry* (Berkeley, California: U of California P, 2000), 59–82.

3. Lyn Hejinian, "Continuing Against Closure," *Jacket* 14 (July 2001): e-journal. Available at <http://jacketmagazine.com/14/hejinian.html>. Citation from page 2 of transcript.

4. Lyn Hejinian, letter to Carolyn Andrews dated 20th November 1984, Hejinian Papers, Mandeville [74, 1, 16].

5. Konstantin Paustovski, cited in "Ivan Bunin (1870–1953)," author profile available at <http://www.kirjasto.sci.fi/ibunin.htm>.

6. Ivan Bunin, cited in introduction to *Russian Views of Pushkin*, ed. and trans. D.J.Richards and C.R.S.Cockrell (Oxford: Willem A Meeuws, 1976), x.

7. Ivan Turgenev, "Speech on Pushkin," *Russian Views of Pushkin*, 71–72.

8. Alexander Pushkin, *Eugene Onegin: A Novel in Verse*, trans. Babette Deutsch (Harmondsworth, Middlesex: Penguin Classics, 1964), 9. Different translations use the names Evgeny Onegin or Evgenii Onegin.

9. Fyodor Dostoevsky, "Pushkin," *Russian Views of Pushkin*, 77.

10. Pushkin, *Eugeny Onegin*, 20.

11. Introduction to Charles Johnston's "Penguin Classics" translation of *Eugene Onegin*, cited in Marjorie Perloff, "How Russian Is It: Lyn Hejinian's *Oxota*," *Poetry On & Off the Page: Essays for Emergent Occasions* (Evanston and Illinois: Northwestern UP, 1998), 224.

12. Hejinian, *Oxota*, 123.

13. Lyn Hejinian, "A Local Strangeness: An Interview with Lyn Hejinian," conducted by Larry McCaffery and Brian McHale, *Some Other Frequency: Interviews with Innovative American Authors*, ed. Larry McCaffery (Philadelphia: U of Pennsylvania P, 1996), 128–129.

14. Pushkin, *Eugene Onegin*, 215. The 'missing' chapter later was published separately as "Excerpts from Onegin's Travels" with an explanatory note by Pushkin.

15. Lyn Hejinian, "On Russia: Why Russia Affected Me So Deeply and What is Going On There in Literature," 5 page unpublished manuscript, Hejinian Papers, Mandeville [74, 13(U), "1983—notes for talk on Russia at Tassajara Bakery"], 3.

16. Hejinian, "On Russia," 3.

17. Jim Kates, ed., *In the Grip of Strange Thoughts: Russian Poetry in a New Era* (Newcastle Upon Tyne: Zephyr, 1999), 265.

18. Kates, *In the Grip of Strange Thoughts*, 265.

19. Hejinian identifies "signs of a new cultural era" in a letter to Charles Bernstein dated 14th February 1987, Hejinian Papers, Mandeville [74, 2(U), "Charles Bernstein"]. In the eventual "5+5 project" of September 1990, Clark Coolidge, Kit Robinson, Jean Day, Michael Palmer and Lyn Hejinian translated works by Aleksei Parshchikov, Nadezhda Kondakova, Ilya Kutik, Ivan Zhdanov and Arkadii Dragomoschenko. See Hejinian Papers, Mandeville [74, 3(U), "5+5 project"].

20. Lyn Hejinian, letter to Clark Coolidge dated 15th December 1983, Hejinian Papers, Mandeville [74, 2, 21].

21. Lyn Hejinian, letter to Carolyn Andrews dated 6th May 1984, Hejinian Papers, Mandeville [74, 1, 16].

22. Lyn Hejinian, letter to Fanny Howe dated 12th April 1984, Hejinian Papers, Mandeville [74, 4, "Fanny Howe 1978–1984"].

23. Lyn Hejinian, letter to Clark Coolidge dated 29th March 1989, Hejinian Papers, Mandeville [74, 3(U), "Clark Coolidge"]. Hejinian's translations of Dragomoschenko's poetry include Arkadii Dragomoschenko, *Description*, trans. Lyn Hejinian and Elena Balashova (Los Angeles: Sun & Moon, 1990); Arkadii Dragomoschenko, *Xenia*, trans. Lyn Hejinian and Elena Balashova (Los Angeles: Sun & Moon, 1994); and *Phosphor* (in process). Excerpts appear in "From Phosphor," *Postmodern Culture* 3:2 (1993): e-journal. Available at <http://muse.jhu.edu/journals/postmodern_culture/v003/3.2dragomos.html>.

24. "The Lyn Hejinian Papers," (MS0074), Mandeville Special Collections Library (Archive for New Poetry), University of California, San Diego.

25. Hejinian "Soviet Diary," 3, 13, 19 and 28.

26. Lyn Hejinian, letter to the author dated 4th November 2001.

27. See for example Kirill Kovaldzhi, "The 'New Wave' at the End of an Era," *Crossing Centuries: The New Generation in Russian Poetry*, ed. John High et al. (Jersey City, New Jersey: Talisman House, 2000), 165. Kovaldzhi cites Evtushenko: "The poet in Russia is more than a poet." Similar observations appear in Hejinian's first written responses to Russia: "For these writers a decision like mine, to devote one's entire life to poetry, is serious in a way that we can't even imagine." Hejinian, "On Russia," 4.

28. Hejinian, *Oxota*, 292.

29. The painting is by Ostap Dragomoschenko, who is Arkadii Dragomoschenko's son.

30. Lyn Hejinian, "Redo," *The Cold of Poetry* (Los Angeles: Sun & Moon, 1994), 93.

31. Lyn Hejinian, interview with the author, 3rd August 1998.

32. Michael Davidson, Lyn Hejinian, Ron Silliman and Barrett Watten, *Leningrad: American Writers in the Soviet Union* (San Francisco: Mercury House, 1991), 47 and 104.

33. Dragomoschenko, "Accidia," *Description*, 89.

34. Dragomoschenko, "Accidia," *Description*, 85.

35. Lyn Hejinian, "Forms in Alterity: On Translation," *Language of Inquiry*, 305. Hejinian is citing first from a letter by Arkadii Dragomoschenko and secondly from a play by Samuel Beckett.

36. Hejinian, "A Local Strangeness," 134.

37. Hejinian, interview with author, 3rd August 1998.

38. Hejinian, letter to author, 4th November 2001.

39. Hejinian, letter to author, 4th November 2001. Poet Clark Coolidge has used the same phrase for a book title; while Hejinian's husband Larry Ochs and the ROVA quartet have made a CD named "This Time We Are Both" that was recorded live in the U.S.S.R. "We three agreed that the confusion caused by our all using this notably odd phrase was delightful and appropriate," writes Hejinian in her letter.

40. Lyn Hejinian, "The Poetics of Exploration," audio interview conducted by Charles Bernstein for *LINEbreak* programme, Electronic Poetry Centre, 1996. Available at <http://wings.buffalo.edu/epc/linebreak/programs/hejinian>. Citation from page 1 of transcript.

41. Hejinian, "Forms in Alterity," *Language of Inquiry*, 304. Dragomoschenko's letter, dating from 13th March 1995, is included in Hejinian's essay.

42. Lyn Hejinian, unpublished draft notes on "American Literary Realism," Hejinian Papers, Mandeville [74, 11(U), "American Literary Realism 1981 talk at New Langton"]. Hejinian's essay "Language and Realism" is an excellent exemplar of Hejinian's inquiries into a "perceptual" realism (*Language of Inquiry*, 83–105).

43. Lyn Hejinian, "Lyn Hejinian / Gertrude Stein," from "9 Contemporary Poets Read Themselves Through Modernism" Lecture Series, 12 October 2000. Sound recording available online at <http://writing.upenn.edu/%7Ewh/9poets.html >. Citation from page 2 of transcript.

44. Michael Molnar, "The Vagaries of Description: the Poetry of Arkadii Dragomoschenko," *Essays in Poetics* 14.1 (1989): 78.

45. Molnar, "Vagaries of Description," 78 and 87; "reality is all there is" cited from Lyn Hejinian, Preface to "Thought Is the Bride of What Thinking," *Language of Inquiry*, 8.

46. Dragomoschenko, *Xenia*, 111–112.

47. My close readings of Dragomoschenko's poetry are subject, of course, to the immeasurable drifts of translation. Critics Michael Molnar and Jacob Edmond read Dragomoschenko's poetry in its 'original' Russian state, which lends a different and advantageous perspective. See

for example Molnar, "Vagaries of Description," 79–85; and Jacob Edmond, "Locating Global Resistance: The Landscape Poetics of Arkadii Dragomoschenko, Lyn Hejinian and Yang Lian," *AUMLA: Journal of the Australasian Universities Language & Literature Association* 101 (2004): 71–98.

48. Peter Nicholls, "Phenomenal Poetics: Reading Lyn Hejinian," *The Mechanics of the Mirage: Postwar American Poetry*, eds. Michel Delville and Christine Pagnoulle (Liège: Université de Liège, 2000), 246.

49. Hejinian, "A Local Strangeness," 128.

50. Hejinian, "Introduction," *Language of Inquiry*, 2.

51. Louis Zukofsky, "An Objective," *Prepositions: the Collected Critical Essays of Louis Zukofsky*, 2nd edition (Berkeley, California: U of California P, 1981), 15.

52. Lyn Hejinian, "Grammar and Landscape" in "Two Stein Talks," *Language of Inquiry*, 112.

53. Hejinian, "The Guard," *The Cold of Poetry*, 11. Although Hejinian began "The Guard" in 1982 before travelling to the U.S.S.R., most of the poem was completed following her initial visits to Leningrad. Fragments of Dragomoschenko's letters are incorporated into final versions of the poem.

54. Hejinian, "Grammar and Landscape" in "Two Stein Talks," *Language of Inquiry*, 116.

55. Hejinian, "Grammar and Landscape" in "Two Stein Talks," *Language of Inquiry*, 109.

56. See for example Jacques Derrida, "Structure, Sign and Play in the Discourse of the Human Sciences," *Modern Criticism and Theory: A Reader*, ed. David Lodge (London and New York: Longman, 1988), 122.

57. Hejinian, "Language and 'Paradise,'" *Line*, 87. The first section of this passage does not appear in Hejinian's revised version of "Language and 'Paradise'" for *The Language of Inquiry* (67).

58. Brian McHale, "Telling Stories Again: On the Replenishment of Narrative in the Postmodernist Long Poem," *Yearbook of English Studies* 30 (2000), 261–262.

59. Hejinian, *Oxota*, 161, 94, 65 and 266.

60. Hejinian, *Oxota*, 165, 168 and 205.

61. Hejinian, interview with author, 3rd August 1998.

62. Lyn Hejinian, "Strangeness," *Language of Inquiry*, 157; my emphasis.

63. Hejinian, *Oxota*, 136. The phrase "common spacing of time" is cited from Jean-Luc Nancy, "Finite History," *The States of "Theory": History, Art and Critical Discourse*, ed. David Carroll (New York: Columbia UP, 1990), 157.

64. For Gertrude Stein's famed technique of creating a "continuous present" see "Composition as Explanation" (1926) in *What Are Masterpieces*, ed. Robert Haas (New York: Pitman Publishing Corporation, 1970), 31–34.

65. Viktor Shklovsky, "Art as Technique," *Modern Criticism and Theory: A Reader*, ed. David Lodge (London and New York: Longman, 1988), 20–21 and 24–27.

66. Hejinian, *Oxota*, 136. This line is from Chapter 121 of the poem entitled "Zina Calls Me Her Sister."

67. Lyn Hejinian, "Some Notes toward a Poetics," *American Women Poets in the 21st Century*, eds. Claudia Rankine and Juliana Spahr (Middletown, Connecticut: Wesleyan UP, 2002), 235.

68. In her "Soviet Diary" at pages 8–9, Hejinian records these fascinating observations: "I ask Arkadii about the word Xenia, and write, as if from dictation, what he says: the title is derived from many meanings of the word—its Greek stem—many roots as in gift, the short poem (shortness and longness are completely phenomenological entities), the difference in similarity (site, from a vocabulary of foreign words—seeds and fruits which are distinguished from other seeds and fruits of the same plant, their colour, form, size, and other qualities), growing up at least in the meanings of each other and at the same time marriage: 'the intersection swirls when

the flower of one plant is swirled by the pollen of the flowers of another plant of the same species. Cross pollination, and the power of unachieved meanings.['] And so forth."

69. Julia Kristeva, *Strangers to Ourselves*, trans. Leon S. Roudiez (New York: Columbia UP, 1991), 11.

70. The Russian word *oxota* has two principal connotations, 'hunt' and 'desire.'

71. Hejinian, "Strangeness," *Language of Inquiry*, 157.

72. Jean-Luc Nancy, *The Inoperative Community*, ed. Peter Connor, trans. Connor et al. (Minneapolis and London: U of Minnesota P, 1991), 33–34.

Hejinian's Ethics
Barrett Watten

Poetic language is [...] a language of improvisation and intention. The intention provides the field for inquiry and improvisation is the means for inquiry. Or, to phrase it another way, the act of writing is a process of improvisation within a framework (form) of intention.

—Lyn Hejinian, *The Language of Inquiry*[1]

An anecdote is perhaps the best way to begin to account for a complex and evolving relationship. I remember, from the period in which Lyn Hejinian and I began working collaboratively on *Poetics Journal* in 1981, a moment of decision.[2] We agreed that Lyn would write a review of Paul Mariani's biography of Williams—it seemed the right thing to do—and she was stuck for a title. "I'm thinking of 'An American Opener,' but I don't know if I can get away with it." "Why," I said. "You know, everyone will think I'm talking about a *can opener*, an Ameri*can* Opener." And the essay appeared with that title. What is the relation between that "can opener" to American openness, in Lyn's work? It is an irreducible particular, a clunky object of material life that does not quite intersect a capacious horizon of imagined totality. In terms of grammar and semantics, as well, it is unclear whether the relation between the can opener and openness is one of parallelism or opposition. It is frame conflicts such as these that excite Lyn, so that "getting away with it" is all to the point. This is an effect I see everywhere in her work: a device of "partial local coherence" that produces a dissonant chord of unreconciled frame conflict and a dynamics of prospective irresolution.[3]

[MORAL: WE ARE THOSE WHO LOVE TO BE ASTONISHED.]

A Border Comedy, the fourth of Hejinian's book-length prose poems to appear, is what one might call a nonnarrative "exterior monologue" founded on the global use of partial local coherences.[4] The poem shifts frames often from line to line, but just as often sets off provisional zones of argument that either are enclosed or radically undermined in the continuous pressure of statement. Some of these provisional zones of argument are intended as instructions to the reader (or even cues to the philosophical critic) on how best to process the unfolding sequence. These instructions, notes left on a refrigerator door for the agreeable (or skeptical) reader, are often dismantled as well, while the reader is stirred by a strange and uncanny energy emitted from the gaps revealed in the poem's frame shifts, a comedic effect that is guaranteed to be literary (cf. *The Psychopathology of Everyday Life*) but that produces a life-affirming energy, a desire to continue nonetheless. Interpretive delirium is followed by provisional investment in orienting interpretants; once hooked, the reader is set up for a *tour de force*, an education in the philosophical use of that which does not necessarily follow:

> We couldn't do anything today
> I fell asleep in a rubber suit
> You bathed in sugar and were hospitalized for shock
> Allegories are told with a purpose whose possibility is lost
> Until a potato-eater appears and eats potatoes
> In the hotel just across the border from the concert hall
> In a feather bed which holds the sweat
> The complement to up is down, to between is between
> Connections can help us to slip in (*BC*, 17)

The parallelism/opposition of the lines defers the discord of their divergent frames to the next cognitive level, where the last two lines meet in constructing an interpretant. A kind of conceptual stichomachia (verse fighting) leads the reader into a scene of decision, in which a succession of binary oppositions is confronted with an anticipated outcome as identical to the unfolding form of poem—as that which *will have been* but is yet *to come*.

[MORAL: ANYTHING CAN ENTER THE POEM, BUT ONCE THERE IT MUST BE TRANSFORMED.]

Such passages of continual frame shifts are only an opening gambit in a carefully staged argument in which relations between intentionality and interpretation construct not an image of the anarchy of production but an argument of value and ethical relation. The project of an ethics arising in partial intentionality is telegraphed in so many words:

> And actually, it's a lot of fun
> Related to experience
> And its correlate, the ability to follow a story

Of travelers whose only homeland was an ethics
They arrived and departed from history untotalled
The landscape was postcard perfect (*BC*, 19)

Here, as in many such zones of local coherence, a decision is necessary. Narrative is associated with "an ethics" brought to us by travelers from somewhere outside of our totalized history, if only we could follow them. On the other hand, what they present could be as pretty an illusion as a postcard, in which case we are left only with a yearning for ideality. Yet the poet has asserted that everything is under control, that this has been anticipated:

And I can see that in these narrative distortions false inevitabilities appear
Ordinary motifs, like patterns in linoleum which we discern and know to
    have no meaning but which seem nonetheless to assert themselves as if they
    were determinate, necessitated, and harbingers of moral significance
And meaning
Design (perhaps by definition) seems to guarantee outcome
Better yet
Each outcome is intermediary—the very purpose of the pattern is to be
    reassuring (*BC*, 14–15)

What is the moral significance of a sequence of patterns in linoleum tile? The poet claims that it is not the motifs themselves but their pattern that is purposive, edifying. But what if a pattern has not yet emerged, and we are left with a decision about the assertion itself? As the poem suspends the outcome of this decision, it will be gradually revealed in its unfolding, in which the moment of evaluation becomes equally a principle of continuity.

But this attention to ethics doubles my enthusiasm
By admitting willfulness (with its many digressions)
And where strength isn't enough, one has to resort to invention (*BC*, 24–25)

[MORAL: AN EXAMPLE IS THE BEST PRECEPT IF WE DO NOT YET
KNOW WHAT IT MEANS.]

One could continue to read Hejinian's work at these local moments of chiasmus, as may be found everywhere in *A Border Comedy*, and build larger arguments about the ethical relation of incongruity to pattern, and their dialectical resolution in meaning, as the poet's intention to value. This is not the politics of readerly construction that has been overturned as an inadequate account of the poetics of the Language School; rather, Hejinian intends a genuine "border comedy" that is enacted in moments of self-undoing in another (which could be simply the co-presence of the reader). To be fair, there has been a stepwise progression away from those early formulas: in Hejinian's work, this is evident in a series of essays, from the optimism of "The Rejection of Closure" as offering a formal analogy for value (open works are better than closed ones) to the more reflexive moments of "The Person" and "La Faustienne," where open form is implicated in processes of objectification and self-undoing—especially in the figure of Scheherazade, who after each of the thousand and one nights could be put to death, as a figure for narration itself.[5] The materiality of signification in the work, as opposed to the theory, of the Language School has always entailed an ethics of total form, a relation misunderstood when dicta such as "the reader is empowered" or "language is material" are taken as immanent claims to value. Such claims may in fact be no better than philosophical anecdotes, internalized frames distributed throughout the more capacious argument; one of the pleasures of the many incursions of theory (or philosophy or ethics) in *A Border Comedy* is the way in which they are immediately reduced, at points of local argument, to hinges of narrative. If simple assertions of material signification and readerly construction are circular as arguments of value, we must look for a more specific account of the *motivation* of the work's constructedness—of the self-positing (or -negating) intentions of the ubiquitous frame conflicts that are everywhere the work's principle of continuity. But circularity is encountered here as well, as the work is composed entirely of a series of frame conflicts: they are the material guarantee of its openness of construction. We will need an exterior as well as immanent approach to this writing to explain the value of its formal strategies.

You and I will never have the difference right
Between visibility and its moral
Our suspicions are too reasonable
But they make good excuses—sporadic boundaries—the difference between us
On the scale of poetry, the pan containing 'I' must never dip lower than the
    pan containing 'not-I'
It's true [...]
Can that be ethical? (*BC*, 45)

[MORAL: REDUNDANCY OF LANGUAGE MEANS WE OUGHT TO LOOK
ELSEWHERE FOR AN ARGUMENT OF VALUE.]

We might also approach a work such as *A Border Comedy* from the "outside" in terms of genre (what kind of work it is; how it relates to works that are like or unlike it) rather than author and form (how self-focusing intentionality is built up in the work). *A Border Comedy* is a singular example of genre, a unique masterwork but also centerpiece of a series of Hejinian's "open" prose poems from *My Life* through *The Cell* and *Oxota: A Short Russian Novel* (a series that continues through *The Book of a Thousand Eyes*).[6] Each is a generic hybrid: *My Life*, still in process, is an autobiographical poem using a stepwise construction first worked out in Ron Silliman's book-length poems *Ketjak*, *Tjanting*, and *The Alphabet*, and which recalls as well the discontinuous narration of Viktor Shklovsky's three autobiographies.[7] *The Cell* is accurately described as a "lyric diary" but one focused on relations of language rather than of person, while *Oxota* draws from the form of Pushkin's verse novella *Evgeny Onegin* and investigates dynamics between persons and cultures in a form that depends on and disrupts the continuities of narration. *A Border Comedy* synthesizes the concerns of the latter two works as it defers the overtly autobiographical horizon of *My Life*. Comprised of fifteen books of roughly the same length, it constructs a border between discontinuity and sequence that unites features of lyric atemporality and narrative form. Rather than being composed as a discrete series of lyric units, *A Border Comedy* is nonlinear in the sense that all of its books were written simultaneously, not one after the other. In the poem itself, the poet describes this process of construction in a moment of *metalepsis* (an internal reference to the total form of the poem, used as a recurring orientation device):

> That's why I've kept this writing of fifteen books unfinished
> Fifteen underway
> I move from one to the next
> In the course of many days adding every day
> A few lines to a book
> Each of which takes a long time and considerable thought
> And that passage of time facilitates forgetting
> Then forgetting makes what's been written unfamiliar
> As if some other writer had been writing
> And each of my returns to each of the books is prompted
> To immediates in a sudden present (*BC*, 151)

An anti-narrative logic of forgetting, a discontinuity of personal identity, is the principle of continuity here. Later, the person may be recuperated at the level of the total form—but that is what we are reading to find out. The person of the poem is not given but constructed.

QUESTION: It is not clear what "total form" means here, since the fifteen sections are simultaneous. Could the whole text be longer or shorter, or does it have to be exactly the length as "planned"? What is the ethics of its particular length vis-à-vis the directive to "plan ahead"?[8]

ANSWER: The anticipated total form of fifteen sections is importantly deferred yet always present in the work's construction. The arbitrariness of the pregiven length is ethical in a way that, to begin with, might seem to override or challenge the aesthetic necessity of a form that is unified with the material it conveys. From the standpoint of the reader, and in terms of both aesthetic appreciation and formal "unity," as once was said, the work could certainly be shorter—but certainly no longer. There is not a little self-assertion in an ethical horizon that initially seems to override any aesthetic realization, in the sense of what kind of anticipation is imagined toward the poem's completion. But even so, the author acknowledges (if it is not possible for her to determine in advance) the necessity for the confirmation of a reading, even one a bit impatient with the work's anticipated unity. This trade-off between the ethical and the aesthetic is implicit in the genre of the long poem, in its anticipation of structural completeness as identical to the work's vision of comprehensiveness, from Homer to *Ulysses* to Ron Silliman's *The Alphabet* and Bruce Andrews's *Lip Service*. It is the disparity between anticipation and total form that becomes the site for the ethical—in that we do not yet know how the work will turn out, as it is being written, even as the status of our not knowing gives a precise value to the realized outcome.

[MORAL: PLAN AHEAD.]

There is a complex genealogy, from American modernism to the present, of the hybrid forms Hejinian works in, though they are typically discussed as part of (or identical to) the author's *oeuvre*, with little said about their historical development or relations between them. For the Russian Formalists, literary works exist against a background of generic conventions (though they had in mind conventional genres rather than a series of idiosyncratic ones); in this sense, the series of formally innovative works that leads to *A Border Comedy* is an equally valid basis for discerning its ethical stakes as any elucidation of intentional claims to value. The crucial modernist examples for such a register of Hejinian's formal values are Gertrude Stein's *The Making of Americans*, for its process of "beginning again and again," and Louis Zukofsky's *"A,"* for its horizon of "The words are my life."[9] Both examples lead to the obdurate materiality of *A Border Comedy*'s form, even as the differences between members of the series are equally crucial.[10] We may compare Stein's notion of process, which is temporal and involves shifts in affective cathexis in persons and pronouns, with Hejinian's:

> My ambition being to unite the process of transformation with that of
>   interpretation
> And if that's taken as didacticism
> Then what have you learned from this poem
> And what have I learned as I'm writing it
> Through a sequence of willed culminations, in the culmination of will
> Whispering for disturbance
> Of my consciousness (the best partition)
> Which is all that lies between what I did yesterday and what I'll do next
>   (*BC*, 73)

Nothing is further from Stein's notion of a "continuous present" than "a sequence of willed culminations," which is not identical to the narrative unfolding but rather a principle of discontinuity in default to the reader, whose presence is required to complete the transformative act. Hejinian is not "beginning again and again" but "not ending again and again." Similarly, language in *A Border Comedy* cannot be said to demonstrate "the words are my life" in that they present a demand for mediation by another. In the constructed horizon of Zukofsky's work, everything adds up to what it *will have been*—the author as identical to the strictures of form; the unfolding horizon of the personal epic as increasingly identical to its opacity of reference and elliptical continuity. Key moments in the transition in *"A"* from constructed text to authorial unity occur, as is well known, in *"A"*–9, which rewrites the poem's Marxist-Hegelian teleology as Spinozist immanence, and in *"A"*–12, which formally attempts to equate the work's textuality with the detritus of lived experience. Zukofsky's attempt to "do away with epistemology" left words to present the truth of their own evidence in a way that guaranteed—because it could not be contradicted—the truthfulness of the life. In Hejinian's work, there is a movement outward, of self-qualification and skeptical inquiry—that may have begun with an assertion of identity in *My Life* but that is continually returned to as a moment of decision in which the very nature of literariness is placed in question. There is, as there ought to be, a radical reversal of polarity in the authorial construction in Hejinian's work: we move from author through form to a scene of decision that defers to another.

QUESTION: How is a "'sequence of willed culminations' which is not identical to the narrative unfolding but rather a principle of discontinuity in default to the reader, whose presence is required to complete the transformative act" different from "the reader is empowered"?

ANSWER: Hejinian is recognizing the place of the reader as encoded into the construction of the text, not just giving over to whatever the reader would make of it. Ethically, she cannot anticipate what any reader would make of her text in an entirely unrestricted form of reading, and so is not content simply with the gesture of openness. Rather, the possibility of the reader is anticipated as a part of the structure, even if the final horizon of that reading cannot be determined in advance. The anticipation breaks off midway, as it were. That anticipation seems to be one way of accounting for the continuously revisionist impulse in the work's construction.[11]

[MORAL: WE MAY NOT "DO AWAY WITH EPISTEMOLOGY."]

Relations to contemporary writers working in similar forms are crucial as well in the genealogy of *A Border Comedy*. A series of postmodern long poems that invert the authorial immanence of modernism toward a constructivist ethics provides a background for the argument of form in Hejinian's work, beginning with Clark Coolidge's *The Maintains* and Ron Silliman's *Ketjak* and followed by many others.[12] As well, a related series of works that interpret narrative toward a more cultural register of poetics has been important in the development of Hejinian's work, as exemplified by Leslie Scalapino's *Defoe* and Carla Harryman's *Gardener of Stars* and *Adorno's Noise*.[13] These relations, under the aspect of genre, lead to a career-long challenging of the boundaries of the author in the writing of a number of collaborative works, including work with Harryman in *The Wide Road*; Scalapino in *Sight*; and multiple collaborators in *Leningrad* and *The Grand Piano*.[14] A theory of multiauthorship is necessary for any account of Hejinian's ethics; at many crucial points, her work has invited the participation of another writer into the understanding of its own self-making.

QUESTION: How would a theory of multiauthorship treat collaboration at the site of production differently from "collaboration" at the site of reception? I would think it would need to. Which are you referring to when you say that Hejinian's work "invites the participation of another in its understanding of its own self-making"?

ANSWER: I am claiming that Hejinian is influenced by her experience of multiauthorship; what she learned from it (in improvisation) is one of the aspects of her work's construction. There are particular idioms that enable as well as follow from collaborative work. This seems more precise than simply "the reader makes meaning," because in collaboration both are sited toward a mutual outcome. And there has to be a sense that that outcome occurs within the limits of anticipation—not the mere assumption of anti-authoritarian openness, where the claim to being democratic often means the work can be anything I want it to be. Rather, the work's elaboration of its own making ethically includes the co-presence of others. Jackson Mac Low's work is also structured on the co-presence of others, but in a more "collective" sense that takes into account the dynamics of group processes of decision making.

[MORAL: A FRIEND IS A PHILOSOPHICAL CONSTRUCT.]

I want to extend this account of Hejinian's literary genealogy in two related directions. The first is to point out the ways that the Russian Formalist theory of literary evolution (not only its key insights into defamiliarization and the materiality of the sign) is crucial for understanding Hejinian's difference from modernist authorship, as well as for her proximity to her peers. The Formalists, it should be remembered, saw literary works as constructed in terms of "the warehouse of cultural materials"; formal analysis of prose leads immediately to the notion of motifs held in common in a culture at large, as these may concretize or undermine stability of genre at a particular historical moment.[15] *A Border Comedy* is suffused with an understanding of narrative as a mode of the culture at large, as evident in the many disjunct "narratemes" placed in counterpoint to its developing argument:

AESOP (*begins*): In the days of old, when horses spoke Greek and Latin and
    asses made syllogisms, there happened an encounter on the road
Then a burst of rain, a moment of invention, shelter was found in a cave,
    conversation, and in time the experience was passed along—as the

experience of the experience—exchanged
There's nothing more to explain
The story is that the listener understood one thing, relayed it, it was
    understood as something else, but everything worked out (*BC*, 70–71)

Narrative, not existential phenomenology, is the privileged means for think-
ing through an ethics of alterity: narratives are co-produced by narrator and
narratee; they come from the culture at large and will return there, but with
a difference marked by "there's nothing more to explain," a self-consciousness
not reducible to telling stories but identified with their construction. Here,
another component of the genealogy of *A Border Comedy* is anticipated by the
Formalists' concept of the "knight's move," where the succession of literary
meaning is never a matter of direct transmission but always cycles back into the
matrix of culture in "the canonization of peripheral forms," what the Formalists
saw as the nonliterary series.

QUESTION: Does the construction of *A Border Comedy* out of disjunct "nar-
ratemes" open the work to culture as follows: 1) narrative is one of the
main components in the "warehouse of cultural materials"; 2) *A Border
Comedy* is constructed from bits of narrative qua narrative; and therefore,
3) *A Border Comedy* is open to culture, i.e., the "nonliterary series"?

ANSWER: Narrative as much as collaboration provides a register for the
other—others' lives, destinies, fates, conditions are brought into the
making of the poem (within its own conditions, which are not necessar-
ily narrative). The border between reflexive nonnarration and narratives
(which are both imported, thus affirmed; and decontextualized, and so
problematized) is a major site for the active thinking and construction of
the poem. The principle of continuity in the poem likewise has to do with
the narrative/reflexive divide. Narrative frame shifts offer a "kick" of dis-
placement and othering that engenders consciousness as a gap between
elements and thus as constituting the work's unfolding. Otherness as a
site for negativity becomes a constructive device.

[MORAL: ACT AS THOUGH YOUR INNERMOST THOUGHTS
WERE OF CONCERN TO EVERYONE, AND VICE VERSA.]

We should consider as well the relation of Hejinian's work to American
composed and improvised musics, and their influence on the construction of

open forms. There is a persistent and willful pursuit of the ethical implications of cultural dissonance, questions of cultural specificity, translation, and misunderstanding, in Hejinian's work that refers to a tradition of American composers like Harry Partch, Lou Harrison, and Alan Hovanness, who are likewise interested in preserving the awkwardness and overlapping implications of the colliding motifs of multiple cultures at variance. In listening to Harrison's appropriation of Balinese *gamelan*, for instance, one hears an effect similar to the frame shifts of Hejinian's work in her incorporation, particularly, of Russian motifs. The consequences of such cultural relativism are central to *A Border Comedy*, as exemplified in its meditation on xenophobia, which foregrounds (even as it pokes fun at) the work's thematization of "otherness":

Sometimes it just happens that one finds oneself alone and out of character
Stendhal on xenophobia: You just start feeling it [...]
Velimir Khlebnikov on xenophobia: It's a single word, and now it has raised
    its animal head to look at me but its mouth is sealed, the word is muzzled
Aristotle on xenophobia: In gatherings of men on public margins, there are
    some who are known as obsequious and others as churlish, and neither can
    be said to debase foreigners less than the other [...]
Sigmund Freud on xenophobia: I pondered whether or not I should spend the
    night in Cologne—the thought of doing so was favored by a feeling of piety,
    for according to family tradition, my ancestors were once expelled from this
    city (*BC*, 128)

Drawing materials from different cultural matrixes aligns xenophobia with the impossibility of pure self-consciousness; in a cultural inflection of the uncanny, the gaps in transmission between registers of otherness is seen as a (strange and estranging) principle of continuity. It is neither the radical contingency of the other nor a stabilized hybridity that one hears; the gap between cultures is not simply addressed as content or quoted as intertext but is a principle of construction predicated on a moment of nonidentity. From the exoticism of quoted registers of cultural difference to the constructivist ethics of improvised music is a short but necessary step: Lou Harrison's self-conscious use of East Asian motifs leads to the syncretism of John Zorn's *East Asian Bar Bands* (which includes a poem by Hejinian translated into Vietnamese). Even more present for Hejinian's sense of improvisation is the free radicalism of black avant-garde tradition, from Thelonious Monk to Anthony Braxton, which have provided cultural and formal models for her (and the Rova Saxophone Quartet) from the 1970s to the present. Hejinian chronicles in detail the formative influences of the black avant-garde on San Francisco improvisation in "Taking to the Music," her contribution to *Grand Piano* 7.[16] There are many registers of improvised music's ethics of alterity in the construction of Hejinian's work: the ethical ideal of co-production, as listening; the structuring of pre-given materials, a repertoire of cultural knowledge, in the immediate present; and the alternation of "carrier waves" of shared convention leading to bright moments of revelatory content. Jazz artists who work in improvisatory frameworks must learn the mastery of each: listening to each other; referring to and transposing motifs; and cooperating toward the result. Hejinian's work at the borders of cultural contact in *Oxota* is exemplary of this effect: cross-cultural dissonance is preserved as an aesthetic strategy, provoking a decisive encounter between the knowledge one brings to a cultural text and the knowledge one gains from it—a fluid encounter with imagined alterity derived directly from improvised musics.

[MORAL: THE STATUS OF THE UNCONSCIOUS IS HISTORICAL.]

In locating registers of interpersonal exchange and cultural openness in Hejinian's work, I do not mean simply to reproduce a polarized account of the ethical in terms such as those suggested by Charles Altieri, who sees a basic contradiction between "ideals of opening ourselves to otherness and those calling for perfectionist versions of the self."[17] Clearly, there are many ways in which the construction of *A Border Comedy* is a profoundly self-focusing act where value is recuperated, precisely at the level of the overall form of the poem, as a mastery of competing intentional states. However, it is also true, as Altieri suspects, that the formal construction of Hejinian's work does not easily align with what he calls an "expressivist" ethics, in which purposive agency maintains its positivity "as a specific mode of dynamic intentionality inseparable from how we inhabit the sentences we speak."[18] For Altieri, self (as opposed to subjectivity) is the positivity of intentional states one discerns at the level of language, particularly in such irreducible markers of temporal and spatial deixis as *now* and *this* (in contrast to the shifting subjectivity of the pronoun *I*, perhaps). As much of the work of the Language School has been written in terms drawn from exactly such insight, the fit between Altieri's language-centered ethics and his readings of language-centered writers is not fortuitous. At the same time, there is a problem when the positivity of such a reading can only yield overly complex, often arbitrary or speculative, accounts of intentional states as they are built up in a practice of close reading. The pay-off, of course, is great for the philosophical critic, whose joy at the nuances of self-consciousness in language-centered writing must be great.[19] But philosophy in the poem is finally one discourse among many, and the gap between languages and discourses is fundamental to its construction as well.

QUESTION: What is the negativity of self-consciousness, referred to above? How is it opposed to the "positivity" of Altieri's reading?

ANSWER: In *A Border Comedy*, the negativity of self-consciousness occurs often in the gaps between positive elements, which also may align with repressed content (the unrepresentable that gives the work energy and purpose, in a latent state). This is thematically explicit: there is a great deal of reference in the poem to dreams and the unconscious effects Freud locates in jokes, though the poem is not really meant to be overtly funny. Rather, gaps in self-consciousness (as with the uncanny) become sites of the negative. Altieri does not have a place for the unconscious in his account of intentionality, as it would need to be subsumed within what he means by being self-present. But Hejinian wants to take it into account literally as both constitutive agency and constructed effect of the frame shifts in the poem. This is arguably one of the hallmarks of the genre of the long poem to which *A Border Comedy* belongs.

[MORAL: ETHICS OUGHT NOT TO BE A CONCERN ONLY FOR THOSE WHO UNDERSTAND THE WORD "ETHICS."]

What Altieri's reading needs is a constructive use of negativity that does not end in a simple logic of opposition or total threat of destruction. Here, Paul Mann's notion of "anethics" is useful: the moment of redundancy of ethical thinking, its impossibility as a condition of ethics itself.[20] In "anethics," all discussion of ethical agency is caught within the horizon of ethics itself—so that ethics can only keep repeating versions of its past. Bracketing the long history of ethical reflection as a necessity for any account of ethics, anethics is then most concerned with the debacle of agency caught at the crossroads of a moment of decision that can only be prefigured—by fate, in the classical account, or by description, in his. Apart from a model for thinking through the old problem of the "recuperation of the avant-garde" (by structures that it seemed to oppose but that now have entirely absorbed it), what is of interest is the relation of agency to description here as a problem for poetry. "Anethics" also sees negativity as central to ethics—the impossibility of judgment as expressed in the acts of agents, leading to Jacques Lacan's dictum that "the status of the unconscious is ethical," which cannot be pursued further here. The self-canceling progression of intentional states in Hejinian's work, as well as the foregrounded redundancy of terms such as "philosophical" and "ethical," certainly supports reading her poem as an "anethics" as much as for its ethical argument in positive forms. If we find a way of including the negative in our ethical thinking that is not simply holistic or totalizing, we may be able to overcome the impossibility of assigning value to intentional states at the level of the word, and relocate value at the level of the total form. In other words, even if we cannot say what the good is, we can act in such a way that we produce good works—by taking into account that which questions our ideal of the good.

[MORAL: OPPOSITION IS TRUE FRIENDSHIP.]

I would like to pursue a constructivist ethics as not simply reducible to the pitfalls of neopragmatist or poststructuralist "construction," one that is primarily informed by the way the literary work is made (and what it cannot fully contain). One route to such an ethics may be found in the way that the concerns of narration, collaboration, and the construction of discourse in both linguistic and Foucauldian senses takes place at the ethical horizon of *A Border Comedy*, exactly where its title would suggest: as a cultural poetics as much as an affirmative will. In Hejinian's work, an ethics of listening to the other permits a disciplined practice of self-consciousness that is not simply an effort of self-perfecting but is generative for others. Her work certainly has had that effect; it is my every wish to keep its borders open.

[MORAL: IT OUGHT TO BE A BENEFIT TO US.]

1. This essay was presented at a session devoted to Lyn Hejinian's writing at the Modern Language Association meeting in Washington, D.C., December 2000. In the years between that occasion and the present publication much has taken place, in poetics and the world at large. The present version is lightly edited and updated from the one originally revised in 2001—which turned out to be an important one for me, as it allowed me to think through some of the questions of poetics I would develop in essays in *The Constructivist Moment: From Material Text to Cultural Poetics* (Middletown, Conn.: Wesleyan University Press, 2003). Lyn Hejinian, *The Language of Inquiry* (Berkeley: University of California Press, 2000), 3.

2. In summer 2001, Hejinian and I were at the outset of a productive decade of collaboration. We were trying to decide how best to anthologize the work of *Poetics Journal* for a projected volume commissioned by a university press, which is just now appearing as *A Guide to Poetics Journal: Writing in the Expanded Field, 1982–98* (Middletown, Conn.: Wesleyan University Press, 2013), followed this year by *Poetics Journal Digital Archive* (2015), an e-book that will bring the entirety of the journal back into print. In 2001 we were also just at the beginning of the collaborative writing project, with eight other poets, that led to the ten volumes of *The Grand Piano: An Experiment in Collective Autobiography, San Francisco, 1975–80* (Detroit: Mode A, 2006–10),

originally imagined to be part of the present volume—though everyone agreed it should not be published as part of any one author's biography or reception: hence, the subtitle "An Experiment in Collective Autobiography."

3. A succinct discussion of the use of concepts such as "frame shifts" and "partial local coherence" can be found in an article in George Lakoff's "Continuous Reframing," from the first issue of *Poetics Journal* (January 1982: 68–73; *Guide to Poetics Journal*, 111–18). He writes:

We make sense of our experiences by categorizing them and framing them in conventional ways. A frame (as the term is used in the cognitive sciences) is a holistic structuring of experience. Each frame comes with a setting, a cast of characters, a collection of props, and a number of actions, states, and/or images. These may be related in various ways, for example, spatially, temporally, by cause-and-effect, means-and-end, plan-and-goal. [...] Framing requires categorizing; the objects, characters, images, and events must all be of the right kind to fit a given frame. And just about everything we do requires framing of some kind, most of it done so continuously and unconsciously that we don't notice it. (68; 111–12)

4. New York: Granary Books, 2001; hereafter cited as *BC*. The work was in MS and then galleys when I presented my talk and first revised this essay.

5. Lyn Hejinian, "The Rejection of Closure," *Poetics Journal* 4, *Women and Language* (May 1984): 134–43; in *Language of Inquiry*, 40–58; "The Person and Description," *Poetics Journal* 9, *The Person* (June 1991): 166–70; in *Language of Inquiry*, 199–208; "La Faustienne," *Poetics Journal* 10, *Knowledge* (June 1998): 10–29; in *Language of Inquiry*, 232–67. "The Rejection of Closure" is reprinted in *Guide to Poetics Journal*, 87–97; the rest of Hejinian's essays from the journal are available in *Poetics Journal Digital Archive*.

6. Lyn Hejinian, *My Life* (Providence, R.I.: Burning Deck, 1900); 2nd ed., (Los Angeles: Sun and Moon, 1987); *Oxota: A Short Russian Novel* (Great Barrington, Mass.: The Figures, 1991); *The Cell* (Los Angeles: Sun and Moon, 1992). Since 2001, Hejinian has also published *The Fatalist* (Richmond, Calif.: Omnidawn, 2008); *The Book of a Thousand Eyes* (Richmond: Omnidawn, 2012); and *My Life and My Life in the Nineties* (Middletown, Conn.: Wesleyan University Press, 2013).

7. Ron Silliman, *Ketjak* (San Francisco: This, 1978); *Tjanting* (Berkeley: The Figures, 1981); *The Alphabet* (Tuscaloosa: University of Alabama Press, 2008); Viktor Shklovsky, *A Sentimental Education: Memoirs, 1917–1922*, trans. Richard Sheldon (Ithaca, N.Y.: Cornell University Press, 1970); *Zoo; or, Letters Not About Love*, trans. Sheldon (Ithaca, N.Y.: Cornell University Press, 1971); *Third Factory*, trans. Sheldon (Ann Arbor, Mich.: Ardis, 1977).

8. The question is adapted from Marjorie Perloff's response to the present essay; Perloff to Barrett Watten, 18 June 2001.

9. Gertrude Stein, *The Making of Americans* (1925–26; 3rd ed., Normal, Ill.: Dalkey Archive Press, 1995); Louis Zukofsky, *"A"* (Berkeley: University of California Press, 1978).

10. For the "obdurate materiality" of the long poem, see Peter Baker, *Obdurate Brilliance: Exteriority and the Modern Long Poem* (Gainesville: University of Florida Press, 1991).

11. This and the following questions were put to the author by Libbie Rifkin by e-mail; Rifkin to Barrett Watten, 2 January 2001.

12. For the language-centered long poem, see Clark Coolidge, *The Maintains* (San Francisco: This Press, 1974); *Polaroid* (Bolinas, Calif.: Big Sky, 1975); *A Book Beginning What and Ending Away* (Albany, N.Y.: Fence Books, 2012); Bernadette Mayer, *Memory* (Plainfield, Vt.: North Atlantic Books, 1975); Steve Benson, *Blue Book* (Great Barrington, Mass./New York: The Figures/Roof Books, 1988); Steve McCaffery, *The Black Debt* (London, Ont.: Nightwood Editions, 1989); Bruce Andrews, *I Don't Have Any Paper So Shut Up (or, Social Romanticism)* (Los Angeles: Sun & Moon, 1992); *Lip Service* (Toronto: Coach House, 2001); Beverly Dahlen, *A Reading (11–17)* (Elmwood, Conn.: Potes and Poets Press, 1989); Rachel Blau DuPlessis,

Drafts 1–38, Toll (Middletown, Conn.: Wesleyan University Press, 2001); and Barrett Watten, *Progress/Under Erasure* (Los Angeles: Green Integer, 2004); *Bad History* (Berkeley, Calif.: Atelos Press, 1998); and *Zone* (in progress).

13. Leslie Scalapino, *Defoe* (Los Angeles: Sun & Moon Press, 1994); Carla Harryman, *The Words, After Carl Sandburg's Rootabaga Stories and Jean-Paul Sartre* (Oakland, Calif.: O Books, 1999); *Gardener of Stars* (Berkeley, Calif.: Atelos Press, 2001); *Adorno's Noise* (Athens, Ohio: Essay Press, 2008).

14. The ten volumes of *The Grand Piano* were completed in 2010; Harryman and Hejinian's *The Wide Road* was also published in 2010 (New York: Belladonna). Other published collaborations include: Hejinian and Leslie Scalapino, *Sight* (Washington, D.C.: Edge Books, 1999); Michael Davidson, Ron Silliman, Hejinian, and Watten, *Leningrad: American Poets in the Soviet Union* (San Francisco: Mercury House, 1992); Hejinian and Kit Robinson, *Individuals* (Tucson, Ariz.: Chax Press, 1988); Hejinian and Ray DiPalma, *Chartings* (Tucson, Ariz.: Chax Press, 2000); Hejinian and Jack Collum, *Sunflower* (Great Barrington, Mass.: The Figures, 2000); and Hejinian and Emilie Clark, *The Traveler and the Hill and the Hill* (New York: Granary Books, 1998).

15. There is a large bibliography of work on and by the Russian Formalists in English. For discussion of key concepts, see Viktor Erlich, *Russian Formalism: History–Doctrine*, 3rd ed. (New Haven: Yale University Press, 1981); for a constructivist poetics that invokes a notion of a cultural "warehouse of materials," see particularly Shklovsky, *Third Factory*.

16. 51–74; the musical and cultural influences from that formative period she chronicles are indeed complex, providing a second register for the *content* of *A Border Comedy*, namely the multiple strands of culture that collide with each other in the space of improvisation.

17. Charles Altieri, "Lyn Hejinian and the Possibilities of Postmodernism in Poetry," in *Women Poets of the Americas: Toward a Pan-American Gathering*, ed. Jacqueline Vaught Brogan and Cordelia Chavez Candelaria (Notre Dame, Ind.: University of Notre Dame Press, 1999): 146–55; 148.

18. Charles Altieri, "Contemporary Poetry As Philosophy: Subjective Agency in John Ashbery and C. K. Williams," *Contemporary Literature* 33, no. 2 (1992): 214–42; 215.

19. Altieri has a field day discerning the strategic deployment of intentional states in Lyn's poetry. For his other discussions of her work, see "What Is Living and What Is Dead in American Postmodernism: Establishing the Contemporaneity of Some American Poetry" and "Some Problems About Agency in the Theories of Radical Poetics," in Altieri, *Postmodernisms Now: Essays on Contemporaneity in the Arts* (University Park: Pennsylvania State University Press, 1998), 23–52; 166–94. I discuss Altieri's use of Hejinian's work in a recent essay, "Poetics and the Question of Value; or, What is a Philosophically Serious Poet?," *The Wallace Stevens Review* 39, no. (Spring 2015): 84–101, which my discussion of Hejinian and Altieri here anticipates by a mere fifteen years.

20. Paul Mann, "For *Anethics*," in *Masocriticism* (Albany, NY: SUNY Press, 1999), 195–274; see also my review of this work in *Textual Practice* 14, no. 1 (2000): 209–22.

Something I'm Dying to Tell You, Lyn
Jalal Toufic

A Border Comedy:[1] *First Lapse*: "The heavy sleep within my head was smashed / by an enormous thunderclap, so that / I started up as one whom force awakens; / I stood erect and turned my rested eyes / from side to side, and I stared steadily / to learn what place it was surrounding me" (Dante Alighieri, *Inferno*, beginning of Canto IV, trans. Allen Mandelbaum).

As the airplane in which he was traveling to Egypt entered a zone of extreme turbulence, he was seized by apprehension. Unlike the passenger next seat, who was worried about going to hell were the plane to crash, he was worried, in a flash of illumination, about not being able to bear the paradisiacal state. He resolved to become initiated into such a state, to be ready for Paradise. Naively and conceitedly, most people assume that while they would not be able to bear the suffering of hell, they would be able to bear the paradisiacal state. But this is certainly not the case. It is not because they would be prohibited by God from entering Paradise (the moral interpretation) that most people do not dwell in Paradise, but because they are unprepared to stay in it (the ethical viewpoint). How many people are able to sit through the paradisiacal experience of watching Sergei Parajanov's *Sayat Nova* (aka *The Color of Pomegranates*), 1968, Yuri Ilyenko's *The Eve of Ivan Kupalo*, 1968, Andrei Tarkovsky's *The Mirror*, 1975, Aleksandr Sokurov's *Whispering Pages*, 1993, Patrick Bokanowski's *L'Ange*, 1982, and *La Femme qui se poudre*, 1972, Stephen and Timothy Quay's *Rehearsals for Extinct Anatomies*, 1988, Jan Svankmajer's *Dimensions of Dialogue*, 1982; and of listening to Yozgatlı Hafız Süleyman Bey's *Bozlak and Halay* (in *Masters of Turkish Music*, Rounder CD 1051, 1990), Tanburi Cemil Bey's music (in *Tanburi Cemil Bey*, Traditional Crossroads, CD 4264, 1994), and Sabahat Akkiraz singing *Ağıt*, *Ne Ağlarsın* and *Arguvan* (in *Sabahat Akkiraz: 'Alawite Singing*, Long Distance, 2001)? If people are unable to bear these lower levels of Paradise, how would they be able to bear those they will experience in the subtle body in *'âlam al-khayâl*, the Imaginal World? It is possible that we are on this rather drab earth because we were unable to stay in Paradise. Musicians, dancers, artists, poets, writers, and thinkers train their audience and readers to accept and inhabit Paradise (I hope I deserve the appraisal of Richard Foreman [the playwright and director of, among other plays, *Hotel Paradise*]: "He [Jalal Toufic] documents the moves of consciousness in a way that leads the reader ever deeper, from impasse to illusion to new impasse—turning the trap of 'what can't be named' into a true paradise").

He arrived in Cairo, which he was visiting for the first time, at 5 AM. He was told at the hotel that his room would be available at 11, when its present occupants were scheduled to check out. He felt like a homeless person. He decided to saunter in the city until his room was ready. The streets were virtually empty since the vast majority of the city's inhabitants were still sleeping (gradually, from feeling excluded, he felt that the whole city was his).

The first section of my video *The Sleep of Reason:*[2] *This Blood Spilled in My Veins*, 2002, shows sleeping humans,[3] who are revealed as dead through the two epigraphs: "On the authority of Hudhayfa and Abî Dharr, may God bless both: The Apostle of God, may God bless and save him, would say on going to bed: 'In your name, O God, I die and live'; and he would say on waking up: 'Praise be to God, Who hath revived us after putting us to death, and to Whom is the Resurrection'—narrated by al-Bukhârî" (Al-imâm an-Nawawî, *Gardens of the Righteous*), and "Our friend Lazarus has fallen asleep; but I am going there to wake him up" (John 11:11) (When Jesus' disciples replied, "Lord, if he sleeps, he will get better," he told them plainly, "Lazarus is dead" [John 11:12–14]). And the second section of the video shows animals who are being slaughtered and who are revealed to be "dreaming" through the following words of Pascal Quignard: "Animals dream while sleeping as they dream while standing as they dream while leaping" (*Vie Secrète* [Secret life]). If animals "dream," even while standing and leaping, it is in the sense that they are captivated, not having beings manifest as such:

> It has been observed that if its [the bee's] abdomen is carefully cut away while it is sucking, a bee will simply carry on regardless even while the honey runs out of the bee from behind…. The bee is simply taken [*hingenommen*] by its food…. When the bee flies out of the hive to find food it registers the direction in which it stands in relation to the sun…. If we … take the box in which the bee has been imprisoned back to the hive and place it some distance behind the hive, then the newly freed bee flies in the direction in which it would have to fly in order to find the hive from the feeding place, even though the hive is relatively nearby, and it does so for the appropriate distance once again…. [The bee] flies back in a pre-established direction over

a pre-established distance without regard to the position of the hive. It does not strike out in a given direction prescribed for it by the place in which it has found itself. Rather it is absorbed by a direction, is driven to produce this direction out of itself—without regard to the destination. The bee does not at all comport itself toward particular things, like the hive, the feeding place and so on. The bee is *simply given over* to the sun and to the period of its flight *without being able to grasp either of these as such*…. The animal … is taken, taken and captivated [*benommen*] by things.[4]

I've placed quotation marks around *dreaming* because, notwithstanding Quignard's words, properly speaking the animal does not dream, for dreams are the apanage of mortals, and the animal is not a mortal. In Arabic, the word *Hayy* means "*Living, having life, alive*, or *quick* … and *hayawân* is syn. with *hayy* [as meaning *having animal life*]…. *Hayât*: … *Life* … And *fa'inna al-dâr al-'âkhira lahiya al-hayawân* in the Qur'ân [xxix. 64] means [*And verily the last abode is*] the abode of *everlasting life: (Tâj al-'Arûs:)* or *al-hayawân* here means *the life that will not be followed by death:* or *much life;* like as *mawatân* signifies *much death: (Misbâh al-Fayyûmî:)* and it is also the name of *a certain fountain in Paradise,* [*the water of*] *which touches nothing but it lives, by permission of God.* (*Tâj al-'Arûs.*) *Hayawân* an inf. n. of *hayiya*, like *hayât*, (Ibn Barrî, author of the *Annotations on the Sihâh*, with Al-Bustî,) but having an intensive signification: (*al-Misbâh*) …—Also *Any thing*, or *things, possessing animal life*, (*al-Misbâh*, *al-Qâmûs*,) whether *rational* or *irrational;* [*an animal*, and *animals;*] used alike as sing. and pl., because originally an inf. n.; (*al-Misbâh;*) *contr. of mawatân* [q.v.]."[5] While the animal does not really dream, since it is not mortal, in his or her dreams the human is closest to the animal, since in the dream, he or she is captivated, absorbed, without having himself or herself manifest as such, and poor in world. Heidegger: "It is only from the human perspective that the animal is poor with respect to world, yet animal being in itself is not a deprivation of world. Expressed more clearly: if deprivation in certain forms is a kind of suffering, and poverty and deprivation of world belongs to the animal's being, then a kind of pain and suffering would have to permeate the whole animal realm and the realm of life in general. Biology knows absolutely nothing of such a phenomenon. Perhaps it is the privilege of poets to imagine this sort of thing."[6] We can say that, contrariwise, humans, to whose essence, according to Heidegger, belongs world formation, do indeed feel this deprivation and poverty in world when they are dreaming, in the dream. We can reread Heidegger's paragraph in a poetic way by substituting "human dreamer" for "animal": "If deprivation in certain forms is a kind of suffering, and poverty and deprivation of world belongs to the human dreamer's being, then a kind of pain and suffering would have to permeate the whole human dreamer's realm ..."

A Border Comedy—Second Lapse: "5 May.—I must have been asleep, for certainly if I had been fully awake I must have noticed the approach of such a remarkable place" (Bram Stoker, *Dracula*, beginning of chapter II).

While walking in Cairo's "City of the Dead," the zone of cemeteries where hundreds of thousands of destitute people live, he was amazed to see children playing amidst the tombs, laundry hanging, people coming in and out of the makeshift habitations they had made. It was difficult for him to navigate this zone, since he was visiting it for the first time and since there were no detailed maps of it. He felt a stab of pain and passed out (*Third Lapse*). She called him, but her call (in this case "Alexander!"), which usually was the only thing about her that turned heads, fell on deaf ears. The one called couldn't for the life of him turn: trying to turn in response, he took a turn for the worse by undergoing an over-turn. Was he in a labyrinth, since he did not know which way to turn? Although he saw nobody in the City of the Dead, which was "presently" indeed an empty agglomeration of cemeteries,[7] quite desolate, he overheard the whispers of those of the dead who had passed the Opening of the Mouth ceremony. One of the voices said: "But one can't gossip without a body to betray."[8] Another said to him in French: "*Tu a été nommé Alexandre à vie*" (You were called Alexander for life). He realized that if he's already dead, then he could no longer claim the name Alexander. She thought that if he is not responding, he must not be Alexander. What is his name then? Should she name names? But how to delicately name names without calling him names,[9] without name calling the one who no longer showed his face anywhere? Can one call the dead without calling him names? For example, how to respond to one of the letters Friedrich Nietzsche wrote between 4 and 6 January 1889 without calling the author of *The Anti-Christ* "The Crucified" and "Prado" and "(Henri) Chambige" (the latter two were criminals who had been tried for murder in Paris and Algeria)?[10] The same voice resumed: "*Ta mort est sans appel*" (Your death is without appeal [literally: your death is destitute of any call]). Repeatedly unable to turn when called, he wondered in exasperation whether he should call it quits or a day—or a life for that matter. But to do the latter he would have to sign his own death warrant. With what name to do so when he no longer knew or remembered his name? He could no longer mind his own business, be it suicide. But was his death his own business? The dead can no longer mind his own business and/or death is not the dead's own business. He came to the realization that the dead cannot sign his own death warrant, cannot die. Given that he was now "in" a spatial labyrinth, when he reached a dead end and retraced his steps to the crossroads to take a different path, he did not feel that he had been at that particular crossroads; but given that he was also in a temporal labyrinth, he sometimes felt sure about his whereabouts even when arriving there seemingly for the first time, and moreover felt that he knew for certain the path to take. *Those doubts were certainties*[11]—being thought-insertions. *Anxious moment / I don't mention betrayal / Leave that to dream.*[12] *I'll throw down the mirror and name it ship.*[13] *Perhaps, in my absent-mindedness—my being foreign—I'm not constantly losing the key but (in my absent-mindedness) constantly finding it*[14]—*the key to dreams.*[15] On finding "himself" "outside" "the City of the Dead," he saw people frozen still in the same postures as those he had seen on the walls of the ancient Egyptian cemeteries of Luxor. When he at last found *her,* he dreaded that she would *cut him*—who had passed the Opening of the Mouth ceremony and was dying to tell her two or three things—*dead.* Why is the living woman in T. S. Eliot's *The Love Song of J. Alfred Prufrock* settling her pillow to sleep when she encounters the undead? Why is she so sleepy then? What disclosure is she thus trying to elude (during the non-rapid eye movement [NREM] stages of her sleep)? "Tell you all," Lazarus says in Eliot's poem, and would that "all" not also include himself? Did Lazarus come back to tell himself about death? Did he find himself sleeping dreamlessly then?[16] I wager that Shahrazâd would not have settled her pillow to sleep had the ghost of one of the previous one-night wives of King Shahrayâr appeared before her, but would have listened to the tale that the latter was dying to tell her. "I woke myself when the / ghost came in / Actually I spoke to myself / saying, 'Wake up, you (I) / are afraid of ghosts'"[17] (how wonderful is the courage of this fear).[18] What the specter of King Hamlet says to his son is certainly something he is dying to tell to him, not only in the sense that he desires greatly to tell it to him (*die*: "*informal* To desire something greatly: ... *She was dying to see the exhibit*" [*American Heritage Dictionary*]); but also in the sense that it is only once he has told him that he was murdered treacherously by his brother,[19] and once Hamlet has settled that unfinished business by killing the usurping king that the former king's soul can rest, i.e., stop dying. Due to the consuming revengefulness that constitutes him or her, the revenant is oblivious that, at one level, it is always *My Life,*[20] but the other's or others' death: "I am Prado, I am also Prado's father, I venture to say that I am also Lesseps ... I am also Chambige ... every name in history is I"[21] (from Friedrich Nietzsche's 5 January 1889 letter to Jacob Burckhardt, which he wrote during his psychosis, i.e., dying before dying—*Oh, as Nietzsche said, those humans of old knew how to dream / And did not need to fall asleep first*[22]).[23]

Dead, immemorially before *Ash Wednesday, Narcissus cannot face himself*[24] in the limpid water of the pool: "Because I do not hope to turn again / Because I do not hope." Notwithstanding *the ineffable poise of the cadaver*[25]—which while falling ("*Cadaver*: Middle English from Latin *cadāver* from *cadere* to fall, die")[26] seems balanced, and which gives the impression that it is nameless—there's *something I'm "dying to tell you,"*[27] who lived after Jesus Christ, "the resurrection and the life" (John 11:25): *A name trimmed with colored ribbons*[28] (such colors have *the musics of the spouse*[29] for synesthetic accompaniment). The one called turned again *back to front / On death's bed*,[30] that is, was resurrected,[31] i.e., was no longer subject to the imposition of betrayal but open to the possibility of dedication: "It's the jump that separates the earth from the earth. The jump is the real mountain. The bird flew (like a zipper that is being unzipped), the far away mountain became a valley." These lines from the first edition of my first book, *Distracted* (1991), are absent from the book's second edition (2003) by Tuumba Press, whose publisher is the poet Lyn Hejinian. They are dedicated to Hejinian, who wrote in "Book 8" of her *A Border Comedy*:

"It's the jump that separates each instant from the earth
The jump is the real rolling wall
The bird flies like a zipper being unzipped
And the mountain becomes
A valley"[32]

Indeed *Distracted* is listed in the section "Sources" for "Book 8" at the end of *A Border Comedy*. Had I already cut these lines from the second edition of *Distracted* prior to 2001, the year *A Border Comedy* was published? In that case the following words from *Distracted* would apply to them: "A line written with the possibility of evading receiving it, but read in the absence of such a possibility only became real when it was thus read; if a copyright is to be attributed to anyone at all, it should be to the one who read it in such a manner." Or is it on seeing these lines in Hejinian's book not placed in quotation marks that I decided to cut them from the second edition, thus dedicating them to a fabulous friend?[33]

A Border Comedy: Trying to join two cliffs with a phrase. But the phrase itself has a chasm, stops in the middle.[34] "Morning overtook Shahrazâd, and she lapsed into silence.... The king thought to himself, 'I will spare her until I hear the rest of the story; then I will have her put to death the next day.'" Thus starts what, we are told, went on in this guise for "a thousand nights" of storytelling. Why a thousand nights? When he was told by his brother that the latter killed his wife and her paramour in flagrante delicto, King Shahrayâr said: "By Allâh, had the case been mine, I would not have been satisfied without slaying a thousand women, and that way madness lies!" On witnessing his own wife's adultery, King Shahrayâr slew her then "sware himself by a binding oath that whatever wife he married he would abate her maidenhead at night and slay her next morning, to make sure of his honor." And indeed, thenceforth, each morning, following his orders, his minister struck off the head of his latest wife. "On this wise he continued for the space of three years, marrying a maiden every night and killing her the next morning ... till there remained not in the city a young person fit for carnal copulation. Presently the King ordered his Chief Wazîr ... to bring him a virgin ... and the Minister went forth and searched and found none. So he returned home in sorrow and anxiety, fearing for his life from the King. Now the Wazîr had two daughters; the elder of whom was named Shahrazâd." It is at this point that Shahrazâd volunteers to be the next wife of the king. In his translation of *The Thousand and One Nights*, Edward William Lane writes: "And thus, on the first night of the thousand and one, Shahrazâd commenced her recitations." This line is not in my copy of the Bûlâq Arabic edition, the edition on which Lane based his translation. I think that it was an error to add it. Borges too errs when he writes: "Why were there first a thousand [the apparently Persian version: *Hazar Afsana*, the thousand tales] and later a thousand and one?"[35] It is confounding that despite all his flair Borges should miss the displacement from *tale* in the Persian version to *night* in the Arabic one: I consider that the first title refers to the stories Shahrazâd tells, while the second refers to the nights, the one thousand nights of the one thousand unjustly murdered previous one-night wives of King Shahrayâr plus his night with Shahrazâd, a night that is itself like a thousand nights ("one night of sweet love is as one thousand and one nights" [*dî laylat hubb hilwah bi-alf layla wa layla*], as Umm Kulthûm sings in her song *Alf Layla wa layla* [The thousand and one nights]). Were I to become the editor of a future edition of *The Thousand and One Nights*, I would place "The Thousand-and-First Night" as the heading of Shahrazâd's first night with the king; and I would make sure that one of the so-called nights is missing, i.e., that the edition is incomplete. Todorov: "The speech-act receives, in the *Arabian Nights*, an interpretation which leaves no further doubt as to its importance. If all the characters incessantly tell stories, it is because this action has received a supreme consecration: narrating equals living. The most obvious example is that of Scheherazade herself, who lives exclusively to the degree that she can tell stories; but this situation is ceaselessly repeated within the tale."[36] By volunteering to be the next wife of the murderous king, Shahrazâd offers herself as the ransom for her father and for the young women of her city, ending up saving, along with herself (and her father), (at least) a thousand of the kingdom's young women, who must have become "fit for copulation" during the "thousand nights" Shahrazâd spends telling stories to the king; yet, notwithstanding her having "perused the books, annals, and legends of preceding kings, and the stories, examples, and instances of bygone men and things," "collected a thousand books of histories relating to antique races and departed rulers," "perused the works of the poets and knew them by heart," and "studied philosophy and the sciences, arts, and accomplishments," she could not have come up with these lifesaving stories except by drawing on the deaths of the previous one thousand one-night wives of King Shahrayâr. Therefore, it is inaccurate to write that narrating equals living in *The Thousand and One Nights*: while narration is a way of postponing the death of the narrator—though only for a while since old age is meanwhile advancing inexorably—it itself draws on death. We could not write were we as mortals not already dead even as we live; or else did we not draw, like Shahrazâd, in an untimely collaboration, on what the dead is undergoing. If Shahrazâd needed the previous deaths of the king's former thousand one-night wives, it was because notwithstanding being a mortal, thus undead even as she lived, she did not draw on her death. That is why she cannot exclaim to Shahrayâr: "There's something I am dying to tell you." And that is why past the Night spanning a thousand nights, Shahrazâd cannot extend her narration even for one additional normal night;[37] it is on the thousand-and-second night, i.e., the night when this collaboration with the previous thousand one-night wives of the king has become discontinued, that Shahrazâd asks the king to release her from telling stories, being no longer able to come up with additional ones.[38] If "the greatest of all night works is the one called *The Thousand and One Nights*" (Lyn Hejinian),[39] this cannot be simply because it has a myriad nights, but because its night is the greatest. The exemplary Night and Day: "Were there to remain only one day, God would extend that day until the Mahdî (the Muslim messiah; aka *al-Qâ'im*) would issue from my children" (tradition traced back to the prophet Muhammad); and were there to remain only one night, Shahrazâd would still tell stories for a "thousand nights"—until a (messianic) child is born to the childless king? Borges: "For us the word *thousand* is almost synonymous with *infinite*. To say *a thousand nights* is to say infinite nights, countless nights, endless nights.[40] To say *a thousand and one nights* is to add one to infinity."[41] But the infinity, if there is one, is implied not in the thousand (nights of the unjustly murdered previous wives) but rather in the one (night of Shahrazâd). Since the "thousand nights" of storytelling are the extension by Shahrazâd of one night, there is something messianic about *The Thousand and One Nights*. I gave my beloved Graziella a copy of *The Thousand and One Nights* in the Arabic edition of

Dâr al-Mashriq, rather than in the Bûlâq edition republished by Madbûlî Bookstore, Cairo, certainly not because it is an expurgated edition, but because it does not contain at least one of the nights—night 365 is missing. "According to a superstition current in the Middle East in the late nineteenth century when Sir Richard Burton was writing, no one can read the whole text of the *Arabian Nights* without dying" (Robert Irwin, *The Arabian Nights: A Companion*).[42] Borges: "At home I have the seventeen volumes of Burton's version [of *The Thousand and One Nights*]. I know I'll never read all of them ..."[43] How ambivalent must be a man's feelings toward his beloved for him to give her a complete edition of *The Thousand and One Nights* before the time of redemption! His wife died just as she finished it. When, melancholic, he descended to Hades to resurrect her, she asked him to tell her a tale, "for instance the story of that Greek, Orpheus. What was it he was dying to tell (again) to his dead wife, Eurydice? Was it: 'Till death do us part'?[44] Or did he die to become an oracle?" Until the worldly reappearance of *al-Qâ'im* (the Resurrector), there should not be a complete edition of *The Thousand and One Nights*. The only one who should write the missing night that brings the actual total of nights to a thousand and one is the messiah/*al-Qâ'im*, since only with his worldly reappearance can one read the whole book without dying.[45] How can Shahrazâd escape slaughter once she can no longer come up with new stories? Past the customary exordium in a Moslem book, consisting in the main of the *basmala* ("In the name of God, the Compassionate, the Merciful"), praise and thanksgiving to God and invocation of blessing on the Prophet, *The Thousand and One Nights'* first words are: "In tide of yore and in time long gone before, there was a King of the Kings of the Banû Sâsân in the Islands of India and China, a Lord of armies and guards and servants and dependents. He left only two sons." We then learn that after becoming kings, and after ruling over their subjects "with justice during a period of twenty years," these two sons, the eldest, Shahrayâr, and the youngest, Shâh Zamân, discovered that they were being betrayed by their two wives. What could have been a factor in this betrayal? It was probably that the two kings were sterile: at no point is it mentioned that they have any children. Would this explain in part why Shahrayâr kills every morning the latest wife with whom he's had sexual intercourse the previous night? Indeed, to spare her life would soon enough reveal his sterility. It may also explain why it is that after hundreds of nights during which they repeatedly had sexual intercourse, we are never told that Shahrayâr asks Shahrazâd whether she is pregnant yet. What is he waiting for during his many nights with Shahrazâd?[46] Is it only the continuation of each of the previous nights' interrupted stories? It is also and mainly to have a (male) child, miraculously or magically. It is not only the embedded stories of *The*

Thousand and One Nights that are permeated by magic—even the frame story is: the jinn who keeps the woman he abducted imprisoned in a casket set in a coffer to which are affixed seven strong padlocks of steel and which he deposits on the deep bottom of the sea for fear of being betrayed by her. *The Thousand and One Nights* ends with Shahrazâd presenting the king with three male children—"one of them walked, and one crawled, and one was at the breast"—and informing him: "These are thy children …" Isn't there something disturbing in this riddle-like formulation? Does it actually describe a single child rather than three children, since in some of the various editions of *The Thousand and One Nights* Shahrazâd presents the king with one child as his son? Does it not remind us of the Sphinx's riddle to Oedipus: "What creature has only one voice, walks sometimes on two legs, sometimes on three, sometimes on four, and which, contrary to the general law of nature, is at its weakest when it uses the most legs?"? Does this augur ill for King Shahrayâr, who was betrayed by his first wife? Will he be betrayed by his thousand-and-second wife, Shahrazâd, this time with his own son (in which case, this uncanny betrayal would be a humorous lesson for him regarding his failure to keep his "binding oath that whatever wife he married he would abate her maidenhead at night and slay her the next morning to make sure of his honour; 'For,' said he, 'there never was nor is there one chaste woman upon the face of earth'")? In this case, the latter would be that negative messianic figure, the Antichrist.

Notes

1. The title of a Lyn Hejinian book published by Granary Books in 2001.

2. Obviously, the title comes from Goya's print *The Sleep of Reason Produces Monsters* (plate 43 of *Los Caprichos*, second edition, ca. 1803).

3. If I chose to place myself among the sleepers, it is partly because unlike Brecht, who is pictured in a poster—hung on the wall behind sleeping Lebanese theater director Rabih Mroué—holding the mask of a sleeping person while he himself is "wide awake" (to "wide awake" Brecht, someone could have exclaimed: "Dream on!" [indeed the mask that the ostensibly insomniac Brecht is holding seems to be the product of dreaming]; Brecht might have awakened then!), and whose work stresses critical consciousness, my work draws considerably on the unconscious in its construction of concepts.

4. Martin Heidegger, *The Fundamental Concepts of Metaphysics: World, Finitude, Solitude*, trans. William McNeill and Nicholas Walker (Bloomington: Indiana University Press, 1995), 242–247.

5. Edward William Lane, *An Arabic-English Lexicon*, 8 volumes (Beirut, Lebanon: Librairie du Liban, 1980), entry *hâ'yâ'yâ'*. I feel boundless gratitude to Lane for this monumental work.

6. Heidegger, *The Fundamental Concepts of Metaphysics*, 270–271.

7. The City of the Dead is conjointly the most populated city and the most deserted city: it fits many more people than a city of the living can, but each person is alone in it, apparently the only survivor.

8. Lyn Hejinian, *A Border Comedy* (New York: Granary Books, 2001), 109.

9. *"Traiter quelq'un de tous les noms*: to call somebody everything under the sun" (*Le Robert & Collins Senior, Dictionnaire Français-Anglais/Anglais-Français*, 5th ed.).

10. From Nietzsche's 5 January 1889 letter to Jacob Burckhardt: "I am Prado, I am also Prado's father, I venture to say that I am also Lesseps…. I wanted to give my Parisians, whom I love, a new idea—that of a decent criminal. I am also Chambige—also a decent criminal…. every name in history is I…. This autumn, as lightly clad as possible, I twice attended my funeral, first as Count Robilant (no, he is my son, insofar as I am Carlo Alberto, my nature below), but I was Antonelli [who was papal state secretary under Pius IX] myself."

11. Hejinian, *A Border Comedy*, 54.

12. Ibid., 61–62.

13. Ibid., 71.

14. Ibid., 62.

15. Magritte's *The Key to Dreams* (*La clef des songes*), 1927 and 1930 versions.

16. See Jalal Toufic, *Over-Sensitivity* (Los Angeles: Sun & Moon Press, 1996), 171–174; 2nd ed. (Forthcoming Books, 2009; available for download as a PDF file at: http://www.jalaltoufic.com/downloads.htm), 40–43.

17. Lyn Hejinian, *The Cell* (Los Angeles: Sun & Moon Press, 1992), 100.

18. For another take on the courage of fear, cf. my book *(Vampires): An Uneasy Essay on the Undead in Film*, revised and expanded ed. (Sausalito, CA: The Post-Apollo Press, 2003; available for download as a PDF file at: http://www.jalaltoufic.com/downloads.htm), 125–126: "We fear fear because often fear either discloses to us or makes us sense what we know (i.e., we fear fear because we are basically gullible enough to think that what we did not know that we know is the truth)—fear is courage. Courage is not the absence of fear, since it partly resides in confronting what fear discloses; but the absence of the fear of fear, of the swish pan that hides what fear could have revealed."

19. The ghost, who asserts a unique identity (in Shakespeare's *Hamlet*, he says to Prince Hamlet, "I am thy father's spirit") is not the dead, who feels *every name in history is I*, but the messenger of the dead. But this messenger of the dead cannot be a revenant asking for a specific retribution without having forgotten about (at least) one of the secrets of his prison house, namely, "every name in history is I"; consequently, he is unable to disclose this secret even in an *aparté*. "But that I am forbid / To tell the secrets of my prison-house, / I could a tale unfold whose lightest word / Would harrow up thy soul, freeze thy young blood, / … But this eternal blazon must not be / To ears of flesh and blood" (Shakespeare's *Hamlet*, 1.5.13–21). The notion that he is forbidden to tell, rather than oblivious about this secret is probably a thought-insertion. What is one of the secrets whose unfolding would harrow up Prince Hamlet's soul and freeze his young blood? That in the undeath realm, where he feels *every name in history is I*, his undead father sometimes exclaims: "I, Claudius, miss my Queen Gertrude." Thus, it is Gertrude who esoterically initiates her son Hamlet into some of the secrets of the undeath realm.

20. The title of a Lyn Hejinian book.

21. See *Selected Letters of Friedrich Nietzsche*, trans. Christopher Middleton (Chicago: University of Chicago Press, 1969), 347.

22. Hejinian, *A Border Comedy*, 17.

23. From another perspective, "dying … is essentially mine in such a way that no one can be my representative" (Martin Heidegger, *Being and Time*, trans. John Macquarrie & Edward Robinson [New York: Harper & Row, 1962], 297); while life is never my life, "for death is that whereby all successive forms of the living are deposed and terminated to the advantage of the single formless power of life, *élan vital* for Bergson, inorganic life for Deleuze, blind folds of DNA molecules for contemporary biology. The infinite value of life affirms itself only through

death…. Death is, for any particular living thing, the transcendence of life in it. Death is that whereby, beyond the derisory being-multiple of living individuals, the existence of life affirms itself. Every time that a living thing dies, what is silently spoken is: 'I, life, exist'" (Alain Badiou, "Existence and Death," trans. Nina Power and Alberto Toscano, in "Mortals to Death," ed. Jalal Toufic, special issue, *Discourse* 24, no. 1 [Winter 2002]: 64–65).

24. Hejinian, *A Border Comedy*, 44.

25. Ibid., 103.

26. *American Heritage Dictionary*.

27. Hejinian, *A Border Comedy*, 14.

28. Lyn Hejinian, *My Life* (Los Angeles: Sun & Moon Press, 1991), 14.

29. Lyn Hejinian's dedication to her husband, the musician Larry Ochs, in *The Cold of Poetry*. Certainly the model spouse is the musician and singer Orpheus.

30. Hejinian, *A Border Comedy*, 49.

31. As far as I am concerned, and as is clear from the title of my seminar "Saving the Living Human's Face and Backing the Mortal," the face is linked to life (*"Muhayyâ* [from the root *Hayy*, Living]: *The face* [*al-Sihâh, al-Qâmûs*, at-Tibrîzî's *Exposition of the Hamâsah*, 23] of a man, because it is specified in salutation; [*Exposition of the Hamâsah* ubi suprà;] a term used only in praise" [Lane, *An Arabic-English Lexicon*, entry *hâ' yâ' yâ'*]), while the back is related to the mortal, who is subject to over-turns.

32. Hejinian, *A Border Comedy*, 108.

33. The following words, "the consequence of using large time intervals is that most, if not all of the fluctuations in images and perceptions cancel out, one ending up having the gross approximation that normal perception is," which appear on page 3 of the first edition of my book *(Vampires): An Uneasy Essay on the Undead in Film*, published by Station Hill Press in 1993, and on which these words by Lyn Hejinian are based, "But no matter what avoiding the larger time intervals / Since they would cancel out all strange fluctuations and less probable connections / Leaving only a gross approximation" (*A Border Comedy*, 52), are not dedicated to Hejinian, as they are still (p. 14) in the second edition, published by the Post-Apollo Press in 2003.

34. Jalal Toufic, *Distracted* (Barrytown, NY: Station Hill Press, 1991), 18; 2nd ed. (Berkeley, CA: Tuumba Press, 2003; available for download as a PDF file at: http://www.jalaltoufic.com/downloads.htm), 18.

35. Jorge Luis Borges, *Seven Nights*, trans. Eliot Weinberger; introduction by Alastair Reid (London: Faber and Faber, 1984), 49.

36. "Narrative-Men" in Tzvetan Todorov, *The Poetics of Prose*, trans. Richard Howard; with a new foreword by Jonathan Culler (Oxford: Blackwell, 1977), 73.

37. This makes clear that the "three years" in "On this wise he continued for the space of three years, marrying a maiden every night and killing her the next morning" is a round expression for "one thousand nights."

38. I presume that the king must have, early on, asked at his court whether any of the historians and scholars of the kingdom and any of its oral storytellers knows the continuation of the story Shahrazâd had interrupted telling him the previous night; had any of them known the end of the story, he would have told it to the king and the latter would have proceeded to behead Shahrazâd. Therefore, while the collection of stories titled *The Thousand and One Nights* draws on previous stories from various cultures (India, Persia, Moslem Egypt, Iraq and Syria, etc.), within the diegesis, Shahrazâd does not simply retell stories she would have culled from "the books, annals, and legends of preceding kings, and the stories, examples, and instances of bygone men and things," the "thousand books of histories relating to antique races and departed rulers," and "the works of the poets," but invents, in an untimely collaboration with the previous one thousand one-night wives of the king, the stories she tells King Shahrayâr.

39. Lyn Hejinian, *The Language of Inquiry* (Berkeley, CA: University of California Press, 2000), 251.

40. "If you were stranded alone on a desert island, what is the one book you would take along with you?" My first choice is Ibn al-'Arabî's *The Meccan Openings* (aka *The Meccan Illuminations*), this great multi-volume exegesis, aided by spiritual taste (*dhawq*) and unveiling (*kashf*), of one book, the Qur'ân. My second choice is *The Thousand and One Nights*—how many islands there are in this book, especially in the tales of Sindbad the Seaman! In the tale of his first voyage, we read: "O Captain, I am that Sindbad the Seaman who traveled with other merchants, and when the fish heaved and thou calledst to us, some saved themselves and others sank, I being one of them. But Allâh Almighty threw in my way a great tub of wood, of those the crew had used to wash withal, and the winds and waves carried me to this island ..." And in the tale of his second voyage, we read: "When I awoke, I found myself alone, for the ship had sailed and left me behind, nor had one of the merchants or sailors bethought himself of me. I searched the island right and left, but found neither man nor Jinn, whereat I was beyond measure troubled, and my gall was like to burst for stress of chagrin and anguish and concern, because I was left quite alone, without aught of worldly gear or meat or drink, weary and heartbroken."

41. Borges, *Seven Nights*, 45.

42. Robert Irwin, *The Arabian Nights: A Companion* (London: Penguin, 1994), 1.

43. Borges, *Seven Nights*, 50.

44. Nietzsche writes of those who are sovereign that they "give their word as something that can be relied on because they know themselves strong enough to maintain it in the face of accidents, even 'in the face of fate'" (*On the Genealogy of Morals*). Is it the case that accidents and the inversions of "fate" are obstacles to keeping the promise, or is it rather that one really promises only that which is likely to be upset by accidents, even by "fate" (in which case, one tempts fate by giving a promise)? That is, has one really ever promised other than the impossible? Have I not once promised a woman: *Till death do us part*, i.e., to love her beyond her natural demise until the labyrinthine realm of death with its over-turns parts us (as it did Orpheus and Euripides)?

45. Thus, during *al-Qâ'im*'s occultation, were someone to read an edition that asserts itself to be the complete edition of *The Thousand and One Nights* and not die, we would have to deduce that at least one of its stories does not belong to the actual book, but is a spurious addition.

46. Every work that deals with waiting in a genuine, essential sense is in some degree a messianic work, leads to or draws on messianism. That the messiah has not appeared on earth yet implies either that we have not yet learned to wait properly (in which case, what we are waiting for is to reach the proper state of waiting, the right way to wait); or else that the messiah's coming is not to earth, that the messiah has already appeared where he should go (see my book *Undying Love, or Love Dies* [The Post-Apollo Press, 2002], 30–34).

Beginnings and Endings
LYN HEJINIAN
STEIN THING
Kevin Killian

"When This You See Remember Me," staged by Lyn Hejinian on 17 November 1995 at New College in San Francisco, was one of those marathon readings where a zillion poets get up and read, in this case from the work of Gertrude Stein. Oh dear, I was a participant, I was there, and yet the event itself has nearly escaped me—I remember only the lights and darknesses that surrounded it fore and aft. Still if one could conjure up those light and dark patches, signs of experience attendant to the experience itself, one shall at least have cleared space for the memories of others to come flooding in, for history to reseat itself. Ten years ago isn't a very long time, is it, and yet San Francisco was a slightly different place, and we who wrote poems here slightly different people. In fact the event might have been called something slightly else entirely. But first, as with everything else, the back story marches forth insofar as I, Kevin Killian, am prepared to write it down.

Lyn's teaching, both at New College and at UC Berkeley, had been fostering an extraordinary exchange between two groups of young poets whom she introduced to each other—so Renee Gladman on the one hand, the New College hand, got to meet Pamela Lu on the other (the Berkeley hand you might say). Students from San Francisco State came to join in, and some tough-minded independents joined the fray, Anselm and Edmund Berrigan were both living here and became natural leaders in a new movement. Lyn had formed an alliance with Travis Ortiz and together they had started work on a new publishing venture, Atelos Press, whose publishing list seemed to symbolize Lyn's new trajectory, one foot firmly in the old Tuumba crowd and another among the young friends of Travis. She had also become close to a young couple, the Neo-Ex painter Emilie Clark, and her husband Lytle Shaw, then a towheaded graduate student at Berkeley, both of them brilliant, both devoted. One's impression was that Lyn, after a protracted period of inactivity, was totally, fully in her element; one worried for her for that reason, how could she stretch herself any further? And yet she had never looked so beautiful nor so at ease. There are some people whose generosity turns them crabbed, haggard—not so in Lyn Hejinian's case.

"When This You See Remember Me" was largely carried out by Lyn's students at New College, where she was giving a class on Stein, and in particular by Tim Krafft, endlessly energetic, speedy and enthusiastic. His hair was strawberry blond, he had that sweet, wholesome effulgence of being one associates perhaps wrongly with UC Santa Cruz, "the Deadhead look," as Dodie calls it. Tim Krafft, also a graphic designer, made a wonderful poster and really did up the publicity so that nobody could have missed it. And a bright yellow T-shirt some of us still have lying around in a bottom drawer. (I looked at mine the other day and noticed, it's not really bright any more. It had once been the color of a banana peel, now it's more like the fruit itself, that pale still lovely shade, less pop perhaps, more muted, like the pastels of San Francisco houses.) This, Lyn's, bringing together of beginnings and endings intrigues me as a novelist and a reporter; I remember from my days writing the life of Jack Spicer how often I wished someone would have "written up" many past events for the benefit of future historians. My abilities as a social historian shine while I'm standing outside the building stealing a cigarette, or on the couch next to you making sure no one else can hear, on paper I'm nervous as I locate Lyn at the center of a shifting nexus of Bay Area poetry communities. Indeed only she could have marshaled us all into one tent. As I think back, there was at any rate a large turnout from us who represented the "New Narrative" counter-movement, for Bob Glück was there, Camille Roy gave a fine showing, Dodie explained how Britain was the "island where they invented explanation," from Stein's "History of English Literature," although today she can't remember doing so, and I read "Miss Furr and Miss Skeene." Theorists and film-makers Jalal Toufic and Trinh T. Minh-Ha performed an electric duet, then disappeared into the night's shadows to cast their intensity elsewhere. Kathleen Fraser read from "Composition as Explanation," while Beverly Dahlen, who had once worked with Fraser on *HOW(ever)*, read affectingly from *Lifting Belly*. Having lived in the Bay Area for so long, and being aware of all the undercurrents, the ways in which we had all lived and opposed our poetry to one another's, I can appreciate the tact with which this project proceeded. This was the year in which we were all more energized; and maybe some of this extra energy came from the widened use of the internet, how it seemed that the delay between thought and act had been bridged, not always to one's advantage as it developed, but there it was, all of a sudden, or so it seemed, everyone was linked and in consequence, surely, our world was going to change for good or bad. Attendant on this increase in speed arrived a slight acceleration in— anxiety, too. Henceforward there would be no time to reflect or pause or even count to ten. You wished it, there it was.

A shifting regret ran through the auditorium of, yes, this is great, but what a shame this date coincides with—well, it was almost unspoken but omnipresent. Across the Bay, at Mills College in Oakland, on that very same weekend was a large John Cage conference, "Here Comes Everybody," featuring Marjorie Perloff, Jackson Mac Low, Lou Harrison, Joan Retallack—all these interesting figures any one of whom would also have been a terrific addition to the line-up here in San Francisco. Were we in fact to see and hear the figures that had not qualified to discuss John Cage but were presumed up to the task of reading from Gertrude Stein? If so, wasn't it a bit—natural—maybe—to feel that one was getting the second-best? If you have never been to the auditorium at New College you're missing an architectural oddity stained, for me, by the radiance of so many memories. Half a funeral parlor, half a gymnasium, with mirrors along the wall á la the sinister dance academy in Dario Argento's *Suspiria*, this hall always reminds me of the pulpit Father Mapple preached from at the beginning of *Moby Dick*, and also of the fact that Robert Duncan founded the Poetics Program here at New College back in the 1970s—it just reeks of auras, not all of them pleasant, it's underlit, with bleacher seats and an absurdly large playing space; padded mats like the kind we used to wrestle on in junior high are often thrown around the floor, too big to shove aside, their blue vinyl too bright to shut out. One by one we lumbered into the spotlight and tried to put our best foot forward.

Thank God for the Buffalo Poetics List Archive, which I can mine to retrieve more details about this event. Interviewing people who were there is one thing, but no one remembers the same thing twice, and although the event was videotaped you'd have to be James Bond and Pussy Galore combined to break that tape out of Fort Kush. Thus I rely on the contemporary reportage from the List, and what I read there jars with my own recollections to a mild degree, like banging one's head against a screen door. Makes me miss Steve Carll, who used to come to everything before moving to Hawaii and he'd write down what everybody did, said, read and gossiped about afterwards. And he did it on the spot so it bears still the wet marks of accuracy. But list or no, I always remembered as the highlight of the show Nick Robinson, Laura Moriarty and Leslie Scalapino acting out Stein's oratorio "Doctor Faustus Lights the Lights." Nick Robinson had been one of the founders of the San Francisco Poets Theater back in the 70s, and I had not seen him acting in many years. He took the small part of the dog, a wise move as it allowed his co-stars to give the play its musical quality. Laura, with her sharp, throbbing voice, and Leslie, improvising delicate vocal lines of her own invention around Stein's text. This was the first time I heard Leslie sing, or even knew she could sing, and after that I put her to work singing in my own plays as often as possible. And also I decided it was high time that Nick Robinson, who for so long had retired from the public eye into librarianship, should make a more frequent appearance on our stages.

A bald man reached over to me and took my hand, and I'm like, "Who is this bald guy with his hand in mine?" It was like a scene from Whitman, only in Whitman, I guess, you don't think of anyone bald, on the contrary, you think of hair, lustrous hair, lots of it. Anyhow it turned out to be Geoff Young, visiting from the Berkshires, and I, going through one of those embarrassing and completely obvious contortions to try to say, of course I knew it was you all the time, how could I forget? Carla Harryman and Barrett Watten were also back for a visit from Detroit, and each gave a big performance. Harryman put the full weight of her theatrical presence into Stein's text "If you had three husbands." To the Poetics List Dodie reported, "It was hilarious the way she'd look individual audience members in the eye and say with conviction, 'If you had three husbands.'" As usual when Barrett Watten took the stage the evening gained even more drama, more contest. He framed his reading from *The Making of Americans* with spicy bits of *Anti-Oedipus*. It was the longest reading of the evening, stretching to twenty minutes or more, one's thumb kept resting on his name on the program with the sight of many more readers to follow him, and yet you couldn't help thinking that he really understood what he was doing, he just wasn't able to bring it all out in a way that communicated itself freely.

From Bolinas Stephen Ratcliffe picked up where Watten had left off, on page 800 of *The Making of Americans*. From Bolinas also, we heard from Robert Grenier and from Bill Berkson. Enormous energy filling the room, battling enervation; you know how it is when a reading lasts four hours or more, after awhile you're just dizzy but your brain is flashing away, you may miss some things, but you're in the groove. If Jeff Conant read from "Ada," as Steve Carll reports, I must have missed it, but I had to have a cigarette, to keep the beat. Though one couldn't have known that this was to be the last time Larry Eigner appeared in public, one might have guessed. I never could understand only every third or fourth word Eigner ever said to me, but there was something particularly fey about his presence that night. You knew he wouldn't be long with us. He must have been accompanied by Jack and Adelle Foley, who took such good care of him before his death, and the Foleys must have also done one of their patented high-speed, maniacal renditions of poetry, but I'm blanking out right now. I can see them doing it, but it's beyond words to describe what it's like. Eigner's appearance, along with that of Thom Gunn, signaled to me, ridiculously enough, a genuine link to another bygone era of poetry, one that had only to stretch out its fingertips to have touched Stein's own. And Eigner, reaching way back to "Melanctha" and the beginning of Stein's career, seemed thus to carry in his bent up old body a whole century's worth of experience via language, a shameful age in many ways but one distinguished by its poetic achievement. The night I heard of his death I dreamed of a leaf falling from a tree, green, browning, brown, curled tight up fragile as a fist.

Your eye invariably strays to the double doors through which you entered, on your right, and when they open up after the reading has started you're always "Who's coming so late?" The doors slid open and there stood a haggard Dan Davidson, dressed in black, flaunting a cape. It was like the initial appearance of Dracula in the Tod Browning film. Dan's face gleamed an unearthly white, his eyes like black raspberries in his pale Byronic face. His hair was a tangle of wet ringlets, long as a 70s rock star. I hadn't seen him in a year or more. He muttered a few words to the young woman who stood beside him, and they closed the doors and left without ever having come in. As far as I know, this was the last time he appeared at a poetry event before his suicide.

I remember Tim Krafft, dressed as a sunflower, his head poking out between the petals, a megaphone at his lips, reading Stein's words as though he had written them himself; and another skit in which he led all Lyn's other students in a slow, circular dance around the stage, very Al Carmines, hilarity condensed by precision. The very next night he, Tim, died of an accidental drug overdose. Bad heroin and he, or so it was said, had only tried shooting up once before. His death rocked us all in shock waves. Even those of us who didn't know him who had seen him on stage, so vital and filled with so much potential, felt robbed. There was something eerie, also, in having played such a large part in such a grand success, and then twenty-four hours later, death stealing in, taking him out.

The atmosphere thus was thick with a sense of beginnings and endings— thick as taffy sometimes, with the personal ambitions of the participants as well, which one could guess at dimly. Maybe we all felt a bit inferior to Lyn, whose comprehensive knowledge of Stein left the rest of us markedly incomplete, grasping at pieces of this huge Buddha whole which only Lyn herself with certainty obtained. What did it mean, why had Lyn asked Robert Hass and Brenda Hillman to participate? This was one of the first publicly played moves of Lyn's alliance with the so-called "bridge poets." We, her admirers, could hardly comprehend the serene audacity of her reach. As doyenne of the Language poets, she had accumulated vast reserves of cultural capital—and thus could do whatever she pleased? That is, find worth in the poetry of the US Poet Laureate, as he was at the time, and in Brenda Hillman, whose move toward a more avant-garde diction had gotten her into trouble with both camps, the mainstream and the experimental. There were some—many to this day— who just couldn't see it, who resented her alliance with Lyn and Lyn's world.

Five years later, at the Page Mothers Conference in San Diego, we were all creeping through some campus forest from one event to another, like weathered GIs in *A Bridge Too Far*, when the darkness was shot through by an unearthly cry, "My God, why did they invite Brenda Hillman!"

I'm leaving so many of the players out of this account. Is Stein a subject large enough to account for one's feeling, sitting on those darn bleachers, that we were all putting, or trying to put, our best foot forward? I credit Lyn Hejinian with forging common ground where no common ground existed. I'm not one who can honestly say I read Gertrude Stein every day of my life. Maybe a good thirty days will go by without me even thinking of her, from time to time. Lou Harrison would have been a much better choice than I, to celebrate Stein's genius. I was there because I lived in the community. I speak personally, anecdotally, and perhaps inconsequentially, but I want to suggest something of the world of feeling that underlines the social world in which writing is made and presented. It's a world composed of gravity, hurt, shame, embarrassment, fear, guilt, defiance, but also one of elation, pleasure, discovery and compassion. In their very different ways Stein and Hejinian have written often of this locus. I write more tentatively than they, I'm the little mouse in the stable skittering under the hooves of the big ... what are they?

The Value of Getting There Slowly
Pamela Lu

One unyielding fact of life for poets, writers, artists, and other hyper-conscious types is our essential separateness from the world—from the world, that is, of all the sensations, phenomena, and people that we would want to know. When the limits of external experience loom up against the desire to know, imagination reaches out to make these limits themselves a realm of experience, for provisional understandings of the physically unknowable or un-experience-able, or for alternative visions of what the world might become, after improvement and change.

Managing the interplay between imagination and the world is a major part of the working process that we're involved in on a daily basis. Between the extremes of feeling overburdened by a world that seems untransformable and unresponsive to our actions (despair) and feeling saturated by an imagination that flies off the handle of what's relevant to real life (delusion), there lies a continual negotiation of the reality/self boundary that we would commonly know as healthy existence, a healthy and productive experiential state.

Somewhere in this productive, daily middle can be found two of Lyn Hejinian's recent projects: *Slowly* (Tuumba, 2002) and *The Beginner* (Tuumba, 2002). Both projects are manifest in the world as books. The physical details of each book are quite arresting and worth a digression.

Slowly is 5 inches wide by 7 inches tall; its cover is predominately royal blue and etched with white lettering. The top two-thirds of the front cover is occupied by a striking black-and-white photograph of stones, which, as the copyright reveals, was captured by the author herself. The stones are not boulders, but they are not pebbles either. They appear to be fist-sized rocks of various shapes and shades, generally but not regularly rounded at the edges, perhaps chips from some ancient granite or flint now packed and latticed together in a groundwork that's unarguably "rocky." Yet despite rockiness, there is a real comfort in the texture, in the bumpy pressure of rock fragments against the soles of your feet as you walk over this terrain at the unhurried pace suggested by the title. You readjust and recalibrate your balance with each step. The bumpy pressure is familiar yet unpredictable. It is both different and new every time.

The Beginner has a predominantly white cover with slender royal blue lettering. In the front cover art by Emilie Clark, overlapping images of birds surge toward their apparent purpose—to drop nourishment into the wide, waiting mouths of their newborns. The feeding goes on indefinitely; it repeats in a series that starts long before the book does and shows no sign of ending. *The Beginner* has the same height and width dimensions and roughly the same heft as *Slowly*—just over 40 pages in length, not counting front and end matter. This makes for a slim, palm-sized volume that is easily tucked inside a jacket pocket or slipped between envelopes and papers in a day bag. Both books, in fact, can travel light, can go where you go, can be picked up and reread at different times and different places without ceasing to be relevant. Each book has the closeness and immediacy of a local guidebook that you might consult at different times throughout the day.

Slowly and *The Beginner* also mark a return to the local terrain of Hejinian's own Tuumba Press, the first time she has self-published under this imprint since 1984. In the years between, Hejinian has traveled widely in the publishing world and produced, fairly recently, the large-scale adventures of *A Border Comedy* and (in collaboration with Carla Harryman) *The Wide Road,* as well as the career-surveying essay collection *The Language of Inquiry.* In these projects she uses the characteristic freedom and expansiveness of her language to inhabit multiple positions at once—whether as critic and poet (always), off-the-loop yarn-spinner and erudite reader (*A Border Comedy*), essayist of the moment and contextualist of the historical (her pairings of original essays with carefully framed introductions in *The Language of Inquiry*), trans-formational brainiac and trans-utopian hedonist (*The Wide Road*), or self and other (*The Wide Road*). In all cases, giant steps are undertaken to cover the partial ground of an ungovernable, epic existence, with its ferment of events and situations percolating just beneath the surface. The poignant inadequacy of summary only heightens the urge to embark on more exotic variety and feats of enthusiasm and to build, through this process, a microcosm of the world's coincidental overabundance and incompleteness.

The microcosm of the recent Tuumba books feels both closer to home and more ordinary. In *Slowly* and *The Beginner,* as in all Hejinian projects, imagination is cast out like a wide, loose net over the actual world, then pulled in and examined with the point-by-point objective ethos of a scientific explorer. What's different is that the holes of this net are smaller. The objects caught are also smaller, finer-grained, at once more mundane and more focused. Mental gears are downshifted to the power and speed of the near observation. The topic determines the size that writing synchronizes to and cuts its teeth on.

The topic, incidentally, is not an object. Rather, it is an attitude, a direction, a particular cognitive approach—of perambulation and circumnavigation in

Slowly, of serial initiation and commencement in *The Beginner.* The topic has expansive potential, but the practice of writing remains dedicated and highly trained, closely considering the topic's broader movements while staying anchored to its human source, its kernel of hopefulness, if you will. (Here *writing* itself deserves pronoun status, for it is the trace and footage of the writer's travels, and so qualified to play the role of limber conversationalist in the moving mind of the reader.) Writing occupies a shifting space of attention devoted to what the topical approach can achieve in the face of limitations:

> I wake to the waking shadow of the world the waking have in common for one long visit slowly
> I walk rather than speed up the ordinary unfolding
> One has to wait for the lateness of the day with recalcitrance circulating to stop in the midst of traffic in a blindspot that flows around one smoothly to regard the dark buildings without apology
> Movement prolongs the finitudes a person moving achieves which lacks finality imperceptibly
> Out the dark door over black leaves putting into motion what painters have known for years I see that the night is in the mind before it ever gets to day
> (*Slowly*, 9)

These are the liminal lines with which *Slowly* begins to survey the perimeter of daily life, circumscribed, neither tragically nor hurriedly, by the long shadow of mortality. To "wake" and to "walk" are parallel efforts undertaken to forge transitions through mortality's two big immutables: time and space. Between the time of sleeping night and the time of wide-eyed day, between the space of stillness and the space of motion, there awaits a slow mode of reckoning that is deeply attuned to what can be known through the transitional passage, "the ordinary unfolding." What thoughts, feelings, and experiences are registered while "Movement prolongs the finitudes"? It is the role of the realist writer to perform somnambulism's opposite: the practice of wake-walking, or equivalently, walk-waking.

Hejinian wake-walks (walk-wakes) all around her perceptual neighborhood, taking in the variety of the local world with all its commonplace detail and immediacy. Among the ordinary things that appear throughout *Slowly*: a skyscraper, a dachshund, a snowball, moths, the "bird we saw yesterday in the tree," a wristwatch, a backgammon board, a head of lettuce, peaches, a camera, dreams, walls, doors, clouds, pigeons, a "silent child," soup, lions, a "taxi cruising at midnight," a garbage truck, a "pedestrian with a schnauzer," a singer, grass, music, and fog. Also, moods and positions that alight on the moment: omens, fate, love, inertia, dexterity, impulse, anticipation, kindness, freedom, abandon, optimism/skepticism, credulity/incredulity, uniqueness, determination.

Returning to the daily is a slow, repetitive ritual, yet one which extends the promise of an enduring understanding:

> The hardest knowledge to acquire to continue is that of unfleeting characteristic incidents
> Strange tales can be quickly heard
> (*Slowly*, 12)

What incidents *can't* be comprehended quickly? What phenomena must be revisited again and again, in circular fashion, until they gradually begin to sink in? Well, the un-strange, arguably dismissable ones, the ones that can't be classified as gripping drama in the popular sense, the ones that don't usually get written about, at least not as platforms of inquiry in themselves. If the quotidian is to have any spiritual, philosophical, or even ethical credibility in advancing an understanding of life and the world, it can't boast the quick summarizable boundaries of the fetish object. Its commodity-value can't be used to glorify the sensitivity, pathos, or moral standing of the writer's consumable persona. Contemporary realist writing (of which *Slowly* and *The Beginner* are examples) is not a demonstration of, but an attempt of, the writer's life. The writing must continue to ask and become that which the writer herself has relinquished possession of—namely, the world at the time of the writing.

> Something is happening.
> To the book?
> Yes, to me.
> (*The Beginner*, 13)

> To be a self is simply to be something in the world and yet yearning for it.
> (*The Beginner*, 40)

> Naturally circumnavigators achieve circularity
> It is no one departing from herself
> Pursuit can't be separated from routines, clothing, meals, and

eventually music which is never made for others alone
   ...

     Circularity, says the circumnavigator, slows to allow the time of a
place to appear
     (*Slowly*, 25)

To inhabit time, to pursue the newness and freshness of time even as it ages—
this is the challenge of the second-millennial realist. How can the world be
entered, encountered, and grasped, when so many heavy pieces of history lie
piled up against the entrance? *The Beginner* proposes an approach which may
or may not be a solution, depending on the practitioner, but which is, irregard-
less of outcome, something that works. It generates and permits real work to
happen. In short, *The Beginner* proposes a continuing awareness of beginnings,
of participating in something for the first time. Like the newly born, the begin-
ner opens her eyes wide and stumbles into a world of reckless simplicity, filled
with the pre-grammatical language of every possible possibility.

     Even when nothing happens there is always waiting submerged in the
task of beginning and task it is in thoughts to begin afresh.
     The beginner makes a beginning, and if optimism is in the air (or
pessimism, that mordant state of mind that says things can't possibly im-
prove), the beginner proclaims it is a good place to begin.
     This is beginning.
     Something and other things in a sequence simultaneously.
     Ants on a white sill buried.
     A harbinger in the light.
     A child composed nudely.
     A side of a tree cut into squares at a shout from a man under an
umbrella.
     A furtive marked moth fluttering into a beam of light.
     A woman at a door falling.
     The beginner is diverted.
     Follow me.
     (*The Beginner*, 11–12)

This is not the *beginning* of foregone conclusions, as in "beginnings and
endings"—but *beginning* as continuous action. This beginning is a process, a
practice of renewal and possibility, or just as fluently, of creation and inquiry.
Answers are not provided to the many questions posed in the writing ("What

can we say in ignorance?", "But what are the emotions?", "Can we hesitate?"),
but the questions themselves forge passageways into the world, toward growth.
The beginner is not just someone who begins, but someone who *wants* to begin.
The site of beginning, always, is arbitrary:

> This is a good place to begin.
> From something.
> (*The Beginner*, 9)

Unlike the deistic movement of creating something out of nothing, the begin-
ner starts with something in the world and creates something else, and then
something else again, as in "Something and other things in a sequence simulta-
neously." The act of beginning (like the act of creation) belongs to ordinary life
and returns to ordinary life to gather its necessary materials:

> I would never want to suggest that one begins by oneself and not in
> conjunction with one's own life and with all the rest of life besides, with its
> conflicting tendencies.
> (*The Beginner*, 15)

—which might very well be another way of saying that the beginner is an
ordinary person with an extraordinary gift for attention, for identifying the
somethings in the world that have the potential to lead to something else. The
beginner's writing is less about making a composition than about charting the
beginner's progress through the world and through time. This is in firm opposi-
tion to the unimaginative, deadening brand of boredom that can find nothing
in the world to make something of. On the contrary, the beginner casts her
lot with the something that is there (though this something might be hidden,
"waiting submerged in the task of beginning"), and effectively enters into a part-
nership with the forces of change, and with change itself.

The Beginner and Slowly are unclassifiable texts with a classic feel to them.
In them, Hejinian takes up the 19th-century realist commitment to the
commonplace as opposed to the extraordinary, the Modernist correlation
of aesthetic form with progress, and the postmodernist resistance to grand
schemas and closure, while ultimately wrapping all these positions up in the
B.C.E. philosopher's reliance on raw materials and immediate experience. The
B.C.E. philosopher calls upon her innocence—which does not preclude the
simultaneous, even collaborative, exercise of her intellectual or emotional so-
phistication—to remain sensitive to the nuances and subtle markings of the

world. The B.C.E. philosopher uses her neutrality as a virtue, a collecting agent for real things and real happenings. In this state of diligence, the mind stays open and responsive, hardy and observant, spontaneous and flexible:

> Listening, especially at dawn, to birds, seductive facts, we listen to their songs as to the song of brains.
> We wake and dream wanting a great accumulation of adventures, as complex a thought as possible and all there, if only for a minute, nothing but passage.
> What things know no one knows, what we were we don't remember, nothing stops, clarification is constant and ubiquitous even if things are unclear and occasions don't endure.
> (*The Beginner*, 16–17)

> All day subjectivity is an endurance awaiting objects for a minute digressing
> And it hopes for objects eager and unbaffled in spaces somewhere near eye level to greet it with comprehension during its waking hours
> (*Slowly*, 17)

If—as Hejinian has posited in her 1985 essay "Language and 'Paradise'"—the "sentence represents the entirety of a perception, a complete thought" and the "line represents ... a unit of consciousness," then each stanza section of *Slowly* and *The Beginner* can be seen as the space of occupation required to unfold the shifts of consciousness around a particular idea or situation. As such, the stanza represents a unit of experience, while the transitional white space between stanzas ultimately corresponds to change—31 changes in *Slowly*, 20 changes in *The Beginner*. When the changes themselves are ready to change character, the book is closed. It's okay for the reader and writer, however, to take their time getting to this point.

> I don't know if this can be called slowly or quickly
> Changes proceed and perhaps they cling to their cause or causes or perhaps they break free but whichever it is I can't determine, determination proceeds
> (*Slowly*, 35)

A Form of Lingering
Rosmarie Waldrop

To rub together green names and yellow sense-perceptions with thought and feeling. The thing itself transcending language. And nevertheless possible only in language. If not material can it still, in a sentence, be placed next to?

Bronze horses, you write, encounter, possible confusion, thought toward the unthinkable, as spring to cruelty, foxtail, pair of socks, not very wide.

Whether our actions—or was it words—issue from us or come flying like birds to multiply the moment. It isn't now that you could answer.

How to recall the body to itself, with lines discontinuous, metonymy restless, the mirror in back of the head? The sayable may remain unsaid in what is said, but still pulls. The force of gravity or tears.

The sun underlined, you write, not an edge, conjunction, iron filings, feathers, hedgehog, half an egg, cloud, context, launched into, and went west.

Words emitted like knots undone in time. Motes, eyes, neighbors, beams, ownership, weapons of mass destruction.

Not only have we heard all, but still can't prove the length of coastlines by the length of our ruler. Wild horses rush across the plains.

Windmills, you write, Chinese, parachutes, person, nuisance, white curtain on a rod, the full moon falls, black with life, as it continued.

As a subject cut off from everything alien would become blind residue, the line lives through its own estrangement, pause or rose. Relationships of practiced loss then shift within the skin.

A measure of the planetary system. Even if the knowable gets lost in what is known, being a woman means impetus, velocity if not location, or else whistling in your ear.

Learned to type, you write, blankets, pigs, bricklayer, lonely in the foothills, forest fire, discursive from the center, outside pronoun, a moment yellow, and most pleasing discord.

On Solitude and Writing: A Memoir of Working with Lyn Hejinian

Katy Lederer

On the first day of her class—it was my sophomore year of college—I observed her sitting stiffly in a straight-backed wood and metal chair, twirling an orange plastic pencil, the kind you can click like a pen, gazing out on all of us, her first class at Berkeley, where, some years later, she would end up a professor with tenure and a half-time load. I want to start the story here because, though I didn't understand it then, Lyn was riding on the crest of an academic wave that would transport her and several other members of the Language Movement from marginal positions as adjuncts or working at regular jobs into the heart of the Academy, and this was a trend that would inflect my relationship to poetry for the next several years. If one can allude to the "Poetry Wars" with a straight face (the idea of poets "selling out"—on either end of the aesthetic spectrum— seems artificial to me now), then I was a casualty of them. I had no idea that by taking her class, I was in point of fact enlisting, and that, no matter how aesthetically open or accepting she may have been, by dint of becoming her student I'd be taking a side.

But that would come later. Back in 1993, she was simply an intriguing new professor who could speak with a seductive intellectual power even as she kept her features friendly and at ease. She had, I felt, a lovely face: round periwinkle eyes, broad friendly smile. At once feminine and intellectually tough, I thought of Lyn as somehow better than the rest of us; spiritually inured to her particular predicaments (as an outsider poet, a woman, a mother of two), she came across as exceptionally happy, and it was this quality, more than any aesthetic inclination, that drew me to her. I was reading Harold Bloom's *Anxiety of Influence* at the time, and I immediately placed Lyn in the company of Ashbery and Stevens—two of Bloom's "poets of the air," their intellects burning with ether— while I, who couldn't help myself (oh, how I wanted to be more like them!) was a poet of earth: vegetal, dark, full of longing and anger.

But it is hard for me to write a memoir about Lyn because her entire sensibility, at least by reputation, is anathema to lyric and memoir as I write it. She is, after all, the author of *My Life*, which deconstructed the genre of the memoir before it had really come into its own. I have tended to use the genres of lyric and memoir in order to "make sense" (if not always beauty) of my emotional and intellectual experiences. Lyn, on the other hand, has always come at her writing from a more deliberate source. Her early work in particular is constructed in a game-like way, complete with rules and strategies that, though they are buttressed on all sides by philosophical ideas (about syntax and meaning and the way that language operates), I have never been able to fully align myself with. Though I have always wished I could practice my writing as Lyn does—so prolifically methodical, so properly formal—it is impossible for me.

Perhaps, then, this memoir is an accounting of envy. My envy of Lyn's intellectual method, my envy of her taut formal control. Though I am always aware that writing is a comprehensively emotional act, an act that, no matter how its practitioners may choose to articulate or calibrate its purposes, is at base an intervention in the world and thus an expression of will, I am also always aware that some writers are more "in control" of their output than others. Lyn has always struck me as a writer of impeccable control, able to begin with a project that she works through systematically until it is completed, meticulously tracing her work's implications, even as she sets it out in rich, seductive tones. In the classes I took with her in those early years of my writing life, she tended to discuss student work under the assumption it was conscious, instructive, a product of the intellect; hers was an enlightenment mentality, an aesthetic cleanly minted by the bright white fires of reason. As a young protege of Lyn's, and a striving intellectual in my own right (I was an obsessional student of social and aesthetic theory) I was highly attracted to the idea that one could set out projects for oneself, that one could theorize and synthesize—that writing could be so rational, so abundantly under control. But whenever I set about working on such projects, each of which was an almost erotic attempt to emulate my mentor, Lyn, I would feel like a fraud and a failure, veering off in some direction or other—too lyrical or intellectually oddball. It was in my second class working with Lyn, my senior year in college, that I began to think of my repeated and failed attempts to imitate her work as a form of misprision— Bloom's word for the inevitable misreading a poet will do of the work of his or her mentor. After two years of trying to write like Lyn, I became painfully aware that my writing would never be Lyn's, or even be anything like it. It was a great loneliness that suffused this misprision, this difference.

The difference between air and earth, good and evil, light and dark. I think of myself and my writing as earthy; of Lyn and her writing as lovely, divine. While I am Manichean, Lyn thrives on ambiguity. Change, for her, a pleasure; the rejection of closure, a cause. It was as I tried to be Lyn that I discovered the fundamental loneliness of poetic sensibility. There was the loneliness of my parents' divorce, of my much older siblings' departure from the house, of the loss of my mother to the depths of New York. But this was a new kind of loneliness, more hopeless, more impossible. This wasn't the young child suffering at the hands of life's vicissitudes, rather it was the young adult forced to face her sensibility.

Lyn had taken a road I could not follow. She had set for herself the task of writing through philosophy, of casting sensibility as theory. She was trying to communicate in very different ways—in much more formal ways (it seems to me)—than poets had traditionally done. It is incredibly ironic, when I look back on it now, that she was considered by the poetry establishment part of a scandal. What had always been an art of the scandal—lyric poetry, with its rhetorical seductions, its admittance of the dregs of our deepest inner lives to the vaunted white page—was now scoffing at the most proper movement to have come along in decades. Where was the threat in it, in this Language Poetry? It was thoughtful and political, even, sometimes, banal. Let's write a sentence a day about the sky, thinks Ron Silliman. Let's write in fragments, attempting to ventriloquize the disenfranchised voice, thinks Susan Howe—and the world of lyric poetry is scandalized? Proper: this is what Lyn's work was not considered then, in the middle 1990's, and what mine—dark, organic, full of longing and anger—was. It makes no sense to me.

This last year—ten years after that first day of class—on the eve of my thirtieth birthday, I found myself frightened and alone in my room. I was living in Brooklyn, in a rent-controlled apartment at the corner of Henry and Second, sleeping on a single bed I'd bought from a couple with a very young son. I didn't have a job and I was finishing a book, a full-length memoir about my family. I had never felt easy about the project, but I had figured that a memoir would be as good a way as any for me to support my poetry habit, which had continued during two years of study at the Iowa Writers' Workshop, then several years of living on no money in New York. I had recently made what amounted to a pilgrimage at the start of the project to see Lyn back in Berkeley. I asked her point-blank if it was "OK" for me to write a "mainstream memoir"—you see, I thought that she'd disown me if I did.

"Of course," she replied. "You should write whatever you want or think you need to write."

I was taken aback by her complete disinterest in the matter. I went back two more times in the years it had taken to finish the memoir, each time asking her permission; each time receiving the same vaguely puzzled approval. But now here I was at the end of the line, in my very dark bedroom on a beautiful

August morning. I couldn't bear the thought of finally finishing the thing, let alone its publication. Lacing the massive guilt I felt for having written fifty thousand words about my family was the prospect of aesthetic betrayal.

Regardless of skepticism I felt about the whole notion of an "experimental poetry," I'd been publishing a magazine that, though it had a distinctly lyric bent, was considered avant-garde. I had done my stint at Iowa being known primarily as an experimentalist, which, in its largest sense, reflected the fact that we were all—all young poets in the academy—expected to take a side. Iowa was an interesting place back then. Devoted to no single "school," a hodge-podge of very readily identifiable aesthetic inclinations, it anticipated the direction American poetry and its institutions would take in the next several years. There was the New York School poet, the formal poet, several young Sylvia Plaths, a James Merrill. It was something like a mock United Nations of Poetry, and over two full years of representing a particular faction (I was immediately labeled a Language Poet and was expected to explain all things Language when appropriate in workshops), I lost my way. I'd mistaken my identity as a poet - as someone who'd responded to a deep internal call—for this other, far less interesting institutional (or, sometimes vociferously and almost inevitably hypocritically, anti-institutional) identity. In retrospect it angers me, that what should have been so personal—the painful and frustrating process of breaking away from a mentor and learning to write as oneself—became a politicized matter. From the moment that the discourse of poetry is cast into the language of "camps," which is a military metaphor, to break away from the mentor (which under this rubric means ranging away from her "camp") is to give up real strategic ground, something that, if one is allied with an avant garde or otherwise protean movement is at best a retreat, at worst, a betrayal. This was the destructively cynical line of reasoning I'd caught myself on, and, just like a well-hooked fish, the more that I thrashed, the more aesthetically panicked and trapped I became. I no longer remembered the Lyn I'd met in sophomore year—the one who, if I had thought about things more or remembered that time in more accurate detail, would never have judged me for writing a memoir, was truly "experimental" in that she saw all writing as based in experiment. I have never met anyone so eager as Lyn to have her mind completely changed.

And so, as I sat in my dark little room, I decided to write her an email and ask her advice. I told her I was terrified. That I hadn't known what I was getting into, but that now I'd signed this contract, and what was there to do? My family, I told her, was furious with me, the writing, I told her, was not very good; though really, of course, these were all just excuses. What I really wanted, plain and simple, was to get out if it—to get out of the writing, to get out of the personal risk. As one might expect to feel about any full-length work based on one's life, my feelings about my memoir were ambivalent, and, after two years of working on the thing, I had lost all perspective. Lyn had always been for me an aesthetic and ethical ballast. Not trusting my own artistic judgment, I looked to her, my mentor, to tell me what was right and wrong, something I knew even then no artist can ever be fairly expected to do for another.

"There is nothing wrong with writing down a life," she replied. "As I think you're aware, I have all my personal letters at the library down in San Diego, and I know how you feel, the idea of people being able to paw through your experience, to know your private life. It can feel awful, but it's truly a generous thing. We need to know of others' lives. If you think, of course, that this will follow you, then don't publish it."

She was equivocal, trying to find the right level with her student who was desperately wanting an out.

I'm embarrassed now to admit to the loss of nerve I had then, but the conversation that resulted was one of the most important I have ever had—Lyn on the phone talking all about not just her life, but also the ways in which she'd written about it—written through it—and the importance of that. I think of this as the first time—no matter how much I may have adored her, no matter how much I'd looked up to her in all my years of school—that I realized she wasn't by nature a pedagogue. No, she too had a life, had equivocal, hard-earned desires: to write a few really good books. To be happy in her life and in her work. To make, as they say, a contribution to her art. She was, I could see, just a person, a human.

"Influence" originally meant an "emanation from the stars that acts upon one's character and destiny." It's related to astrology—the ways in which the heavens come to shape our very lives. In this, it reflects our basic notions of both religion and art: we imagine that our teachers are like angels looking down upon us, their purity and enlightenment guiding our way. And in some sense, this is accurate, a metaphoric portrait of the mentor and her protege. Yet as the history of literature attests, things are neither so simple nor so poetic: aesthetic grounds shift, sensibilities clash, the mentor and her protege grow apart with the passage of time. As in life, even the most intimate spiritual and artistic relationships remain unfixed, and no matter how often I return to that image, of Lyn, there in front of the class with her pencil and generous face—no matter how eagerly I try to embrace a personified version of art, an unstintingly affectionate, welcoming version—I am writing this alone.

Face/
Lisa Robertson

A man's muteness runs through this riot that is my sentence.

I am concerned here with the face and hands and snout.

All surfaces stream dark circumstance of utterance.

What can I escape?

Am I also trying to return?

Not the private bucket, not the 7000 griefs in the bucket of each cold clammy word.

But just as strongly I willed myself towards this neutrality.

I have not loved enough or worked.

What I want to do here is infiltrate sincerity.

I must speak of what actually happens.

Could it be terrible then?

I find abstraction in monotony, only an object, falling.

Gradually the tree came to speak to me.

I heard two centuries of assonance, and then rhyme.

Had I the choice again, I'd enter whole climates superbly indifferent to abstraction.

I saw amazing systems that immediately buckled.

Here I make delicate reference to the Italian goddess Cardea who shuts what is open and opens what is shut.

I conceived of an organ slightly larger than skin, a structure of inhuman love minus nostalgia or time.

Honeysuckle, elder, moss, followed one another like a sequence of phrases in a sentence, distinct, yet contributing successively to an ambience that for the sake of convenience I will call the present.

I experienced a transitive sensation to the left of my mind.

I am concerned here with the face and hands and snout.

Was I a plunderer then?

I am interested in whatever mobilizes and rescues the body.

I saw the sentiment of my era then published its correspondence.

I am satisfied with so little.

I felt pampered by the austerity—it pushed my hip so I rolled.

I become the person who walks through the door.

The air goes soft and I'm cushioned as by the skin of an animal.

I can only make a report.

Womanliness knows nothing and laughs.

I can't live for leaves, for grass, for animals.

All surfaces stream dark circumstance of utterance.

I can't say any of these words.

Gradually the tree comes to speak to me.

I collaborated with my boredom.

I write this ornament yet I had not thought of men.

I come to you for information.

Sometimes I'm just solid with anger and I am certain I will die from it.

I conceived of an organ slightly larger than skin, a structure of inhuman love minus nostalgia or time.

If only I could achieve frankness.

I could be quiet enough to hear the culverts trickling.

I'm talking about weird morphing catalogues and fugitive glances.

I could have been wrong.

I subsist by these glances.

I desire nothing humble or abridged.

I'm using the words of humans to say what I want to know.

I did not sigh.

I have no complaints.

I feel some urgency.

I confined my thievery to perishable items.

I do not want to speak partially.

I loosened across landscape.

I doubt that I am original.

I've been lucky and I'm thankful.

I dreamt I lied.

I stole butter and I studied love.

Something delighted me.

And if I am not cherished?

I endlessly close.

But just as strongly I willed myself towards this neutrality.

I enjoyed that pleasure I now inhabit.

I collaborated with my boredom.

I experienced a transitive sensation to the left of my mind.

I stood in the horizontal and vertical cultures of words like a bar in a graph.

I feel like the city itself should confess.

With the guilt that I quietly believe anything, I dreamt I lied.

I felt pampered by the austerity—it pushed my hip so I rolled.

I desire nothing humble or abridged.

I find abstraction in monotony, only an object, falling.

Yet I enjoyed sex in the shortening seasons.

I had at my disposal my feet and my lungs and these slimnesses.

I am satisfied with so little.

I had insisted on my body's joy and little else.

I wish not to judge or to dawdle.

I had no plan but to advance into Saturday.

I had a sense that I'd strengthen, and speak less.

It was a chic ideal.

Look, I'm stupid and desperate and florid with it.

I have a representation of it.

Had I the choice again, I'd enter whole climates superbly indifferent to abstraction.

I have been like lyric.

I withdrew from all want and all knowledge.

I have myself defined the form and the vulnerability of this empiricism.

I heard that death is the work of vocables towards silence.

I have no complaints.

I could have been wrong.

I have not loved enough or worked.

I have myself defined the form and the vulnerability of this empiricism.

I have nothing to say,

I come to you for information.

I burn, I blurt, I am sure to forget.

In the evening I walked through the terrific solidity of fragrance, not memory.

I heard that death is the work of vocables towards silence.

Honeysuckle, elder, moss, followed one another like a sequence of phrases in a sentence, contributing successively to an ambience that for the sake of convenience I will call the present.

I heard two centuries of assonance, and then rhyme.

I may have been someone who was doing nothing more than studying the Norman flax bloom.

I let myself write these sentences.

I needed history in order to explain myself.

I loosened across landscape.

I raised my voice to say No!

I made my way to London.

I made my way to London.

I must speak of our poverty in the poem.

I can't live for leaves, for grass, for animals.

I must speak of what actually happens —

I'm a popstar and this is how I feel.

I only know one thing: I, who allots her fickle rights.

I feel like the city itself should confess.

I only wanted to live on apples, in a meadow, with quiet.

I can only make a report.

I permit myself to be led to the other room.

I have nothing to say, I burn, I blurt, I am sure to forget.

I preserved solitude as if it were a wood.

I am ignorant, but I know.

I raised my voice to say No!

I was almost the absolute master.

I saw amazing systems that immediately buckled.

I enjoyed that pleasure I now inhabit.

I slept like these soft trees.

I'm wondering about the others, the dead I love.

I speak as if to you alone.

Am I also trying to return?

I stood in the horizontal and vertical cultures of words like a bar in a graph.

I can't say any of these words.

I subsist by these glances.

Still I don't know what memory is.

I think of it now as mine.

Here I make delicate reference to the Italian goddess Cardea who shuts what is open and opens what is shut.

I took part in large-scale erotic digressions.

The present has miscalculated me.

I want to mention the hammered fastenings in ordinary speech.

I want to mention the hammered fastenings in ordinary speech.

I was willing to suppose that there existed nothing really.

But what I want to do here is infiltrate sincerity.

I was wrong.

I'm for the flickering effect in vernaculars.

I will construct men or women.

I had insisted on my body's joy and little else.

I will not remember, only describe.

This is the first time I've really wanted to be accurate.

I will write about time, patience, compromise, weather, breakage.

I sleep like these soft trees in sleep are sweeping me.

I wish not to judge or to dawdle.

I took part in large-scale erotic digressions.

I wished to think about all that was false.

I'm really this classical man.

I withdrew from all want and all knowledge.

In the strange shops and streets I produce this sign of spoken equilibrium.

I wrote this ornament yet I had not thought of men.

This is emotional truth.

I'm crying love me more.

Its landscapes are cemeteries.

I'm just a beam of light or something.

I only know one thing: I, who allots her fickle rights.

I'm using the words of humans to say what I want to know.

I did not sigh.

I'm wondering about the others, the dead I love.

I dreamt something delighted me.

I've been lucky and I'm thankful.

I only wanted to live on apples, in a meadow, with quiet.

If only I could achieve frankness.

I had no plan but to advance into Saturday.

In the evening I walked through the terrific solidity of fragrance, not memory.

Life appeared quite close to me.

In the strange shops and streets I produce this sign of spoken equilibrium.

I could be quiet enough to hear the culverts trickling.

In the year of my physical perfection I took everything literally

Still, the problem was not my problem.

It was the period in which ordinary things became possible.

I am interested in whatever mobilizes and rescues the body.

Life appeared quite close to me.

I will construct men or women.

Limbs, animals, utensils, stars

I crave extension.

Look, I'm stupid and desperate and florid with it.

I do not want to speak partially.

My freedom was abridged.

I speak as if to you alone.

O, to quietly spend money.

I let myself write these sentences.

Of course later I will understand my misconceptions.

I doubt that I am original.

Sometimes I'm just solid with anger.

I have been like lyric.

Still I don't know what memory is.

I have a chic ideal.

Such is passivity.

I will not remember, only describe.

The present has miscalculated me.

I do feel some urgency.

Instances of Optimism in Hejinian's *The Fatalist*

Jean Day

Waking involves one in a dangerous transition from the dark
of the theater to the bright daylight of the public square. You find something
there—but that's a lovely thing about you, you always do
manage to find something.

Spilling out into evening sun from Ang Lee's *The Hulk*, Isaiah (age eight) admitted he found the science scary but didn't mind the monster. The monster, after all, is just a baby gone haywire in this version, a sympathetic if not exactly lovable type. A product of post-traumatic stress (memory) and Faustian scientific inquiry (prolepsis), he's "what happened" to his alter-ego, Bruce Banner. If fate, as Hejinian says, is "whatever's happened" (72), her own Faustian negotiations flourish by dint of an optimism that is both philosophical and practical. I take this optimism to be a form of muscular sympathy based in her idea of fate.

"Destiny is simply a good excuse for experience" (10), she says early on, pedantic, serious, and enthusiastic at once. Her method in *The Fatalist* follows from this; having limited her material to text from her own correspondence with disparate others (students, friends, relatives), she begins with an original "fated" slab of text, a record of chronological experience as it's happened to unfold. But then lines, syntax, time—and varying levels of intimacy, mood, and subject matter—are enjambed by subtraction, pared away bitwise to reveal (or create) "destiny" —which may, in Hejinian's terms, be fate in its overdetermined form: a "limiting condition" (7) toward which a life might point. As a result, *The Fatalist* is both retrospective and propositional. Its slightly torqued theses are posited as though logic, and especially the logic of experience, were by definition a sort of aleatory cut-and-paste:

> … Experience
> doesn't reveal one's own reality but the reality of things
> alien to one, the sea lost in the sky, the sky lost in a sequence of paragraphs
> and the wind blows—do I have that
> right? the only thing to offer posterity is life? (11)

Such a logic is tempered by a self-consciousness that allows Hejinian to ask questions like "do I have that right?" meaning both "do I have that freedom" and "do I have it correct" (elsewhere in the work she asks "Will this work?" [21] "What would Freud say?" [23] "Is that elitist? Is it night? Is it / morning? What is a good poem?" [37]). And this agitation to know, this doubting as investigation, sets the poem up as a kind of dialogue: these are questions addressed to an interlocutor, if not to the reader, specifically, herself. The self-reflexivity of *The Fatalist*, the play of asking and advising, experimenting and recording, works as a way of resisting the temptation to totalize or essentialize experience ("... it has seemed as if the situation requires / us to express a world view but / that would require us to view the world / and that's impossible"; 50), effectively leaving it open to "fate."

Or to digression, the most open of semantic possibilities. Diderot's digressions, and his and d'Alembert's encyclopedomania, quiver throughout *The Fatalist*— in the enthusiasm of the poem's many essayistic definitions and in the sheer messy pleasure of digression as both topic and method. A kind of backward coming to the point, digression is semantically "emptying" (entropic) but philosophically "full of possibilities" (hence, optimistic):

>   ... these are the things that excite
> the world and enter the encyclopedia
> which like fog, gathering and luminous, appears at dawn
> over the ridge.... (55)

Life, "it turns out," is an encyclopedia, full of definitions/digressions that are ultimately what it all comes down to. "Few of the ideas are mine. Thank you again" (14), Hejinian graciously admits, feinting at one of many endings that simply lead thought in a new direction. Digression too is a function of time, the passage of which produces meaning or fate ("Some days have gone by that were 'good'"; 9), and in its recursiveness it becomes a marker for time's uncontainability:

> ... The purport comes all at once
> at the end in such a way that one is thrown back
> to the poem again to carry out the "again" that the poem is
> about.... (10)

> Everything that works does so in time and testifies
> to time's inability to stop life.... (1)

Uncontainable time would be of no interest, however, if it weren't a recordable feature of human experience, a true fact of life. In practical human terms, the most significant practical feature of the optimism of *The Fatalist* is the sense in which living in time is collective and social:

> ... As of Sunday
> I'll be ... wondering what thinking can excite
> discoveries that in turn can lead to relevant pleasures, relevant propositions.
> And then the friend reciprocates
> and recounts his or her experience. Each person is an experience
> for others.... (14)

Hejinian the optimist believes in an inherent value (if not outright good) in contingent and plural experience (relevant relatives). That value is neither transcendent nor abstract; suffering and fear coexist with freedom and pleasure in The Fatalist's world, but no individual experience is defining, tells the "whole story." The fatalist/optimist moves from one experience to the next with the logic of determined luck:

> ... which reminds me that life is terrifying and to forget this
> is to miss much of life and so spend a day out
> hunting with a pair of falcons in love
> with a big guy who walks around Scotland with an eagle on his arm
> across fields accompanied by the birds.... (16)

That transformative logic, that sympathy in time (of the falcons for the big guy, of the fields for the birds, of the fatalist for them all), is the byproduct of purposive digression's constant meeting-up with stepwise and simultaneous chronologies:

> ... Every metamorphosis, after all, is a history of time
> regained by chance.... (68)

And one could hardly proceed without some sense of reversibility, however highfalutin or absurd:

> ... The upended woman on her head on a potato
> is exactly what is needed to devise
> an elegant argument in which the limiting condition
> known as "fate" and the limiting condition

known as "beginning" merge to create
an unfated ongoing incipience into which fate can accumulate
without determining anything, not even my mother's name. (7)

The fatalist, finally, is also a beginner—a Hejinian archetype from a previous work and another optimist by virtue of the fullness of time "ahead"—and all around—her. Eventful but plotless, "daily life provides us with numerous situations / but no explanation of how anyone got into them." (62) "If life is real," the fatalist/optimist says, "we aren't wasting our time living it." "You can't discourage me" (69), she concludes, "My goal / is to follow myself into the present" (70)—like an infant, lining up the punctuality of the present with the bath of continuation:

Little persons who don't exist suddenly do, becoming
a permanent part of the "forever" that is all we will ever know (17)

Optimism, if I understand it in this work, then, is the unsentimental but clearly happy living of massive, illimitable "reality" and time—their "ongoing incipience." An expression of *amor fati*: not minding whatever the monster turns out to be.

I Will Write Two Lines
Anne Tardos and Lyn Hejinian, 2005

1

I will write two lines, knowing that you will insert a third line between them
Late one afternoon in a café. I'll offer you a sequence and you won't foresee the
  consequence—
Therefore my second line's connection to my first will depend largely on you

And that will be the poetry we make. Music will intervene, but we won't complain
About interventions, but accept what happens happily, while hoping
That non-sequiturs don't make any sense. When I write, I'll attach my lines

To whatever music these strings will form—we won't complain
About the things we can't control (aggressive friends, traffic jams, the neighbor's dog);
The other speaker, who could be me, will intersperse her thoughts with mine

Just as laughter wafts through tragedy. I'm not referring to the nervous giggles,
The repressed hysteria, beads of sweat, and the twitching bladder contractions
I used to get when my shell-shocked uncle shed tears recounting the horrors of war.

Imagining future horrors is a popular pastime, which is only worthwhile
If people have other expectations, exciting plans. The imagination then can play
  with horrors and
If such an imagination prompts us to act in their prevention

(Since pleasures, too, are products of invention), then more power
Will be needed after the lightning storm that forced me to disconnect all com-
  puters and pay attention
To it. Awhile back, for instance, I imagined you in a French café

Where I sat, sipping a kir royale and imagined you in your garden—
The cineraria are stellar—myriad too—and you'd delight in nibbling at the nasturtia,
Your every move surreptitiously watched by the neighbor's cat

Being watched in turn by another cat. Historiography must be like that—the product
Of feline obsession with the art of observation they use in the gauging
Of a line of watchers producing a lineage of watchers, some hardly distinguish-
able from others

And so these nasturtia-nibbling cats wait until you leave your garden to do their nibbling
So very like rabbits that I expect to see them stop, sit up, turn ears, and hop.
But they are cats and happy
While keeping perfectly still and invisible for as long as is required.

You are far away and invisible too, as is the wind, though it is close, making itself
Known by moving lines that are the branches of the visible trees.

2

You are far away and invisible too, as is the wind, though it is close, making itself
And others feel a sudden shudder of excitement at being alive
Known by moving lines that are the branches of the visible trees.

Cactus sensibilities searing hellfire balloons
Celebrate drought life that humans fear
Paying homage to tension and attention at once.

Lizards levitate, newts secrete, salamanders serve as exemplars
Of cold-blooded stoicism, icy endurance, and a dim view
Of soil citizenship shared with spineless worms

Whipped along by life's demands into a deeper layer of the earth
Which they aerate, fecundate, and churn like clouds raising roots to the wind,
Or as cheerfully perceive as no layer at all.

But as odor and abstract (invisible) color, theirs, a whole world
Awaits them at the other side of the worm hole
Lacking perspective, they burrow through directional hollows

Not knowing how to navigate through this new parallel,
Stretching without human meaning under a human's meaningful garden
Universe in which everything seems a little different and yet the same

As it might have been before the surrounding buildings rose
Their pink stucco the color of a rose
To hide the horizon and make the distance invisible.

Invisible distance becomes a matter of imagination
Extended by memory, itself extending over facts, casting images into
Imagination—a function of consciousness, what Bergson calls the "fabulation
    function."

Though it's not the function of animals to speak
When they speak, we must listen to what
They do so sometimes as we read or sleep

Dogs will sleep anywhere, sometimes circling
Around and around before falling down to sleep.

3

Dogs will sleep anywhere, sometimes circling
Like a boa around a pig or like the hand of someone winding a clock
Around and around before falling down to sleep

Among the secrets of the sleep world that can't be shared
Is that we seem to be free of any judgment
And it's the sole truly apolitical realm we have

Yet the recurring nightmare of many
Has entered reality and is taking place now in the nation we inhabit
Finding ourselves naked in public

And unable to run, gravity holds us down
The one true transitory power
And the sand on the beach is dirty

Yes, the sand on the beach is dirty
And at low tide mud life burbles from the mudflats as bugs buzz
I rejoice that things are as they are

On the fringes of what I experience I verge
On the edge of unspeakable irritation
As my thoughts sink after my stick

Deeply probing the improbabilities
Which happy gamblers and good improvisers take advantage of, delighting in
Things going wrong or reaching incoherence

Or achieving unmanageable density—destiny
As galaxies proliferate across the cosmos
In the intricacy of a roar

Quasars' tonal quality as they starburst
Free of the foreshadows that get dreamt up in retrospect when time
Luminously zooms seemingly toward the viewer's telescope

Though it's pointed toward the horizon like a microphone set to catch a distant
    song
The telescope like a long Tibetan horn catches time, then lets it go

4

Though it's pointed toward the horizon like a microphone set to catch a distant
    song
Ledey-da-lee, ledey-da-ley   teeraloo teeralah
The telescope like a long Tibetan horn catches time, then lets it go

As far as it will go into another dimension
As flat and round as words on a page or the gray grim plane that fields
Another universe, where only certain worms can travel to and fro

On the tracks of grimy fingerprints smudged on a sheet of glass
Repulsive and beautiful at once
In which we see a human face, or its echo, a visual ghost

It all depends on who does the seeing
Through the glass by day or of the glass at night
And how the seer's imagination functions at that moment

Black or bright determines whether the seeing is sight or insight
Through a glass darkly
Or a vision of another kind, prophetic, grave, mad, or blind

Blind blob bleak black blond
As it says in an old song adrift like blue smoke in the air:
Scratch a terrier and soon find cat vomit on a desk chair

Abandoned on a street outside an empty building
In a non-local field of decoherence
Occupied now by ghosts where Billie Holiday sang

Haunted in her solitude and reveries of days gone by
By sounds that can't save themselves, they're given instead to times in places we
    remember later
Unaware of Schrödinger's non-local cat who can be dead *and* alive at the same time

In a boxwood box, close-grained, hard, and heavy
Like its inhabitants, the ideas of a hypothetical feline
As the representatives in dreams of whole events that have been condensed

Condensation is where two or more concepts are fused
So that a single symbol represents the multiple components

5

Condensation is where two or more concepts are fused
Suddenly in strongest secrecy and strangest shape, like this or that—no one will
    tell—
So that a single symbol represents the multiple components

Woven into it by the spinning thoughts of a splendid thinker
Battling with a powerful internal struggle
Who may feel that her feet are moving on their own when she walks

Transferring her body weight via her spinal column to each leg alternately
Placing left heel on a leaf as right leg swings, right toe on a scrap of writing as
    left leg swings, she exults in the weather
While balancing herself on the very top of the thigh bones, with an easy see-saw
    action in her feet

As she heads west, symbolic site of freedom and said to be the direction
Every young "man" should go
In which lies the homeland of the dead on the Islands of the Blessed

The White Isles, the Elysian Fields, where Homer tells us of shrill-blowing West
    winds that cool men
When they rage and trumpet their claims, seeing enemies lurking everywhere
    there are men,
Not designating adult males, but human beings, as mortal entities

Cast as mortal enemies and wearing symbolic masks (one white and ghostly
Barely human, stoic and expressionless,
Another red as if depicting blood or, better yet, embarrassment—or love)

Symbolizing not Eros, but bloodshed, carnage, and decimation
Savagely inflicted and sadistically prolonged, so that
Instead of promoting joy, equanimity, love, and compassion

Men heated by history before the West winds blow throw themselves
At the mercy of who knows what bloody horrors and
Into marshlands of despair where all through the night frogs sing

Dwelling in the slimy pool of anguish and dejection, the frogs
In moonlight climb onto dark lily pads and there, each forging phrases of their
    dirge, they
Make loud "thok" sounds as though a hammer were hitting an anvil

On a clear, breezy day when sounds carry and the rhythmic clop of a passing
    pedestrian's step
Seems set to the rise and fall of sirens in the distance, thought's accord's a chord
    (a cord).

On a clear, breezy day when sounds carry the rhythmic clop of a passing pedes-
trian's step
And when the clippety-clop of a trotting horse's hooves on the cobblestones
Seems set to the rise and fall of sirens in the distance, thought's accord's a chord
(a cord).

Striking resemblance to effervescent Mogador impediment
In a little port of peach is suddenly revealed, battered by wind
Cordially characterizing tittle-tattle frenzy

In a trance produced in part by derring-do drums, in part by mountain air
Where nothing is lacking and nothing is superfluous
False memories of childhood arise and we're taken out of linear time

And thrust into awareness of the present moment where our life becomes available
If only we'll recognize that patience and presence are the same, a sort of prescience
As in the Chinese proverb: "The best time to plant a tree was 20 years ago. The
second best time is now."

It's Thursday and July and it isn't until late this afternoon that the sun

Like a surreal cinematographer came out of the fog to see the fog coming in
again from the sea

Which has nothing to do with *The Fog of War*, a film I just saw
Starring Robert McNamara, whom Zukofsky in "A"-18 called "Secretary
Offense," remember him? I did,
Last night a little belatedly. If you saw it too, what did you think of it?

His apologies have come more than a little belatedly from his "bulletproof mouth"
"Raising the promise of 200,000 draftees"
Sporting (according to the poet) "hinny's teeth"—so he bit the grass while wan-
dering on all fours.

Today a midsummer Sunday as it's supposed to be: warm, dry, and serene
As the inexplicable patterns infinitesimally devised by the busy lives of everyone,
    as in a meadow—
Central Park full of children and birds and dogs surround the carousel.

The fiery horses rise and fall eternally unable to pass the spinning boat of girls
Encircling, revolving and rotating vertiginously around a time frame
In which one announces to the others "Three Spinnings: one thing spinning on
    another thing that's spinning on another thing which is the world."

The cover of this week's *New Yorker* shows "The Son of Kong" spraying the city
    and its inhabitants with his watergun
And people gratefully receiving the cooling spray, holding up their children and
    dogs to be nearer the source.

7

The cover of this week's *New Yorker* shows "The Son of Kong" spraying the city
    and its inhabitants with a huge water gun
Under a blazing sun. "Is this normal?" one might ask, referring to the summer
    heat, "or is it global warming" to have monsters delivering water
And people gratefully receiving the cooling spray, holding up their children and
    dogs to be nearer the source

Of monster culture. They want to be cool, i.e., they want to be around what-
    ever's current and hot
They join a line before even knowing where it leads to, they are drawn to
    attractions
As the movie reviewer points out: gazing at a naked body can make us more,
    rather than less, eager to know the soul "that it enshrines"

As if the soul, the essence of our personality, was entombed within our bodies
But very much alive, though no more eager to be disembodied than its stink
    wants to leave the skunk
Even though this is exactly what appears to be the case

When from a Wal-Mart in LA one imagines that one's in a French café with un
   coup de rouge and a beret

Or in bed with a lover, wrestling together with each other's soul.

Wrestling and fawning and swinging and yawning after coming
Upon one's lover's secret, namely that she or he has no secret and merely leaves
   one
Wondering how California lovers differ from French ones

Who may or may not differ from Melanesian ones but certainly do from apple
   trees
And onions and chocolate and puppy dogs and all kinds of measurements and
   video art ...
Is the last thing I said to myself (vague and yet incontrovertible) last night as I
   fell asleep in the heat.

Woke up this morning with a sigh, a certain sadness at having to cross to an-
   other realm once again
As I do each time the lights in the theater come on and the gulf between fantasy
   and reality yawns—so I do too as I mournfully leap
As if going to work wearily, hardly noticing the enormous joie de vivre and
   power flaming inside me.

The features, real or fantastic, that are not part of the plot surround it
With an intrusion upon the senses where the characters
Are the best (because shadow-casting?) of what's on the screen or the street

And a character like Lucio in *Measure for Measure* is described in the dramatis
   personae as a Fantastic
"Honest in nothing but in his clothes"
Which meant a rake or an improvident young gallant ...

"All their petitions are as freely theirs
As they themselves would owe them."

8

"All their petitions are as freely theirs,"
 Once a lowlifer, as some might say
"As they themselves would owe them."

Or as Buddha once told: Three things cannot be long hidden:
(Or four if you count the rain, five an infant's hunger)
The sun, the moon, and the truth.

"Truth is a process," says Alain Badiou, "and not an illumination."
"It is the subjective development of that which is at once both new and universal"
But the sun and moon are both

And Blake tells us, "If the Sun and Moon should ever doubt, they'd immedi-
    ately go out"
Since, as Marvel says, "we cannot make our sun / Stand still, yet we will make
    him run"
By which he must have surely meant something other than what I understood

Since the Sun is not a city light, and the Moon
At least can be gazed at as long as it reflects the sun's rays
And Rae Armantrout says, it is "none of our own doing!"

We are not responsible for everything under the stars
Nor do the stars, though they're said to be dead souls, think about us
Lest we feel ultra paranoid and self important

As we move about, stuck on the ground
Bound to the earth by the chains of gravitational forces
Even when in flight, seatbelt on, east-, west-, north-, or southward bound

Reading MOND to be the German word for moon
(Which doesn't rhyme with lune but kind of does with pond and sounds a bit
    like mount)
Or else the acronym for modified Newtonian dynamics

E.g., a flat sheet's turning up, then turning down
Demonstrating how time can curve around itself
And turning flatly round (a very dark matter

By any means of the imagination).
This is both the last line of part 8, and the third line of part 9

9

By any means of the imagination).
A parenthesis is transparent (like a window) whether it's open or closed and
This is both the last line of part 8, and the third line of part 9

Which is a wondrous number on which, as well as with which, to count
To nine is never-ending magic:
Nine women without vanity, nine horses running wild, nine bubbles—

Doesn't everything we do emanate from something we did previously?
Obedient to chance more than to causes in a world of constant changes and
    effects?
And doesn't that imply that there is no starting point—no singularity?

But then again, isn't every entity, every situation, every event unique
As is the visual representation of what "nothing" might look like
However much it's bound to other things and always found amidst them

Things that by their simple being there acquire their authenticity
From contingencies—the shadow of a flock of geese honking far above the
    street
As a creature that mimes its creator or a poem that resembles the poet

As this one would, if instead of binary semi-symmetry our body parts came in
    threes?
Could they? Don't they?
And perhaps they do since we are ourselves by virtue of our thoughts nestled
    between our eyes.

A gentle and gradual, yet inevitable transformation of certainty into a total col-
    lapse of any system
Is the outcome we intuit but cannot study systematically since many of the
    pages of the book of time are lost, which means that the sum of chapter two
    and one
Will appear all the more terrible if its occurrence is sudden, radical, and
    unexpected

As it can't help but be, though we keep the windows shut
To protect our serenity and to make sure that we remain intact
Drowning out the sounds of traffic, kids shouting, and a homeless woman's rant.

The homeless disturb the homeowners with their misery and anger
Living outside in unaddressed alleys or in front of 247 Lily Street or 938 37th
    Avenue
While inside the living room an angry man rants in front of his terrified children.

Nine miles out to sea, invisible from the city's windows, bouncing between
    waves like a word within parentheses
Bob eight fishing boats, trailing twenty-nine lines.

Thinking and Being / Conversion in the Language of Lyn Hejinian's *Happily* and *A Border Comedy*

Leslie Scalapino

Conversion: A physical transformation from one material, state, or condition to another—as in alchemy … Physical, structural transformation to effect change in function.

A primary issue of poetics in 'avant garde' or radical practices in US poetry from the late 1970s to the present is that of writing's relation to authority: the use of sources as the authority of the writing intended as exterior to or an elimination of self-expression and subjectivity; or the writing may use *identification* of subjectivity itself as a source of *critique* of subjectivity (as it's authority) in its activity of being illusion and social construction. In both of these modes or possibilities, in various 'avant garde' or radical practices, the direction has been the rejection of the assumptions of 'confessional' writing and a change in the sense of what constitutes 'self' (rejection of concept of entity of self, possibly even rejection of 'self' as the data of sensory phenomena, substituting doctrine) and thus also a change in what constitutes a basis of authority.

For example, the issue of what constitutes authority may be played out in the mode of poetry's language whose characteristic is intellectual construct, possibly doctrine-based (thus centrally motivated, in the sense of being 'idea' or description of ideas rather than, or being outside of, the language in which it is expressed); or the language of the poetry may be syntax and structure that initiates movement and change *as* its language (thus writing which *is* 'only' its language, similar to music)—or *both* of these possibilities together.

My own basis is that language which *is* the thought-sensory process, in its abstraction of 'motion' as syntax/sound (rather than representation, as the writing describing its ideas), is an occurrence itself which only takes place in reading. Yet there are subtle differentiations: writing may be a description of its ideas which as such is the *illusion of their 'occurrence'*. Further, in the contemporary poetic conversation, the language of intellectual construct proposes being free from self by marking it visibly, whereas individuated thought-sensory process of poetic language *marks itself* as subjective (that is, subjective which may be the examination as also at once the *vehicle* of examination). The latter concept of critique of subjectivity by its inclusion undertakes examination of the social conventions of language, such as the division itself—of 'self' into the category of "personal," rather than the 'self' being regarded as phenomena of senses. Language of subjectivity as its own critique undertakes also examination of the corollary assumption of such a division (of "personal" as psychological, rather than phenomenal): critiquing the view that intellectual, ironic, paratactic syntax can be separate from "personal," that intellect can be free of subjectivity. On the other hand, intellectual construct's critique of subjectivity or subjectivity's supposed elimination may be the view writing which is socially rebellious—outside of a Marxist or otherwise formal in the sense of acceptable presentation of social change—as subjective and individualistic in an egoistic manner. Thus current poetic discourse undertakes a basic American cultural dichotomy of division between thinking and being, the division itself being a determination of thought, description, and experience.

Considering two of Lyn Hejinian's works of poetry, *Happily* and *A Border Comedy*, I'm viewing her work as demonstrating aspects of US cultural conversation on dichotomy of thinking and being: Her synthesis, maintaining dichotomy, is a sense of a conception of reason articulated by her to be both a faculty and a formal element of writing. Reason (in her sense of it) is free of 'self-expression' yet has emotional and moral characteristics: She conceived of works of her writing, in the light of this conception of reason, as a form that is social harmony and experience of happiness. As such, there's the suggestion in her work that writing that is examination of thought as dichotomy would be outside social harmony.

In Collaboration

Lyn Hejinian and I collaborated on the book-length poem, *Sight*, for four years (Edge Books, 1999); we are continuing on *Hearing*, our projection being to write the five senses. Hejinian set the formal parameters of both poems, in *Sight* units of two (which could be two lines, paragraphs, or stanzas); in *Hearing*, a unit of one (usually one paragraph, which may be lengthy). The choice in advance of the formal parameters or rules of the work is an example of procedural writing, a characteristic of Hejinian's poetry, also a poetic mode of various avant garde practices (such as in the works of John Cage and Jackson Mac Low) based in the intention to go past one self's imposition (or in the older view of the Surrealists, to overcome the inhibiting control exercised by the conscious mind) on the writing. The use of procedure, obviously, is to open a work of writing to chance, to unknown change under the effect of its imposed formal directives that are to be the work's 'rules' not determined by personal will and intuition. A contrasting poetic mode (also common as basis of current radical practices) is syntax created contingent on a sense of the shape and the conflicts of whatever engagement is being 'foreseen' (an intuitive sense of the matter of or that which is arising in the writing, grasped as language-shape) appearing and changing as the work continues. An example of this mode (language-shape) is Robert Creeley's poetry in *Words* and *Pieces*. In that my own method of work is to use no advance method of determination of the language, I found the choice of the formal mode of the writing for *Sight* and *Hearing* as a determination of form in advance to have the effect of limiting the language's capacity to alter itself to allow disruption of its own determination. Change 'had to be' intellectual in the collaboration, rather than: the poet having the sense of being 'as' the language, 'inside' it, formed by it.

Usually Hejinian and I sent the poems of *Sight* by fax, frequently accompanied by letters in which we discussed elements of daily life, texts we were reading, and our conjectures considered alongside the poems influencing them. Our discussions were sometimes aesthetic debates. For example, one such discussion (initiated by myself in this case) was about Nagarjuna, early Indian Zen thinker, whose utter deconstruction of any stable entity or any basis I took as a model appropriate for poetry now. Hejinian's responses were always engaged demonstrating her characteristic intellectual curiosity. To my attempts at viewing Nagarjuna's dismantling of any logic by requiring the mind to hold direct contraries at once (which would then take each other's place/there would be no place in space then/no *then* even), she replied that this would be conflict, outside social bounds, outside harmony (precisely the point of it, I thought, since harmony is an imposition, and if so, fixed, the same as suffering). I was trying to imagine and articulate change that is not even any relation between events or any being in itself: What would 'constitute' no entity? In that conversation, I used the word "struggle" as the language gesture of 'apprehension' in comprehending such, the motion that would be entailed as language. Negative connotations of "struggle" (moral) are/were not to my point; yet that is entailed in what 'struggle' *is*. That is, struggle is inherent in apprehension of there being no entity, a contradiction.

Interestingly, I think the implication of this as language gesture (which would constitute, if one could do it, no closure, as in her "Rejection of Closure") is not dissimilar to Hejinian's statements of intention in *Happily* and *A Border Comedy*.

Hejinian's tendency is to harmonize and bring to a rational state of balance. Responding to my rendering of Nagarjuna, she stated: "Doubt is a co-participatory state of mind, whereas when one struggles, one struggles against the flow, struggle is divisive—one struggles in separation from something (as a butterfly from the chrysalis?)." In other words, a butterfly cannot struggle with its chrysalis, logically. It's true that if there is no relation as memory or structure, the butterfly does not struggle with the chrysalis. Yet—though the butterfly and the chrysalis are 'a' negative space (which can't be, they are *not* one creature)—I could still reply that the word "struggle" in this has to do with 'investigation' 'energy' of what must take place—not in either the butterfly or chrysalis? Then where?

Though this issue was of particular interest to myself, it was typical of our discussions; some centered around issues suggested by Hejinian also. Part of collaborating is to change the other person's meaning. Sometimes in our collaboration I thought harmonizing by omitting (harmonize thereby omitting) changed the meaning in the direction of happiness. So, the issue of harmonizing or happiness as a boundary was a matter of investigation and discussion as both of our points of view in *Sight*. The issue is part of both of our processes, anyway.

In a good collaboration, the other poet, the other side, is present so the harmony of one is naturally disrupted and expanded to meet the other, a characteristic of Hejinian's practice.

Conversion in the Language of Happily

Happily is language which, by being conjecture, out-runs any determination of itself, of event, or mind. The writing (poem) becomes the producing of chance. Occurrence is 'created' 'before' us/one; at the same time, the writing being its present-time — is the mode by which it has no determinacy: "I sense that in stating 'this is happening'/Waiting for us?/It has existence in fact without that." That is, statement that 'this is happening' isn't even determined by anything occurring even, is expectancy. The writing is a series of statements, and 'happening' is also outside, existing outside those statements, which are 'alongside' as it were.

Her poem is a language of determinacy that's a series of definitions (of "reason," of "happiness"), but these as changing according to their manifestation at the instant—thereby the terms' definitions/language are the means by which the writing out-runs its having determinacy (a form of holding contraries but which produce rather than cancel). For example, 'happiness' in the following sentence is a quality or event; it is a moral state, a state of being, and an action (by the sentence being a question) which occurs by its being defined (but not stable, the question mark) as distinguished: "Is happiness the name for our (involuntary) complicity with chance?"

Similarly, reason is (only): "Sentence meaning reason." Reason occurs as the structure of the (any) sentence (otherwise it's not a sentence), it's inherent in (reading) that clause of language itself. Yet joy (in us) is existing without us, is *outside* 'us' ('us' is social; so 'joy' is outside reason [which is social], outside the sentence?)—while occurrences are going on outside of us, and are only recurrent as our (her) language: "The visible world is drawn/Sentence meaning reason/ Without that nothing recurs/Joy—a remnant of an original craziness we can hardly remember—it exists, everything does, without us" (8).

The space in which one has the experience of happiness (joy) is being created (not determined) by a logic of language in which logic is not existing *then*, or outside. Happiness or joy being the sole tool of conversion, compressed in a space where no other quality or action or event is allowed by her into contemplation or occurrence (no existence of suffering comes into the space of this poem, though it exists outside—'outside' is a space the poem acknowledges) enables the poem-space to be "pleasurable run-on regeneration," a sky that's a language conversion: "Imagining ourselves under a gray sky shining so brightly our eyes can't establish any connections, a sky so bright that the option of connection isn't open, this puts us in mind of beginnings that reason can motivate but not end" (23).

The latter line as paragraph is an endless line, a language conversion in which reason can't determine or order by one making connections (as it's one endless line), nor can meaning be concluded thus finalized. In *Happily,* Hejinian views pleasure as having the potential to be endless as regeneration without determinacy, a particular definition of pleasure: distinct from, for example, the pleasure principle of the rat pushing the bar for more sugar and returning addicted to this stimulus. In other words, her definition of pleasure itself excludes, separates pleasure entirely from suffering *then* (when experiencing pleasure): time is prolonged as pleasure that is seeing—the endless time/the line in space there does not hold to suffering.

In *Happily,* Hejinian's use of the basis of happiness (a sensation/a space/ an emotion as language) is not just the desire to escape suffering, but the investigation of *there being* any such basis (of happiness), as if at all, basis that's the openness of the future of all the positions of things, for people and in phenomena—a matter or question of 'being' as urgency.

And 'happiness' can exist only if it is seen and entered into by itself (a process of elimination: "accidental wanderings having to wait widening the view between optimism and pessimism?/ Until they terminate? deny?" p. 38). That's as if a backwards Nāgārjuna (in his logic, which I'm using as a foil, everything is interdependent—there is no thing single, no entity and so not either its beginning or its ending); Hejinian's view is here akin to Nāgārjuna? Hejinian's saying happiness only exists 'as itself' without suffering *there* (in her text), the text bringing this about. 'Happiness' is 'dependent' on (and defined as) experiencing it there without end: "The one occupied by something launched without endpoint" (p. 7). In *Happily*, 'suffering' is not excluded *conceptually*, conceding its existence in fact (without this allowance Hejinian would be pretending, merely avoiding the *subject* of suffering). In a negative space she creates in which suffering is not seen, happiness is seen independent of us, and dependent on relation to *outside*: "Happiness is independent of us bound to its own incompleteness sharply" (p. 24). "Nearly negative but finite it springs from its own shadow and cannot be denied the undeniable world once it is launched—once it's launched it's derived" (p. 25–26). Rather than the gamut of experience being viewed as if anyone's actually, that unfolds in real-time, here experience being seen as 'happiness' is a mode of the writing: 'happiness' being illusion of a state/experienced (in reading) occurring as if an action of writing.

Conversion in/to Thought as Traceless Collaboration

Thus "happiness the name for our (involuntary) complicity with chance" is Hejinian's particular definition of happiness as an intention, invention. She also makes a tie between 'thinking' and 'happiness' (if 'happiness' is complicity with chance), "I am among them thinking thought through the thinking thought to no conclusion;" and a tie between 'thinking' and 'knowledge.' The latter word, however, implies something more settled than chance; in *Happily* the word "knowledge" is not used, and there is a balance of the senses with (and as thinking) apprehension: "I always thought time burning any cargo one can't take along where I gladly stood in the middle would be scholarly but it is packed to the doors with impressions and makes wild sounds or it moos" (*Happily*, p. 32).

Hejinian's *A Border Comedy* is a book-length poem with the trajectory of her present-time thinking being, in the poem, an exchange with philosophers and theorists, listed as sources for each book of the poem at the end of the poem. The structure of her poem is based on Ovid's structure and conception in *Metamorphosis*. She described her method as working at once on all fifteen books of her poem, duplicating the fifteen books of Ovid's poem, a method intended to induce her *not remembering* a narrative of any book of her own poem—but intended rather, for her to be in the present instant of her thought writing on the computer, working on all of the books or sections by returning to one after a sufficient time of forgetting (63). Hejinian is taking a gesture (from a source) and translating *their* gesture so that it is a thought of hers (a form of metamorphosis) in a form of exchange as her thinking in *her* instant. She refers to a gesture/idea of a source (though not directly by quoting) but which 'is' not the same thing as itself.

Her poem is a form of appropriation, translation which changes its sources but is experience as 'the experience of other's thought *only as hers*' (yet) in which barriers between faculties, events, and time are to disappear.

In *A Border Comedy*, there is a sense of a central presence, the life and nature of a person (the writer) referring to events and relation to others, doing a push of a buoyant stream to see how far it will go. She reaches a peak level (of holding onto ideas, stories, aphorisms within stories at once), then undercuts this maxed accumulation with boisterous humor or digression of a different thought intruding where it may, so that the writing (only its trajectory itself) takes off afresh on as if an endless horizon line of digression as narration. She makes a distinction between emotion-event, and thought-event—the effect being the sense of the poem being an attempt to convert event in thought. The conversion creates a sense of a distinction between thinking and being, as if to get 'outside' self, this separation seen as being outside of limitation, achievable as the mode of thought (20, 23).

In *A Border Comedy*, the reader isn't inside the writer, apprehension moves as the text only. Hejinian creates this present-future by the writing being: instructions always outside of the state of being—because any state of being would be (only) *one* self. There is a trajectory movement outside of any one. That 'syntax of *having* to be outside,' as it were, is intended I think to create the actual experience of being free, in the sense of being in a limitless future of beginnings, as the lines. There's also the sense of a reverse (backwards movement) from thought back into the event created by it. She carries on a debate in which her language of expository statement is at odds with enactment in language: "sensation of time (or of present time, of 'now') must also be a sense that *this is happening* (i.e. a sense of experience)" (94) . Thus, in the latter statement: nothing can happen because there is only being outside occurrence. In her mode, the self is never endangered by having to be actually *in* one self (there is a barrier to being in present event/sensation as the poem, a protection of thought going *before* it).

But we *are* realistically in a self phenomenally, any one. That is, in this poem, she is not making the reality or sensational experience of being within a self, nor does that appear to be her intention (though sometimes it *is* her intention when she speaks about writing having to have the sensation of experience, speaking then *about* writing rather than that being itself sensation). Rather, one is to be as an exchange of minds in relation to the outside. Specifically, the speaker in her poem, while sometimes accounting her life, is not a person through whom the reader experiences, she is identified as superior, exchanging in reference to the field of philosophy and theory. Hejinian's source list of collaborators, at the end of *A Border Comedy*, includes hundreds of names such as Aristotle, Gilles Deleuze, Andre Breton, Sartre, Plato, Heraclites, Martin Heidegger, Jean-François Lyotard, Freud, Williams James, Emerson, Derrida, and many others. Almost all men, her 'exchange' with them is linked to the conception of creating a history of the present: "But here's an ambitious undertaking/An attempt to account for the twentieth century!" There's a tension or conflict, I think, between her conception of knowledge as *representing* the exchange between great minds/being that, and the sense that her exchange with the ideas of these silent collaborators is not static rather, as the poem's avowed purpose, is a pole of action that is a mode of modifying experience itself (what I'm calling 'conversion').

If in *A Border Comedy* the structure, as a centered speaker/thinker (Hejinian), creates analogies describing the meaning of (as) states of being, states which as such can only be outside—this process occurring by her attempting to forget what she has written, adding lines while working on the computer, writing at the particular time within that present only, one receding into the future ahead, a sense of self coming up with thoughts so nothing's still and there's always hope—yet she suggests language cannot actually change the space. A crucial passage stresses this space as social definition: "Art is not free to innovate but is subject to semiotic constraints, rules of language it shares with its audience/In its leap" (102).

Sentence structure in this poem, being descriptive language, is hierarchical structure rendering separation of thinking and being (the conversion of being into thought): the intention is to *make* that separation (between thinking and being) as reading in the future lines. There is a hierarchical conception in Hejinian's division between knowledge which is the province of great minds, and *apprehension* which could be that of anyone. Thus a hierarchical construct is also mirrored in the border which is set up between the "border ghosts" listed as the sources who are Hejinian's silent 'collaborators' and the readers, as also in the distinction made between those listed as sources (the philosophers and theorists) and those thirty listed in the acknowledgments (placed separately at the book's beginning, the list including women) who are poets and artists not considered by Hejinian to be sources though echoes of their concepts and works sometimes occur in the poem. (For example, Carla Harryman's utopian theory seems to be echoed in references to "the Utopian man" in Hejinian's Book Two,

p. 28–40 and Books Three to Four, p. 45–65. Harryman is included on the list of friends, but not on the list of sources-collaborators.) Only seven men who are living poets are listed in her sources. As far as I can tell no women who are living poets or artists, only a few who are critics and philosophers are listed as sources for *A Border Comedy*. "When I was young, for example, whenever I wrote I was a man/So I mentally imitated men/But in the end the form was too hierarchical" (187). Though she there disavows this hierarchical view, even her interjecting the distinction that imitating being a man *is* hierarchical (men are hierarchical and women not? men being at the top? She adds that her choice was based on men having power), is itself hierarchical *there* because aspects of this relation, as in the very statement of it, are still in place. Thus there is a social space that is also reflected in the sentence structure; *both* social implication and written structure are making a division between thought and being.

Another aspect of this division (between thinking and being), a corollary, is the conception of knowledge as cerebral, rather than apprehension occurring from all of the senses. She broaches the dichotomy as if the senses had to be reversed as (to be) the intellect in order for experience to occur: "Let's up to sleep! Between the sample and the meal/How difficult it is to experience anything! How difficult it ought to be!" Experience is a sample to demonstrate thought. She sometimes uses statement that by its form is inarguable (only because there's no talking back/it's non-participatory), and in its content is separation of thinking and being as separation of mind and body, inaccurate statements (considered by this reader): "Before this, science declared that we are physical machines that have somehow learned to think/Now it transpires that we are thoughts that have learned to create a physical machine/At the first hint of light in the morning/Everyone appears 'likely to express'/There's an ancient belief that after too many words/The body runs out and lies empty" (99). Every point in this layered statement is I think inaccurate: that science is a single entity which at some point declared we were physical machines who have learned to think; that it's now found that we all, like machines, are likely to express (as if *expression* were robotic, separate from *thinking* that is free); and that physicality derived from evolution, as separate from thinking, is the source of *expression* (which would therefore be only physical and emotional rather than 'of being' as such). Even in her questioning a mind/body split, it is rigorously reinforced: "Diderot may have been right/The mind may be nothing without the impulse-ridden body." (130.) As if to have impulses is to be "ridden," rather than sensations and concomitant impulses all being part of mind.

A metamorphosis that is outside of mind/body dichotomy is linked to her particular process of collaboration as abstraction. Dissolution of the narrative she sees as tied also to dissolution of sensory apprehension, the rendering of that in writing: "Excessive change in time will destroy the sensing body parts" (23). She comments on conversion into thought that is exchange with others who are "border ghosts" establishing a relation between using the ghosts' part of the exchange, their secret contents in almost an overflow to surpass the individual, and her intent of changing apprehension as the space of the poem itself: "the number of events it takes to create the probable sequence/Necessary to cause a change in any person's state" (13). "We share in the capacity of narrative to submit to the desires of this or that mind/Without giving up its secrets/And speak when no one answers." (12)

An example of minds meeting outside one's own mind: she describes a dream meeting conscious life as the subject of the poet's experience (in the passage below) and the structure of the poem as *that* experience. Yet she states what our experience *is* in reading rather than rendering sensation or impression of dreams meeting waking occurrence. She makes an image of dream meeting waking life given only as an idea in one isolated spot, pushed then into the beginning of the next book of the poem: "In sleep/My dream would be to create a sort of eye on the tongue/Then speaking the broken edges of my conscious life would meet/And merge over the gap in which I'd see/Half my life/Meeting my other half" (88). Statement shapes the whole rather than our having the sense of experiencing this perception. In *A Border Comedy*, by the very form of the work, she does not carry on a conception for long; but rather, as her purpose, drops or applies ideas at will, a 'random' reference to ideas as they come up (working on the various books on her computer at once) but with the intention that this 'random' process of the writing get through to a different level (akin to Andre Breton breaking down conscious control over the writing; except, the opposite of Breton: Hejinian is emphasizing 'the rational' overcoming the other side that is emotional and physical) (89).

The conception of "truth" apparently bound up with the view of knowledge as exchange between great minds in which the poem is thus a form of history (of their thought as being hers in metamorphosis in which, repeating an unnamed object it loses its antecedents (24))—even real-time history is converted into her thought. The poem introduces truth, in the sense of "History Introduces Truth," by its ideas being assumptions of other beings: "*One feels oneself to be one's own self and another.* Such a Truth can only be corroborated through terrifying degrees of empathy. *And this original crisis is the eternal moment of metamorphosis.*" (28) The latter idea may be rendition of Nietzsche or Jalal Toufic's discussion of Nietzsche, Hejinian is conveying that the original crisis cannot be *rendered* as the language (citing the struggle of attempting to render is stated descriptively)—precluded by the hierarchical separation itself between thinking and being as in the sentences quoted above. Nor can the experience that arises from that crisis be rendered—the reader can not feel terrifying degrees of empathy by reading Hejinian's text. For the text is by intention a metamorphosis that is a change taking one out of feeling that is emotional, sensory apprehension, or intensity of terrifying empathy.

The nature of realism is a central issue of Language writing, with differing outcomes but usually with the weight on critique of subjectivity. Hejinian's intentional splitting of thinking and being defines her particular conception of realism: she associates isolation of 'one as entity' with the "lyric program" (whose credo is to disguise as beauty, recurrence concealed). Thus, she stresses, beauty emphasizes the individual object or event, submerging the recognition of its narrative that is actually only interdependence of movements, such as jumps and mind-process (which is an event's *non*-existence as single entity). I'm phrasing this as elucidation as negative space. She makes an association of beauty with dichotomy, the tendency of the proponent of beauty to isolate negative things that happen, such as atrocity: the effect of which is that 'atrocity' may be *merely witnessed* by the feeling individual—rather than its accurate/realistic basis being *engaged*: perception as relation in context, atrocity is only in relation to other events in a stream when seen in its interdependence, akin to Nagarjuna's view. In the following lines, beauty (the lyric program) is described as implicated in being outside merely 'witnessing'—and "atrocity" is reduced to its thought in her only, a minor level almost non-existent or only part of harmony, as if there *were not* real atrocities? these *not* having great significance? Her distance from particularity of event, and that as removal of tension between events, produces an imbalance by its very balance: "Repeating like squirrels/In a lyric program meant to beautify the interstate/And disguise recurrence/So that an awful thing that's happened, an atrocity, can be isolated/"Witnessed"/And at that a kindly gardener who never says a word comes to push my sled" (62). While her intention is to show the submerging of egoistic seeing as failure to accurately see atrocity, there is in those lines not *time* to see the particularities of some atrocity.

In other words, in this passage unintentionally she smoothes over, not dissimilar from beautifying the interstate, not disallowing but not bringing up the subject that there are real atrocities. Harmonizing is more depersonalizing than dissonance, precisely because dissonance allows *all*, aberration as well as a norm (contradictory factors—all can—occur as dissonance).

Examples of hierarchical structure in language which transforms detail as experience of event into a *description of its meaning*: Hejinian proposes the idea of "Lodging the dream of the night before into the action of the day ahead/ In accordance with the laws of time we provide/Having yearned to follow our soulful thoughts out beyond the world and then having found that we've turned around to face and follow the world instead" (69–70). I compare her image of the dream pushed into the action of the day to a method of writing as well as active use of dreams in my prose work, *Defoe* (68–82), dream meeting waking life, halves of both as run-on process of night and day collapsing on each other. The writing of this part of *Defoe* is to push a random dream, as any (in real-time) occurred, into the day ahead of it until it meets the day and is in it, *is* it, though the day is also only itself realistically. The text makes a space: the dream as a space (rather than the dream's content) pushed into waking space grasped by the mind; there isn't any barrier that would be time/location/ as mind or self that's distinct from that space. There's a difference between real structure as *a real-time action (real dreams and real days) that's also a writing syntax* and Hejinian's description that is the *idea* as *image* of lodging the dream into the action of day, then described in intellectual statement as one having sentiment, "soulful thoughts." Her image is also *summary* of an emotion, occurring as sentiment (rather than a line of writing that does/is an action). My emphasis is her construct as division.

I'm comparing action and thought, considering what Hejinian conceives sensation of experience to be, and considering how this relates to her conception of knowledge:

A dream in the future of an eye on the tongue where her conscious life meets the gap of her other half, startling as physical, sensational (88), becomes a conversion of the event of the dream to thought which then appears to be pushed into the beginning of the next book (summarized, however, as its meaning or purpose): "And at each step let what passes for reality rise/To assimilate the day/And complete the transmutation of what would otherwise forever cling to its objects/Into an approximation/A promise/An imperfect proximity/Or premise/Like this, that every authentic poetic project is directed toward knowledge" (89). Hejinian takes the imaginative construction (and/ or the activity) of the dream pushed into the day ahead or the other half of oneself, appearing in Books Five and Six, and reiterates this once in a further chapter, Book Seven, as if we've been continuing to experience this all along without recognizing it: Describing it therefore gives the sense of 'experience'— interpreted by Hejinian there, however, as being for the purpose of "knowledge" ("knowledge" is not elucidated except as a goal) which is accumulation socially defined in the sense of defined by that which is outside of oneself/is outside of what is given *there* in the text. The experience is for a purpose other than itself.

This is the opposite of its source in *Defoe* where day and night transformed *there* there is nothing outside these.

Writing as abstraction of other's ideas or dreams and events being intentionally degraded experience that is a kind of transformation of herself (oneself) is, in the terms of Hejinian's poem, a metamorphosis into an exteriorized as such completely different version akin to an invisible exquisite corpse which she likens to the game of "Telephone" in which an original sense is changed by someone else repeating it: "shelter was found in a cave, conversation ensued, and in time the experience was passed along—as the experience of the experience—exchanged/There's nothing more to explain/The story is that the listener understood one thing, relayed it, it was understood as something else, but everything worked out/Who then is the victim of semantics?" (70–71)

In the following three lines Hejinian identifies the problem that descriptive language can state *anything* as having taken place, the language always elusively false: "The sudden but complete recognition of reality that produces serenity/ And if ever a man breaks my heart with his indifference, then I will break my mirror/It will be punished for its sincerity/I'll throw down the mirror and name it ship." (71) That is, if the writing is not *actually* producing serenity, and the mirror of the writing reveals that, then the mirror can be broken to substantiate a lie (the lie being, in that case, that one is in serenity): under these conditions writing can be anything. Following these (above) lines, she embarks on, by introducing the conception of, lampooning her own system: "unsystematic lampoons of systems, and all manner of reversed reveries ... We are stunned by the riches of the riches if and when they (the rich) have too many museums/... The object was (to be) stunning/So that all the mind's faculties might overcome the mind's limits" (71). Her method is a describing being bombarding of all the faculties in order to overcome their limits. Yet she still holds thought as actual basis. To include the recognition that language merely names and can change the name, outside of and regardless of 'the real,' is to bombard the illusion of language's truth—but in so far as she lampoons her own method it is *as* that logic (hers), *not* transgression *outside* it. She also suggests, and apparently endorses, that the context is only illusion improved by text, whose standard is social definition: "The improbable environment/Which is improved with telling ... Perhaps that's because, in the end, what most of us most desire these days is to be /Recognized /How religious!" (66–67) Elsewhere in the poem, statement as didacticism to "unite the process of 'transformation with that of interpretation' in a sequence of willed culminations" (73) is also a state of being free of self akin to happiness (82, 83, 84–85).

I use the word "didactic" to refer to the distinction that: interpretation of the text, within it, is given (as from authority) rather than the reader deciphering the text as phenomena.

A Border Comedy attempts to outrace finality of 'experience'—substituting experience or event with 'thought,' which, as if that were more permanent. While allowing the presence of others as her collaborators, Hejinian interprets change as a metamorphosis of all *to be* her scheme. Although the very material of the poem is the constructs and ideas of a multitude of others *within her*, by filtering out (by not identifying, except as unattached list of references, her collaborators, at the end of the book) the contexts of their gestures, the effect/action of these gestures or conceptions is also eliminated, creating an absorptive text which states ideas, including her imposition of resolution of conflict. Though she is broaching the issue of 'experience' as the writing's process itself, the poem can't embody/render that—in that its premise is 'thought as gesture itself,' a metamorphosis of event to be abstraction *to transcend the impermanence of constructions of self* (20). Producing a border of 'experience' and language, the author separates the reader's apprehension from this border by the poem's very sentence structure, as well as by the text's whole structure and conception (such as reference to outside-silent sources), as hierarchical frame. The poem ends with a sense of resolution which is description of the single individual, the author and her life, as made up of experiences of pleasure and suffering.

A Border Comedy creates a bind in the very problem it seeks to broach: By converting sensations, exchanges with others, their gesture, etc. into 'thought' in order for these to be experience(d), they can't be experience. *One* can't be (in) 'experience'—because, for one thing, "knowledge" is regarded as outside oneself and an acquisition (acquired from philosophy and theory). Hejinian's intent was to write "a poem that kept itself apart from me/And from itself" (63). The idea of sensation or impression, always separate from the sensations or experiencing these, thus giving the reader the impression of *having had experiences which they haven't had*, is a divide whereby one is both eternally separated, and, as part of that hierarchical construct, defined by structures and allusions which emanate from a centered self (writer), who is therefore separate from the reader, the reader separate from phenomenal experience. Thereby, one could neither be outside social definition nor be oneself. *Happily* was written after *A Border Comedy* and as an engagement of being is without the latter's conflicts. The later poem is almost the 'reverse' as gesture. Yet *A Border Comedy* is interesting for broaching a range of Hejinian's aesthetic ideas and characteristics of her language, as well as being demonstration of our cultural dichotomy of division of 'self' from phenomena.

In both *A Border Comedy* and *Happily*, Hejinian's project is the engagement of being. In *A Border Comedy*, the description of someone else's idea already transformed as hers without citing the particular reference *in* her text (nor conversing with the reference), in a series of such continuous descriptions or rendering of references, is removed from its traces; her poem itself is as if past-times, discoveries already formed outside of *A Border Comedy*. The instant of discovery as interaction with these references is not in the poem, which gives the poem a personal orientation. This suggests a comparison and also an addition to Walter Benjamin's "Art in the Age of Mechanical Reproduction": Rather than the discovery's originality as its defining or crucial characteristic (Benjamin citing the demise of a particular sense of originality), I'm considering that by omitting the connections that were made in *coming to* a discovery, the discovery isn't duplicated—only the summary of its meaning as a product is given. A discovery is its process throughout, being *its connections of all of its times*.

In *Happily*, the text is directly engaged *as* the process of making an accumulation of comparisons, even between contraries, the process being the sole activity. Effortless in the sense of utterly attentive. Her mind converses with her mind, even by omissions and additions brought into that converse. 'Being' is not only the subject but the activity; 'being' (as if 'being there' or 'being in the act of' as well as 'a being') is neither solely idea nor solely mind leaps that take place as if space between connective points. All of these occur as one. The text's activity thus is its inner life, free of addressing terms of social definition outside itself.

Similar to Walter Benjamin's observations on the degrading of experience (the individual's experience in the modern time having no authority, in Benjamin's essay "The Storyteller"), theory because of its generalizing function has the quality of authority. Dualism turns the act of occurrence 'back' into composed description of its meaning as part of a 'then' composed whole seen as given, a division between oneself and phenomena and between writing and subject matter. The alternative to dualism is not seamless occurrence (or in writing, not seamless narrative), but rather the acts of occurrence being seen making the structure in which they are—and the acts at once seen to be separate from the structure, free in the sense of the structure unknown not formed yet.

In summary, Hejinian's recurrent theme or intention is a version of 'happiness' that is defined loosely as without closure, a complicity with chance as a state of (in) the language. This version of 'happiness' includes a conversion of phenomena into (as) thought. As such Hejinian's project is 'visionary' to bring about a type of experience, not typical or a summary of a period of poetry, though its *ideas* are indicative of this period's ideas.

Dipping back into earlier works, such as "The Green" (choosing it at random in *The Cold of Poetry*), the hierarchical balance (such as authority of speaker/poet and sources) of *A Border Comedy* is not the frame in the earlier poem (nor of *Happily*, as I'm indicating, which is most recent). "My dream life is lit by a eulogistic flicker. The belated heavenly bodies orbit. Dreams don't waste the present. The air moves around, holds time, carries sound. Skywriting marks the air with pressing shadows of a thousand trees" ("The Green," p. 133). There, present dreams are as if outside the present, as are heavenly bodies. The air which moves around (around what?) holds time (is thus separate from time). Everything separate from everything else is simultaneous present (by being present together) non-hierarchical. It is not possible to separate sky writing trees.

In regard to writings' relation to authority: The introduction of hierarchy occurring even as the mode of *A Border Comedy*'s procedural process (use of authority as references from philosophy and theory—in descriptive language of intellect rather than observation or sensation), in a poem which is a scheme of history, reinforces the sense of history as hierarchy. That is, the procedural method of composition, apparently individual (in the sense of being open, not composed in advance, the poem described as written in separate, continual beginnings intended to be without imposition by the writer's conscious control— the sense of use of time to forget the narrative of any particular book, the author working on all fifteen books on the computer at once) gives the impression of the poem's hierarchical structuring itself as a description of uncomposed reality. The writing as statement of ideas, continually separate from its experience, is a sense of a virtual reality creating this period's ideas, indicative of the phenomenon in this period of conception of authority as itself changing reality.

Works Cited and References

Benjamin, Walter. "Art in the Age of Mechanical Reproduction" and "The Storyteller." *Illuminations*. New York: Schocken Books, 1969.

Creeley, Robert. *Words*. New York: Scribner's, 1967.
____. *Pieces*. Los Angeles: Black Sparrow Press, 1968.

Hejinian, Lyn and Scalapino, Leslie. *Sight*. Washington DC: Edge Books, 1999.

Hejinian, Lyn. *Happily*. Sausalito: The Post-Apollo Press, 2000.
____. *The Border Comedy*. New York: Granary Books, 2001.
____. The Cold of Poetry. Los Angeles: Sun & Moon, 1994.

Scalapino, Leslie. *Defoe*. Los Angeles: Sun and Moon, 1995.

Figuring Out
Lyn Hejinian

"Don't you hear that terrible screaming all around us, that screaming
that men call 'silence'?"
   (Werner Herzog, epigraph to *Every Man for Himself and God Against All*, or
The Mystery of Kaspar Hauser)

In *Dahlia's Iris: Secret Autobiography and Fiction*, Leslie Scalapino describes her
As: All Occurrence in Structure, Unseen—Deer Night as a "physiological-concep-
tual tracking of—that is—reoccurrence" and as "a particular schism/gyration of
'the inside of the inside' *being* 'the outside of the outside' (at once)."

"The text," Scalapino says, "is syntax of split or shape, a schism/gyration (of an
earlier event—which was: 'getting it' that there's death—*experienced* by me as a
kid at age fourteen, it has a particular past). [...] The text is reoccurrence of that
particular earlier conceptual (spatial) configuration but in *Deer Night* it is syntax,
not transcription of events as content of that earlier time (rather, events as 'interi-
orized' then, not 'known'). This is for one the inside of the inside of the outside.
Seeing history outside 'that person' (one), *in* oneself—later, in a crowd."[1]

This text is a physiological-conceptual figure precisely as motion is in cinema.
The inside of the inside of a movie is its moving, and that moving is what pro-
duces the phenomenological creation of the outside of the outside. In just this
way, the text of *Deer Night* is a motion-figure. Its action occurs on the inside, as
action in a film occurs between frames, and what we read is not something be-
coming something else but change (described as a schism / gyration) itself.

Though it would have been more salient, perhaps, to talk about Scalapino's
writings in conjunction with *The Invasion of the Body-Snatchers* (discussion of
which takes up a long section of the *Secret Autobiography*, it being, as Scalapino
has told me, one of her favorite films [the remake, with Donald Sutherland]), I
am instead going to point to Werner Herzog's 1974 film, *The Enigma of Kaspar
Hauser*, or, as it is more properly titled [when the German title is translated
literally], *Every Man for Himself and God Against All*. Though very different art
works coming from very different sensibilitites, both Herzog's *Kaspar Hauser*
film and Scalapino's *Deer Night* are expressive of certain similar views regarding
the state of things, among them that so-called civilization (culture, the social)
is full of pitfalls, and that landscape is not mere background but is itself the
shape / gyration of what happens in it. And in both Herzog's and Scalapino's

view, it is extraordinarily difficult, perhaps even impossible, for a person either to find his or her place in the landscape or to separate from it. In this regard, Scalapino's view is particularly radical. Existing occurs simultaneously both as what's identifiable, distinct and separate, and as what is, by definition, non-separate (here Scalapino follows Nagarjuna's precept that nothing has inherent existence, there is no distinct independence). "People are everywhere but are part of the existing calm endless terrain."[2]

If I had time, I would want to make the move between *Deer Night* and *The Mystery of Kaspar Hauser* via the epic theater of Berthold Brecht and the operas—*Parsifal*, in particular—of Richard Wagner, an odd pair, I know, and the Wagner, especially, must seem an unlikely context for understanding something about Scalapino's work, but I believe that there is something to be said within the context it provides. In *Parsifal* the plot, the drama, is entirely interior, and the sole site of real motion is in the music. The shape of the movements of the characters is driven from within, as a manifestation of radical inner conflict rooted in a past that has become the inner shape of the outer present, its wound.

To an only slightly less noticable degree, the drama of Herzog's hero, Kaspar (whose innocence parallels that of Wagner's Parsifal) is also an interior one, the drama of existential wonder (astonishment at the not-necessary but possible character of all that appears) and of social suffering (Kaspar's wounded state is social and all evidence indicates that it was the result of social forces—a dynastic battle over competing heirs to the house of Baden, one the rightful heir who was said to have died as a very young child and the other his cousin, who became the heir after the death of the child and in fact became prince of Baden).

Suffering has been a persistent concern in Leslie Scalapino's work. She can quite accurately be said to be at work on the problem of suffering, a problem that is always under scrutiny by Buddhist philosophy, which originates in pondering the causes, interior (in the mind) and exterior (in the world), of suffering, and the possibility for freedom from it.

Buddhist philosophy, which Scalapino has studied for many years in great depth and detail[3], makes two observations of particular relevance: first, that pain and suffering are ubiquitous and that living as we do in their midst we cannot help but be in a state of terror; and second, that empirical reality is solely phenomenal—a matter of appearances—and we can never see anything as it is (per se, to use Scalapino's term, or as a thing-in-itself, to use Kant's), first because it doesn't show itself as it is and second because, after a space of time no greater, according to Nagarjuna, than 1/65th of a finger snap, our perceptions are immediately taken over by our intellect, a constructed (or, in Nagarjuna's terminology, karmic) formation, the result of and force for conditioning (and thus also taking over) by the force of previous experience, including, perniciously, social conditioning.

In several respects, the conflict faced by someone in quest of clear seeing but trapped within karmic formation is related to the familiar conflict between individual and society that was the central preoccupation of the 19th century novel and of crucial concern to the Protestant, capitalist, middle-class. This middle-class was heir to the imperialism that was an intrinsic part of the Enlightenment, whose values seemed to justify colonialism and which in turn made the rise of the middle class possible. But to the degree that Scalapino's *Deer Night* participates in the tradition of this conflict, it does so in a particularly radical way. It carries out a challenge both to individuation and to the social, attacking the assumptions on which both sides of the conflict were premised.

It is in this context that, in *Deer Night*, Scalapino has rewritten *The Tempest*, which she views as a drama of imperialism.

Her rewriting of *The Tempest* is extreme—it is absolute. Scarcely a trace of *The Tempest* remains. It is, she has said, "a total rewriting—that is, without using the plots, characters or language of Shakespeare. The writing is not a 'lyrical' 'meditation' on Caliban's colonized state.... It is perspective that is rearrangement.... It's rearrangement of one's thought, by demonstrating its rearrangement."[4]

With the stakes as great as they are (and it is because so much is at stake that Scalapino's writings have such emotional intensity), such a rearrangement must be total—it must rupture as well as shift. It involves wrecking the mind. As Scalapino says, "I just want to wreck your mind."[5]

Wrecking mind—or "continual conceptual rebellion," as Scalapino terms it—is not something to be undertaken casually; this is not gestural, it involves no glib theatricality, and the syntactic layering and the conceptual difficulties—the mind-wrecking devices—are not mere avant garde gestures; Scalapino's work is not about surface aesthetics.

Scalapino feels that it is her *obligation* to wreck mind: one's own mind, since in exercising its powers of interpretation, it obscures experience under clouds of illusion, nullifying empirical haeceity and blinding us to reality; and the mind of others,' since in interpretating us, others perform acts of deformation and even, potentially, of destruction.

"Continual conceptual rebellion," she has said (in conversation with Dee Morris[6] and me), is a means of outrunning the forces that would re-form (conventionalize) one. If you stay in one place too long you'll be taken over—either by your own fixating ideas or by those of others, either of which can immobilize and re-form you. To survive (the body snatchers) one must always be outrunning the destruction of the world. It is for this reason that travel is such an important motif in Scalapino's work[7]. Travel does the urgent work of changing everything at once. It undoes the world and it undoes the traveler.

Travel is a motif, not a theme; it is a motif in the Russian Formalist sense—an integral part of the dynamic that structures the work by propelling it. Likewise, and for similar reasons, surgery (and related procedures—such as the scan requiring that the body, one, be injected with dye) appear as a motif—as the site of the non-separation of physical and psychic suffering (pain is terror, terror pain) while also bringing about an undoing, not in the form of a demise but in the form of transformation, metamorphosis, outracing. "Seeing the blue dye within myself (and therefore seeing not on my eyes) I was running at dawn."[8]

The writing being 'on' an early split in one's psyche is not 'about' one's psychology. It's a way of there being no difference between occurrence in the outside and as the inside. So that one is not separate from occurrence. *As: All Occurrence in Structure, Unseen* is reenactment of political discourse as it's being also a form of silence: people's expression that is not recognized or comprehensible as 'discourse.' It is expression that is excluded.

The refusal to be defined, by the action of out-racing 'one being defined'— and not 'being' that action either (of out-racing), though that's all that occurs—'to be' out racing (as a form of silence that 'isn't' 'inarticulateness'). Writing 'could be' leaping outside the 'round' of being interiorly/culturally defined (at all) (by oneself or outside) …[9]

The full title of *Deer Night* is *As: All Occurrence in Structure, Unseen Deer Night* and if we take all that follows the colon as a subtitle of sorts, we are left with a title consisting of the single term "as," a word that withstands a great deal of scrutiny, a word that, according to the linguist Ann Banfield[10], isn't even, properly speaking, a word at all. It has function but no meaning. It is what is known as a hyperfunctional element, operating variously and, as one book on grammar puts it, "often ambiguously," which is to say that its functions are not always mutually exclusive. It can serve as an adverb (Webster's offers "*as* deaf as a post" is an example) or as a conjunction (and Webster's offers the phrase "as deaf *as* a post" for this, too, though with the emphasis on a different "as," as well as "spilled the milk as she stood up" and "she stayed home as she had no car"); it can serve as a preposition ("works as an editor," "appeared as Hamlet"), as a pronoun ("she is a foreigner, as is evident from her accent)," as an intensifier (for example, adverbially, as in "I came as quickly as I could"), and as a complementizer ("Fury is smart as horses go"). It can register temporal relativity ("as the doorbell rang, I put on my coat") and causative relativity ("as it was cold, I put on my coat") and often there is ambiguity as to which it is doing; the difference between sequence and consequence is blurred. *As* is a site of relationships—it is neither one thing nor another but, in Scalapino's sense, it is "occurrence in structure, unseen." It is prevalent in metaphors, and by virtue of its presence it produces metamorphoses. It is "syntactically impermanence," cinematic motion, the shift / gyration of semantic transmutation.

"Yes," Scalapino wrote in a fax to me (June 5, 2000)—"Yes, complete meta-morphosis—the urgency of necessity for that utter change literary (so that 'one does not = one' at all nor is 'one inside social construction' 'while being that') is in all of the works I find, including over and over in "Deer Night"—such as pages: bottom 31–32, p 90 and 91, p. 94." I'll quote from page 94: "The black butterflies as the worms on the red wheat fields—irreducible as the black but-terfly/which is the man flying being that. On a hot vast terrain of fields *per se*, there are no people. I could only repeat that. It's its relation."

This relation is the result of what I would like to term the "as effect." In order better to explain what I mean by the "as effect," I want to turn for a minute to a grammatical unit in Russian: what is known (in English) as the instrumental case. Like the particle "as," the Russian instrumental case has an array of func-tions. And it often is optional whether one uses it or some other grammatical construction—to use it, in other words, is intentionally to evoke a subtlety that is inherent in virtually every one of its usages—the "as effect." Thus, one can say, "she sings like a nightingale" in two ways. The first simply uses "kak" (like)—poyot' kak solovei; the second uses the instrumental: poyot solovyom. The first says solely that she sings like a nightingale, the second says that but in the sense that she sings as a nightingale—in singing, she becomes nightingale. A slightly more radical example is this: one can say "they were walking along the shore" simply by using the preposition vdol (along) (oni shli vdol berega), or, by dropping the preposition and using the instrumental (oni shli berogom), the latter intimating that in walking along the shore one is that shore—one, as it were, shores the body of water beside which one walks. And my final example is a line from a poem by Boris Pasternak, whose English translations says: "Through the snow I walked, followed by fading footsteps," which is accurate as far as it goes but misses what is most powerful in the Russian, where "fading footsteps" is in the instrumental case—suggesting that his walk in the woods exists in and as the fading footsteps that follow him. He is, in the language of the poem, walker becoming his tracks, walker in his tracks, walker as his tracks.

What I am calling the as effect is not a trope but an "occurrence structure." Within its realm, everything is what it isn't and isn't what it is.

In contemporary Western philosophy, one might look to the work of the most radical of the deconstructivists to find an analytic method capable of disclosing the prominence of "as" occurrences. But it is to ancient Eastern philosophy that one should look for the account of it that most closely corresponds to that of Scalapino, and in particular to that of the highly sceptical Madhyamika school of Mahayana Buddhism, known as the Middle Way.

The notion of the Middle Way of Madhyamika as developed by the second century (AD) philosopher, Nagarjuna, is not to be confused with the notion that Aristotle termed the Golden Mean. It is not about moderation. It is, rather, an extreme and relentless mode of analysis that discloses the impossibility of characterizing the nature of anything because it denies the possibility of anything's being something per se, that is, on its own, independent of everything else. "The content of the world is not an established order or form, but a process of ordering and form-giving, and [...] every order must make way for another order, every form for another form."[11]

Or as it says in *Deer Night*:

> Because all belonging—in the contemporary society—is the creation of actions that are the society—any is to violate actions
> Violating one's own actions in oneself—inner—dawn—as volatile rim, only, then.

> Present as disjunct per se only—that space / time cannot be 'their' narrative—or one's. Event is between.[12]

Since nothing can have independent, self-contained existence, nothing can exist as the terminus of analysis and nothing definitive can be said about anything. Things only exist *as* what they are. It is in this sense that the Middle Way of Nagarjuna can be said to lead neither here nor there and be seen to be about neither this nor that. It has the formal properties of emptiness—it is *as* emptiness.

These properties in *Deer Night* appear as images in order that they have particularity and be given substance as thought, since it is substance and substance alone that bears sensuousness. They appear as images because the work is addressed to the world of appearances, the world of becoming, the world in which things arise, endure, and decay, the world that excites our longing and eludes our grasp.

The poetry does not split itself off from that (this) world, and in fact it can't—it's in language, and language is entirely of this world. The only things for which we have words are appearances.

But even while being restricted, bound, to the world of appearances, the poetry can (and does) allude to thought between the words—thought which is still "in" the poem but not worded, just as motion is "in" a movie but not in any of its frames.

This thought lies between the images—at points of metamorphosis. These are the most obvious "as" points, where the copula "is" has been transmuted into "as," itself now functioning as a copula, revealing the inseparability of everything, and, I should add, using that inseparability as a means of outracing closure.

It is in this context that I would like to propose that Leslie Scalapino's work is a study in the problem of freedom. She says as much in a "Note" that follows the text of *Deer Night*: "*Deer Night* was instigated by the idea of a complete transformation of *The Tempest*, a construct of Western and Asian conceptions as the motions of the mind, only the mind *being* action or phenomena *as* writing. The intention was for the work to be a state of freedom (eventually), subverting capitalism's 'imperialism' from the inside."[13]

It would be erroneous to say that *Deer Night* **is** *The Tempest*; *Deer Night* outraces *The Tempest*.

The as effect is performative: Geilgud as Hamlet, man as brown indigo butterfly, woman as ibex. This is acting; from it, actions occur. But the performance is of "as"—a performance of minimal overt stagey drama but of maximal complexity. It takes superior acting skills—to be "as"—namely to be being. And yet it is accomplished by everything that is. One may respond with wonder, but also with terror. Acts are being put on everywhere, that's all there is, that's reality—a non-reality—the confusion is awful. We are each and all in numerous casts of mind. Furthermore, not everyone gets to chose her/his/its role. Some of us get cast: for example, as a girl sold into a brothel.

Or as a toddler who, when somewhere between 3 and 4 years old, is imprisoned in the windowless cellar of a stable, where he will remain for 12 years, the rest of his childhood.

This is what happened to the youth known as Kaspar Hauser.

Werner Herzog's film very closely follows the text of a small book called *Kaspar Hauser* written by Anselm Ritter von Feuerbach, a famed jurist (he was responsible for banning the use of torture in Bavarian prisons) who was responsible for the disposition of Kaspar Hauser after his sudden appearance on May 26, 1828, in a small square in Nuremberg, unable to talk and barely able to walk. Feuerbach's book was completed not long before his sudden death, probably from poison, in May, 1832. Kaspar Hauser was murdered in December, 1833.

Neither crime has ever been solved, but there is ample reason to believe that the princely house of Baden had reasons for wanting Kaspar Hauser out of the way and that Philip Henry, Earl of Stanhope was complicit in bringing this about. Jeffrey Masson gives a rather spirited account of the affair in his introduction and commentary to the English translation of Feuerbach's book, published under the title *Lost Prince: The Unsolved Mystery of Kaspar Hauser* (NY: Free Press, 1996).

The film version of Kaspar Hauser's life begins in the landscapeless and all but lightless dungeon, where we can barely see Kaspar; he wiggles his toes and rolls a wooden horse back and forth on the floor. The area is small, everything is within reach; Kaspar neither walks nor stands. (This dungeon was discovered in 1924 at Schloss Pilsach during renovations just after it was purchased by the novelist Klara Hofer; the wooden horse was still there.)

He is visited, usually when he is asleep, by his keeper, "the unknown man," who leaves bread and a jug of water and carries out the pot of waste to empty it. The man also brings Kaspar paper and pencil, and guiding his hand, the man has Kaspar write a name: Kaspar Hauser. He teaches him the word horse. He teaches him to say "I want to be a gallant rider as my father was before me."

Without explanation at dusk one day, the keeper carries Kaspar Hauser from his dungeon. The landscape is verdant, birds are singing, waves are breaking along the shore. It is spring (May, 1828). Landscapes proliferate as Kaspar is carried into Nuremberg, beautiful in the film but terrifying for Kaspar, for whom the light and motion are excruciating. (For all of his life, bright light brought terrible pain and Kaspar preferred the dark, night: doctors claimed that he had developed neurologically so that he could see in the dark as well as a cat).

Kaspar is abandoned, standing in a small square, facing a clock tower; its face is blue, the lower half is obscured, as if in mist.

He is found, and various events occur and are chronicled. He learns to talk but only marginally to remember. He is moved by music; listening to a blind pianist, he comments, "I feel strong in my heart, I feel old."

He learns to play the piano, and he learns to draw and paint—his subjects are almost always from the natural world; he is especially adept at rendering images of flowers.

Georg Friedrich Daumer becomes his teacher. Kaspar never learns to walk except awkwardly, but he goes out with Daumer. He encounters the enigma of space. Daumer points to the tower at whose top is Kaspar's room. But that's impossible. When in the room, Kaspar sees it everywhere around him. When standing below the tower which is said to contain the room, he can turn his back and it is gone; therefore, the room is bigger than the tower.

Kaspar is interrogated by clerics who test his faith. He gestures all around at the things they can all see. "How can God have created everything out of nothing?" he asks the clerics.

He dreams—of the Caucasus. He sees it clearly: "a strange village on a mountainside, with white houses and steps rather than streets, and on the steps there was water running." He says this has dreamed in him from the Caucasus.

He is interrogated by a logician, who poses the following problem: there are two men, one comes from a village of liars, the other from a village of truthtellers; with what one question can one tell them apart?

Kaspar Hauser answers immediately: "Are you a tree-frog."

"Nothing lies inside of me except my life," Kaspar says.

Kaspar is invited into the garden at Daumer's house by a stranger who says he has information about Kaspar's mother. Kaspar is stabbed.

He is discovered, bleeding to death, and carried in to his bed. As he lies dying, he comments sadly that he knows only the beginning of a story, not how it continues. Berbers are proceeding across a desert:

Now the caravan stops
because some believe they are lost
and because they see mountains ahead of them.
They look at their compass but it's no use.
Then their blind leader picks up a handful of sand
And tastes it as though it were food.
My sons, the blind man says, you are wrong.
Those are not mountains you see
It is only your imagination.
You must continue northwards.
And they follow the old man's advice
And finally reach the city in the north.
And that's where the story begins.
But how the story goes after they reach the city, I don't know.[14]

The results of an autopsy carried out after Kaspar Hauser's death are chronicled: "Deformities discovered in Kaspar Hauser's brain and liver." The chronicler announces: "Finally we have got an explanation for this strange man."

The chronicler, of course, is wrong. We have no explanation.

Deer Night has its origin in a specific gyration/configuration that Leslie Scalapino felt in the course of an experience involving something she witnessed, she says, when she was 14 (probably the same age as Kaspar Hauser when he was removed from his dungeon). To know what it was would explain nothing, and Scalapino does not name or describe it. In *Deer Night* she attempts to replicate that shape exactly, the shape not of her psychology but of the occurrence. The gyration/configuration is, in fact, to some extent the shape of unknowing. Like Kaspar Hauser, Scalapino employs gesture, music, and logic as a means of developing this figure. And in her work, as in Kaspar Hauser's dream, the gyration involves voyaging as an inner, as well as outward, undertaking, an outracing which leaves the end behind. This voyaging is, as she terms it, "physiological-conceptual"; she has described it as being like learning a motion in dance—the body learns a motion, not an idea, but the motion is an idea-shape. It is interiorized in the course of being produced outward, performed.

What I've called outracing or voyaging without end might aptly also be termed learning without end or, better, outlearning. As Scalapino sees it, one must (constantly and relentlessly) outlearn what one has been (and is being) taught. One inhabits a culture and is taught that it is the universe and one's own. To go to and then return from a different culture drives a wedge into that universe. The sensation that Scalapino's writing is wedged into the contemporary American version of the universe is accurate; she wants us to outlearn it, to outrace it.

Notes

1. Leslie Scalapino, *Dahlia's Iris: Secret Autobiography and Fiction* (Tallahassee, FL: Fiction Collective Two, 2003), 127, *As: All Occurrence in Structure, Unseen—Deer Night* is published in Leslie Scalapino, *The Public World / Syntactically Impermanence* (Hanover and London: University Press of New England/Wesleyan University Press, 1999).

2. (*The Public World*, 33; LS on Peter Hutton's silent films).

3. She states emphatically, however, "I am not writing a scheme (not writing 'according to' any philosophy, there's just the writing)." Letter to Lyn Hejinian, October 26, 2000.

4. (from "Silence and Sound/Text" in the "Demonstration/Commentary" section of *The Public World/Syntactically Impermanence*, which precedes the trilogy of works that constitute the second half of the volume, called "As: All Occurrence in Structure, Unseen", 31).

5. quoting a remark of Philip Whalen's in her essay "The Radical Nature of Experience" (also in *The Public World*) 5,

6. The entirety of this paper is indebted to extensive conversation with Dee Morris.

7. And, I should add, in her life, which is, in certain ways, inseparable from her writing. Scalapino told me an anecdote which seems salient. She and her husband Tom White were traveling with Scalapino's parents in Mongolia. They were in two jeeps crossing the Gobi Desert, which is largely without roads. Leslie was seated (among pillows, because of her damaged spine) with her notebook and a pen, intending to write as they went along, but whenever she began to write the driver of the jeep, a Mongolian man from the area, would bring the jeep to a stop. "I realized that we'd never get anywhere, and that was a problem" she said, referring not only to

their literal journey but also to the writing, since she is adamant that her writing not function as a snatcher, that it not immobilize anything. It must participate in the outrunning.

8. *The Public World*, 92.

9. *The Public World*, 31–32

10. Brief conversation, April 2000.

11. Herman Oldenberg, *Buddha: His Life, His Doctrine, His Order,* translated by William Hoey; quoted in Karl Jaspers, *Heraclitus, Parmenides, Plotinus, Lao-tzu, Nagarjuna,* edited by Hannah Arendt, translated by Ralph Mannheim (NY: Harcourt Brace Jovanovich, Inc., 1966), 116.

12. *The Public World*, 132

13. *The Public World*, 133.

14. Werner Herzog, *Screenplays:The Enigma of Kauper Hauser; directed by Werner Herzog* (1974), NY: Tanam Press, 1980, 144.

from The Unfollowing (for C. E., elegies)

Lyn Hejinian

Every minute proves that reality is conditional
Sounds paddle the air echoing when I speak my mind
The door opens, I rise naked from the tub
It's strange to return to Abyssinia by train from my bed
I hear Jerome singing below
Sleep?—yes, I sleep in fear almost of the lovely night before
Boom—one—one—one, boom one and boom one and one and one
Only one
A woman appears carrying a pink bag
You stay, okay with the sheets, we'll get a suit, you're in our story
When love can't be composed any better, then love can't be postponed any
       longer
Things predicted are always restricted
Go, smoking pan, with your bacon to window
This afternoon there will be "une grande séance" and everyone will nap

All that the girl thought irrelevant was never to become relevant to her

At the far left in the upper corner we can see the "Blessed Islands," at the bottom to the right it says "The End"

I am horrified, he has been shot, I see the blood on his hands and head, but now I see that the victim isn't who I thought it was, he has turned to beseech me but it's just some blond stranger—I don't care a bit about him and walk away

Time's retraction brings the failure of action

Elbow, richness, auburn, critic, water rising through the plumbing system

Anomalies cannot provide

No dummies, they were experiencing, then experience ceased

A scream from within a circle of chairs, an ascending of stairs, and then the scream's cancellation—all accomplished without any screaming

A sphinx, a grid, and a cyclist in red

It was a warm day, March 8, the co-ed had sweat on her lip, a foretaste of spring

Knowledge is lost in redundant unexpectedness

A field, a flash of emergence, the present, new ideals

A moan

An elf with so many toes on her feet, bam bam, that she couldn't wear boots, dam dam, stepped into hot coals, ram ram

The day comes up from a severed page

Joe has standing whiskers, Jane has a secret

The dancer is ballooning, he's fat and light-footed, he's becoming airborne,
    nothing's in his way

How oppressed the young woman is by her mother's image of the happiness
    that must be hers

Along comes a wave casting spray as it bears—down on a man half-asleep on a
    towel and half-awake in a rowboat adrift on a violent sea

The cold in this luminous season stings

Let us go then, you and I, in pajamas through the sky, in which we'll dine on
    rice and pie, we'll drink from apples made of lace, we'll topple statues,
    invent space

There in her hand is a slice of bread, its surface just beginning to stiffen

Can we question this?

The stars are bits of fire that have broken off from earth

Like ants we must make our choices quickly

Death we cannot people, lens, clock, or declare

Thunder here is rare, no matter how thick the air with things with sides to
    strike into view

Time's flow is dammed and the past comes back

To begin with, I am faced with mountains to circumambulate, since I can't cut
	through them
I enter the folds of a human adventure
On every door there hangs a figurehead and this one comes to face me as the
	door swings shut
I will proceed with good will—the best of wills—anxiously
Bird of daughters, bird flying from the forks, the blurbs, the serials, the time
I saw a golden tadpole, eating apple jam; I saw a sudden whirlpool, sucking
	down a ham
The boughs groan with fruit, an apple falls—false alarm
It's a non-sequitur—that
Sense data sinks
The muscles give out mid-word and a thief stutters while accusing me (his
	uncle) of theft
Lune comes along mounted on a beast called Lequel who is neither more or less
	than a horse as obedient to Lune as the tides are to the moon
Shot of men hurrying toward each other at an intersection with open umbrellas
	none willing to give way to the others, shot of placid camels kneeling
	near a chained dog, shot of sugar maples temporarily obscured by fall-
	ing snow
Tomorrow morning, unless things vastly improve, I'll go in person to the front
	of the caravan and take it *over* the mountain
I thought I saw an earthworm, stirring in the dirt, then I saw it was a sadist,
	wielding a quirt

There goes something, forever lost in context

A Sudanese customs agent halts a caravan carrying rocking chairs into lands
where no rocking chairs are needed

Come lest desire clatter, dance now lest we can't dance later

Here remains as a bridge vanishes, the backdoor shuts, etc. and here cares little
as to which is which

Conjoining unlike concepts (say, birth control and origami) is something mor-
tals do

This does not follow

Danish baby, Danish toddler, Danish mother, Danish father—see them eating
midnight meats

The passengers on prison ships are not allowed to celebrate

There is very little, almost nothing, that …

I order you to feel free to help yourself to ice cream which is melting

At midnight I'll become a merchant mariner again

Is this paper snow, undertow?

It is perceived unconsciously and might have been a spider emerging from a
duck's egg, a cause for excitement provided by the outside world to an
inner world that almost missed it

It's only with clumsy freedom that things appear on people's lips

Smoke is the noun for the thing over the fire, to sting is the verb for what's
       being done
It is only in *this* light that I can see the spider's web
Along comes a girl with mighty thighs astride on equine butter
Nothing rises that doesn't rise
A woman had the finer python and its name was Palm but she called it Call
A blown shell
New consonants are discovered far more often than they can be used
Come rain or shine, *she* takes the umbrella on even days of the month and *she*
      takes it on odd, and whomever the dog loves best, it will follow
Gone is the adjective lost—or was it last
In the Museum called Unless hangs the pelt of a beast that seldom comes to
      hand
That's all
Can we call life falling
We can talk to each other about tiles, snowballs, and camels
In a cave of ice—while wild weather rages outside—she—anticipating the loss
      of her crown—makes a comment, opposed by none

Late at night the insects sing it

Stories do not float

Should maples shade the growing grass, some will pause and some will pass

A footprint on the windowsill has been left by the killer to make everyone think
        he's departed

Once I went to India, in search of grand seduction, next I went to Manchester,
        with spinners, for production

Perhaps leaves fire

Prevented?

The elegy continues

The tree is exactly itself in its accidents

Night on our faces (for we have many) hides from us (there are many of us) our
        fates (we have many of those too)

A viola yields but could she handle it or did she hide it

The world says get out with definition

It did it did it did it

Turning everywhere in unkempt directions we must make now a beginning

Who would perish stronger does and leaves us on the slope some tree or other
    remnant
Reason what of flurry, what of fishes, of fury
This that the body does is unlikely
The wan ants go along and go along through the woods and over the log onto
    leaves that fall into the creek where some ants drown and some ants
    travel
We can only ask as like to unlike ever since
There once was a woman who was allergic to cats and she was also allergic to
    camels
What remains we ask impossibly to bother for
My daughter can speak!
It was said long ago that the stars write the sky, it was said that what enters a
    cloud will exit elsewhere
In the snapshot we find one we find absent
Ask what of fire, fever, sugar, and lag time
Papa, papa, have you come back home?
In the form of a queen, the free fish returns his long lost hook to a poor
    fisherman
And so we see that the here and now that is constantly changing is always cur-
    rent—or is it?

Lids cease moving and experiences fold

The pirouetting motes (saying nothing of themselves but proving that there's air
and that it moves them—they do say that much) seem little but a light
invention in the dark that keeps the world away

Closely written pages litter the tale of the avenue down which the woman
doesn't return Is there any salt, we wonder

Call those clarifying darkroom flickers of a winged thing reasoning flurry

What upright strictly switched such shadow

Hands at her cheeks, lips parted and tip of the tongue just brushing the pink
ridge behind the teeth, she is part way through the word

It's getting harder to accept the whole tamale

Two small girls pad by the bungalow and the older one declares

We come to the often open, the pond

It's widely known that a *monstar* is a magical creature, a haunting figure, a celes-
tial giant, a twinkling beast

A scene is setting

Hundreds remember this

A woodpecker of wood fastened to a piece of wood by a wire and string pecks
when the string is pulled

Floating to earth holding onto an inflated condom down comes a swinging
mouse which may well be an irreverent owl, a statistical pinecone, or a
vestige of melancholy

The hawk, when interrupted, will metamorphose

The woman in the photograph is not to be confused with those she put at a distance and then brought back singly

Some say the stars are burning leaves

The truest story is a short one told "at length" and "step by step" though "all in vain," "all in fun," and "just for your sake"

We could stop here for the unframing, the vague resemblance, the blurring of vision

Her name was Kick, her name was also Crawl

This is full of inexplicable consonants

Between poles lie fallen wires the barbs are melting into

We want a wind that can justify the rattling of the door, the wafting of the scrap twisted inward away from danger

For no apparent reason, the empty sleeves of the gray wool coat that has hung in place for days from a sturdy hook by the door uncannily shift and the coat falls

Perhaps the books should be sealed—perhaps they should be dipped into clear glue or resin

Along comes a herdsman with camels over the plains in a plan that can't be filled

She is at the tile crossroads of the fountain still

An Interview
Lyn Hejinian and Jack Collom

LH: It is spring (March 2002) and fated to be stormy because it has been. Having been writing poems for almost fifty years now, what have you learned about fate from poetry?

JC: Fifty years of trying to write poetry as taut as has taught me that fate is infinitely malleable and it had better be. For example, just now it's my fate to answer a very large question and if I go by "fate" alone I can't avoid pomposity (see above, see below); so I takes me right thumbnail and scrapes around on fate's belly until it turns red & then I scrambles the red into a little machine between me palms and off we go. Who are you?

LH: "I"? I suppose I'm the result of numerous contingencies, most of which I didn't warrant or notice, and the source of a few others, most of which I can't promise or predict. "We," says Thoreau—"we" and "ourselves"—but for the moment, asserting my singularity, I'll say "I" and "myself": "I find myself in a world that is already planted, but is also still being planted, as at first." There is no evidence of progress in the seasonal model. Natural science has to be content with knowledge. And poetry, too?

JC: Well, it depends (like water in a well) on words being repeated twice, which oddly enough gives them an even chance of "survival through substance," since three dimensions are better than one and matter at least lives in memory. Form just lives, but poetry has, meanwhile, gone out, I find. Which indicates it's well. Are you familiar with some of its haunts?

LH: Language isn't ghostly, really. And, with the sun behind me, the shadow of my head on the table bears no relation to the word "head." So poetry, as I see it, has no haunts. But what if, instead, we propose that poetry itself is a haunt—whose would it be, or what's? No; I'll phrase the question differently: Is your waking life very different from the life you dream when asleep?

JC: When I'm awake I dream of the places that the great blue heron frequents; when I'm asleep I think of the heron itself. In the morning I imagine a ghost and the word "ghost" having an argument: "Is!" "Isn't!" "Is!" "Isn't!" "Is!" "Isn't!"

until the heron, whose head casts no shadow, surprises them by coming to a point. Frogs Beware! What's wrong with this picture?

LH: Nothing that isn't wrong with any picture: its stability and the lack of shadow. What I value most about birds (and seek to emulate as best I can) is that they no sooner come to a point than they leave it again. Where they land is never more important than their flying. They are musical in this—more musical in this than in their singing. And because they seek the air, they are always casting changing shadows. I'm reminded of a story (I've told it before) that was told to me by Mohammed Salikh, an Uzbek poet (and hereditary prince). He called it a ghost story and claimed to have dreamed it. He was flying over the desert in search of his mother. He spotted her and tried to land but couldn't because he had no shadow. Then his mother threw her cloak onto the ground to make a shadow for him and he landed. It's our shadow that attaches us to life, he said. Shadow, experience, action, living—writing is about these, not about literature. Would you agree?

JC: I would agree if I weren't in the middle of an unaccustomed cup of tea, which makes me feel that to keep one's undifferentiated energy very close to the bottom every time one turns over a new leaf, i.e., every breath, helps slide things under the plate that says, "Shadow is the opposite of literature." What do you use for energy?

LH: Sleep. Coffee in the mornings, a sense of possibility during the day and exercising possibility by making choices, hurriedly, like an ant, a passenger. Come evening (in the imperative), I'm in love with the dark. I've been dreaming recently of babies (reproduction). Do you have a camera? Are your poems "snaps"—pictures, mementoes, proof that you lived, experienced, thought, cared?

JC: My photos are "instant babies"—interactions with environs. Poems a little more gestated … we men, poor men, must scramble ludicrously among struts of bridges to generate molecular structure, perhaps drop bombs from our bellies, or, mostly, only toss a spitwad into a beerglass to—but now I've forgotten what we're imitating. How much leverage do you bring to insistence?

LH: Trying to discern what you (in the course of positing yourself as one of the gang called "we men") mean by "leverage," I picture a crowbar—a crowbar in the hands of a man in a garden prying loose a rock. And then the seesaw at the park, the seesaw one so enthusiastically mounts and then can't dismount, comes to mind. I remember feeling trapped (as a girl) on the seesaw, unable to get off lest I bring the girl at the other end crashing to the ground. The lesson to be learned is that, if one has leverage, one is bound to it. Do you remember your parents being athletic, playing games?

JC: The game of walking tips up a few stones, and the legs move as a memory of running, which my father did in high school (he never won but often came in second). My mother swam, graceful as an eel, having played basketball for the U. of Illinois. But I get these miles and balls only through their telling. All I can remember them doing athletically together is dancing, Daddy klutzy but determined, Mom as light as a dream. Would you care to dance?

LH: Dancing is a wonderful way to get from A to B. Caring itself is a dance. One dips, turns, flees, responds, returns. From "painted letters" one goes to "puppets." Every good poem dances off the page, as the French poet Dominique Fourcade asserted, each following its own logics. But in every dance there remains something undanced. You have had some interest in evolutionary theory. Do you believe in progress?

JC: There is no overall progress. There CAN be local progress. (Earth is local.) There…. No, seriously, 99% of claims to progress are based on—well, what I mean is, the word "progress" by its plainness seems to me to invite contemplation of ultimate value, and—well, there it went already. See what I mean? (Ingredients: "forward" and "go"; "forward" is localized by definition.) But thought like the above is localized, first in logic, then in repetition, then in wit. That's called "the history of Education." Putting one little foot after another, and another technique would be "just do it," only not say it, just—uh—do it. Would you care for a drink?

LH: If one had nothing to drink, the business of getting one foot swinging after the other would become impossible. I suspect that we are always walking in circles, but the fact that we are doing so would become more and more apparent, until inarticulate and wheeling, like leaves we'd fall. But drowning is not a better option. In any case, though I find myself thinking about death often and intently these days, it's not the ostensible "cause of death" that interests (or confounds) me. "I find myself thinking about death": but that's impossible. Nonetheless, I feel it—but it isn't mine. The impropriety of death is clear. Ownerless and absent, death…. Stymied, I'll take a breath. Have you read Aldon Nielsen's *Black Chant*?

JC: No, but it sounds morbid. I did know an old man named Danielson who, when my wife and I were moving to another part of town, ran up and said, "Butter the cat's paws when you get there, so he won't run away." I guess the butter is meant to prevent the cat from getting purchase, thus from walking or running at all. And of course if the cat were running "away," it would be to what is remembered as home. Place beats people, it seems. Such easy slippage on a repeating surface. Do you ever look in the mirror?

LH: Yes, because it's morbid to ask questions. I was keeping a weather diary for awhile, and was just developing a scale to use in describing the strength of the wind (capable of tossing the branches outside my window an inch, a foot, a yard, etc.), when I forgot to look, missed a few days, and, feeling I'd betrayed the weather, I abandoned the project. At the moment the breeze is a 2-incher but there are occasional one-foot gusts. And now the branches are pulling back, before they relax (now). Those who believe in a deity can thank it for things; those who believe in weather can be grateful to it for … weather. Does your belief system include rain?

JC: My belief system is rain. When it comes (gains emphasis), things grow, but if it dominates for too long everything floods and the living creatures (plants too) drown. Light's skepticism clarifies but simply doesn't provide the "glue" that might make context palpable. Left to themselves, these two qualities (rain and light) tend to go wild. The researcher returns from his or her coffee break and finds dichotomy has become a pincushion of aching flesh. Are you married?

LH: Repeatedly, day by day, and willfully, with artichoke in pot rather than pin in cushion. Conviviality is a splendid context for crossing from Mondays to Tuesdays and beyond. What are your favorite foods? And do they figure in your poetry? And if so, what function do they serve?

JC: I've said for years my favorite food is bacon in order to create the impression of a wild, risky, red-streaked man, but now my favorite food is anything other folks drop on the floor. It goes without saying that these favoritisms, these "roving forks of light," figure in my poetry. Their function is to make a hash of experience. How has your writing changed since you were a tiny child?

LH: I wrote entirely in crayon, avoiding "flesh," until I was nineteen. From 19 to 24 I wrote autobiographies, though they were never my own. From 24 to 27 I used nouns as verbs and verbs as nouns. In 1968 I began to write on a portable

Olivetti and hoped to become as Italian as Audrey Hepburn. Thirty years later I wrote "Yesterday is gone and never was / And here it is / So we can go to bed with unity of purpose / And crave more of the temperament of life in life's philosophy." I have increased my confusion. Did you ever work as a cowboy? Do you like horses? If you had a horse, what would you call him?

JC: I worked as a cowboy but the job at hand was poet. I say "as a cowboy" because I like the rhythm (as a cowboy, as a cowboy) but, too, because in my compositions I twirl a loop at anything that moves. Nevertheless, I have no skills. I like horses in about the way an arctic fox likes the United States. If I had one (horse) I'd call her Mare Nostrum. What is humor, and what is humor to you?

LH: I couldn't answer that right off the bat and looked the word up, and there's a humorous notion, that of looking a word up, or it would be if one were of a lecherous cast of mind and there's another, that of casting a mind, like a fly on a line at the end of a pole or the discus (which I almost wrote as "discuss") thrown by the idealized athlete or the mold for a statue of a general on his horse or admiral on his rock or pensive poet—Rilke, say, or Pushkin. I've seen many statues of Pushkin and none of Rilke. Humor is a temporary state of mind imposed by circumstances. It's an unpredictable and unreasoning inclination. It's a whim, in fact. It's the capacity to discover something ludicrous or incongruous and that brings me to my next question: do you think that, as so many of the best young poets are shifting from verse forms to prose (or, to use Clark Coolidge's term, prosoid) forms, they are doing so so as to write autobiographies?

JC: They are. Let's just get that down plain and then go on: having begun the autobiographical, obviously, spread, into (oh shit) VITAMINS spelled backwards or some such, SO: a bubble of conceptual inebriation leads into vision of white giant house in back fields, sixties, murmurs at the stove, pure bird classification, orange ... how do you chop single words out of history?

LH: Metaphorically, of course, but angrily, too. You can stir the word short, of course; you can try this—you can call the U.S. President a tot whose favorite toy is his shit rot. Probably you should and many do and so it goes. But, returning to history, one cannot see clearly what has been lost. Of course, if feelings of shame result, one can say that what's been lost is self-esteem. And if one is weeping, perhaps loved ones have died. But can one return to history after "single words" have been chopped out of it?

JC: To not return to history is to die, and become history. Which raises various specters, such as one's tininess in the immensity, for one, and living defined as dancing feet for another. Maybe if we combine the two visions we can see consciousness as a flea, wonder as an itch, and life as a scratch. Do you find that "single" words burgeon like (word) in a petri dish?

LH: Just as algae make sense and roses are roses? Yes. Words seem destined to oscillate perpetually among the various forms of sentence. It has been said that there is an inevitable conflict between the aspirations of men (sic) of letters and the chatty public—but the public when in public (which is the only time the public is the public) says hardly anything at all. Think of the people shopping in a mall. Are you thinking of people shopping in a mall?

JC: No, I'm thinking of you saying, "Are you thinking of people shopping in a mall?" But a mall is a sea of variegated speech—no room for the stroller to insert a word even if she (sic) has the breath for it. When they are sitting or standing ingesting something the public becomes a sea of variegated speech itself—actual speech, which is almost indistinguishable from a landfill, not to mention the gulls thronging and squawking upon it. Are you thinking of the gulls thronging and squawking upon it? No, my real question is, How do you feel at parties?

LH: Frantic, eager and apart: "Hysterically convivial and engaged, smiling while talking to myself, I stood alone at the top of the stairs while the brilliant flushed philosopher waved a baby blanket in the air as if signalling–battle? surrender?"—that's a typical festive moment (from my perspective). "Two months later the child, a boy, was born and they called him Leon but his name was George, which disappointed his mother's parents and goes to show that there are many kinds as well as degrees of distance (as of disturbance)." The party goes on just as a story does, and sometimes one gains the greatest pleasure by squeezing one's thoughts into the interstices. Did you ever, as a child, have to be rescued from a cave or trap or cave-in or ditch or snowbank or other literal tight squeeze?

JC: Tight squeeze? Tight squeeze? I'm trying to think. Don't press me! I do have a horror of such a trap. I wouldn't do what Clark does (the caving anyway) for all the gold in Fort Knox. But I—give me a chance!—can't recall a frightening early episode. On the other hand, I used to be remarkably free of acrophobia, a bravery squeezed, perhaps, from an intense desire to be a regular boy (so I could then be eccentric). Once, while working as a surveyor in New York City, I walked a 50-foot I-beam a couple stories in the air. Now, to even peek over a cliff gives me the willies. What's your favorite balance and/or imbalance?

LH: The inescapability of relativity interests me consistently—the endless extensions of history and compelling presence of contexts—but non-equivalencies, uniquenesses, incommensurabilities interest me even more. The relation of one unique thing to another perhaps isn't quite an imbalance as a nonbalance—but my favorite, whether it's an imbalance or a nonbalance, is the non-equivalences of love. Perplexing as the situations this occasions may be, the love one feels for one person is not the same as, nor comparable to, nor in competition with, the love one feels for another. In addition, I am enamored of complex prepositional phrases—e.g., "in and of the moment." You often write diaristic poems—travel poems. What determines whether you use the past or present tense as you go?

JC: As I go, the broad strokes are always present tense but should you examine them closely you'd see that the molecular composition comes entirely from the past. This accounts for the moldy odor. The interesting thing is that the moldy odor gives the "going" whatever flavor it has. The tension between the fact of moldiness and the jogging along—the mixing, or rather unmixing—is all I can hope to mediate. So in a travel poem you have an artificially bestowed physical analog of the mental effort to keep moving, and the challenge is to avoid motion's tendency toward stasis—its inertia. So that time doesn't just spill once into "in" and "of" but keeps on splitting. Do you ever or often find yourself astonished at such things as the miracle of driving a car?

LH: Recently, to the extent that I notice my doing so at all, I've found myself wary that I'm driving a car. Alas, I'm getting old. My own vulnerability is not all that greater than it was when I was young, but the things I encounter seem now more vulnerable to the possibility of my getting and/or doing them wrong. On those occasions I feel nonplussed ("without more"), and then, lest my competency be diminished by my hyperawareness of what's happening and, worse, what could happen, I allow "automatic pilot" to take over. By virtue of that, my car and I are transported (while I am thinking about other things and the car is earnestly dedicated to its task) to our destination. Is there someplace you've always wanted to visit and never been?

JC: Asia. Well. So much for that question. Seems like I have some free time and space here to explore around, even "ramble." Let's see, what speculations shall

I ~~visit~~ wander, as it were? When I picture Asia I see the vast spread of the map dotted with 3rd-grade geography-book scenes. People with comical hats planting rice, etc. I've always wanted to go inside the Earth. Tunnels and hidey-holes were intense delights to me when I was a boy. Now, I get a little claustrophobic. On the other hand—but I'm repeating myself. I want to travel into the legs of my armchair. My favorite image for years was a path disappearing into a wood (from a book of Indian tales, and "Old Man"). What do you think of disappearance?

LH: Disappearance is a conceptual abstraction until we consider what is doing or has done the disappearing, and then it's a literal one—something or one gets abstracted from the scene we call our world. I'm as saddened by loss as the next person and just as aware that the hour at hand immediately and my own right hand eventually will disappear. In fact, disappearance is so common that it's banal. But that's true only conceptually—it's not banal literally. J is gone! O! What do you think of reappearance?

JC: What do I think of reappearance? I think it's never the same, as it were, but enormously heartening. It warms memory. As Gertrude (solid name!) Stein's example teaches us, context is so huge by definition that it's gotta be different all the time. So. So? So repetition is never other than relative, relative relative. Not so relative. But money blurs this, like excessive symbology in poetry blurs things. A sock is a sock. Keeps you warm. Sometimes it looks like a beautiful fish (I think). Do you have any relatives who tend to show up over and over like a bad penny?

LH: None, unless we count myself. But I did have to stop (as you've noticed) to think before answering, since it seemed that I, the author of a family saga, must certainly have noticed relatives like that. In the context of a family saga, after all, one has relatives like everything and anything. I did once spend many hours of a Thanksgiving weekend sorting pennies with my nephew M who was hoping to have a penny for every year of the 20th century when he was only 10, but that's not what you asked. You asked…. Ah. Yes—her name was Daisy, I think, or Charity, I was 10, no, now I remember, her name was Pansy and she was in the Army. Is the U.S. already (3/2/03) at war?

JC: I think we're at war with nature. War is always a matter of degree. And so are we (a matter of degree). It's natural to destroy nature, given that we have exceeded nature in the matter of means. Perhaps baseball is a symbol of what I mean: the ball leaves the pitcher's hand and is meant to fly by a stick wielded by the opponent. Everything rolls out beyond the fingertips, happens beyond the claws. A little boy discovers the principle of the lever and that it multiples pleasure. Next thing you know he's bombing Iraq. But I think he'll find the drawing power of the details within the gesture. Do you, like Levertov, "like to find what … lies within something of another nature"?

LH: What I like is not just "to find" but to please and be pleased by what I find within things "of another nature" (by which I assume you, or Levertov, mean of a nature that isn't my own). I fear I'm more like Isabel Archer than Denise Levertov. I'm given to appreciation. Things that are displeasing demand too much of one— they limit one, they accuse one. Have you ever been guilty of plagiary?

JC: Who? Me? I plagiarize "all the" time. That's the very definition of thought-ful work. Hope so! Appreciation itself is plagiary. Love is a simple thing; love is a diamond ring. But Levertov meant, in her lines, another nature than the one which contains, as "gull feathers of glass / hidden // in white pulp." Same poem she "plays" this beautiful "and the butteryellow glow / in the narrow flute from which the morning-glory / opens blue and cool on a hot morning." Or did she make that up? Do you too have ambivalence about "pleasures"?

LH: My relationship to pleasure is complicated, of course, and ambivalence plays into it, as it does in all complications, but I adjust for that strategically: instead of "ambivalence" I utilize "deferral." It's an economic model. I await pleasure, I expect it too, but first I pay my dues, I work off my debt in advance and in the process do more than required. Having done all this in advance I'm owed plea-sure even before it begins, no need to be embarrassed, no reason to demur. Do you keep a journal? Do you keep a record of what you read? Of what you eat?

JC: Deferral / seems to me / in terms of seasons / to be rural / what you see / for a variety of reasons. I don't keep a journal, but I write so much it hardly matters. Tho' a journal calls out something special in its rhythmic ordinariness. Joanne Kyger recommends a curt journal. I remember visiting some young friends 30+ years ago, with beer, and kissing the star of the place, in the bathroom. The im-possibility of even mentioning this, much less calling it up into notice now, shaves the face of deconstruction…. Journal what I read?! O how have I not known this'd be lovely and necessary to do?! Once again?! (I barely care what I eat.) Do you regret the worldliness that attends poetry? Or rejoice in its scantiness? Or?

LH: I depend on its omnipresence, its ubiquity, its persistence. The world is all we have—or, to put it another way (don't you adore putting things other ways?):

the name for "all we have" is "the world." What else is there to care about? The transcendent God? No. The only gods I can countenance are worldly ones—the gods of (respectively and respectfully) the worldly tree, the worldly river, the worldly spatula, the worldly boot, the worldly eyeliner, set of building blocks, cellphone, lariat, etc. What's the first thing—no cheating here—what's the very first thing that occurs to you when you come upon a silent butler?

JC: Marcel Marceau peering haughtily down Roman cartilage. Just kidding—but I didn't cheat—and the reason to kid is that I can't quite think what a silent butler is, or rather can't think what a silent butler quite is. A machine that—opens the door? Serves drinks? So I guess the very first thing that would occur to me would be a germ of speculation about how the abundance of hybrids currently confuses human thought, that is, how it kicks candy-coated ball bearings into the typical mental stream. Do you like abnormal subdividings?

LH: As in cancer cells? No way! Anyway, hybridity results from conjunction—and I like conjunctions, yes I do! Although meanwhile but then however, etc.—forever. There's a lot of future in any given conjunction, none in a subdivision. Think of the desert—a deserted desert—no one around, not even you or me, unimaginable—hot, the dirt pale, acrid, a mix of dessicated things—got any notion where that thought was going? Ever had the sense that you were reading someone's mind?

JC: No, I have no notion where that thought was going, except it was about to turn the corner into beauty. And that would've shown subdividings as being intimate conjunctions—lit up the old intentional fallacy. As for reading minds, not much beyond the usual perceptions of unworthy motives. I mean (by "usual") that "everybody" "these days" is uncritically involved in this postFreudian interpersonal fascism which consists of invalidating anything anybody says by thinking how that thing-said might be at least tinged with falsity and then assuming the worst. I try to avoid this type of thinking because of my goodness. Do you think men are sweet because they're limited by logic?

LH: I don't think "men," taken categorically, either as the male of the human species or as the human species ("mankind") generally, are sweet, nor do I think that, for the best of you/us, logic is limiting. But you are trying to get at something here—something about the pathos of our (whoever "we" are) attempts to think well, and the melancholy (or even despair) that pervades our awareness of the history of our having not done so. We are failures, and we continue to be so on a daily basis. The self-critical and interpersonal criticism that would help us get things better produces anxiety—is that process—the process of the contentious community—what you mean by "postFreudian interpersonal fascism"? No—that can't be it. What do you mean?

JC: I mean, I mean, it's a question of authority. In order to properly undercut the authority of a statement (anyone's any-statement—as if we could say what-is), many people educated to recognize the subconscious mind have made a virtual statement of the anti-statement critique. That is, the wisdom of interpretive process has been arrogated willy-nilly and in whole chunks by any (inadvertent) listener. This has become routine, and routinization of anything, even rebellion, amounts to unjust authority. After years of study, someone says, "Much of Earth's soil is washing away many times faster than replacement soil can be formed" and someone else cries, "This elitist treehugger wants to deprive good Americans of their livelihoods just so he/she can wallow in a private park!" However, interpretation should depend on a sense of its own relativity as much as on the world's. But someone will say to this paragraph, "You just want to rationalize a social order you're comfortable with." What's your take on confusion?

LH: Confusion is the better part of dialectics. There are countless situations about which each single position, however carefully considered and however in some respects laudable, is properly assailable and ultimately untenable. The really courageous thinkers are those who take up a position and then shovel the sand out from under themselves (or, as they say, deconstruct it) and then take up an alternative position only to do the same, the point being that WE are the site of the confusion. We're the co-creators of the problem. We shouldn't even grow narcissistically self-congratulatory about our embrace of confusion. Do you wake in the middle of the night filled with terror?

JC: No, I don't wake in the middle of the night filled with terror. But I do think that even the finest conversations, unless they are playful, are like the proverbial "ships passing in the night." That is, that's their geometry. The different speech-balloons are only tangentially, temporarily, and partially connected, by a certain liquid expanse. They don't answer to each other; each cherishes its sovereign cluster of lights. Yet they may send across their captains to share a drink and swap lore. To me, the risk with deconstruction is that it places a torpedo in the hands of an alleycat. Too much democracy! Democracy's virtue is its inefficiency. Do you wake in the middle of the night filled with terror?

LH: Yes. Terror that the ships will collide and terror that they will pass just beyond sight of each other. One wants both/neither to be known—exposed in one's cabin eating crackers and butter—and/nor to be a secret. One wants to keep possession of one's secrets but not to be one—or is it the other way around: one wants to surrender one's secrets to a "true friend" but to remain one, even (or especially) to oneself. It is true that though mirrors don't lie, we nonetheless lie to mirrors; old women know this to be true, but I ask myself, do old men? Many writers have spoken, in one way or another, of their love of "easeful death." They mean their own, not that of their child or friend. I am afraid of death, but not of my own. Do you indulge in things that are "bad" for you?

JC: Old men lie to the mirror and more or less know it. I do indulge in things that are "bad" for "me." One could think up a form of magic movie, watching which a squint or wink would bring out another, different, swirling scene—like a bedroom conjured from the fragments of an old-style battlefield. I see myself stumble "innocently" about like the White Knight, then from the gleams of armor an imp of desire manifests with rum-soaked cigarettes to secretly suck and "relax." Do you distinguish between euphemism and detail?

LH: Now that's a question! But after eating an apple and seizing my sword, I'll take a stab at an answer: yes! On the other hand clichés (and the metaphors that precede them) would be impossible if we couldn't merge euphemism and detail ("on the other hand being an example"). Love is a euphemism whose details are least known to lovers. Is there one thing you've loved above all others? And can you guess why I put that in the past tense?

JC: Depends on which shanty/universe I'm living in, since the extreme lovable's a shape-shifter among the basic verbs; poetry, sex, light, self, creative process, love, birds, beer, bacon, ball patterns, crazy sounds, and absurdity are all aspects of the same simple little wiggle. I don't know why you put it in the past tense. Not because I'm old. Perhaps because I can't predict how it will change. How would you build a pyramid to love?

LH: Clumsily and slavishly though without slaves. Still I'd need a lot of help—I'd be forced to admit that. It would stand out—"out"—and within reach of time, which has only increased my love for all that is love of all that I love. And it wouldn't be a pyramid (though there's no such thing as an ugly stone). Perhaps it would be one of the prepositions, they are the very opposite of military. Like "of" or "with" or "by" or "to" my pyramid to love would be very small and it would draw to it things of great importance (to me) and hold them there, delicately. How would you prepare for torture?

JC: By relaxing. But then that would wash out in a trice because torture is much too smart for me. Torture is probably the apex of human cleverness: utter lack of pretense. It's like ground music (picture earth heaves), like musical psychology, like psychological blood, like bloody breath, like breath formed to skin-buttons and pushed pushed pushed pushed pushed. Then pushed some More! More! More! On and on. Like blaspheming light-dark rhythms with a thousand teeth. It's very difficult to think of extremes because "think" falls short. Torture is so smart it goes beyond thinking. In a sweeter way, that's what poetry attempts. Would you put any limits on the word "think"?

LH: On the word or on thinking? The word can think, thunk, thank (or, even, thonk and thenk) to its heart's content. And others can think and thunk and thank as they please. But I do find myself putting limits on my own thinking: I will not think of the worst that could happen to those I love, lest thinking the worst might make it so. And there are some thoughts I will not think since thinking them is tantamount to action: thoughts of vengeance, self-justification, thoughts rooted in self-loathing. I will not think these thoughts—which is to say, I will myself not to think them. Tolstoi came to consider war to be an "absolute social evil"—do you?

JC: "War" ... "absolute" ... "social" ... "evil" ... these are all words of such size they lose touch with physical reality. Nor do they keep a shapely relation with spirit. They are removed; thus only the clumsiest part of our intuition can "go there." Having said that, I do think that war is "natural," though I've read the contrary arguments, and I wonder if any life-form capable of complex organization (social) will not inevitably commit massive destruction. Since I deplore anthropocentrism, I'm less worried about war than about the war against nature (and I realize the ironies and overlappings). The bacteria will survive and, presumably, re-evolve, but everything alive you can touch is going. The bite-size part of time is going. Can people expand care beyond presence and simile? (Ai-yi-I-I-I.)

LH: Can people care beyond the moment in which they can benefit from caring? Can people care for things with which they have no familiarity, for which they feel no similarity? These are the questions you are asking, I think. Or rather, you are asking if people can improve on "nature," resist "the territorial imperative" (there was a book with that title, published in 1960 or thereabouts, by—not Paul Goodman but by a friend of his), be better than their biology. I can only hope that the answer is yes. Alas (perhaps alas) it is precisely by going to words (notions) "of such size they lose touch with physical reality" that we'll achieve this improvement on nature. All principles are abstract, all violence is a physical reality. Shouldn't I rescue the spider in the bathtub?

JC: Rescuing the spider will make you feel good: do it. The act could spread to other rescuings of nature, or (with people in general, not you, my dear) substitute itself for policy.… To hope that we can be better than our biology is to assume that biology exists only in the arena of ug-ug-gimme-dat. Culture is in its entirety descended from biology. Philosophy evolves, whether long-term survival mechanism or wandering by-product. Biology has localized senses too, that give it a "flavor" in our minds, but we should never confuse flavor with definitive causal agency. It's an "everything" word that derives personality from its limitations (which aren't real). To withhold credit from biology for Beethoven's 9th or a Dickinson poem is to focus our values intraspecifically. Alas! That's what we've been doing. The "answers" to care's limits must be limitless metonymy and metaphor—associative poetic procedures—in addition to (science-tested) principles. Or—we'll turn out to be, as it were, a mickey-mouse "death star" (as in the Cretaceous). Did you ever have the feeling we came from outer space?

LH: I've thought that we might end up in outer space (the literal outer space, not "heaven"), but when I "feel" where we've come from, it's not outer space but caves that I picture. But "picture" is too mild—as I've grown older (and have become, by most standards prior to the most recent, old) the realization that the "bog people" and "cave dwellers" and Charlemagne were real has become more real. The palpable presence of their having once been is sometimes overwhelming. Hello! I too …! I say. Did you ever wish you were a girl?

JC: As far as I can plumb my wishes, I've never wished to be a girl. I have wished that energy enter me. I have wished to embrace objectivity, like climbing a tree. I've been refreshed and exhausted by trees' slowness, I've fallen through branches, I've hit the ground, I've wished that somebody else start the talking. I've wished to be as central as a girl or woman is. Did you ever dream or daydream of levitation?

LH: No, quite the opposite. I've dreamed of things' succumbing to gravity, never of something's (or my) defying it. I've dreamed of crashing planes, I've dreamed of the earth's being smashed by a mottled brown and blue spinning malevolent mirror image of itself. I've dreamed that I'm falling. I've dreamed that I've come to the edge of a pit and seen that I've fallen into it and am lying there dressed in white and dead. Sunlight is falling all around. A bulldozer is approaching, bobbing over the rough terrain. Do you believe there is a man in the machine?

JC: A man in the machine. Sounds vaguely familiar … is it "ma" leading, plus later, buried "n" (closure of tongue to alveolar ridge) between vowels and sound the word's end, as if peering over a cliff? Is it a novella by B. Traven? Is it about a teleological universe? Does "man" include "woman" as woman includes man? I believe that when the yodeling robot yelps along our streets, usually at night, there's a man in in in in the machine. Do you think there was a beautiful period of matriarchy overcome by a less beautiful patriarchy?

LH: There either were, or weren't, prehistorical societies ruled by women, and my thinking they existed or thinking they didn't is of no relevance. I suspect it is unlikely that such a society would have been lovelier than those ruled by men, whether then or later. I know that men are afraid of women—afraid in ways that women cannot imagine and that in no way resemble the ways in which women are afraid of men. The fear that men have of women may have made a society ruled by women an unhappy place—for the men but also for the women, who after all would have had to cope constantly with a debilitated, dysfunctional, pathetic segment of the population. Have you ever seen a ghost?

JC: No, I've never seen a ghost. This is because I am a rational gentleman clothed in black and white (and subtle shades of gray), not some hysterical—woops, there's one now! She (I'm judging by the hair) seems to be Italian, is quite tall (67"), supple, is this very second passing through the bricks behind my bookcase. With the faintest of smiles, she's gone. I'm quite sure she was hallucinatory, generated by a questionable olive in my brunch martini. What is childbirth really like?

LH: It's like trying to remember something: the intense mental labor involved in recovering a memory—say, the exact look of a room or a bird or the sound of one's father's voice. I remember what my father looked like, though for years after his death from cancer I only "saw" him in my mind as he was toward the end, gaunt and receding from life: drifting. Then one night in a dream I saw him through a department store window. He turned and saw me and passed flawlessly through the window; I introduced him to L. He was fastidiously dressed except on weekends, when he gardened. What's your favorite household chore? What's your least favorite?

JC: Doing errands lets me shake a leg and cock an eye. I like washing dishes too. Putting things in order is a compulsion but can get too tiring. Large-scale cleaning, I don't take to the end texture; also it's hard on back, and I'm soft on balance. Maybe I don't see the cleanliness except as gleam and prefer my gleams extreme and quasi-isolated like a sunrise. When is passivity OK?

LH: When it is "radical passivity" (see *Radical Passivity: Levinas, Blanchot, and Agamben*, by Thomas Carl Wall), a condition that allows the once-familiar to return in a form that is both still-familiar and scary, i.e. as a ghost. It's not the ghost that's scary but its return—which couldn't happen without the space that (radical) passivity provides. Without that radical passivity music would be meaningless. The ghost that we allow into music—or that is music—is the guest of passivity. And as far as I'm concerned, that's OK and more than OK: "not," as Wall puts it, "an essence, a shining path, nor a destiny, but the sheer possibility of relation in general—a dice throw." Do you tend to win games? Are you lucky?

JC: I tend to win games due to my ricky-tick intelligence type and ability to focus, and to lose them when my blue center spills onto the table. Or somebody else gets hot. I'm lucky I'm alive. Like anyone, I'm lucky to be imperfect. Lucky to shoot myself in the foot when I'm hectored. I'm lucky I can't stand a moment without context. I'm lucky I live for such moments. I'm lucky I'm nervous, I guess. I'm lucky (I think) I wasn't born a fruit fly. Is the life of a human more valuable than the life of a mouse?

LH: I doubt that it is, except to a human. In a cosmos animated by life, life is by definition the most important of all things. Perhaps, if and when we come to learn more about the cosmos of death (if there is such a cosmos), we'll be capable of different urges, different forms of love—or no love at all (which is, after all, just another term for the yearning after life and liveliness). But as it is, we live precisely to live and can care for—and experience love as—nothing more than living. For better or worse, this loving/yearning-for-living is inherently selfish—though perhaps only because death threatens it/us from all sides. In practice, then, we behave as if a human life is more valuable than the life of a mouse. To behave otherwise is self-sacrificial—noble, perhaps, but unlively. Do you have any idea what "C.P.T." refers to in the last stanza of Langston Hughes's poem "Dancer" (from Montage of a Dream Deferred)—"Even a great dancer / can't C.P.T. / a show"?

JC: Conjure-Pirate-Treasure   Colette-Proust-Tanguy
        Conceive-Preach-Time   Cougar-Panther-Tiger
        Completely-Pump-Thump   Compensate-Previous-Thud
        Cool-Prime-Tandaradei!   Carve-Preen-Trickle
        Corn-Peach-Tomato   Click-Prick-Trick
        Connect-Perfection-To   Cock-Poodle-Too

No, I don't. Sorry. What will American poetry be like in 100 years?

LH: Something American, though what "American" will mean in 100 years is hard to know. America is an imaginary site. The native peoples didn't conceive of it as a geo-political entity and the Europeans who did so were dreaming. Lasciviously, in some cases—as in John Donne's wonderful/awful "Elegie: Going to Bed":

> Your gown going off, such beautious state reveals,
> As when from flowry meads th'hills shadowe steales.
> Off with that wyerie Coronet and shew
> The haiery Diadem which on you doth grow:
> ....
> Licence my roaving hands, and let them go,
> Behind, before, above, between, below.
> O my America! my new-found-land,
> My kingdome, safeliest when with one man man'd,
> My Myne of precious stones: My Emperie,
> How blest am I in this discovering thee!

But there was something I wanted to ask you ... Fuck! What were we talking about just before the phone rang?

JC: I think it was golden-ratio reasoning, in which each assertion is 1.618 times bolder than the one before. The precision of it all typically knocks the socks off the interlocutor, who crawls into bed shivering from the top down and begins reading *In the Belly of the Beast* with a flashlight till his/her parents, awakened by the sound of pages turning like the lapping of waves on some Madagascar shore, where two lemurs are gathering coco shells, row into the room and make their macro-micro demands. How do you quiet down a horse after it's been spooked by avalanche or hungry puma?

LH: You ride it again past the site of the fright to show that the danger has moved away. This can take a lot of time—it's like remastering a tape in an old studio with quirky equipment near an airport. If you could spend a week anywhere in the world, where would you do so? And if you could spend a year (a full cycle of seasons) somewhere, where would you do that?

JC: I'd spend a week on a rickety old bright brown luxury bus driving through Mexico, Germany, Libya, Ethiopia, Ecuador, Iceland, and Singapore half-full of friends and strangers, stopping frequently for looks and side trips, equipped with everything and nothing. I'd spend a year right here. Or in Mexico or Germany or San Francisco. Would you like to have a magical device that would process all the sound around you into kaleidoscopelike shifting forms? Discuss.

LH: No! Even as it is (and even as they are), sounds tend to seize control of the things around me. Sound itself is a "magical device," and its magic is, by definition, out of my (or your) control. It would be terrifying to have sound itself "magically" transformed. But I would very much like to know how to play the violin, i.e. to make (magic) sounds in the ways that the violin makes possible. Is grief embarrassing?

JC: Grief is potentially the most embarrassing state. People might think, "You failed to be happy!" But now I see in Webster's that "embarrass" comes from roots meaning "in a noose" (I think of the baracan, which in Libya concealed (or conceals) all but the left eye of the faces of native women). And, further, that the first two meanings refer to "doubt or perplexity" and "financial difficulties," neither of which necessarily addresses the self-consciousness I associate with the word. There's also "hampering the movements of," and "making intricate." To return to grief, luckily people have found ritual expressions for grief and have also developed a respect for the sensitivity grief implies. So that, all in all, and although the opposite is also true, I think a lack of grief is embarrassing, especially in today's world. Do you know the derivation and connotations of the phrase, "around Robin Hood's barn"?

LH: I'll imagine them first and look them up second—which may in itself constitute a form of going round Robin's barn. That's how I've always heard it, by the way: with the verb "to go": "going around Robin Hood's barn." Robin Hood in his heyday didn't have a barn (unless the forest served as such), so the reference must be to Robin in middle-age, when he preferred to tell stories of adventure rather than living them. And who could blame him? Robin Hood lived long and learned that just walking about the ordinary world in an ordinary sort of way is an adventure, since one never knows what's around the corner, even if one put it there. To "go around Robin Hood's barn" is to have the capacity for adventure in situations that the young would consider dull. But I see (from the Oxford Dictionary of Phrase and Fable) that it is indeed "round Robin Hood's barn" that is the phrase, and it means a circuitous route. What do you think of John Kerry?

JC: I don't care for Kerry. He seems too poli-tick. He seems subtle as a subterfuge. Subtle without "admitting" it in his demeanor. I have colossal admiration—and distrust—for his phrasings on sensitive topics. Of course, we "need someone electable," but that's a shoddy perfection of democracy: honing down the idiosyncratic to a polish that's TV-keen but really no smarter than a Wendy's ad. I've always thought Clinton was the best we're gonna get, lately: compromise shines. Only Bush is allowed to be radical, now, since it's balanced by the "dignity" of his position, and it's radicality feeds America like a root cellar in a hurricane. So vote for Kerry. Or emigrate (where??). What's wrong with death?

LH: Its antithesis to life: its absoluteness, its irrevocability, its unchangingness, its truth. One of the "selling points" for cinema in its early days was that, by its means, the dead would never be completely lost to us. Once again one could watch one's father turn to the right, once again one could see one's beloved smile—perpetually returning, but in a form that is deaf to us and blind: approaching intimately, familiarly, terrifyingly. What's your favorite film?

JC: Favorite film. The thin layer of wetness (humor) over my eyeballs. Well, some of my favorite films are "The Art of Vision" by Stan Brakhage and two Hollywood films I've seen recently (again) on TV: "Bonnie and Clyde" and "The Treasure of the Sierra Madre." Also "Mikrokosm" (sp.?), Terry Gilliam's "Baron Münchhausen" movie, "Being John Malkovich," anything with Ava Gardner, a raft of experimental films including Dorsky's and Marie Mencken's and Bruce Conner's (sp.?) and Kubelka's, anything by Georges Meliés (sp.?). Off and on I've loved many kinds of cinema. Docu's. My favorite movie is the passage of the days (what rhythm!). I've seen "New Faces" 15 times. I'll also toss in an Islamic love story I proofread for Jenny (that she recently "retold," cutting it down from 200 pages); even at 42 pp. it is so relentlessly rollercoaster, irrational-rational, moody, it seems to capture biological process, as Brakhage's films capture nonreferential vision. Spoiled Vis and Ramin are as unquenable as life itself. What is your favorite smell?

LH: My favorite smells include that which dry northern California soil emits in summer as dew forms, the light chocolaty smell of a small garage with oil on the floor, the smell of new wood, and the musky smell emitted by some weed or shrub or tree that evokes strong emotions to which I can't attach any memory but was certainly as sporadically present in my childhood as it is now. Kate Lilley (the Australian poet and scholar of "early modern"—i.e. Renaissance—women's writing) and her partner (and fellow scholar) Melissa Hardie recently told me of some 3-volume psychoanalytic work analyzing the personality profile of people given to "disgust" (i.e. a sense of revulsion caused by tastes) versus that of people given to "dissmell" (a sense of revulsion caused by smells, in particular that of shit). People prone to dissmell tend to be authoritarian—that's what the theory is, but I don't remember the details as it all seemed preposterous (and Kate and Melissa's account of their occasion for reading it was hilarious). I wore patchouli oil back in the 60s because I liked the smell; I still do and would wear it again if it weren't so preposterous to do so. Did you as a child have fantasies that you were living in the wrong family—that there'd been a switch, for example?

JC: I don't think I had that particular fantasy-cluster, perhaps because it was so early evident that that fantasy had been co-opted by literature. Fantasies depend on belief, and it was hard to believe one had actually been switched after reading about switches as fantasies. I did believe, for example, in the reality of Oz, and that I'd somehow sometime get there; I believed the animals speak (and that I'd somewhere join their conversations); I believed I'd levitate in some fine moment. In all these cases, though my fantasy has a basis in previous fantasies (which are clearly fantasy), it's possible to construct an algorithm by means of which the possibility "bleeds" its way step-by-step from true to not and back again. Flying and speech are obvious; even Oz has a thousand connections with "reality." Did you ever wonder thus: "Why am I (who must be the universal subjective) me?"

LH: Not in precisely those terms. But the question "why am I this rather than that?" was a question that recurred throughout my childhood and youth, and thinking about it may have provided me with the grounds for empathy later on. The matter of being this particular person was, to me, always framework for considering the arbitrariness (and, often, the cruelty) of circumstances. That is, when I looked at my enviable (so they seemed to me and so they were) circumstances, I was amazed that I hadn't been born into some other harsher set, along with the people that I tended to think about (victims of history's many atrocities), even almost to identify with. Later, in adulthood (even to this day), I have often succumbed to the temptation to wonder how it is that I am not a duck, or jellyfish, or tiger in the wild. Or a cowboy or doctor (both things I once wanted to "be"). If you had another life to live, what would you be?

JC: I don't know. I wanted to be a red fox when I was small. Do you mean reincarnation when you say "another life to live"? If so, I'd like to be, oh, a parrot in the wilds of the Amazon. And, if there's one there may be more: a quicker Jack. Now you may ask yourself a question. What will it be?

LH: I'd like to ask my parents how they reacted to the rounding up and incarceration of California's Japanese-Americans in March of 1942. Were they outraged? Going by what I witnessed later of their reactions to racist paranoia and bigotry, they would have been. But California politicians and the San Francisco newspapers had been waging a virulent anti-Japanese campaign for decades—might they have been somewhat persuaded by it? They were living in San Francisco; my father had joined Naval Intelligence and was awaiting orders; I was 10 months old. About ten years later, when he refused to join a protest against the Greek grocery store owner's purchasing a house on our street, my father was verbally attacked on our front porch by a Berkeley "neighborhood preservations committee" for being a "pinko" and a "nigger-lover." When I once asked my mother about wartime San Francisco, she described a somewhat rough transition into complex modernity of a culture that sounded like something transplanted from New England by a mercantile class that liked proximity to the Pacific and the artifactual culture of Asia. She described cultural "shocks" occasioned by the war but said nothing of the city's Japanese and concentration camps. Do you know the current theory explaining the toppling of the enormous statues on Easter Island?

JC: No. I read about it (if it's still "the current" theory) recently, but memory failed me again, as it does more and more frequently. It's as if I fail to pay enough attention to the factors that feed memory, such as nutrition, good study habits, temperance, the cultivation of an elastic sense of time … what else? It's as if I were chopping down the forest, as it were, of my mental ecosystem in my greed for ceremonial fires and daily luxurious warmth. Following which, of course, my contextual landscape erodes away and the layeredness on which life depends succumbs to the "gravity of the situation." Oh, levitation might create a memory manqué.… I take solace in the fact that even a fallen memory leaves a kind of geometry in the air. Do you think the mental/emotional differences between men and women are partly genetic in origin?

LH: Perhaps—perhaps. But compared to the cultural pressures that are brought into play to produce "gender," genes probably play a relatively minor role. Not even taking queerness into account, we both surely know plenty of men capable of the qualities stereotypically attributed to women, just as we know plenty of women capable of the qualities stereotypically attributed to men. When it comes to humans, it's particularly complicated to separate biological imperatives (the residues from survival-valuable behavior traits) from cultural ones. And it's also important to acknowledge the degree to which people (at least some) have chosen their modes of mental and emotional life. But sadly, on the whole humans don't exercise nearly as much choice as they might. Is there a single poet with whom you would most want to argue?

JC: Yeah, and it's happening in the most amiable way. Aside from you, I would pick the poet, or two, I love the most: Hopkins and (of late years) Gertrude Stein. That there's so much to argue with in each case probably reveals that I make things difficult for myself. But should one make things easy for oneself? What would one be easing the way for? Hopkins, if he sat across the table from me, might inquire, while twirling and measuring a butternut leaf, why I diffuse myself like a minor oilspill. I'd be thrilled. I would ask Stein (if I could crawl into her portrait) why she is so modest. What is (are) your favorite number(s)?

LH: 3 (for dialectics), 7 (for its harping on and then undermining dialects), and 9 (for good luck, rhythm, and rhyme). Under duress—that is to say, when in a real panic, I recite numbers in random sets to myself. The set is limited to numbers under 100: e.g., ten, two, forty, ninety-two, three, etc. Repetitions are permissible, so the sequence is potentially infinite. I'm not allowed to "go back" on a number. It's the equivalent of "automatic writing": the automatic numbering of distress, ever in quest of pattern and, from pattern, information. Do you use all ten fingers when you type or do you, raptor-like, "hunt and peck"?

JC: I hunt and peck, though after fifty-plus years the hunt's become a twitch. I typed while in the Air Force; after I'd got up to sixty words a minute with my forefingers I was sent to a two-week typing school and taught to type sixty-per with ten fingers. But then I reverted immediately to hunt-&-peck because I fancied its idiosyncrasy. Incidentally, Ron Padgett hunts and pecks with a great number of his fingers. Of late, I've been slowed: my left hand's poor at fine movement, from nerve damage, and I hold my left forefinger firmly against thumb and middle finger to strike the keys. Also, my right forefinger has become useless through an infection (tendon damage?) and I've substituted the middle finger. I'm not sure about the effect of all this middle-finger employ-ment on my poetic style. Poor eyesight and the scattering of mental control also play their parts. At any rate it's, if we choose a bird simile, more vulturine than raptor-like, though I prefer a fresh kill. I do love typing inordinately. What are your commonest entertainments?

LH: Typing is one of them, for me too. Sleeping is also an entertainment of sorts (or a sorting of myself from myself that seems, as I embark on it, to open the doors to entertainment [and I do think of going to sleep as an embarka-tion]). Or, to put it more accurately, sleep is an invitation to entertainment. But it seems that I'm formulating "entertainment" as something that comes to one—your question seems to ask what things/actions entertain me. But being entertaining for others must also be of value—as a mode of being hospitable (though, truth be told [and what good is an interview if one doesn't attempt to tell things truly?], while I believe in hospitality I much prefer solitude—which I can then use for typing). Grammar is very entertaining. Have you ever wit-nessed a crime?

JC: Once in Germany I was invited by some low-life acquaintance to visit the apartment of a criminal boss who was temporarily bedridden. The invite was ten-dered, I guess, on the basis of my being an American civilian driving a Leopold Laundry truck and having a taste for the little intrigues of that giant Munich beerhall called Matthäser. I wish I could now examine my interview, but the talk has faded into a single impression (which, suspiciously, resembles part of a Fritz Lang film): I was being felt out for possible use (my mobility, my "in" with the occupiers), and, responding, I wanted to leave the door open to this excitement but at the same time not bend my blue spine, that is, I wanted to keep an honest façade. And I never heard from them again. I've witnessed my own crimes, such as the stealing of a good stapler from the IBM factory and the stealing of a large pair of cutters (1963) from the Seymour Brass Mill. I still have and use both these tools. If you were alone on an island, would you build a boat?

LH: I might build it, but I doubt that I'd launch it. No, I take that back—if, having washed up on a desert island, I built a boat, I think I might indeed set off on it. No, I take that back. The question you've asked, as I see it, is actu-ally about the will to live. I know nothing about sailing and I have no sense of direction, so that to set off on a "boat" (and it would indeed be not a boat but a "boat") would be suicidal, an acceptance of death. Building the boat, on the other hand, would be an expression of liveliness, a demonstration of optimism, an exercise of energy, a "distraction" (and at my age [63 as of last Monday] I have ceased to consider life-affirming distractions, which is to say the stuff of daily business, unimportant); it would be a pleasure and an end in itself. I think I'd remain on the island and keep a lookout for potential rescuers—a passing ship or plane or (as I drifted off into hallucinations) a bird or whale, porpoise, or fish miraculously aware of my plight and wondrously willing to carry me across the ocean and home. Do you own a gun?

JC: No. I've always been strongly against guns. I think it stems from my intense sympathy as a boy for wild creatures. Or the association of guns with "regular" manhood. I once shot a rabbit in the head when my companion, who was going to, for the ranch table, asked me if I'd like to. Nothing wrong. I went through M-1 and carbine training in ROTC. Nothing wrong. But anecdotes are like little shotgun blasts that cluster around or near a perceived target. What was your early experience with TV?

LH: My first TV experiences took place in the basement of a house across the street from ours. Five children lived in that house, and the middle one, Kit, was the one who was my friend. His sister was my sister's age. We watched Hopalong Cassidy and pulled down our pants to show what they concealed. Then my parents got a TV and we watched Hopalong Cassidy at home—without the five neighbor kids. The Hopalong Cassidy movies were soothing. Much of the rest of my early TV watching was traumatic. Seeing some version of "Frankenstein" at night with a babysitter left me with a terror of the dark, of our attic, and of my closet. And being forced to go to bed before the end of some stirring movie about some parentless children and a horse and a medical crisis occasioned my first, strong, indelible experience of loss. Reading a recent essay, I came across the comment, "there is no art without mourning." Do you think that's true?

JC: I think mourning is, to a degree, simply recognition of and memory of pain and loss. Without mourning, then, there could be no humanity, much less art. But to say "there is no art without mourning" lays a particular and undue emphasis on it. So if emphasis is truth, the quoted comment is not, or not much. One can make parallel comments like "there is no motion without dissatisfaction" and they have the fault of truisms, that they're ideas without things. Of course mourning has a more ceremonial air than dissatisfaction. Do you think much about clothes?

LH: I think about clothes very little and about shoes even less. My mother was a beautiful woman—naturally elegant, I think. She never talked about clothes, never exhibited any particular interest in them per se, and didn't have the money to buy expensive clothes (or at least not until late in life), but my father traditionally bought her a dress or "outfit" for Christmas. In retrospect, perhaps I got the impression that they were important, and I most definitely noticed my mother's beauty and elegance. But, be that as it may, they haven't been particularly important to me. Or is the exact opposite the truth of the matter? I think so. Will you be cremated after you die? And if so, will the ashes be scattered or will they rest below a marker engraved with your name?

JC: I picked up the image somewhere of being tied into the upper branches of a tree and letting the birds feast, but of course that's jocular, being illegal. I want the disposal of my remains to be cheap and "no muss, no fuss." Decades ago I wrote a Last Will and Testament Poem asking that my friends have a party on the occasion and play some Blind Willie Johnson and some yodeling. 'Twould be nice. My parents are both buried (ashes), entirely unofficially, in a spot next to a stump up Boulder Canyon on national forest land. Something like that's fine. Will you say something embarrassing?

LH: I'm sure I will—I already have. Doing so seems almost unavoidable, if and as one lives among others, though I try to remain astute, appropriate, aware, attentive. Confidentiality floods in where confidence is lacking and one betrays oneself; slips of tongue, badly timed or badly placed candor, misunderstood social relations—these can all occasion embarrassments, either as they happen or in retrospect. Retrospection brings other pains to self-reflection, too: shame, remorse, regret, guilt. Probably more bad deeds than good have been prompted by these. Did you like school—say 2nd grade, or 8th?

JC: I was twelve in 8th grade and have often considered that year the happiest in my life. I "never stepped on a sidewalk" the whole time; i.e., it was all woods, field grass, tree limbs, alleys and holes in fences. This I suppose was a nonlinear "learning from life" that balanced the surface linearity espoused by my favorite teacher (8th grade), Miss Edgar. She was systematic with the language, in order, perhaps, to infect us with her (nonlinear) love of it. At commencement exercises, she prefaced her awarding of the English prize with a long disquisition on the "oyster-like" qualities of the recipient. My pals and I were joking and poking each other: who is this oyster? (not me, my lowest grades were in English). It was me. My oldest friend Gerard and I still reminisce about Miss Edgar (what could have been her first name)? What does it take to complete a thought?

LH: A period, but that only completes it momentarily, locally, and grammatically. Some thoughts dissipate, of course—thinning into mist and particles that enter into other thoughts which thinking carries on. But it's as impossible to imagine a true completion of a thought as it is of a story or an idea. Thoughts are one and the same as their implications and ramifications. Even a dead thought (one, say, that no longer interests anyone) isn't so much completed as simply abandoned. And even a true thought (one, say, that has achieved the status of a "given," so that no one has to think it any more [e.g., the world is round or cows eat grass]) isn't so much completed as absorbed into a world view to which it continues to contribute. If I weren't feeling slightly lazy at the moment, I'd see what the OED has to say about "complete"—maybe, as sometimes happens, the word has hidden within it its own undoing (in a meaning that is the very opposite of what we've come to understand by the word). What book(s) are you currently reading?

JC: Looking through my chief workroom/bedroom stacks, I find *Natural History* magazine, Alice Notley's Naropa Summer Writing Program handout, "Bed" (Summer Writing Program magazine), *Shirley Shirley* by Alicia Askenase, *High Country News, Sound Nets* by Richard Martin, *I Was Going to Use That* by Rob Geisen, a Michael Moore generic email, poems by Carmen Vigil, *Teachers & Writers* summer issue, *The Invisible City* (ed. Marcella Durand), *The Distressed Look* and *God Never Dies* by Joanne Kyger, *New Goose* by Lorine Niedecker, a Rachel Levitsky ms., *I My Feet* by Gerhard Rühm, *Infinity Subsections* by Mark DuCharme, *An Evolution of Writing Ideas, and Vice Versa*, by me, "Geochemical Evidence for Oxygenated Bottom Waters During Deposition of Fossiliferous Strata of the Burgess Shale Formation" by Christopher Collom, *My Life in the Nineties* by you, *Harper's* magazine (2), *Bombay Gin 30, Austerlitz* by W. G. Sebald, *The Paris Stories* by Laird Hunt, *The Seasons* and *Rivers & Birds* by Merrill Gilfillan, *Guns, Germs, and Steel* by Jared Diamond, *Music of the Spheres* by Guy Murchie (many untouched for somewhile). And these represent just the fin of the shark (don't count new Fish Drum stuff). I'm a mess. I think I have cataracts. Who's winning, in your book, the city or the country?

LH: I remember that some years ago I said to you or wrote to you or thought to say or write to you—I remember wanting you to see (and acknowledge) that environmentalist concerns might be contrary to the interests of ordinary people. In the process of closing down corporate exploitation, real and good people suffer, and not in some abstract sense but really, truly, in the very heart of their lives. I wanted you to see that—and of course now, these years of friendship later, I know that you've seen that. It's a complicated opposition, and probably not a valid one, that of country vs. city. What is either, that it might win? And what might it win? Countrification (sounds like something the British upper-classes did, or that movie star Americans do when buying land in New Mexico). Citification? In my own heart, the country (you do mean rurality, right, and not the USA as a patriot's heaven?) wins—that is to say, in a battle (but there is none) for my devotion. And yet, at the same time, I have had (and have) a good life in the semi-city of Berkeley, California. To live here is not to lose. Have you ever signed a loyalty oath?

JC: Yes, I think so, in the armed forces. Memory is hazy. And perhaps I've re-fused to sign one or two. In 1990, on receiving an NEA Fellowship, I signed (and mentally dismissed) a statement of moral loyalty: I wouldn't use the money to create "homoerotic or obscene" work. I was interviewed by the Boulder Daily Camera and an article resulted from which I'll quote: "Addressed to the thoughtful conservative: … You may quibble about details of change: fads swell and fade, inaccurate claims are made, ego-driven charismas co-opt causes. Fine: quibble. Me too. But to emphasize such quibbles to the point that your main philosophic energy functions in opposition to change itself is like shooting a lifeboat full of holes because its seats are uncomfortable." And so on. What's your favorite sport?

LH: To watch, do you mean, or to play? Either way, the question throws me into a quandary, since I'm not sure just what constitutes "sport." Playing is involved, but not always and not all play is sport. One doesn't play gymnastics, and monopoly isn't a sport (though perhaps it is; the CNN sports channel in-cludes poker matches in its sportive programming). Activities involving physical prowess—is that a definition of sport? Anyway, whether it's watching or doing, physical activity involving horses is just my cup of tea—with the proviso that in horse racing generally the horses are too hard to see and with the added proviso that I myself haven't been horseback riding in years. So, since the equestrian seems to be an ideal rather than realized sports arena for me, I guess I'll say that hiking is my favorite sport, the extended hiking wherein, at some point, one be-comes like a bird. Have you any phobias, mild or severe (fear of spiders, ghosts, airless elevators, etc.)?

JC: Fear of questions that dangle from experience. I don't think I have phobias (or allergies). I'm thinking lately of myself as having neuroses, for example a neurotic relationship to social intercourse. Most conversation I dislike, find myself dreading, though at the same time having an enormous lust for, in some other form. My mother and father didn't talk much, didn't "do" talk as warm contextual flow.... I used to be afraid of water, perhaps the smothering potential. I thought I'd be afraid of losing breath, now that I'm wearing oxygen, but I'm not. I'm afraid of heights, now that I've lost my good balance (I once walked across an I-beam a hundred feet or so, a couple stories up, in New York). I'm afraid of stopping this, afraid of not getting another chance. How close do you like to be to things?

LH: Generally, I like to be close enough to things to see them and know what they are, but there are exceptions to that. I like to keep a good distance between myself and things that stink or threaten. And I like to get very close to things that provoke my curiosity (even, as in the case of the golden orb spiders now abundant in the backyards of Berkeley, when they threaten—which occasionally the spiders do, rearing up, wagging their front legs, and shaking the web) so as to see their obscurer elements or study their particular features. Recently, I have felt myself getting closer and closer to understanding certain complex poems—Zukofsky's "A," for example. Or to put it another way, I find that I have come to a point in time (my time or the world's, I'm not sure which) where I can participate in such poems with feelings that I call "understanding"—exhilarated, in effect. What work of literature that you didn't write do you wish you had?

JC: I often wish, as I read, poetry especially, that I had written or, even more, could write what I'm reading, but I try to shake such feelings as being flare-ups of ego-sickness and not a receptive way to read. (Pause.) Picking from literally thousands of possibles, I'll mention Anne Carson's piece in The Best American Poetry 2004, "Gnosticism." What I envy, miss, is her familiarity with the landscape so that she can, having passed through abstract coherence (of Gnosticism) and through concrete versions of and off it, pass into a glorious, sour chaos, nursing its logic. Work energy, non-dilettante. Have you desired to be a musician, or sublimated such a wish?

LH: My answer to the first part of your question is yes: I've desired to be a musician. It occurs to me, though, that I should say something more about what "being a musician" has meant to me when I've desired it. Sometimes what I've desired in music-making are the immediacy and the ecstasy; I'm thinking back to the days when I thought I could imagine being Janis Joplin, say, or Heifetz, or Piatigorsky—caught up, carrying it (whatever it is) on, being: musical. But sometimes the object of my desire has been the very opposite of that—not the drunkenness but the precision—the practicing—the "math," as it were. As to the second part of your question: probably my answer here too is yes. Writing poetry has been (and remains) for me a means of sounding and sounding out, and I don't regret being a poet rather than a musician. Is there anything in human sexual behavior that has the power to shock you?

JC: Yes: what I haven't imagined (and thus haven't yet been able to surround with soft pillows of thought) but can imagine now, on purpose. Sucking the cock of a rhinoceros, or fucking a baby thus breaking its bones. I'm not shocked by human sexual behavior's inevitability, nor by the deceptions and intricate maneuvers and folkways that grow from this inevitability…. Thinking about this lets me see shock afresh, as a bluntly wielded word, usually meant to cause dismissal or avoidance, like the word "cliché." But behind the gleaming wall protecting each is a little universe. Would you like a free question, that is, to both ask and answer your own?

LH: What if I were to say no? I suppose I'd politely go on nonetheless, trans-muting my "no" into what would become, in effect, a yes. Enter dreams and sadness! "Yes" and "no" scarcely differ. Behold the birth of something now emerging into psychic space! I realize that this is merely an answer. Walking to work a few mornings ago, I heard the sound of music—some recording of a modern work for solo piano, I thought. I was approaching the house from whose windows, I thought, the music was issuing—a brown shingle house with high hedges to the sides and front and a (as I could now see) narrow driveway, obscured until I was right at its entrance. It was from the driveway that the music was coming. A man—eyes closed, hands flying, head and shoulders swaying—was playing a piano that was standing in the back of a battered white pickup truck. Many hours later, walking home from work, I passed the driveway again; the man and piano and truck were gone. Farewell! Why do you suppose the piano was in the truck and where do you suppose they went?

JC: I don't know, I don't know. Maybe the piano represented a black key inside the white-key scope the pickup bed stood for. Did the music seem to form any sort of sonar blueprint for Chinese boxes? The player, you say, seemed like blind flight; could he have been expressing a recommendation for human-ity to organize its realizations into environmental sequences, each step largely predicated on what surrounds it? An opening sphere, a closing sphere? Or per-haps the whole deal was just a rather unusual little wake-up business the man had started: Unmistakable Alarms, Inc. I hope where they went is out across America and the Pacific, multiplying concentrically. Can you swim?

LH: I don't sink in water, I can do a few laps in a pool, and I love being in the water—so yes. I'm delighted by the sense of traveling in an altogether alien medium, and I know how to do so (for short distances). Float bubbles, as the palaces melt! I know an assortment of strokes (crawl, backstroke, breast stroke, side stroke). But I don't swim often. The great adventure would be to embark into the ocean, but the northern California coastal waters are notoriously dangerous—the undertow is strong and can toss one head over heel, the tidal currents are swift and can carry one away, notorious sleeper waves roll in on even the quietest days and sweep people off rocks or tidal pools, and the water is always very, very cold. The adventure is too much of one. And though there are some local public pools I could swim in, I don't. Competing with others in their lanes, by closing time, I'd succumb to weakness. Do you sleep easily and well or do you have insomnia?

JC: A bit of both. Nothing troublesome. I have a little physical discomfort (and now, of course, I'm wearing tubes); I take a trazodone before going to sleep (so I can). I lie on my left side awhile (pillow between bony knees), right leg drawn up, then on my right side, left leg drawn up, etc. I try to keep breathing through my nose, so lie on my back sometimes. Sometimes I lie awake but I don't mind. I try to make my imagination physical, so it'll sink from memories and problems into colors and shapes, which then start dancing on their own. In the morning I no longer leap out of bed immediately but lie there awhile planning poems (or other activities). I usually nap, or at least rest, about mid-day. Do you ever become angry with me?

LH: No. Back when we first started writing works together, I got frustrated sometimes when you took what I took to be a "silly" turn where I wanted a "serious" continuation of something, but I got over that pretty fast. It was just that I couldn't keep up with your imaginative pace. Comedy is serious and the so-called "silly turn" can advance thought at high velocities that "seriousness" can't achieve. The first result of our beginning to write together was our book *Sunflower*; my book *A Border Comedy*—my favorite of all my writings—became the continuation of the truly full "something" you introduced me to. Are you ever angry at me?

JC: No. I've felt fretful at what I've taken to be, or to include, mere serenity. But that's just where I've learned the deepest, dearest lessons, which involve linguistic patience, the forming of a partnership with, rather than a use (abuse) of time, and even the ways work's exercise are endless—but then indeed snap off properly at personality's foot. (Our colloquies sail on silvery tracks; I'm sure if we were tossed together for a time we'd find extravagances of objectionability....) Who are your favorite novelists?

LH: That's easy: Marcel Proust and Charles Dickens and Henry James are my favorite novelists. I enormously admire Melville, too, but his imagination is always utterly unfamiliar to me, so I haven't the warm affection and sense of affinity with Melville's work that "favorite" implies (to me, at least). But, having said that, why do I feel that "favor" requires some kind of "coziness"? Surely it must be because I imagine the social or psychic space in which reading novels occurs to be some kind of happy, untrammeled site. But why should reading novels be assumed to be an intimate activity? I don't think of reading poetry in those terms. If there is a movie/film that particularly terrified you, what is it?

JC: I think of "The Uninvited," with Gail Russell and Ray Milland. The thing was, I saw it as a child, when a movie could terrify me (I've been told, lately, it's a mediocre movie, but I remember, or remember remembering, a sudden door slam that was stunning ((or perhaps wakening))). By now, movie fears have become merely delicious (and maybe that was part of it then). By now, I'm afraid that somebody in a given movie is going to deceive someone else, or be misunderstood (almost the same), and I get so uncomfortable it's almost like terror. Then it's difficult to crawl out of one "parenthesis" and into the next. What do you think/feel about mathematics?

LH: In my imagination (which is the only place it can exist for me), the world of mathematics resembles the world of the stars and constellations—a sidereal world of infinite pattern and pattern variation, a world of countless dimensions, the site of a real (as distinct from sentimental) mystery or mysterium (silence). From my relationship with mathematics, I've learned the cognitive importance of confidence—which is to say that, almost always lacking mathematical (or even arithmetic) confidence, I can only very rarely carry off even the simplest numerical procedures with assurance. But when, giddily perhaps and trusting to the good luck of the novice, I do act mathematically with confidence (intuiting, as it were, the tip in the nick of time as the taxi pulls up at my destination and discovering afterward that it was exactly right), the result is thrilling—I feel that the stars have been with me. Have you enemies?

JC: Enemies (head whips this way and that, apprehensively)? I don't think so. I'm afraid my third son Franz might consider himself my enemy, or, worse, me his. As an emissary of his mother. But I don't think even she's my enemy, rather a crashed friend. Enmity spreads like octopus ink, destroys distinctions. Trying to see through it, step by step, I see as enemy to me first of all Homo sapiens (this shows the aching love and want behind enmity), more particularly a sort of giant "cabal" of those humans who not only destroy nature but do it with pretense of good. Also those who angrily militate for sentimentality or mere convention in any field or, one can say now, even for lack of thought. Going inside those generalities, no specifics arise, except that, tragically but at the same time refreshingly, one's nearest and dearest, from time to time, shine as enemies. What's your earliest memory?

LH: "A moment yellow." That's the opening phrase of my book *My Life* and as far as I know the opening phrase of my conscious life. If it is a memory at all and not some strange brain-buzzed shimmer that stands in for memory, then it records my coming upon a dandelion or buttercup on a tiny patch of grass behind the house on Filbert Street in San Francisco that my paternal grandfather had bought for my parents. I must have been lying on my stomach, legs kicking, head up, nose to nose with the flower. My father may have been in uniform. Or perhaps he wasn't—is it possible that this memory is (as I feel it is) so early that I'm not yet 7 months old (as I was when the Japanese bombed Pearl Harbor)? In any case, the memory is vivid with particular color—nothing like the night (of murky absolutism) "when all cows look black." Will you tell me about your own military service?

JC: USAF 4 years. Polished shoes and blanket tight, AF 16 422 508 reporting for duty SIR. Enlisted in Chicago (to avoid Korean War draft), Basic Training outside San Francisco, where I got my now 52-year-old tattoo. Loved marching, became squad leader. Then they made me a Remington Ranger (clerk-typist). Stateside Greenville, South Carolina, where I was jailed overnight for staggering drunkenly down the sidewalk, lost a stripe; Altus, Oklahoma; ASAP overseas. Tripoli, Libya. Typed Morning Reports all day with 2 fingers, read Moby Dick in a Quonset hut. Wandered endlessly, on pass, among white buildings, Hadrian's Arch, stopping for beers in Italian bars (falling through the roof of one, where I'd clambered, from reading Faust, to watch the foot traffic on Sharia Istiklal). TDY in Athens & Rome, Troop-Carrier Wing Detachments. Reassigned Neubiberg, near Munich, where, in the Havana Bar, I met a hefty Bavarian woman who laughed when I pulled a peanut butter sandwich from my pocket. Whom I later married. 4 years up, released from AD, NYC (cold magnet where I lived, surveyed, attended operas, before returning to Munich).

LH: I have a feeling that you want to ask me something. Am I right?

JC: Yes. What do you do when things go wrong?

LH: It depends on what the things are and how wrong they've gone. Fixing, fretting, falling silent, mourning, justifying, attacking, abandoning, denying, raging, regretting, forgetting, speaking out, etc. are all responses I've made (voluntarily or not) to wrong-going I've perpetrated, witnessed, or endured. Running into bad weather for the duration of a vacation is one order of things going wrong, being diagnosed with terminal illness is another, having one's child killed in war is yet another. I guess the appropriate general response is to go on, vowing to do better, even when things go wrong and even when their wrong-going is ostensibly none of one's own doing. And I guess that's what I try to do. Also I cry. Can you tell me something about the various pets you've had over the course of your life to date?

JC: When I was 5, my father, Village Clerk of Western Springs, Illinois, brought home a young German shepherd for me (a stray the police had found). I named it Points for its sharp ears, but it ran away after one day. There were no other pets till I was married (I think my sense of animal friends was displaced into the wild and into fantasy). Traudl and I had cats, one at a time. I was interested enough to call Muschi Orangehead, but I'm not a "cat person." Cats continued with Mara, and Jenny had three cats (each taken in via necessity) when I moved in, but we didn't replace them and have happily had none for years. Now I have two parakeets, which my daughter gave me. I like the rhythm of caring for them. One, Slider, has attained the age of 14. I think if I were to choose, now, I'd get a reptile.... I think my mother would become too attached to a pet, and therefore was too devastated when it died. If you could go anywhere in the world for two weeks, where might you go?

LH: To sea. Or maybe under it—in an undersea vessel exploring the deeps— but two weeks in such a thing might drive me crazy (I can't sleep without windows open). So I'll say, simply, that I'd go to sea. If I could make some further stipulations, I'd say that I'd prefer to be at sea for the weeks when the moon is minimally present at night—say from the last quarter to first quarter; I'd like to float (or toss about) in the dark, and I'd like to see the reflections of the stars bobbing and torn. Be careful lest what you wish for is what you get, they say—so I'll not wish for those two weeks at sea but only say I might jump aboard if invited. Have you ever felt that some path in life you wanted to follow was closed to you—and if so, why (what closed it off)?

JC: Scholarship. Or being scholarly. It's partly a path, partly a floodplain. I graduated from an unaccredited high school (tiny mountain town) and was told I was only eligible to attend the state agricultural school. Also, my parents had no money (but they bravely, frugally sent me to A & M). Backwaters education has a simpler structure, more like checkers thinking than the (urban) emotional complex of chess. One sees logic more starkly. During four Air Force years I read a lot, but my reading was shaped like a barracks. Then I married and worked; amid that schedule I could write or study, not both. And I've inherited and moistened a memory scattered and Alzheimeresque. Well, boo hoo, but I think a level of laziness was/is more crucial in my failure to become a scholar (just a level or 2, like a layer of water in a stack of plywood). Also excess of eagerness (funny word "eager"; vinegar is eager wine; eager is a point, gives birth to a line, not a web; yet a number of points makes a field, which is eventual ground …). (Philip Whalen became a scholar against great odds—perhaps some scholar should split and classify the types of stubbornness.) What can you say about your moment-to-moment writing process(es)?

LH: For years my processes have been just that, "moment-to-moment," such that all the events that are generated aesthetically and/or philosophically have occurred at the surprising moments where one thing unexpectedly meets another and, as it were, forges a relationship with it. This has been the nature of my process for years—working within microcosmic points of encounter, with very little idea (and very little desire to have an idea) of what's about to happen (or, sometimes, of what it is that has happened). But suddenly that kind of engagement doesn't seem to be working as well as it did for so long, and I find myself having to step back, hold things in mind, sustain some kind of "over view." I don't want to suggest that I am seeking to seize control of the writing; it's just that I can't manage to proceed (at least with my current projects) completely in the dark—though staying in the dark remains as relevant thematically now as it was procedurally before. What's your favorite color?

JC: Sunday-go-to-meeting: orange (Saturday too). Weekdays brown. I used to love chocolate brown but now favor a range of browns, including "dull" ones. In fact, I like odd combinations above all. My favorite color is—not plaid but something holding a knothole to a Matisse might reveal. Is that too precious? Well, slosh some Elmer's glue and sprinkle fine dust on it. Red! When I was a kid, blue was my fave. Lifted me up (he says greenly). Never used to like red. Seemed aggressive. Now I see red's tremble under the extroversion. Bison. Chartreuse. How do you get along with numbers?

LH: Uncomfortably, I suppose, although now and then, without calculating, I may "know" the sum of two numbers the way I "know" the name of some flower ("Henderson's shooting star!" "coreopsis!"). But mostly, though I trust that the name I come up with for a flower is the name it's known by among humans locally, I virtually never, when it comes to numbers, trust that the sum I sense is the right one. Then again, more than sometimes, structurally I use number to organize and shape material. *My Life*, for example, consists of 47 sections/poems each 47 sentences long. I was 47 years old when I wrote it. Now I'm 63, and that number has little bearing on my sense of myself—in my movie of myself, I'm older than that and much younger. Was "the Donald Allen anthology" (*The New American Poetry*: 1945–1960) important for you?

JC: It was as important for me as marriage. I was living in the Polish-Russian factory town of Seymour, Connecticut, with Traudl, working in the brassmill, writing poetry inspired by what I could find in Louis Untermeyer anthologies, when Stan Brakhage sent it to me in 1960 or '61. At first I was shocked by its roughness and what I took to be the carelessness of writing "immediately." I was very soon a convert. In fact, I'd been looking desperately for ways out of convention's deathgrip (not to say the convert doesn't drag all baggage into new room; not to say new room wasn't envisioned; but permissions can be as simple as "Oh, you can write what's in front of you?" "All day long?"). Early enthusiasms were Olson (especially the essay), Dorn, Wieners, Ashbery. Others too, or soon. I took the revolution to be deep-down, that is, aesthetic. It was all a language-allure. Many people are stuck with just one revolution, but I think the opposite is true too: that revolution foments revolution, sometimes dragging it kicking and screaming from reluctant context, as the inclusion of women. Was (is) the Allen anthology important for you?

LH: Absolutely, and I wish I could remember as clearly as you do how it came to me, and when. The binding of my original Grove Press edition fell apart long ago, but I still have the "volume," in its disrepair, held together with a length of string tied in a bow. Releasing the pages, I find no clue as to when or where I was when I read it, but I am almost positive that it would have been Cambridge

(Massachusetts) in 1961 or 1962, when I was still in college. I'd read (and imitated) a lot of e. e. cummings's poems with enthusiasm and a sense of discovery in high school; I'd read *Ulysses* with a sense of being in on a secret and I'd read *Mrs. Dalloway* with a sense of familiarity. In early 1960 I had come across a copy of Ferlinghetti's *Coney Island of the Mind* and Kenneth Patchen's *Albion Moonlight* (along with various slender volumes of his poems), and in May 1962 on my 21st birthday Ken Irby gave me a copy of Creeley's *For Love*. The Donald Allen anthology must have come my way around then: 1961, 1962. Like you, I was drawn to Olson; I loved Brother Antoninus's "A Canticle to the Waterbirds," the McClure poems, the O'Hara poems, the Creeley poems. I thought John Berryman's *Dream Songs* (not, of course, in the anthology) were amazing, and I was just beginning to read Wallace Stevens. It all adds up, I suppose, and can't be reduced down. I didn't notice that there were so few women, I didn't consider the social politics that such a volume represented at all. The poetry was the thing, and I could (so it seemed) identify with anyone writing it. How do you start a poem?

JC: I used to just sit and start. Lately (for years) much of my actual wordage has come via collaborations, so the start is a bargain, relatively responsibility-free. But most of the collaborations serve, it turns out, as keeping a hand in, and as conversation. I do learn from them, over and over (and the repetition's necessary), about multiple causes, multiple input, degrees of out-of-control, uses of spontaneity. The past year especially I've been "collaborating with myself": starting a series of poems but writing only one line into each, until a day has passed and it's time for another line each. Thus I get a more horizontal feel within process. The "rules" with which I begin such a series are meant to be balanced between extremes of openness and closedness—extremes to emphasize the physical, to discourage "humanistic" cogitation. The open/closed approach is developed from my criteria for classroom work with children. Another aspect of starting my poems is that they're usually gotten into before the first light, just after night's-sleep and a little hypnopompic thought and some homely exercises and chores, with black cold instant coffee. Thus primed, I try to seek/allow some lines. No rush (not much). Also, I see, looking through recent mss., I start, or prepare to start (jot), upon having a thought, like "Those four (Gunnison) cottonwoods are both incredibly ragged and incredibly formal...." Open, I hope, to residues of clatter. Excuse my windage. Do you "disagree" with writers as you read them?

LH: Sure. I read for information and of course for confirmation but I read for context, history, too—which is to say to find out what's been written, what's been thought, and inevitably I encounter things to disagree with. I gape at movies, but my critical faculties are alert as I read. So what makes me decide to read no more of a work? Certainly, it isn't necessarily disagreement—I am sure I've given up on books which I've found too agreeable. I'm driven by curiosity, and things that are insufficiently curious frustrate or bore me. So do things lacking credibility—rants emanating from the George W. Bush regime, for example, or accounts of events provided by dilettantes or paranoids. Do you enjoy any sort of crafts, such as woodworking, knitting, ceramics, etc.?

JC: No. Unless you count typing. I used to roll my cigarettes. I'd roll a canful while watching "Sesame Street" or chatting over a kitchen table. I draw some. I photograph but avoid the craft. As a boy I found handwork too grounding; I walked. Then, grown up, I made up for that lacuna by working in factories (making a living too). Instead of table legs I made automatic pressure controllers and coils of brass. Also giant rolls of toilet paper. I write poems, which roll through the craft room. Would you like to "visit the world" a hundred years from now?

LH: Life is enlivened, and certainly it's informed, by curiosity, and since I'm curious now, I'll say yes, which may seem an incautious answer except that your proposition is offered merely (and thoughtfully) in terms of a "visit," not a residency or return (indeed, it would scarcely be a return, given the radical irrevocable changes that the world is disastrously undergoing even now). But I am deeply pessimistic about the future—"the future"; it makes me crazy to think about it. Have you undergone psychoanalysis?

JC: Never have. I've sought snippets of therapy at odd times. The first was in college (forestry school); I remember a nice lady told me I was afraid of success. The next occasion must've been twenty years later, when I went to another nice lady to complain about my wife. I hoped for insight and got some sympathy. Since then I've gone to counselors a couple times when I've wanted someone to talk to. When my second marriage broke up, I was devastated and went to a Jungian counselor for several months courtesy of my employer, IBM. He told me I was an introvert.... I remember when the hippie revolution first broke through I welcomed it as a validation of sensitivity (soon co-opted from within and without). I think keeping reasonably flexible in the face of life's constant mirrorings can amount to self-psychoanalysis. What do you think of Ginsberg's declaration that his work is to ameliorate pain and that anything else is "drunken dumbshow"?

LH: I'm not sure if you are asking me to assess Ginsberg's work vis á vis pain or to pose the question to poetry itself: is it a function of poetry to ameliorate pain? is all other poetry a drunken dumbshow? We can safely say that ameliorating pain is enormously important and valuable. I'm far less confident in agreeing to the proposition that drunken dumbshows are unimportant or not valuable. With your permission (which I will take for granted), I will set aside the drunken and dumbshow issues and take up (the basket of? burden of? hem of?) the first part of the proposition in a very general way: is it the function of poetry to ameliorate pain? Answer: no. The function of poetry is to call life to attention—with all its pains, as well as pleasures. Do you think there is an afterlife?

JC: Not no but hell no. Heavens no. I can't remember a time I didn't think that was silly, and also pernicious, though totally understandable. The somewhat mealy-mouthed consolation is that we live on in the hearts of dear ones and in our works. But as I approach 75 I find that that works.... "Afterlife" is an affective oxymoron. What do you believe now that you didn't ten years ago?

LH: I've grown more pessimistic in the past ten years, my state of mind at any given moment is more filled with contradictions than it was, I believe that life is fundamentally hard and sad and perhaps ten years ago I didn't—or perhaps I did. Certainly I've acquired more negativity, but maybe not altogether different beliefs. On the other hand, none of my beliefs, such as they are, have rigidified; on the whole, I'd say I've come to be less credulous, more doubtful. The danger is that I might become fearful—I won't let that happen (that's a vow). How do you waste time (if you do)?

JC: I waste waste waste waste waste waste waste time by leaping too readily to physical shape when I dwell just as deeply in the rules of grammar. I w. t. by reducing what's new to a hazy memory of algebra. And by not being algebraic enough when it's algebra time. By not being an angel. By being too much or not enough a clumsy flesh fork. By drinking wine, reading the funnies, worrying what people think, letting attentiveness slide, feeling guilty and letting that arabesque the days, being too easily satisfied with language, not reading (not connecting thoughts like rungs of a ladder, and not transcending connection's difficulty and delay), watching TV, following NBA basketball, inefficient correspondence (sitting there fretfully waiting for the "right thought"), explaining, reading magazines, skimming magazines, carrying magazines to Ecocycle, trying to stuff a globe in a brain, turning "waste" to "etwas" (German for "something") but not to "sweat," drinking again, drinking "again" in a sense (innocence), being John Wayne introvert, failing again & again to dance with the left-right-center of things (e.g., dreams, reality), fantasizing hostility, retreating from variety's hug into its announcement, desiring, floating in the blue "center," playing, unplaying, napping before I'm exhausted, disguised whining, forgetting, panicking at forgetfulness, wallowing, counting money, daydreaming sex, rambling, scrambling, "skedaddling." But not by doing this. Can you describe your workroom(s)?

LH: Here it is, extending 6 feet to my left, 18 to my right, 10 behind me, and in front of me just beyond the computer screen are four windows, one of which is open, looking out on the boughs of a redwood tree rooted in the neighbors' backyard and hanging over ours. Along most of three sides of the room runs what I suppose one would call a "work top," giving me about 9 feet of space, 27 inches deep, on which to spread papers and another 6 on which to work on "films" (mixed media drawings/collages). The late afternoon sun is shining on some black and white photos that I'll eventually cut into 1-inch squares for the "films"—I'd better move them, lest the light fade them. And the other (you suggest there might be two)? The other is here on my neck and teeming with thoughts, thick as milk in parts and thin as wisps of an infant's hair in others, moving like the images in a Brakhage film. Do you write down your dreams? Do you have any recurrent dream or recurring type of dream?

JC: I don't, except very rarely, write down my dreams. I think I "should," and have put pen and yellow pad by bed sometimes to facilitate same (the details evaporate so quickly—why is that? Simply because they lack the real-time anchors memory's chained to?) but haven't habituated myself to it. I think the transitive juice of dream is available (like verbs, or verbness, are available, I mean) during awake-time, perhaps more "purely" than if one organized dream representations. Many dream writings, in my opinion, are falsified by the scribes' focus on narrative and on symbolic "meaning." I think a better way to write dream would be to let the syntax catch the dream's atmosphere. I love to catch phrases from dreams—they seem like lines from a, say, Ted Berrigan poem. A recurring dream in childhood was of being on the rough, broken wall of a square ruin and being chased round and round on this wall by a large gorilla. Another was of a bear gradually lightening to my actual window as I opened my eyes. A young-adult image was of inching my way along an I-beam covered with tattered burlap high above a city both mysterious and "normal." And I visited this city again and again (a bit like a cross between Tripoli and Rome). I often dream of being caught in terrific complications with people. If you were beginning-college age again, what would you study that you actually didn't (much)? Discuss.

LH: Biology—botany, probably, or meteorology. Or both—you aren't asking me to imagine a career but only an epistemological adventure. And it would be that—every discipline occupies (or generates) its particular knowledge-ethos. When I was "beginning-college age," however, it was precisely "the ethos" of the sciences (as I, in my ignorance, understood it) that kept me from doing any more than fulfill the "science" requirement in place at Harvard (or Radcliffe, as it was for women until the year of my graduation—I have a "Harvard" degree but went to "Radcliffe"). Prior to that, in the all-girls school I attended, students had to take science every semester, but we were continually exposed to the notion that science was inappropriate for women. This was in the late 1950s—I graduated from high school in 1959—the era of what C.P. Snow called "the two cultures," the humanities and science at odds with each other. The idea that science was antithetical to the imagination prevailed—what a shame! I wish I'd studied philosophy, too (one can do so on one's own, but one is likely to remain an amateur), and Greek. If I were to ask you what was the outstanding moment of today, what would first come to mind?

JC: What first came to mind (when I read the question for the second time, just now) was my early-morning exercises (because it's early morning), especially going outside and doing various stretches while looking at the morning there in some detail, letting myself note some detail not ever heretofore noticed. This morning it was a particular batch of leaves and twigs that stuck up out of the tree straight across Pine St., shaped more or less by the 6:15 light. A little spark of ethos to fan into its counterpart. What can you say about your hands?

LH: You've struck a vulnerable point there. My hands look old—they have been the first parts of me visibly to age, wrinkling and mottling to produce append- ages that I sometimes try to hide from view, sometimes regard as alienages—a new term, I suspect, but I like it. And, indeed, I like or at least am grateful for and to my hands. I mourn their getting old, that's all. They work well, the right far better than the left (except in the garden, where both seem equally adept at pulling weeds). My father's hands had long fingers (and beautiful skin)—it was sometimes said that he could have been a musician (but he was totally tone deaf). I'm often driven to touch things with my hands to learn more about them—or to tempt fate, as when, for example, sitting behind a person with remarkable hair in a concert hall or movie theater, I surreptitiously reach out to touch it. My mother told me that if you cut, rather than file, your fingernails, the nails will get thick and stubby. Experience suggests to me that she was wrong. What household chores are you in charge of, and do you mind them, and what household chores do you particularly dislike?

JC: I'm not sure what counts as household chores, but I do most of the errands (including groceries). I put dishes away (Jenny washes but I sometimes have; we own no dishwasher). I do my own laundry (at a laundromat). I've sometimes cooked breakfast. I make my own lunch (except now; Jenny has us on a diet). I keep office supplies available. I balance checkbook, write about half the checks, keep cash in pocket. I answer the phone. I do the garbage and recycling. I keep the car running and though not clean semi-orderly. I do minor repairs and/ or assemblies (often with wire). I put water in swamp cooler half the time, get up at a given time if there's plan or need. I photograph, edit, birdfeed, bacon-bring…. I don't care for cleaning house (want more "visible" results). Haven't got into gardening because I'm lazy (this is a terrible confession: laziness in the organic) and also have trouble getting in those positions. Otherwise, I usually enjoy all these tasks. How do you feel vis-à-vis the other people of the world?

LH: Much as I feel about myself, I suppose. Regarded as a species, most of us are grotesque in appearance and we behave despicably or foolishly most of the time. And yet, if I picture to myself one of those ridiculous hypothetical situations that professional ethicists like to invent, in which I have to choose between rescuing a drowning pup or a drowning corporate criminal, I'd almost certainly rescue the human, though corporate criminals are among the types I judge most harshly and most hate. Watching people in public spaces, I sometimes disdainfully despise them, but at other times I feel vibrant affinities with them and a sense of our shared fate (that of being human). Sometimes I imagine other humans—strangers—each living his or her human life, and it all strikes me as profoundly poignant. In certain sentimental moments, I think of us all as anxiety-fraught loners passing each other as we all pass through this time and place. Were you ever a member of the Communist Party?

JC: No. Not even close. Don't like parties (though they're so necessary!). Don't like Marx (though he's great!). If there were a party of Thoreau, or Rimbaud, or "O," or Diderot, I'd go. Forgive my facetiousness. What have I ever belonged to? The Open Road Pioneers, as a boy, along with friends Bill and Gerard, an outfit that half-captured the Boy Scouts' tossed-away woodsiness, presided over (through the mails) by one Deep-river Jim. Oddly, Pioneers was on some FBI list of the Dangerous Left, I later learned. What's one of your favorite pieces of music and why?

LH: With your permission, I'll name four favorite pieces of music, rather than one—four from such different musical terrains as not to be at all in competition with each other. They are Shostakovich's String Quartets (all 15); B.B.King's "The Thrill Is Gone"; the longer songs of the Guinean singer Kouyate Sory Kandia; Larry Ochs's "Mirror World" diptych. It's hard to articulate the reasons I love these different works—the reasoning isn't very precise, and probably can't be, since my responses to music occur in experiential spaces that are language-less. But I'll try. I've been listening over and over to the Shostakovich String Quartets for ten years or so, going back to them repeatedly and experiencing them differently each time but always as the expression of "a life"—a reflection of its difficulties, terrors, grief, aggressive willfulness, merriment, etc. I love B.B.King's "The Thrill Is Gone" just for the thrill of it. Its lyrics renounce love even as the music drives one crazy with it, and that, in a nutshell, captures the complexity of erotic passion, especially a longlasting one. Kouyate Sory Kandia is to my ear the "purest" of the West African griot/mandingo singers—though what I mean by that I can't really say and why "pureness" (whose existence is dubious, to say the least) should be of any merit in music (or anywhere else) eludes me. His singing comes from within history, from all that's happened and can't be changed. I guess that's not "purity" but fate (or, as in Shostakovich's String Quartets, life). As for Larry Ochs's two "Mirror World" pieces—I've followed the development of his music for almost thirty years and to me this diptych (premiered in June, 2005) contains within it all the extremes he's been after. (It's dedicated to Stan Brakhage, by the way.) And then there's Beethoven's "Grosse Fuge"—maybe that's my favorite! If you could live a second life—if you could have two lives going instead of one—would you be a geophysicist, or …, well, what would you be?

JC: For years I thought I'd prefer Anthropology. Studying people as if they were animals. Culture as nature. I've also thought: Zoology itself. And I deeply love music, but I'm happy being an amateur musician in semi-professional language (and listening to "everything" from Albinoni to Ma Rainey). Likewise, I'd like Philosophy, or to be more learned in it, not so much hanging out a shingle. Crime? I don't know; last night we watched "Ladykillers" (with Alec Guinness) and, while I adored the little old lady, I wanted them to get away with it and go to a South Sea island and live happily forever. Pretty reductive. As with all these questions, one could write a "book" in response. If you were a taxonomist, would you be a "lumper" or a "splitter"?

LH: Truly fine taxonomy requires that one have the analytical skills of the splitter and the synthetic skills of the lumper, and I would, of course, want to practice truly fine taxonomy. I'd begin with the splitting—discovering the minutest distinctions so as to discover subsets among sets and subsets among subsets. I would delight in discovering veritable singularities. But then, having discovered the dissimilarities abiding between, say, very, very similar flying bugs that make some of them one sort of Pterygota, for example, and others another, I'd lump. I'd lump in the accepted way by gathering them with sow bugs, ants, and butterflies in the class Insecta within the Phylum Arthropoda, and I'd lump them with lobsters, such as the one that Jean-Paul Sartre thought was following him as he walked along the beach. I'd lump Sartre with Aristotle and split him from Camus. I'd lump the beach with my kitchen because sand from a beach is on my kitchen floor. Do you own any valuable furniture? Antique silver? First editions of 18th century books?

JC: No, no, and no. Jennifer does (own things of this kind). I own an old car and a tiny fraction of my old house. I do own a chair I like very much, made in Olathe, Colorado (it may have cost ten bucks). The seat is somehow a wild collage of polished wood fragments pressed into a square, like a sonnet about a hurricane. When we were in Olathe a week ago, I looked for the store in which I'd bought this chair (years ago while working there in Migrant Education). The store had been inside a hill of dirt, but I learned it had been torn down not long ago. I do own a couple shelves of '60s poetry books and booklets which could be worth a lot. I'll have to ask Steve Clay. If you had to be some other living person (than you are), who would you pick? Discuss.

LH: I'm not sure I like being myself, but I can't think who among living persons I'd prefer to be. Once inside the skin of someone, I'd be likely to find things just as uncomfortable or weird or difficult or complicated as they are inside my own. Being someone—anyone—entails all kinds of complexities, but at least I find this one (being myself) workable. I wouldn't dare take on the task of actually being even one of the people I most admire; they each seem more or less tormented, at least some of the time. In fact, the notion that one might suddenly be someone else is terrifying—like a key plot element in a horror film. Being no one is terrifying, too, of course—and that is a prospect we have to accept nonetheless, since that's exactly what being dead is. Do you agree with Gilles Deleuze that "it is the task of language both to establish limits and to go beyond them"?

JC: Yes. Thus language is seen as a living creature; limits are seen as relative; contradiction is seen as life's condition; reduction is seen as arbitrary. With language animal rather than machine, one climbs on (if one dares, if one cares) ready for a ride, not just a plan. Then the niceties of domestication/wildness come into play. The simultaneous action of both becomes possible. Should we respect the rights to life of other animals as we do our own?

LH: That's a tough question to answer, I hardly know where to begin. It's an ethical question, a political one (or an economic one—which in this context is probably the same thing), a biological question, and of course an ecological one. (There are probably numerous other sorts of questions that it is, or numerous other contexts in which one might pose the question, but since I can't imagine how to cope with these, I won't try to evade answering by thinking up more.) At the ecological level, the answer must be adamantly YES. The degree to which the welfare of all things is a result of their carefully (though perhaps not consciously) tended interdependence should be obvious, and thus not to help maintain conditions for non-human flourishing is to undermine human flourishing. (I'm going to avoid your "rights to life" phrase, since I know you aren't invoking an anti-abortion issue here.) At a biological level—NO. Humans depend for survival on being able to consume protein, and where complex humanlife-sustaining proteins are not available from non-animal sources (which is a lot of places), humans have to eat "other animals." Or each other (Jared Diamond, in *Guns, Germs, and Steels* argues that cannibalism arises precisely where other than human sources of protein are insufficient or unavailable). At the eco-political level—I'm in a quandary. At this (dreadful) point in human history, to opt in favor of equal respect for all animate species is, at least in the short term (which is to say, within the life span of everyone alive now), a privilege. The class-blind aspect of the Green movement is truly upsetting. On the other hand, if equal respect for all that lives isn't established, people of all classes will die, and at the moment (when the poor end up being exposed to toxins at far higher rates than the rich and privileged) Green politics is becoming class-conscious. Ethically, meanwhile, YES. And aesthetically, too. And why stop at "other animals"? What about wayside weeds? But those aren't questions I expect you to answer. Instead I'll ask you this—when you say to someone the words in an interrogatory tone, "Isn't this a lovely day?" what exactly are you asking?

JC: I'm asking (and this is based on your stipulated interrogatory tone) for a hand out of the abyss. Or, to put it less dramatically, for companionship in the available joy (which cannot sustain itself alone—or maybe I just can't imagine it doing so for very long). Actually, I don't think I'd say those words in an inter-rogatory tone so much as a declarative tone. Not too declarative, just, y'know, putting it out there. "Isn't this a lovely day." Beginning smile. Maybe it's a pickup line. I'm interested in the time aspect. It feels like an expression of approval not only of one particular day but of days. Of a continuing "thisness." Of rolling on.… Now I think of "this" in the line, as opposed to "it." I think "it" would be just a touch lazy, not up for the "th." This gives it (the line) an energy, bespeaks a bit more effort at perceiving the immediate—which, at the same time, strengthens time. What do you see as the essence of postmodernism?

LH: Despair. Or maybe greed. Or maybe hallucinatory atemporality. The post-modern is the milieu in which the "society of the spectacle" (in Guy Debord's sense) stands established. I'm very gloomy currently about the state of his-tory—the state of history qua history, I mean. There is scarcely any history currently—scarcely any consciousness of how and why things are connected to each other, how and why they came to be as they are, how and why they will have outcomes; there's scarcely any consciousness that they will have outcomes. What's needed are revolutions, however terrifying, to set history in motion again—but postmodernism precludes revolution (for the very reason that revo-lutions are historical). (I want also to say, with respect to revolutions and terror, that I am profoundly opposed to terror, and though it is all but invariably in-trinsic to revolution, I suspect it is at the root of revolutionary failure.) So what about "postmodern poetry," so-called, that notoriously difficult stuff that is said to be understood only in academia? Might it represent (as it did in Russia in the second decade of the 20th century) a revolution of the word? As you can see, I am answering your question with questions—which is cheating, to some degree, but it can also be understood as a manifestation of my inability, finally, to answer your question to my own satisfaction. Do you think it possible for someone to write a "modern epic"?

JC: Well, it'd have to be picaresque. Coherence has been exposed as a phallus of the intentional fallacy with all the structural integrity of tinfoil. If the letters in "epics" traded head for tail we'd have "spice." Whereas, if "epic" were to trade head for tail, it'd be "cpie," shorthand for "cowpie." Thus, the singular epic, under anal isis, leads to fertility, a clear mandate for a rich future. The indica-tion is that a nation like Finland has achieved its leafy prominence in the world via its concentration on the Kalevala. India, on the other hand, with many epics writhing about like a host of arms and legs and supple trunks, winds up with "spice"—long ago traded away, historically, for a mess of pottage, or, worse, plundered, thus flopping the nation on its back. All this is contingent on the validity of the reversal method of determining fate, which may be tested by going back in (epic) history and switching the extremities, front to back, of the archetypal Trojan Horse. What would the reception have been? A long swishy tail atop the equine neck might have been taken for a new and better brain, one of dancing motion, multiple strands. And the eyes, nose, mouth, ears all gathered close to the asshole—what keener way to express the solidarity of sense and system? The Trojans would not only have pulled this wondrous creature in but also immediately proclaimed it king, and hauled it up to Agamemnon's throne! The Greek soldiers, upon leaping out, would have been met with a chorus of adulations—upon which they would doubtless have switched sides (not just ends) and the outcome would have been quite different. Lights! Song of the Co-opted Innards! In contrast, only a lonely figure, punished by Apollo, to be seen, wandering the streets, at last sitting down with Dionysus in the Multicultural Café, inviting the passing Ulysses in for a drink, listening to him spin tales of shape-shifting pigs. What are your first couple of hours after waking like?

LH: Shape-shifting is involved, but nothing like that which you've just described and demonstrated! Of course there is the initial border to cross—the 20 inches or so from bed to floor—but I don't think you are asking about that, nor about the brushing of teeth, dressing, the toast, etc. Typically (and I'm very reluctant to give this up), I spend the first couple of hours after waking reading and taking notes. The notes are sometimes "on" the reading, sometimes they digress from the reading, sometimes they seem entirely unrelated (and prove that I was thinking about something else while (by rote, because I "know how to read") reading). I read somewhere between 30 and 50 pages every morning of poetry and philosophy—and this is reading that I remember and "work" on the next morning. The first couple of hours after waking are promising. Given that "history" is almost synonymous with "the breaking of promises," I regard the first couple of hours as preparation for better history. How much revising (rethinking) do you do—and how much rewriting?

JC: "How much revising (rethinking) … and how much rewriting" seems to break things along a line I'd like to blur. That is, type blurs, and amount depends. Lately it seems I could, given the energy, prophetably change every damn thing I've ever written. The degree to which I haven't focused hard enough, over mottled time, plunges sometimes clear up into a very puerile satisfaction with some instant gallop of the hand (about like this sentence). But I do love to tinker, and I tinker on tinkering's adrenalin when love is gone (or perhaps love = adrenalin), and I've learned that the cold light of morning isn't necessarily the last word. Bullets …

_ Policy: conscious decision, each typewriter space.

_ Ideal: each part comes as a little vision.

_ I used to think up steps more logically.

_ I lie abed in the hypnopompic state, and then try to remember what slid in (even about revision).

_ If it's musical it ain't all bad.

_ Nothing is obvious but obviousness itself (i.e., originality isn't).

_ Revision and cowardice did a little dance together. They talked a bit, tailed off; stepped on each other's feet; exchanged phone numbers (adjacent zip codes). Is the fox ambitious because it knows what to do? The rain?

LH: Being neither an ethologist nor a meteorologist, I can't speak for the fox or the rain. Certainly the rain doesn't "know what to do" in the common sense; it "does" nothing, though it of course has enormous effect. Foxes do know what to do, at least insofar as foxiness is concerned, and no doubt they compete—but (non-human) animal competition is not clearly synonymous with "ambition." But then again ambition, in the human sense, seems not to mean what it once did; our word "ambition" comes from the Latin ambitio, meaning "going around," and certainly foxes do that. One synonym for "ambition" is "strong desire for advancement," and if we imagine the fox to be advancing toward food, no doubt it feels just that: a "strong desire for advancement." The rain may fall on this semantic field, but that's merely coincidental. The rain neither has nor doesn't have ambition. Do you think academic life is bad for a poet?

JC: It's not only bad, it's necessary. When I was on the brink of adult life (feeding myself), just post-Air-Force, I had to decide what to do, with poetry the number one concern: be academic or no. I decided it'd be too danger- ous to my poetry to over-articulate my responses expositionally, as academics do. Workwise, I 'Went manual." Perhaps for too long. My poetic development has been slow. At some point (somewhat Colorado-isolated) I ran out of ideas of what to read next and went back to school (factory days, CU nights), so someone would tell me what to read. But this was all very patchy. I get very frustrated because I can't read, say, *Poetics Journal 10*. I should try harder.

I think academic life at best gives understandings of work, time, and context. Multiplicity. Perhaps there should be a rule: academics spend 4 months teaching and studying, 4 months writing and studying, and 4 months laboring in factory, farm, or diner.

Everyone should be academic (in a grove of trees, but not with Plato), because only a rare genius can be an autodidact and transcend mere crankdom. Because education takes you outside the self. Do you think academic life is bad for a poet?

LH: When I was a university student, New Criticism was in control of academic readings of poetry, and I thought they were awful, not because they were imposing "theory" or "interpretation" on the poetry but because they were excising poetry from the lived contexts out of which they developed. I rebelled accordingly and would have answered most emphatically "Yes!" to that question. But except for a moment just the other night, since the emergence of post-1968 "theory" and what's called "the turn to language," it has been possible again for "the academy" to be a site for the fulminating, debating, developing, and sharing of ideas. It has been so for me. And, to speak of it from another perspective, even if academic life were "bad" for the poet, the kind of work one does in (helping kids think and showing them great things to think about), it is surely something one can believe in. As for the moment of doubt I experienced "just the other night"—to tell the truth, I don't now remember what I was worrying about. It's true that I'm no longer isolated from "the mainstream"—which is to say, in the context of my work I do from time to time hobnob with mainstream poets, and I'm sufficiently polite (and insufficiently angry at them) to do so amiably. Perhaps I was worried that I had "lost my edge." I'm not worried about that right now. Wittgenstein, when he was teaching at Cambridge, encouraged—indeed insisted—that his best students "go manual." Several did (not very happily). Let me ask you one of Wittgenstein's questions: "Can one order someone to understand a sentence?"

Between bibetgekess and 'but...': Lyn Hejinian's *The Book of a Thousand Eyes*

Tim Wood

Writing about Lyn Hejinian's *The Book of a Thousand Eyes* is like talking about someone else's dreams. The poems are peculiar and uncanny, full of surprising leaps and linkages that one might expect from a book written in the dark.[1] Such is the stuff of dreams. Such is the stuff of experience transmogrified through Hejinian's discursive narratives and formal poetic experiments. This tome of interlocutory poems shows how dream gets petrified in the world and then how writing may reverse the process, following the breadcrumbs of language back to where the dream originates, to a place where the poem reanimates a vision that has since disappeared.

The book is a meditation on sleep, which is a meditation mediated through dream:

> Dreams don't provide the thrill of sleep
> Waking does
> Sleep only exists in memory
> It's imaginary
> I can sleep my sleep but I can't observe it[2]

The conscious reflection on the condition of sleep underlies the interplay between the narrative logic of our days and the dream logic of our nights, between the liminal state of the apprehending self who sees the self as other, and, conversely, and perhaps more importantly, the other as the self. Sleep also accounts for the gaps in time in the spaces between the lines, between the stanzas, and between the poems. Accordingly, the gaps temporize the space between the spoken and the unspoken "because the gap between the said and the unsayable is temporal."[3] Finally, then, while the lines stress the importance of being alive, the spaces address death—sleep's doppelganger.

As "a night work,"[4] the poems in *The Book of a Thousand Eyes* have keen night vision (even in the day), allowing us to see what is hard to discern or is even invisible in broad daylight. The book wanders the mind's dark wood remarking and thus remaking the world by recounting and so reencountering daily events through nightly reveries. But as Hejinian insists of tales replete "with the kinds of transmutations and metamorphoses which occur in dreams," these poems "are not private fantasies or psychological displays but public stories—embodying social norms, cultural values, and ultimately moral advice."[5] The poems are neither solipsistic nor confessional, but appear in the form of fables, nursery rhymes, and fairytales; they are bedtime stories, kindred spirits with the oldest forms of storytelling, and they speak to an imagined community.

1.

She wants to abolish this whole aspect of the story, this sequence in chronology, and my heart goes out to her. She cannot do it without abolishing the sequence between the sentences. But this is not effective unless the order of the words in the sentences is also abolished, which in its turn entails the abolition of the order of the letters or sounds in the words. And now she is over the precipice.—E. M. Forster on Gertrude Stein

The Book of a Thousand Eyes is compelled by the idea of the story and explores what it means to tell one. Although it is a book of poems, Hejinian is a storyteller in the tradition Walter Benjamin describes in his classic 1936 essay, "The Storyteller: Reflections on the Works of Nikolai Leskov." Ostensibly a paean to Leskov, Benjamin's essay is also his elegy for the dying art of storytelling in the twentieth century:

Less and less frequently do we encounter people with the ability to tell a tale properly. More and more often there is embarrassment all around when the wish to hear a story is expressed. It is as if something that seemed inalienable to us, the securest among our possessions, were taken from us: the ability to exchange experiences.[6]

In *The Book of a Thousand Eyes*, the stories are in verse and very often dream mediates the exchange of experience; yet, these formal methods are what keep the poems most true to Benjamin's conception of the story. Hejinian uses the line to break up and break into the conventions of syntax and logic that organize the pragmatic, information-laden sentences of our days; similarly, dream rearranges typical sequences of images and events, intervening in the temporal conventions that gird the stories we tell ourselves—those disposed cultural narratives—in order to disrupt preconceived habits of thought. By redeploying traditional story forms to the theater of experimental poetics, the poems press us to examine the means by which we come to understand what happens in the world and how, out of that understanding, we create what we know.

Cultural knowledge has customarily come from stories, and so to this Hejinian returns. However, if Hejinian's methods seem unfamiliar to readers who tend to shy away from experimental poetry (but still think to like a good story), it may be because, as Benjamin suggests, language has long since been repurposed. The kinds of storytelling Hejinian conjures up in *The Book of a Thousand Eyes* have fallen into general disuse, relegated to hasty, sanitized renderings from the lips of a tired parent tucking a child into bed. According to Benjamin, there has been a fundamental shift away from the story to another cultural mode of communication:

> With the full control of the middle class, which has the press as one of its most important instruments in fully developed capitalism, there emerges a form of communication which, no matter how far back its origin may lie, never before influenced the epic form in a decisive way. But now it does exert such an influence. And it turns out that it confronts storytelling as no less of a stranger than did the novel, but in a more menacing way, and that it also brings about a crisis in the novel. This new form of communication is information.[7]

Throughout his reflections, Benjamin exposes how information erodes storytelling by replacing interpretation with explanation, communal truth with verifiable fact, and an ongoing polysemic open-endedness with the immediacy of a single, transparent meaning—all of which Hejinian's work resists.[8]

Benjamin points to the rise of the novel as the primary symptom of storytelling's decline. Fermented in an environment where a class of people exists with the leisure to read in isolation and where the culture depends on information rather than literature for knowledge, the narratives carried by novels turn out to be antithetical to those unraveled by a storyteller:

> The storyteller takes what he tells from experience—his own or that reported by others. And he in turn makes it the experience of those who are listening to his tale. The novelist has isolated himself. The birthplace of the novel is the solitary individual, who is no longer able to express himself by giving examples of his most important concerns, is himself uncounseled, and cannot counsel others. To write a novel means to carry the incommensurable to extremes in the representation of human life. In the midst of life's fullness, and through the representation of this fullness, the novel gives evidence of the profound perplexity of living.[9]

According to Benjamin, the novel offers an incommensurable if perplexing portrait of human life but gives up the ability to instruct; as a result, no matter how complex or realistic, a novel can never contain "the slightest scintilla of wisdom."[10] As a writer who likes "playing idea against idea, genre against genre"[11] and who authored *Oxota: A Short Russian Novel*, Hejinian might take issue with Benjamin's conception of the novel. In *The Book of a Thousand Eyes*, Hejinian expresses the opposite view of the incommensurable:

> The incommensurable is that which resists or eludes assimilation by way of comparison (e.g., "that is just like Y!"). The incommensurable can't be incorporated into the realm of exchange value, of the commodity, it resists the submergence of everything into that system of equivalence, which nullifies uniqueness and compels us to exchange, for example, this beautifully made table for that tenderly nurtured cow.[12]

The incommensurable to which the novel accedes may reach similar ends to a story by deflecting the exchange value given to language by "fully developed capitalism." While Benjamin makes the novel a foil for his ideas about both storytelling and a market-driven economy, Hejinian views the novel as another cultural form of expression whose potentialities can be reworked, played with, exposed, and redirected: "Poetry may be didactic; it is certain that it's the best place to mix genres."[13]

The novel may not be the *genre non grata* for Hejinian; nevertheless, her writing practice remains consistent with the basic contrast Benjamin draws between the way the story and the novel use information. Like Benjamin, Hejinian's work interrogates the terms by which information becomes exalted. For example, by calling *The Book of a Thousand Eyes* "a source work,"[14] Hejinian critiques the encyclopedia, information's grand exemplar. A capacious textual form, the encyclopedia represents the Enlightenment's drive to contain and organize information in such a way that knowledge becomes decontextualized, transparent, and consumable. In contrast to encyclopedic containment, *The Book of a Thousand Eyes* spawns other texts, most notably her 218-page poem *A Border Comedy*. As a source text, *The Book of a Thousand Eyes* is open-ended, refuting the encyclopedic idea of a totalizing system. In this respect, the book may also be a send-up of high modernist projects like Pound's *Cantos*, which, through exempla, takes up the encyclopedic ambition to construct such a system in poetry. Pound's lament is Hejinian's unapologetic *cris de coer*: "I cannot make it cohere!"[15]

Instead of atomizing information, *The Book of a Thousand Eyes* creates knowledge by comingling information with experience. Knowledge taken from experience and made into the experience of others[16] is contextualized rather than excerpted, generative rather than acquisitive. Hejinian expands on the point in her essay "La Faustienne" when she discusses "the relationship between narrative and knowledge":[17]

> Changes are occurring likewise to notions of the author—the writing self— and therefore the genres that attempt to represent the intentions of the author are changing. It is precisely because definitions of the self have changed that the traditional genres that speak *for* the self (lyric poetry, for example) or *of* the self and its development (the novel) are either being consigned to an increasingly "old-fashioned," conservative, or nostalgic position or are being subverted and reinvented to accommodate contemporary experience of being a person—a zone. The sense of independence must now include, where it hasn't been replaced by, a sense of interdependence, and, in writing, interest in free expression may be giving way to interest in free knowing.[18]

According to Hejinian, the author's relationship to the reader fundamentally changes when the self is understood not so much as an identity than as "a zone." The self as a zone becomes a network of names and naming, and throughout *The Book of a Thousand Eyes*, the poems name names—Janet, Misha, Viletta, Ed, Joanne, Mary Ann, Josh, Franco, Maureen, Phil, Xavier, Sam, Lola, Nestor, et al. The litany of first names creates a feeling of privacy, intimacy, and friendship as well as a sense of congregation, population, and community as public as any crowded street. These people are both individuals and, because no first name is ever really unique, also allegories of a collective. Ultimately, the preponderance of names complicates the little poem "Lyn? Lyn? Come here! Is that you? Lyn?" (146). Is this the author imagining herself as a third person? Or is this another person calling her, perceiving her the way she perceives the Janets, Mishas, and Vilettas, and Eds? Or is this another Lyn altogether? Her name as a fixed identity—and identity itself as an idée fixe—is cast into doubt and erodes. This identity crisis recalls a similar moment in Whitman's "Song of Myself" when he asks, "Who need be afraid of the merge?"[19] In both, a stolid sense of self falls apart.

In *The Book of a Thousand Eyes*, the autonomous self finally gives way and ratifies the sense of a person as "a zone" when, over a hundred pages later, we get to another tiny poetic gesture: "Guys! We need a password!"[20] This may be an updated version of Whitman's "password primeval" which is also for Whitman "the sign of democracy."[21] The line is about access and interpretation, a question Hejinian's work always raises; here, the line suggests that interpretation is a communal or "democratic" effort. The collective, informal, spoken "guys" resonates with the function of Benjamin's storyteller who is present to both the story and the audience. Additionally, the technological associations that the line evokes expand the sense of a communal space that is both collaborative and interactive. Given this conceptual shift of "being a person," the author can no longer be the repository and disseminator of knowledge but must account for the experience of the reader and allow for the reader's participation in the construction of meaning. Contrasting the figures of Faust and Scheherazade to distinguish between two antithetical approaches to storytelling and authorship, Hejinian writes, "Where Faust sells his soul for knowledge, Scheherazade saves her life by offering it."[22] In other words, "a scientific model for the acquisition of knowledge (along with the very idea of acquisition in relation to knowing and its value)" must give way to "mediated knowing" or "embedded knowing" or "knowing something in the context in which it is meaningfully known."[23] So rather than extract information and present it as "news," the story contextualizes rather than explains:

> Just as the second hour meets the first I dream an explanation but the
>   explanation ramifies
> I extrapolate and that's conditional
> There is nothing unconditional—there is always room
> It spreads like the shadow of knowledge over a sleeping person
> Immortal before, immortal after, but mortal now[24]

The condition of morality *is* conditionality, and therefore subjectivity means that "the explanation ramifies." There is never only one explanation; there are a thousand.

Compare Hejinian's statement about genre and authorial intention quoted above to Benjamin's definition of a "real story" and the connection between her poetics and his idea of the story becomes clear. The story, Benjamin argues,

> contains, openly or covertly, something useful. The usefulness may, in one case, consist in a moral; in another, in some practical advice; in a third, in a proverb or maxim. In every case the storyteller is a man who has counsel for his readers. But if today "having counsel" is beginning to have an old-fashioned ring, this is because the communicability of experience is decreasing. In consequence we have no counsel either for ourselves or for others. After all, counsel is less an answer to a question than a proposal concerning the continuation of a story which is just unfolding. To seek this counsel one would first have to be able to tell the story.[25]

Hejinian's idea of "free knowing" is akin to Benjamin's idea of "having counsel" in that the purpose of writing moves away from self-expression or authorial intention (a type of hyperindividualism[26]) to a communal sense of coterie where writing emphasizes shared experience as the foundation for knowledge. What Hejinian consigns to changing "definitions of the self," Benjamin assigns to the alterations in the capacity to tell a story, but both tellingly frame their critique of contemporary language use in terms of genre. Hejinian notes that even novels and lyric poetry have the capacity to feel passé if not "subverted or reinvented," and hence the penchant for the experimental, revolutionary, and generically hybridized in her work.[27] However, these inclinations are not necessarily new but rather hearken back to the traditional function of the story where "a man listening to a story is in the company of the storyteller" which, as Benjamin points out, is also the traditional function of poetry: "For even the reader of a poem is ready to utter the words, for the benefit of the listener."[28]

Benjamin anticipates the way in which events will increasingly become grist for the information-mill and come to us prepackaged as "news" stamped with the imprimatur of truth. Separated from context (and, as a result, the process of constructing meaning), events feel "objective" as personal experience gets replaced with sanctioned, institutional forms of explanation. Readers are made into consumers, which is one reason Benjamin associates information with the structures of capitalism. Under these circumstances, it should not be surprising if we begin to feel as though both what happens and what it means are inevitable. Coming to us as a fait accompli, the objectivity of information in the guise of news mimics knowledge; however, real knowledge, as it functions within the story—and this is how it is in *The Book of a Thousand Eyes*—replaces a sense of inevitability with a feeling of possibility. Knowledge is heuristic and creative; it is understanding in an active, provisional mode.

Adhering to Benjamin's idea of a story, *The Book of a Thousand Eyes* replaces "free expression" with "free knowing"[29] by fostering a sense of unfettered access to interpretation. The potential for knowledge comes through an engaged imaginative process. One might argue that all texts, and especially all literature, invite interpretation; however, there are different kinds of interpretation and different degrees of authorial control over meaning. The news gives us one extreme to which we've become accustomed: "Every morning brings us the news of the globe, and yet we are poor in noteworthy stories. This is because no event any longer comes to us without already being shot through with explanation."[30] *The Book of a Thousand Eyes*, in contrast, is designed for reader intervention, encouraging the reader to enter into a linguistic exchange where the positions of "writer" and "reader" are interchangeable. Hejinian performs this exchange in the book's opening lines:

> I'll write
> and I myself can read
> to see if what I've written is right.
> Sleep offers an excuse
>   for substitution.
>
> But who else would dream
>   the world one thinks?
> It's only there
>   the world repeats.
>
> Many days are often mine.
> Do I feel that
>   timeless satisfaction?[31]

There is something of the Seafarer's solitary "I" in the first lines ("Mæg ic be me sylfum / soðgied wrecan").[32] Only the dreamer can tell the dream—who else? But as the lines progress, the certainty of the speaker is replaced by uncertainty. A question mark appears. The type of authorial control insisted on by the Seafarer is substituted for Chuang Tzu's identity paradox: When the writer wakes and reads what she has written, has she been a writer dreaming of herself as a reader or is she a reader now dreaming of herself as a writer?[33] The writer is to the reader as waking is to the dream or the experience is to writing. One reality replaces another and both are illusions, substitutions for "the world one thinks." The poem like a dream is capable of being transported and therefore transposed into other minds, places, contexts, and times. Perhaps it is this transitive quality that lends our days that feeling of "timeless satisfaction"? The activity of writing in Hejinian's book is in fact geared toward transforming the writer into a reader, an interpreter of experience, a creator of knowledge through contextualization. The writer doesn't tell the reader anything but writes in order to read, rattling the conventional correlations between the self and text by putting the reader and the writer on the same plane in relation to the story.

Hejinian treads along the fault line of a paradox: as sanctioned explanations fall away, we become increasingly responsible to the associations our minds make even as we are forced to embrace uncertainty about the validity of those connections. Reading *The Book of a Thousand Eyes* requires us to substitute provisional, contextualized forms of knowing for the assurances given by sound bites that inform to convince rather than to inquire. Although contextualized knowledge may seem more unstable, it is when meaning becomes discursive that events recover their capacity to be useful, applicable, and personal. Instead of exhuming a world of our own construction, the activity of writing these poems, as much as the poems themselves, provokes us to move beyond our previously held beliefs about the world. Because of what Keats famously described as our "irritable grasping after fact and reason,"[34] there may be a tendency to take refuge in binaries like author and reader because they feel stable and unchangeable. But from the beginning, Hejinian problematizes such staid, distinct dichotomies. An innate discomfort with confusion may make information attractive, but poetry such as Hejinian's promotes interpretation which, as Benjamin notes, "is not concerned with an accurate concatenation of definite events, but with the way these are embedded in the great inscrutable course of the world."[35]

2.

Those who dream of the banquet may weep the next morning, and those who dream of weeping may go out to hunt after dawn. When we dream we do not know that we are dreaming. In our dreams we may even interpret our dreams. Only after we are awake do we know that we have dreamed. But there comes a great awakening, and then we know that life is a great dream. But the stupid think they are awake all the time and believe they know it distinctly.—— Chuang Tzu

The Book of a Thousand Eyes is a thousand titles and one title, both plural and singular. It is *the* book of *a* thousand eyes, not *a* book of *the* thousand eyes. E plurbis unum? What are the epistemological implications of the "the"? What are the ontological implications of an "a"? There are either a thousand books with one reader or one book with a thousand readers, a thousand books with a single eye, or the book with a thousand eyes.

There are many—a thousand?—implications inherent in this title. Hejinian offers a history of it in her brief interview with Rusty Morrison, the editor of Omnidawn and publisher of *The Book of a Thousand Eyes*:

The title of the book makes a nod to *The Arabian Nights*, one of whose equally well-known titles is *The Thousand Nights and A Night* (the title that Sir Richard Burton, creator of its greatest English translation, gave it). It also alludes to "The Night Has a Thousand Eyes," a popular Victorian-era poem by Francis William Bourdillon, whose opening lines are "The night has a thousand eyes / And the day but one." The poem goes on to offer a parallel statement: "The mind has a thousand eyes / And the heart but one." Bourdillon's point is that the sun (as the one eye of the day) and love (as the one eye of the heart) are superior to the thousand eyes of night and the mind; I suggest that the multiple views available to the night and to the mind have something in their favor, too. [36]

Here's another possible interpretation: Once, Avalokitshvara, Buddha of Compassion, finding himself on the cusp of enlightenment, chose to forgo nirvana[37] so that he could return to the world and free all other sentient beings from their suffering. The depth of his empathy made him think he could singlehandedly rescue all souls from the condition of samsara.[38] So he goes back and starts to draw others toward enlightenment. But for every one soul that achieves nirvana, ten more appear. In his increased effort to keep up, his head explodes into eleven pieces. Amitabha, the Buddha of Infinite Light, puts him back together and gives him nine heads and a thousand arms. Amitabha also gives each hand an eye in the center of the palm; this way, Avalokitshvara can see all who suffer and work faster. And so, Avalokitshvara commits himself to the world of illusion and the ineluctable desire for the well-being of others. While there is some debate about the meaning of his name, all scholars seem to agree that Avalokitshvara means in one way or another "the god who looks." Avalokitshvara is the Buddha of a Thousand Eyes.

3.

Erotic play discloses a nameless world which is revealed by the nocturnal language of lovers. Such language is not written down. It is whispered into the ear at night in a hoarse voice. At dawn it is forgotten.—part of an excerpt from Jean Genet's "The Thief's Journal" on the flyleaf of John Zorn's *Elegy*

One way to think about *The Book of a Thousand Eyes* is as a postmodern version of Benjamin's traditional story; another is to understand the relationship of the book to its generative model, Sir Richard Burton's translation of Scheherazade's tales, *Book of the Thousand Nights and a Night*. Benjamin only mentions Scheherazade in passing, but she remains a key figure for his conception of the storyteller:

It starts the web which all stories together form in the end. One ties on to the next, as the great storytellers, particularly the Oriental ones, have always readily shown. In each of them there is a Scheherazade who thinks of a fresh story whenever her tale comes to a stop. This is epic remembrance and the Muse-inspired element of the narrative.[39]

Benjamin latches onto Scheherazade's form of story because it offers episodic continuation, which not only creates "the chain of tradition which passes a happening on from generation to generation" but also presents "*many* diffuse occurrences" where multifarious stories replace the authoritative history of the "*one* hero, *one* odyssey, *one* battle." Benjamin also alludes to Scheherazade when identifying the origins of this form. Identifying traders and their travel tales as one key foundation for his conception of the story, Benjamin states that "their task was less to increase its didactic content than to refine the tricks with which the attention of the listener was captured. They have left deep traces in the narrative cycle of *The Arabian Nights*" (101). More than a foreclosing lesson, a good story depends on suspense because suspense keeps the story going.

Scheherazade provides the elements of story on which Benjamin's conceptions are based, but Benjamin never addresses the conditions that give rise to her inventions; in neither of these crucial asides does Benjamin take note of the fact that Scheherazade is a woman speaking for women.[40] Hejinian, on the other hand, recognizes the effect a female storyteller has on the story's purpose, meaning, and means of being told. Hejinian applies the strategies of storytelling that Benjamin identifies (postponement, discursiveness, and intrigue) to a feminist poetics that is partly derived from Scheherazade's example. So while seeing the link to Scheherazade further illuminates the flame of the story glowing at the center of Hejinian's poems, *The Arabian Nights* also provides a context for understanding what it means to say that *The Book of a Thousand Eyes* is a book written in the dark.[41]

What allows for the story to exist as a social and feminist critique of patriarchal power is the context in which the story is told. Hejinian elucidates this point in her essay "La Faustienne": "Scheherazade's nights begin voluptuously and it is after she and Shahryar are satiated each night that she takes up her stories. It is thus narrative not sexual suspense that Scheherazade sustains."[42] Hejinian uses the figure of Scheherazade to critique Western Enlightenment's conception of female power as purely sexual, since it is not Scheherazade's body but her knowledge that keeps Shahryar in suspense.[43] But Hejinian does not deny Scheherazade's sexual power: with regard to both sex and storytelling, Shahryar is clearly left wanting more. In *The Book of a Thousand Eyes* as in *The Arabian Nights*, the interrelationship between the erotic and the political, the body and the story, is explicit. The narrative strategies, therefore, resist the kind of Platonic split between mind and body that underpins the tradition of Western philosophy. As Hejinian insists, "philosophy should not be hostile to the eyes."[44]

In Hejinian's book, this "erotic and dramatic context" [45] amplifies the shouts of "You f-ing cultural pimps!" and emboldens the plots of "the wife of the merchant George" and heightens the suspicions of "the women in line after 5 pm at Blockbuster's."[46] *The Book of a Thousand Eyes* reworks the relationship between sex and knowledge in terms decisively opposed to the binary split between the body and the imagination: "I am writing now in preconceptions / Those of sex and ropes / Many frantic cruelties occur to the flesh of the imagination."[47] Her knowledge is embodied; the story remains inseparable from the storyteller: "The mouth is just a body filled with imagination." Unlike Benjamin's view of the storyteller—"he is the man who could let the wick of his life be consumed completely by the gentle flame of his story (108)—the female storyteller undergoes a threat of physical violence that accompanies the traditional patriarchal impulse to suppress her tale. In "La Faustienne," Hejinian offers the example of the Little Mermaid who has her tongue cut out so that she can't sing. The female hero occupies a dual position. In order to tell her story, she must overcome a physical threat, as she must derive her power both from her body and her song: "The silencing of the fairy tale maiden renders her inner being (her thoughts, her feelings) secret. She embodies her secret; she is a nocturnal inscription, both writer and what's written in the dark."[48] Scheherazade's narrative strategies are ultimately a means to overcome both physical and intellectual domination.[49]

So considering *The Book of a Thousand Eyes* "a night work"[50] in the tradition of *The Arabian Nights* not only designates a particular time for the text to be written but also a particular kind of writing activity. The when and where cannot be separated from the writing's purpose. As Hejinian observes, "Scheherazade tells her tales in bed, but their milieu is public."[51] The stories graft an intimate space to the public sphere. Likewise, Hejinian's poems, while presented as dreams and therefore private, run counter to a confessional mode: instead of making intimate stories public, these poems unravel the political in an intimate setting. Sex becomes erotic foreplay to the more seductive and climactic story rather than the story using sex as a prurient form of suspense. When Hejinian says that the stories of Scheherazade are "part of that public and political tradition, though with the unique feature of being, finally, a night work,"[52] she points to the subversive nature of the female storyteller. This "unique feature," this context of privacy and darkness, marks Scheherazade's narrative methods as forms of feminist storytelling to which *The Book of a Thousand Eyes* takes part and should be added. "Sentences in bed are not describers, they are instigators"[53] and in their telling, the stories embodied by the female storyteller are transgressive and therefore potentially transformative.

While providing narrative tension, the arousal sustained by an "epistemological suspense" maintains a moral purpose. Hejinian espouses the discursive as a means of creating such postponement:

> The narrative momentum, how one thing leads to another, thus could be said to be digressive, but not in the linear sense; the temporal linear context is, in fact, precisely what has to be reoriented if Scheherazade is to save "the daughters of the Musulmans," herself included, and the way this is accomplished is with performative concentricities and spirals. To achieve this redemptive outcome, the tales and Scheherazade's strategies for tale-telling defer conclusions, prolong suspense, and interiorize meaning."[54]

The reordering of time is not only an aesthetic postponement but also a survival strategy. Scheherazade tells stories to stave off death, which is ironically associated with dawn: "death hovers at the edge of dawn on the horizon of light when all stories come to an end, inscribing her end as well."[55] The feminist tale reverses traditional poetic tropes and, as a "night work," counters the masculine tradition of poetic forms like the aubade by putting off the morning for a more urgent reason than "sweet reluctant amorous delay."[56] The redemptive end to which the story is addressed is nothing less than making a tyrannical ruler wise by transforming his lust for death into "an appetite for life."[57] The story, therefore, becomes a personal means of exerting political influence; as Hejinian explains in her interview with Morrison, "the Scheherazade story is about an Eastern woman's generous gift of knowledge to a tyrannical ruler who is made kind and wise by it."[58]

The stories are embedded in a story as the days are embedded in the night, which changes both their meaning and their purpose, and it is this frame—the night work of Scheherazade herself—to which Hejinian attends and her poems extend. Political action gets exerted through the bedchamber and night gets extended into diurnal activity through story. The night work uses this intimate domestic space to inform, interrupt, and finally intervene in political discourse, working to break down the opposition between day and night, public and private, personal and political. Hejinian says, "*The Book of a Thousand Eyes* is a night work, in that my interest is in the processes of assimilation and assessment that take place in the figurative dark and silence of night, where opposites as such can't exist because they always coexist."[59] In a profound sense, what Hejinian shares with Scheherazade is this radical sensibility to make apparent opposites coexist through the dissolution of binary categories—man and woman, us and them: "Daylight tests the imagination; the imagination, in turn, targets the dark."[60]

Like Scheherazade, Hejinian utilizes the imagination to affect political change. Scheherazade's private fate is tied to all "the daughters of the Musulmans"; likewise, Hejinian's dream-poetic counters "our fucked up structures of thought."[61] Both use narrative to alter the power dynamics engendered in both personal and political relationships. To a great degree, altering the dynamic of personal relationships effectively changes the dynamics between politics. It was Pound's dream, too, for the poetry to become the instrument of enlightened leadership in this way, although his idea of exempla (forging one hero, one odyssey, one battle out of many) runs counter to the narrative strategies described by Benjamin and utilized by feminist writers like Hejinian. Mimicking the culture narratives he opposes, Pound constructs an alternative history but one that is nevertheless superior, exclusive, sanctioned, and which carries an expectation that it be properly explicated by an elite reader. To some extent, Benjamin is in line with Pound. His storyteller stands in opposition to "fully developed capitalism"; yet, as someone "who could let the wick of his life be consumed completely by the gentle flame of his story,"[62] Benjamin's storyteller seems relatively comfortable within its systems, maintaining a secure place in its structural hierarchies. Contrary to Pound, Hejinian uses narrative to extend outward from one incident to many, from one person to a plethora of people. And unlike Benjamin's storyteller, Hejinian's Scheherazade fights being consumed; rather than incinerating in the story's blaze, she passes it on like a flame from wick to wick, and, through this accretion of small flares, illuminates the dark.

4.

Cautious—We jar each other—
And either—open the eyes—
Lest the Phantasm—prove the Mistake—
And the livid Surprise

Cool us to Shafts of Granite—
With just an Age—and Name—
And perhaps a phrase in Egyptian—
It's prudenter—to dream—
   — Emily Dickinson

Reading *The Book of a Thousand Eyes* is also a good way to understand the recidivistic power of the unexpurgated fairy tale,[63] which Benjamin identifies as the primum mobile of the story: "The first true storyteller is, and will continue to be, the teller of fairy tales. Whenever good counsel was at a premium, the fairy tale had it, and where the need was greatest, its aid was nearest."[64] Hejinian reassembles the fairy tale to update "good counsel" and test whether "the synthesizing tendency of the syllogism and the aphorism"[65] can be made compatible with "radical *openness*." More simply stated, can a decidedly closed form be put in the service of an open-ended text?[66] Since morals, maxims, and advice have become signs of authorial tyranny and even the hallmarks of "bad writing," for Hejinian's experiment to work, the poems must become instructive without being reductively didactic and illustrative without being linearly explanatory. Hejinian deconstructs the moralizing impulse of the fairy tale through multiplication, discursiveness, and non sequitur, shattering the acquisitive Faustian impulse toward knowledge where good counsel curdles into pedantry.

As Benjamin argues, the chief end of the story—its moral—is not didacticism but is always open-endedness: "After all, counsel is less an answer to a question than a proposal concerning the continuation of a story which is just unfolding."[67] Or, as Hejinian writes in *A Border Comedy*,

> the epic accumulation of good advice called 'Happenstance'"
> Can tell its own history in its own terms
> In one thousand thinking sleeps[68]

Aligning "good advice" with chance operations makes the accretion of advice or counsel a matter of incessant activity, which is more a function of continuous recontextualizing than a static collecting of exempla. Writing, then, offers advice by demonstrating a way of being in the world:

> I wrote almost daily just
> As the waves ring against the sand
> Like quickly sinking sacks
> All identical and each alone
> At sea[69]

Writing day by day—or, in this case, night by night—each poem testifies to the specific context in which it was written as the particularity of any wave is unrepeatable; at the same time, the accumulation of the poems creates a book like the cumulative repetition of waves forming the surface of the sea.

As a book that started out as a one-page addition to *The Book of a Thousand Eyes*,[70] *A Border Comedy* is a good example of how this accumulation functions. The book as a whole works in very much the same way as the stories of which it is comprised:

One anecdotal fact would be followed by another
And many together would make a story
Consisting of "separate facts tenuously connected"
And conspired
Story to story
To which everyone should add and be added[71]

Because "an anecdotal story is merely a span / Consisting of separate facts / Each tenuously connected to the next,"[72] it reaches beyond the limits of its pages where it becomes part of yet another, larger text. And so it goes, extending onward and outward, toward an idea of the infinite.

Whether or not they overtly adapt the form of the fairy tale, the poems in *The Book of a Thousand Eyes* exist between the temporal coordinates of the fairy tale's "once" and "ever after." The "once" is not just a casting back into the past, a reminder that things were not always as they are, but also an admonition that—and here one feels the drag of Heraclitus's river—the story like the experience it recounts happens once and once only:

This tale like many others happened once and only once and I will tell it only once and then no more so listen well and if you do you will understand why I have filled my basket with sand[73]

The story can be repeated, the poem reread, but the situation itself does not recur. So the moral that attends to the story will always address the particular circumstance of its hearing in a peculiar way:

That is the tale, and if you have listened well, you will understand that the four girls have lived happily ever after[74]

But opposed to the incommensurability of "once," there is the continuity of "ever after." "Ever after" is the last temporal coordinate of the fairy tale and offers an alternative to the other ending: *finis*.[75] As opposed to "THE END" which defines a goal as a terminus, the fairy tale's counsel—"the continuation of a story which is just unfolding"[76]—maintains an open-endedness and a receptivity to chance:

The point of such moral instruction is, of course, the continuation of happiness:

Let's think of happy people going to sleep
Like Pythagoras to music. When they wake
They become persons and require clothes

And that's what we term wakefulness.[77]

Happiness, by definition, is dependent on good fortune and "the future, like fortune, is to be found not in events but in their meanings."[78] The moral of the story depends on a dream logic that offers unexpected outcomes and dodges the type of rigid identities that "require clothes." Moreover, the disjunction of dream allows for an interpretive atmosphere that promotes the giddy surprises we often associate with being happy:

> She had it in mind to go up the fir tree to watch the nude
> pigeons, or angels if transparent, or a flea, like a man in mental
> wind churning in the creek, two men on the road bouncing by on
> glass with the greatest pleasure but not until then able to say,
> it's on the floor. I am a laconic and I have a truck. My statuette
> not then and cannot now do better than a tree trunk or a wrist.[79]

The stability of the fairy tale's fabulist structure might make us feel secure, but it is the errancy, digression, and surprise within the fairy tale—its infinite possibilities and meanings—that make us feel free.[80] These are the poles of the story in between which Hejinian operates.

The two impulses—the beginning and the end—come together in the narrative crisis, frequently marked in *The Book of a Thousand Eyes* by the word "suddenly." The critical hinge in any story, "suddenly" is both the inevitable turn of events and the liberating surprise, the expected unexpected leap. In *The Book of a Thousand Eyes*, Hejinian frequently uses the fabulist's well-used trope to shift away from the sequential logic of chronology that falsely sutures experiences together into one long slog. "Suddenly" cuts and splices images and events together in an unforeseen way:

> Suddenly a film
> Weathering a film
> Shareably a film, shakily a film
> A film about a man who's framed
> Action![81]

"Suddenly" juxtaposes contexts and provides multiple, simultaneous frames for what we think of as experience. "But," as Hejinian qualifies early on in *The Book of a Thousand Eyes*, "The word *suddenly* is always relative."[82] Suddenly, too, requires a specific, limiting context to furnish its surprise; so, if Hejinian's conscious and conscientious use of the fairy tale's conventions do not entirely free us from the conventions themselves, the poems reveal how these structures might at times unnecessarily confine us.

5.

I was in Paradise or in the vain fantasies of a dream. —Sir Richard Francis Burton, *The Book of a Thousand Nights and a Night*

The Book of a Thousand Eyes took almost twenty years to write. In contrast, Scheherazade told stories for about three years. These are the living contexts, the "real time" of the storyteller who tells the tale within which the time of the story expands and contracts. There is the dream that may last a few minutes and the time within the dream which may feel like forever. There is the time it takes to read a book and the time it takes to write it. The story outlasts both. As far as poetry books go, *The Book of a Thousand Eyes* is a long book (333 pages) and therefore requires time to read, and therefore accrues meaning over time, and therefore changes as it is read and reread, since its entirety cannot be retained by memory.

Taking twenty years to write, *The Book of a Thousand Eyes* is a postmodern, deconstructed epic akin to Zukofsky's *"A."* Beyond the deft blending of the political and the personal, the shifting between an autonomous "I" and a communal "Thou," the book mediates temporalities, as epics tend to do whatever their ostensible subject matter. The poems flit between classical temporal conceptualizations—carpe diem and tempus edax rerum, tempus filia temporis and tempus fugit (often figured allegorically as the Fugitive). There's Kronos and Chairos as well as the proverbial *tic toc*.

It is a book of hours, its length a reminder of the extent of our days and of Scheherazade who told a story every night in order to survive. The poems are short, circuitous, cross-pollinating. There are no hierarchies or chronologies beyond the inevitable order of the pages. Titles, numbering, chapters are absent; the poems are separated by a symbol that looks like an asterisk in full bloom or some type of astral flower, or perhaps it is a sleeping, celestial eye.

The index of *The Book of a Thousand Eyes* is its most telling poem. It is a compendium as well as an alphabetically ordered reminiscence (a gesture toward an open-ended totality). It reveals the affects of order on randomness (and randomness on order) by restructuring the sequence of the poems and decontextualizing the first lines. These lines, which function as the last poem in the book, offer new connections that accrue fresh meaning in their indexical context. As both a foundry and a foundation, a means of finding and recalling, collecting and recollecting, the index is the book's memory: it both contains the book and is contained by it.

The index refutes the book's ostensible end on page 333 where we wake into an unspeculative dawn, its rosy figures reaching out to strangle the book's protean dream. So the index becomes the continuation of a dream from which you have already awoken. The index begins:

Accident and necessity renew their fatal pact,
A dream, still clinging like light to dark

And ends 282 lines later:

Wild wind,
With fish fault thought,
Wobbly deeds possess vitality
Written descriptions are no more than tickets,
Yesterday has arrived and remains,
Your brain is like a lake,
You've taken off your socks,

If "When they wake / They become persons and require clothes / And that's what we term wakefulness,"[83] then *The Book of a Thousand Eyes* is a book of no shoes, no shirts, and full service.

6.

I'll let you be in my dreams if I can be in yours.—Bob Dylan

The Book of a Thousand Eyes makes happiness a moral imperative. Benjamin writes, "The wisest thing—so the fairy tale taught mankind in olden times, and teaches children to this day—is to meet the forces of the mythical world with cunning and with high spirits."[84]

Hejinian echoes this: "Though they may not be redemptive in effect, the diverse works that comprise *The Book of a Thousand Eyes* argue for the possibilities of a merry, pained, celebratory, mournful, stubborn commitment to life."[85] The accretion of poems is both a matter of endurance and a means to make matter endure. To put it in Viktor Shklovsky's adamantine terms, they make the story stony and the stone storied.

In the end, Hejinian's writing proves that we are not real in any absolute way. We do not last and, eventually, we leave no trace. One of the great literary fictions of which even the scientific bent of the Enlightenment did not rid us is that writing's perpetuity makes us indelible. Perhaps it was even part of the project of the Enlightenment to foster this assurance of immortality. But not even writing can prevent our eventual disappearance. Writing can, however, replace us. Not by becoming a relic that outlasts the body—although it might be that sometimes for some—but, more profoundly, by becoming an erratic reality that takes the place of an illusion we call variously the world, experience, memory, reality, the self. The story substitutes the fantasy of the perpetual self with the perspicacity of a dream that sees through the "seems" of what otherwise appears to us as a seamless continuity. Because, as *The Book of a Thousand Eyes* demonstrates, writing that has at its heart "a commitment to life" is different in kind than writing that intends to perpetuate by memorializing. As Benjamin states, "the statement that makes no sense for real life becomes indisputable for remembered life."[86] In life, the insensibility of death expresses itself as nonsense or as non sequitur; otherwise, life appears as remembrance and, from the vantage of death, as a totality that is always already completed. As Hejinian quotes in "La Faustienne," "Being (or the actual being of each and any entity) exists not because it is the opposite of non-Being but because it is 'true of its own accord.'"[87] In *The Book of a Thousand Eyes*, being alive is clearly not the opposite of being dead but rather an aporia of which dying cannot make sense. If "A man ... who died at thirty-five will appear to *remembrance* at every point in his life as a man who dies at the age of thirty-five,"[88] then a commitment to life means resisting finality and finding, through the forms that language allows, ways of writing that depend on change and chance and express plenitude rather than a plenum:

Everything changes but perhaps the whole remains although it seems unlikely as well as undesirable

There is nothing but reality
Once there was a man named Task-in-Life and there is no perhaps

about that

There can't be perhaps about anything that is

But perhaps there is[89]

Notes

1. Lyn Hejinian, "La Faustienne," in *The Language of Inquiry* (Berkeley: University of California Press, 2000). Hejinian writes, "*The Book of a Thousand Eyes* is a night work ... I have wanted to write in the dark, so to speak, when the mind must accept the world it witnesses by day and out of all data assemble meaning" (250).

2. Hejinian, *The Book of A Thousand Eyes* (Richmond, CA: Omnidawn, 2012), 65.

3. Hejinian, *A Border Comedy* (New York: Granary Books, 200), 51.

4. Hejinian,"La Faustienne," 250.

5. Ibid., 260. Hejinian makes this comment in reference to *The Thousand and One Nights*.

6. Walter Benjamin, "The Storyteller: Reflections on the Works of Nikolai Leskov," in *Illuminations*, ed. Hannah Arendt. (New York: Harcourt, Brace & World, 1968), 83.

7. Ibid., 88.

8. Benjamin writes, "Information ... lays claim to prompt verifiability. The prime require-ment is that it appear 'understandable in itself.' Often it is no more exact than the intelligence of earlier centuries was. But while the latter was inclined to borrow from the miraculous, it is indispensable for information to sound plausible. Because of this it proves incompatible with the spirit of storytelling" (89).

9. Ibid., 87.

10. Ibid., 88.

11. Hejinian, *A Border Comedy*, 108.

12. Hejinian, *The Book of a Thousand Eyes*, 70.

13. Ibid., 27.

14. "A Brief Interview with Lyn Hejinian," by Rusty Morrison (http://www.omnidawn.com/hejinian2/index.htm). Hejinian states, "The *Thousand Eyes* project proliferated; it might be thought of as a source work, one element of a larger process, as well as a creative compendium in its own right."

15. Ezra Pound, *The Cantos of Ezra Pound*, 14th ed. (New York: New Directions, 1998), 816.

16. Benjamin writes, "The storyteller takes what he tells from experience—his own or that reported by others. And he in turn makes it the experience of those who are listening to his tale" (87).

17. Hejinian, "La Faustienne," 232.

18. Ibid., 235.

19. For context, see page 17 of "Song of Myself" (http://www.whitmanarchive.org/published/LG/1855/whole.html).

20. Hejinian, *The Book of a Thousand Eyes*, 285.

21. For context, see page page 29 of "Song of Myself" (http://www.whitmanarchive.org/pub-lished/LG/1855/whole.html).

22. Hejinian, "La Faustienne," 260.

23. Hejinian, "The Quest for Knowledge," in *The Language of Inquiry*, 214, 220.

24. Hejinian, *The Book of a Thousand Eyes*, 23.

25. Benjamin, "The Storyteller," 86.

26. In *A Border Comedy*, Hejinian writes, "The term 'I' is a narrative cliché" (47).

27. Hejinian's publishing project Atelos is "devoted to publishing, under the sign of poetry, writing which challenges the conventional definitions of poetry, since such definitions have tended to isolate poetry from intellectual life, arrest its development, and curtail its impact. All the works published as part of the Atelos project are commissioned specifically for it, and each is involved in some way with crossing traditional genre boundaries, including, for example, those that would separate theory from practice, poetry from prose, essay from drama, the visual image from the verbal, the literary from the non-literary, and so forth." (www.atelos.org/info.htm)

28. Benjamin, "The Storyteller," 100.

29. Hejinian makes this distinction while discussing authorial intention in "La Faustienne": "The sense of independence must now include, where it hasn't been replaced by, a sense of interdependence, and, in writing, interest in free expression may be giving way to interest in free knowing" (235).

30. Benjamin, "The Storyteller," 89.

31. Hejinian, *The Book of a Thousand Eyes*, 15.

32. The line can be translated variably: Burton Raffel translates it, "This tale is true, and mine." Raffel's translation emphasizes the two key words—"true" and "mine"—that inflect each other through the poem. Ezra Pound combines the gritty Old English sound with connotations of reckoning when, punning on *wrecan*, he famously transposed the line as "May I for my own self song's truth reckon." The word "reckon" not only connotes the sense of fate underpinning the poem (i.e. a reckoning) but also gets at the spoken quality of the poem by selecting a colloquial Americanism for recall. My own translation is "I myself must a true tale tell." While similar to Raffel's, my emphasis is different. I want to stress "myself" in order to evoke the solitariness of the Seafarer and also "tell" along with "truth" to suggest storytelling as a third term that negotiates the "true" and the "mine." I also try to capture the alliteration that formally organizes the Anglo-Saxon line. However one translates the line, the sense of the storyteller using personal experience as the basis for discerning truth seems analogous to what Hejinian explores in *Book of a Thousand Eyes*.

33. For the original version, see *The Book of Chuang Tzu*, trans. Martin Palmer with Elizabeth Breuilly, Chang Wai Ming, and Jay Ramsay (London: Penguin, 2006), 21.

34. Letter to George and Thomas Keats (December 22, 1817). (en.wikisource.org/wiki/Letter_to_George_and_Thomas_Keats,_December_28,_1817)

35. Benjamin, "The Storyteller," 96.

36. Morrison, Interview. (www.omnidawn.com/hejinian2/index.htm)

37. According to Random House Dictionary, nirvana is "freedom from the endless cycle of personal reincarnations, with their consequent suffering, as a result of the extinction of individual passion, hatred, and delusion: attained by the Arhat as his goal but postponed by the Bodhisattva." The world literally means "to blow out, a blowing out ('not transitively, but as a fire ceases to draw')."

38. According to Random House Dictionary, samsara is "the process of coming into existence as a differentiated, mortal creature." It is also "the endless series of births, deaths, and rebirths to which all beings are subject." The word literally means, "running together."

39. Benjamin, "The Storyteller," 98.

40. Despite the passing references to Scheherazade, Benjamin's storyteller is

decidedly male. Benjamin places a notable emphasis on "him" and "his." The emphasis is, of course, partly due to the fact that he models his storyteller on Leskov; yet, more broadly, Benjamin conceives of the political arena for the story in fairly patriarchal terms.

41. In "La Faustienne," Hejinian writes, "I have wanted to write a book in the dark, so to speak, when the mind must accept the world it witnesses by day and out of all data assemble meaning" (250).

42. Ibid., 255.

43. Ibid., 254.

44. Hejinian, *The Book of a Thousand Eyes*, 250.

45. Hejinian, "La Faustienne," 255.

46. Hejinian, *The Book of a Thousand Eyes*, 295, 90, 120.

47. Ibid., 28.

48. Hejinian, "La Faustienne," 249.

49. In this context, we can see that the aesthetic move to occupy both the reader and writer positions and liberate them from their adversative relationship becomes yet another strategy to overcome the patriarchal suppression of feminist narratives by occupying both the subjective and objective positions.

50. In "La Faustienne," Hejinian uses the phrase to refer to both *The Book of a Thousand Eyes* (250) and to *Thousand and One Nights* (258), forging an explicit link between the two texts.

51. Ibid., 260.

52. Ibid., 258.

53. Hejinian, *The Book of a Thousand Eyes*, 17.

54. Hejinian, "La Faustienne," 254.

55. Ibid., 260.

56. John Milton, *Paradise Lost*, 4.311.

57. Quoted in Hejinian, "La Faustienne," 255.

58. Morrison, Interview. (www.omnidawn.com/hejinian2/index.htm)

59. Hejinian, "La Faustienne," 250; also see pages 249–50 for Hejinian's statement regarding "the postmodern critique of binarism."

60. Hejinian, *The Book of a Thousand Eyes*, 74.

61. Ibid., 71.

62. Benjamin, "The Storyteller," 108.

63. The connotations of recidivism may seem oxymoronic in relation to "good counsel"; however, by calling the fairy tale recidivistic, I would like to suggest that good counsel tends to resist rather than reinforce social conventions. The resulting poetic repetition and reconfiguration of traditional forms, therefore, is not conservative but pursues radical social transformation.

64. Benjamin, "The Storyteller," 102.

65. Hejinian, "Language and 'Paradise,'" in *The Language of Inquiry*, 68.

66. Lyn Hejinian, "The Rejection of Closure," in *The Language of Inquiry*, 40–58. Hejinian writes, "Form does not necessarily achieve closure, nor does raw materiality provide openness. Indeed, the conjunction of *form* with radical *openness* may be what can offer a version of the 'paradise' for which writing often yearns—a flowering focus on a distinct infinity" (42). She then goes on to define "open" and "closed": "We can say that a 'closed text' is one in which all the elements of the work are directed toward a single reading of it. Each element confirms that reading and delivers the text from a lurking ambiguity. In the 'open text,' meanwhile, all the elements of the work are maximally excited; here it is because ideas and things exceed (without deserting) argument that they have taken into the dimension of the work" (42–3).

67. Benjamin, "The Storyteller," 86.

68. Hejinian, *A Border Comedy*, 90.

69. Hejinian, *The Book of a Thousand Eyes*, 158.

70. Morrison, Interview. (www.omnidawn.com/hejinian2/index.htm)

71. Hejinian, *A Border Comedy*, 31.

72. At one point in *A Border Comedy*, Hejinian calls the poem "a writing in lost contexts" (63): by "mov[ing] from one [of the poem's fifteen books] to the next / In the course of many days adding every day / A few lines to a book / Each of which takes a long time and considerable thought," Hejinian "facilitates forgetting" (151). Along with allowing for continuous recontextualizing, forgetting becomes a means of retention as well as repetition. For example, with regard to the story, Hejinian writes,

> An anecdotal story is merely a span
>
> Consisting of separate facts
>
> Each tenuously connected to the next (27)

Several pages later, Hejinian writes,

> Just as, in the old days (to quote Viktor Shklovsky)
>
> One anecdotal fact would be followed by another
>
> And many together would make a story
>
> Consisting of "separate facts tenuously connected"
>
> And conspired
>
> Story to story
>
> To which everyone should add and be added
>
> And be confused (31)

73. Hejinian, *The Book of a Thousand Eyes*, 322.

74. Ibid., 323.

75. Benjamin again uses the novel as contrast to the story's "ever after": "[T]he novel reaches an end which is more proper to it, in a stricter sense, than to any story. Actually there is no story for which the question as to how it continued would not be legitimate. The novelist, on the other hand, cannot hope to take the smallest step beyond that limit at which he invites the reader to a divinatory realization of the meaning of life by writing 'Finis'" ("The Storyteller," 100). To extend the point further, we can turn to Viktor Frankl's *Man's Search for Meaning* (Boston: Beacon, 2006), where he reminds us that "The Latin word *finis* has two meanings: the end or the finish, and a goal to reach" (70). In terms of Benjamin's genre categories, this means that the story resists the kind of teleological ending that gives meaning to a novel.

76. Benjamin, "The Storyteller," 86.

77. Hejinian, *The Book of a Thousand Eyes*, 160.

78. Ibid., 21.

79. Ibid., 326.

80. Cf. Benjamin's discussion of Montaigne in part XV of "The Storyteller," 100.

81. Hejinian, *The Book of a Thousand Eyes*, 327.

82. Ibid., 24.

83. Hejinian, *The Book of a Thousand Eyes*, 160.

84. Benjamin, "The Storyteller," 102.

85. Morrison, Interview. (www.omnidawn.com/hejinian2/index.htm)

86. Benjamin, "The Storyteller," 100.

87. Hans Blumenberg, qtd. in "La Faustienne," 250. Hejinian cites Hans Blumenberg's "Light as the Metaphor for Truth" in order to argue against the dialectical categories of the Enlightenment that oppose Being to non-Being (cf. 249–50).

88. Moritz Heimann, qtd. in Benjamin, "The Storyteller," 100.

89. Hejinian, *The Book of a Thousand Eyes*, 101.

Lyn Hejinian
A Bibliography

poetry:

The Unfollowing (forthcoming, Richmond, CA: Omnidawn Books, 2016)

My Life and My Life in the Nineties (Middletown, CT: Wesleyan University Press, 2013)

The Book of a Thousand Eyes (Richmond, CA: Omnidawn Books, 2012)

Selections from The Unfollowed (Boulder: Kavyayantra Press, 2011)

The Wide Road (with Carla Harryman; Brooklyn: Belladonna, 2010)

Etel Adnan, Lyn Hejinian, Jennifer Scappettone: Belladonna Elders Series (5); three authors (Brooklyn: Belladonna Books, 2009)

Saga / Circus (Richmond, CA: Omnidawn Books, 2008)

Situations, Sings (with Jack Collom; New York: Adventures in Poetry, 2008)

Lola (Brooklyn: Belladonna, 2005)

The Lake (with Emilie Clark; New York: Granary Books, 2004)

My Life in the Nineties (New York: Shark Books, 2003)

The Fatalist (Richmond, CA: Omnidawn Books, 2003)

On Laughter: A Melodrama (with Jack Collom; Boulder: Baksun Books, 2003)

Slowly (Berkeley: Tuumba Press, 2002)

A Border Comedy (New York: Granary Books, 2001)

The Beginner (New York: Spectacular Books, 2000; Berkeley: Tuumba Press, 2002)

Happily (Sausalito: Post-Apollo Press, 2000)

Chartings (with Ray Di Palma; Tucson: Chax Press, 2000)

Sunflower (Great Barrington: The Figures, 2000)

Sight (with Leslie Scalapino; Washington, D.C.: Edge Books, 1999)

The Traveler and the Hill and the Hill (with Emilie Clark; New York: Granary Books, 1998)

Wicker (with Jack Collom; Boulder: Rodent Press, 1996)

The Little Book of a Thousand Eyes (Boulder: Smoke-Proof Press, 1996)

Guide, Grammar, Watch, and The Thirty Nights (Perth, Western Australia: Folio, 1996)

Two Stein Talks (Santa Fe: Weaselsleeves Press, 1995)

The Cold of Poetry (Los Angeles: Sun & Moon Press, 1994)

The Cell (Los Angeles: Sun & Moon Press, 1992)

The Hunt (La Laguma, Tenerife: Zasterle Press, 1991)

Oxota: A Short Russian Novel (Great Barrington: The Figures, 1991)

Individuals (with Kit Robinson; Tucson: Chax Press, 1988)

My Life (second version; Los Angeles: Sun & Moon Press, 1987)

The Guard (Berkeley: Tuumba Press, 1984)

Redo (Grenada, MS: Salt-Works Press, 1984)

My Life (Providence: Burning Deck, 1980)

Gesualdo (Berkeley: Tuumba Press, 1978)

Writing Is an Aid to Memory (Great Barrington: The Figures, 1978; reprinted, Los Angeles: Sun & Moon Press, 1996)

A Mask of Motion (Providence: Burning Deck, 1977)

A Thought Is the Bride of What Thinking (Berkeley: Tuumba Press, 1976)

poetry books translated into other languages:

Gesualdo, tr. into Turkish by Uygar Asan (Istanbul: Nodyainlari, 2015)

Ma Vie (My Life), tr. into French by Maïtreyi and Nicolas Pesquès (forthcoming, Dijon: Presses du réel, 2015)

Minha Vida (My Life), tr. into Portuguese by Mauricio Salles Vasconcelos (São Paulo, Brazil: Dobra Editorial, 2014)

Felizmente (Happily), tr. into Spanish by Gidi Loza (Playas de Rosarito, Baja, CA: Editorial Piedra Cuervo, 2013)

Mi Vida (My Life), tr. into Spanish by Tatiana Lipkes (Mexico City, Mexico: Mangos de Hacha, 2012)

Mi Vida (My Life), tr. into Spanish by Pilar Vazquez and Esteban Pujals (Tenerife, Spain: Acto Ediciones, 2011)

Gesualdo, tr. into French by Martin Richet (Marseilles: Jacataqua, 2009)

Lentement (Slowly), tr. into French by Virginie Poitrasson (Paris, 2006)

Mitt Liv (My Life and My Life in the Nineties), tr. into Swedish by Niclas Nilsson (Stockholm: Modernista, 2004)

Mit Liv (My Life), tr. into Danish by Jeppe Brixvold with Line Brandt (Copenhagen: Borgen, 2001)

Jour de Chasse (The Hunt), tr. into French by Pierre Alferi (Paris: Cahiers de Royaumont, 1992)

critical prose:

The Grand Piano: An Experiment in Collective Autobiography: San Francisco, 1975–1980 (ten volumes; with Rae Armantrout, Steve Benson, Carla Harryman, Tom Mandel, Ted Pearson, Bob Perelman, Kit Robinson, Ron Silliman, and Barrett Watten; Detroit: Mode A, 2006–2010)

The Language of Inquiry (Berkeley: University of California Press, 2000)

Leningrad (with Michael Davidson, Ron Silliman, and Barrett Watten; San Francisco: Mercury House, 1991)

translations:

Description, poems by Arkadii Dragomoshchenko (Los Angeles: Sun & Moon Press, 1990)

Xenia, poems by Arkadii Dragomoshchenko (Los Angeles: Sun & Moon Press, 1994)

edited volumes:

Poetics Journal Digital Archive (with Barrett Watten; ebook; Middletown, CT: Wesleyan University Press, 2015)

A Guide to Poetics Journal: Writing in the Expanded Field, 1982–1998 (with Barrett Watten; Middletown, CT: Wesleyan University Press, 2013)

Ghosting Atoms: Poems and Reflections Sixty Years After the Bomb (with Olivia Friedman; Berkeley: Consortium for the Arts and UC Regents, 2005)

Best American Poetry 2004 (New York: Scribner's, 2005)

poetry in anthologies:

The Pushcart Prize XXXIX: Best of the Small Presses, Bill Henderson, ed. (Wainscott, NY: Pushcart Press, 2014)

Short: An International Anthology of Five Centuries of Short-Short Stories, Prose Poems, Brief Essays, and Other Short Prose Forms, Alan Ziegler, ed. (New York: Persea Books, 2014)

Kindergarde: Avant-garde Poems, Plays, Stories, and Songs for Children, Dana Teen Lomax, ed. (Lafayette, LA: Black Radish Books, 2013)

Postmodern American Poetry: A Norton Anthology (second edition), Paul Hoover, ed. (New York: W. W. Norton & Co., 2013)

The Best of the Best American Poetry, Robert Pinsky, ed. (New York: Scribner Poetry, 2013)

The Arcadia Project: Postmodern Pastoral, Joshua Corey and G. C. Waldrep, eds. (Boise, ID: Ahsahta Press, 2012)

The Alchemist's Mind: A Book of Narrative Prose by Poets, David Miller, ed. (Hastings, East Sussex, UK: Reality Street, 2012)

Conversations at the Wartime Café, Sean Labrador y Manzano, ed. (San Francisco: McSweeney's, 2011)

American Hybrid: A Norton Anthology of New Poetry, Cole Swensen and David St. John, eds. (New York: W. W. Norton & Co., 2009)

Women's Work: Modern Women Poets Writing in English, Eva Salzman and Amy Wack, eds. (Bridgend, Wales: Seren, 2009)

The Reality Street Book of Sonnets, Jeff Hilson, ed. (Hastings, East Sussex, UK: Reality Street Editions, 2008)

Saints of Hysteria: A Half-Century of Collaborative American Poetry, Denise Duhamel, Maureen Seaton, and David Trinidad, eds. (Brooklyn: Soft Skull Press, 2007)

Nineteen Lines: A Drawing Center Writing Anthology, Lytle Shaw, ed. (New York: Roof Books, 2007)

The Oxford Book of American Poetry, David Lehman, ed. (Oxford University Press, 2006)

Bay Poetics, Stephanie Young, ed. (Faux Press, 2006)

The Longman Anthology of Poetry, Lynn McMahon and Averill Curdy, eds. (Pearson/Longman, 2006)

Best American Poetry 2005, Paul Muldoon, ed. (New York: Scribner's, 2006)

Vanishing Points: New Modernist Poems, Rod Mengham and John Kinsella, eds. (Cambridge, England: Salt Publishing, 2005)

The Addison Street Project, Robert Hass and Jessica Fisher, eds. (Heyday Books, 2004)

Norton Anthology of Modern and Contemporary Poetry (vol. 2: Contemporary; New York: Norton, 2003)

Great American Prose Poems: From Poe to the Present, David Lehman, ed. (New York: Scribner's, 2003)

California Poetry: From the Gold Rush to the Present, Dana Gioia, Chryss Yost, and Jack Hicks, eds. (Berkeley, CA: Heyday Books, 2003)

Poetry from Sojourner: A Feminist Anthology, Ruth Lepson and Lynne Yamaguchi, eds. (Urbana and Chicago: University of Illinois Press, 2002)

The Best American Poetry: 2000, Robert Hass, ed. (New York: Scribner's, 2001)

Poems for the Millennium, Jerome Rothenberg and Pierre Joris, eds. (Berkeley: University of California Press, 1998)

Moving Borders: Three Decades of Innovative Writing by Women, Mary Margaret Sloan, ed. (Talisman Press, 1998)

Out of Everywhere, Maggie O'Sullivan, ed. (London: Reality Street Editions, 1996)

50: A Celebration of Sun & Moon Classics, Douglas Messerli, ed. (Los Angeles: Sun & Moon Press, 1995)

The Gertrude Stein Awards in Innovative American Poetry, 1993–1994, Douglas Messerli, ed. (Los Angeles: Sun & Moon Press, 1995)

A Salt Reader, John Kinsella, ed. (Perth, Western Australia: Salt, 1995)

Artes: An International Reader of Literature, Art, and Music (New Jersey: Ecco Press and Stockholm: Natur & Kultur, 1994)

Postmodern American Poetries, A Norton Anthology, Paul Hoover, ed. (New York: W. W. Norton & Co., 1994)

From the Other Side of the Century: A New American Poetry 1960–1990, Douglas Messerli, ed. (Los Angeles: Sun & Moon Press, 1994)

The Best American Poetry: 1994, A. R. Ammons, ed. (New York: Simon & Schuster, 1994)

Subliminal Time, Leslie Scalapino, ed. (Berkeley: O Books, 1993)

Out of This World, Anne Waldman, ed. (New York: Crown Publishers, 1992)

Resurgent: New Writing by Women, Lou Robinson and Camille Norton, eds. (Urbana and Chicago: Illinois University Press, 1992)

O One, Leslie Scalapino, ed. (Oakland: O Books, 1988)

The Pushcart Prize XII: Best of the Small Presses, Bill Henderson, ed. (Wainscott, NY: Pushcart Press, 1987)

"Language" Poetries, Douglas Messerli, ed. (New York: New Directions, 1987)

Everyday Life (Detroit: In Camera, 1987)

Epiphanies: The Prose Poem Now, George Myers, Jr., ed. (Westerville, OH: Cumberland Press, 1987)

Up Late: American Poetry Since 1970, Andrei Codrescu, ed. (New York: Four Walls Eight Windows, 1987)

In the American Tree, Ron Silliman, ed. (Orono, ME: National Poetry Foundation, 1986)

A Century in Two Decades, Keith and Rosmarie Waldrop, eds. (Providence: Burning Deck, 1982)

The Pushcart Prize VI: Best of the Small Presses, Bill Henderson, ed. (Wainscott, NY: Pushcart Press, 1981)

Networks, Carol A. Simone, ed. (Palo Alto: Vortex Editions, 1979)

The Big House, Michael Slater, ed. (New York: Ailanthus Press, 1978)

These Women!, Mary Mackay and Mary MacArthur, eds. (Washington, D.C.: Gallimaufry, 1978)

Omens from the Flight of Birds, Stephen Vincent, ed. (San Francisco: Momo's Press, 1977)

Doctor Generosity's Almanac: 17 Poets, Ray Freed, ed. (New York: Doctor Generosity Press, 1970)

poetry in anthologies published in other languages:

Los Mejores Poetas Americanos Contemporános: Charles Bernstein, Lyn Hejinian, Ron Silliman, Barrett Watten, Manuel Brito, ed. and tr. (Madrid: Ediciones Literarias Mandala, 2011)

Nuova Poesia Americana, Luigi Ballerini and Paul Vangelisti, eds. (Milan: Mondadori, 2006)

Antologija novije američke poezije, Vladimir Kopicl and Dubravka Đjurić, eds. (Belgrade: 2001)

Antologia de Poesia Norte-Americana Contemporânea, José Roberto O'Shea, ed. (Florianópolis, Brazil: Editora da UFSC, 1998)

Une "Action Poétique", Pascal Boulanger, ed. (Paris: Flammarion, 1998)

La Lengua Radical, Esteban Pujals Gesali, ed. (Madrid: Gramma Poesia, 1992)

Ruski Almanac, Dubravka Djuric, ed. (Belgrade: 1992)

49 + 1, Emmanuel Hocquard and Claude Royet-Journoud, eds. (Paris: Editions Royaumont, 1991)

Double Rainbow/Dvoinaya Raduga, Marat Akchurin, ed. (Moscow: Molodaya Gvardiya, 1988)

Rosa Disibilita (Milan, 1981)

anthologized translations:

Crossing Centuries: The New Generation in Russian Poetry, John High, ed. (Jersey City: Talisman House Publishers, 2000)

Re-Entering the Sign: Articulating New Russian Culture, Ellen E. Berry and
  Anesa Miller-Pogacar, eds. (Ann Arbor: University of Michigan Press, 1995)
Third Wave: The New Russian Poetry, Kent Johnson and Stephen M. Ashby,
  eds. (Ann Arbor: University of Michigan Press, 1992)

essays included in collections of critical writings:

"Sun on the Avant-Garde," in Lily Hoang and Joshua Marie Wilkinson, eds.,
  The Force of What's Possible: Writers on Accessibility & the Avant-Garde (New
  York: Nightboat Books, 2014)

The Idea of the Avant Garde, Marc James Léger, ed. (Manchester, UK:
  Manchester University Press, 2014)

Thinking Poetics: Essays on George Oppen (Modern and Contemporary Poetics),
  Steve Shoemaker, ed. (University of Alabama, 2009)

A Best of Fence: The First Nine Years, Rebecca Woolf, et al., eds. (Fence Books,
  2009)

Poetry and Pedagogy, Joan Retallack and Juliana Spahr, eds. (Palgrave
  Macmillan, 2006)

"Some Notes Toward a Poetics," in Jerry Harp and Jan Weismiller, eds., *A
  Poetry Criticism Reader* (Iowa City: University of Iowa Press, 2006)

"Stages of Difficulty in the Difficult Poem," in *Poetry and Pedagogy,* Joan
  Retallack and Juliana Spahr, eds. (Palgrave Macmillan, 2006)

Lofty Dogmas: Poets on Poetics, Deborah Brown, Annie Finch, and Maxine
  Kumin, eds. (University of Arkansas Press, 2006)

"Introduction" to Gertrude Stein, *Three Lives* (Los Angeles: Green Integer, 2004)

"Afterword" to Viktor Shklovsky, *Third Factory* (Normal, IL: Dalkey Archive
  Press, 2003)

"Gertrude Stein," entry in *World Poets,* editor in chief, Ron Padgett (New
  York: Scribners, The Scribner Writers Series, 2000)

"La Faustienne," in *By Herself: Women Reclaim Poetry,* Molly McQuade, ed.
  (Saint Paul, MN: Graywolf Press, 2000)

"Forms of Alterity," in *Translation of Poetry and Poetic Prose,* Sture Allén, ed.
  (Stockholm: Swedish Academy and World Scientific, 1999)

An Anthology of New Poetics, Christopher Beach, ed. (Tuscaloosa: University
  of Alabama Press, 1998)

"A Local Strangeness," interview with Larry McCaffery and Brian McHale,
  in *Some Other Frequency: Interviews with Innovative American Authors*
  (Philadelphia: University of Pennsylvania, 1996)

"Rejection of Closure," in *Onward: Contemporary Poetry & Poetics,* Peter Baker,
  ed. (New York: Peter Lang, 1996)

"The Quest for Knowledge in the Western Poem," in *Disembodied Poetics,*
  Anne Waldman, Andrew Schelling, eds. (Albuquerque: University of New
  Mexico Press, 1995)

"Interview," in *A Suite of Poetic Voices*, Manuel Brito, ed. (Santa Brigida: Kadle Books, 1992 [actually published 1994])

"Past Lights," for *Past Lives*, Martha Casanave (David Godine, 1990)

"Line," in *The Line in Postmodern Poetry*, Robert Frank and Henry Sayre, eds. (Urbana and Chicago: University of Illinois Press, 1988)

"Rejection of Closure," in *Writing/Talks*, Bob Perelman, ed. (Carbondale: Southern Illinois University Press, 1984)

poetry published in literary journals and magazines (partial list):

"I can't concentrate for long …" (from *The Positions of the Sun*), *Axon: Creative Explorations*, vol. 4, no. 2, December 2014, Jessica L. Wilkinson and Ali Alizaden, eds. (www.axonjournal.com.au)

"Tacit Knowledge" (from *Wild Captioning*), *Mantis: A Journal of Poetry, Criticism & Translation* 12 (2014)

"Melancholia: a Triptych" (3 poems from *The Unfollowing*), *Hysteria*, issue 1, Bjork Grue Lidin, ed. (London, UK, 2014)

"Preface" and "The Unfollowing Spring" (5 poems from *The Unfollowing*), *Jelly Bucket*, Lisa Schmidley, ed. (Bluegrass Writers Studio, 2013)

"Sleep Requires a Lot of Space," *American Poet*, vol. 42 (Academy of American Poets, spring 2012)

"Barbarism" (from *The Language of Inquiry*), "The Altitudes" (from *The Cold of Poetry*), "It's hard to turn away from moving water" (from *My Life*), tr. by Arkadii Dragomoshchenko, *Novoe literaturnoe obozrenie*, no. 113 (in Russian)

"Children Love Color" (from *Wild Captioning*), *Conjunctions 58: Riveted: The Obsession Issue* (spring 2012)

12 poems from *The Book of a Thousand Eyes*, *Bombay Gin*, vol. 37, no. 2 (fall 2011)

"Walking to Wick" (with Jack Collom), *Volt* 16, 2011

"The Slow Parade," *Grist: The Journal for Writers*, issue 4, spring 2011

"City Under Sun," *Conjunctions: Urban Arias*, 2010

"Five Elegies (The Unfollowing)," *Hambone* 19, fall 2009

"The Shifting Position of the Sun," *Kulturo* (Tema: Sociale Fantasier), no. 29, August 2009 (Copenhagen, Denmark)

"Six Positions of the Sun" (Belladonna Elders Series 5, 2009)

From *The Fatalist* (in French, tr. by Martin Richet), *MIR: Revue d'Anticipation*, spring 2009

"from The Book of A Thousand Eyes" (9 poems), *Parthenon West Review* 6 (January 2009)

"Nine Nocturnal Fragments" (9 poems), *Colorado Review* 35.3, fall/winter 2008

"First Night of a New Year" (a set of 7 poems), *No: a journal of the arts* (issue 7, 2008)

"Two Nights Near Shore" (a set of 4 poems), *Abraham Lincoln* # 3, August 2008

"Define" (work written in collaboration with Jack Collom), *Bombay Gin*, vol. 34, summer 2008

Two poems, *Parmentier*, vol. 17, no. 2, spring 2008 (The Netherlands; tr. into Dutch by Ton van't Hof)

"A Bit of Nocturnal History," in *Conjunctions* 50: *Fifty Contemporary Writers*, spring 2008

Cal Literary Arts Magazine, spring 2007

Zoland Poetry: An Annual of Poems, Translations & Interviews, spring 2007

Traffic, spring 2006

Nea Synteleia (Athens, Greece), 2006

Conjunctions: 25th Anniversary (anthology issue), fall 2006

Coconut (online journal), fall 2006

Court Green 2, spring 2005

Berkeley Poetry Review, spring 2005

Fulcrum: An Annual of Poetry and Aesthetics, fall 2005

Hambone 17, fall 2004

Fire, no. 23 (Oxford, England, 2004)

Pom2 (2004)

ZYZZYVA (2004)

Action Restreinte (tr. into French by Martin Richet; Paris, 2004)

PEN America: A Journal for Writers and Readers, Issue 5: Silences (2004)

Conjunctions: Cinema Lingua (2004)

Rattapallax (2004)

Conjunctions: 40 (2003)

Van Gogh's Ear (Paris, France, 2003)

Sal Mimeo (2003)

Bomb (2003)

580 Split, spring 2002

Crowd (2002)

Meanjin, vol. 61, no. 3 (Australia, 2002)

Antennae 3 (2002)

Rapidfeed (2002)

Barrow Street (2002)

Journal for Theoretical Studies in Media and Culture (2002)

Discourse 24.1: "Mortals to Death," 2002

Shiny 9/10, spring 1999

Boundary 2, spring 1999

The Colorado Review, fall/winter 1999

Lingo 8, fall 1998

Private Arts 10, spring 1997

Hambone 13, spring 1997

Terra Nova, vol. 2, no. 2, spring 1997

Prosodia 7, spring 1997

Explosive Magazine 2, spring 1997

Modern Language Studies 27.2, 1997

Bellingham Review, vol. xx, no. 1, spring 1997

The Germ, fall 1997

Phoebe, vol. 25, winter/summer 1996

Chain 3, spring 1996

lyric &, spring 1996

New American Writing 14, summer/fall 1996

Chicago Review, vol. 42, no. 2, summer 1996

Iowa Review, vol. 26, no. 2, 1996

trembling ladders, issues 2 & 3, 1996 (Australia)

The World 52, fall 1996

Zurgai, spring 1995 (in English and Spanish, tr. Manuel Brito)

Berkeley Poetry Review, spring 1995

Proliferation 2, spring 1995

Chain 2, spring 1995

tinfish, fall 1995

Volt 2, fall 1995

Antenym, December 1995

Antithesis, vol. 7, no. 2, 1995

Sojourner, vol. 19, no. 6 (February 1994)

Black Bread 4, spring 1994 (collaboration with Leslie Scalapino)

Prosodia, spring 1994

Tessera, vol. 15, spring 1994 (collaboration with Carla Harryman)

River City, vol. 14, no. 2, spring 1994

Lingo 3, summer 1994

Proliferation 1, fall 1994

Raddle Moon 13, fall 1994

Southern Review, vol. 27, no. 3, September 1994

Chelsea 57, 1994

Green Z 12, spring 1993

Grand Street 44, spring 1993

Lingo, spring/summer 1993

Prosodia 3, spring 1993

Black Bread 3, spring 1993

Hot Bird Mfg, vol. ii, no. ii, September 1993

Black Warrior Review, 18, 2, spring/summer 1992

Obdje, October 1992 (in Serbian)

The World 45, December 1992

Pequod 31, 1991

Avec 4, spring 1991

Hot Bird Mfg., vol. 1, no. 17, 1991
Meanjin, vol. 50, no. 1, 1991 (Melbourne, Australia)
Socialist Review, vol. 21, no. 9, 1991
Logos (Leningrad), vol. 1, 1991
East Bay Guardian, October 1991, p. 58
Aerial 6/7, fall 1991
Big Allis 2, 1990
Aerial 5, 1990
Archive Newsletter, no. 45, spring 1990
Sequoia, vol. 33, no. 2, winter 1990
Verse, vol. 7, no. 1, 1990 (UK)
Raddle Moon 9, 1990
Five Fingers Review 8/9, 1990
Polja (Belgrade, Yugoslavia; in Serbian), December 1990
Paper Air, vol. 4, no. 2, 1989
zuk 17 (France), February 1989 (in French)
Rodnik (Riga, Latvia, USSR) January 1989 (in Russian)
Mirage 3, 1989
o•blék 5, spring 1989; 9, 1991
Sonora Review, spring/summer 1989
Motel 1 (Canada) 1989
screens and tasted parallels 1, 1989
Artes 4 (Stockholm), 1989 (in Swedish)
Action Poetique 117 (France), 1989 (in French)
New American Writing 5, fall 1989
Tyuonyi 4, 1988
Dagens Nyheter 27, November 1988 (in Swedish)
Ghandabba 5, 1987
Caliban 2, 1987
Ironwood 30, 1987
Gendaishi Techo (Tokyo), 1987 (in Japanese)
Sink 3, 1987
Occident, vol. cii, no. 1, 1987
Notes 1, 1986 (France)
Parnassus: Poetry in Review, 1986
Boundary 2, fall 1985/winter 1986
Ghandabba 4, 1986
Bomb, 1986
Temblor 4, November 1986
Writing (Canada), 1986
Sulfur, 1986
Feminist Studies, 1985

Predlog (Leningrad), 1984 (in Russian)
This 12, 1983
Annex, 1982
Sulfur, 1982
Grosseteste Review (UK), 1982
Hills, 1981
Sun & Moon, 1981
Change (Paris), 1981 (in French)
Action Poetique (Paris), 1981 (in French)
Sulfur, 1981
QU, 1980
This 10, 1980
Sun & Moon, 1979
L=A=N=G=U=A=G=E, 1979
Roof, 1979
Alembic (UK), 1979
This 9, 1979
Hills, 1978
Roof, 1978
Sailing the Road Clear, May 1978
Tottel's 17, 1978
This 8, 1977
Telephone 12, 1976
Sailing the Road Clear, December 1975
Telephone 14, 1975
Big Deal 4, 1975
Newsletter a la Cafard, 1975
Occurrence 4, 1975
Center 7, 1975
Telephone 10, 1975
Ironwood 4, 1974
Truck 14, 1974
Telephone 9, fall 1973
Beyond Baroque, vol. 1, no. 4, 1971
Amphora, no. 1, 1970
Boss, 1970
Bowery Press Broadsheet 4, 1969
Arx, vol. iii, no. 5, 1969
Quixote, vol. 4, nos. 8 and 9, 1969
Epoch, vol. XVIII, no. 1, fall 1968
The Minnesota Review, vol. VIII, no. 4, 1968
The Galley Sail Review, no. 20, 1968

Wordjock, no. 4, 1968
Cardinal Poetry Quarterly, vol. iii, no. 7, 1968
The Goodly Co, no. 13, 1968
Beloit Poetry Journal, vol. 19, no. 1, 1968
Poetry Northwest, vol. vii, no. 3, fall–winter 1967
Arts in Society, vol. IV, no. iii, fall–winter 1967
The Eventorium Muse, no. 5, 1967
Approach, no. 62, 1967
Beloit Poetry Journal, vol. 17, no. 2, winter 1966–67
The Laurel Review, vol. vi, nos. 1 and 2, spring 1966, fall 1966

poetry published in foreign-language journals:
"Children Love Color" (from *The Positions of the Sun*), in French, tr. by Martin Richet, in online journal *Jongler* 2, forthcoming 2015
Selections from *The Fatalist*, in French, tr. by Martin Richet, in online journal *Jongler* 1, 2015

essays published in literary and scholarly journals:
"A Small Theory," *FPC* (*Formes Poetiques Contemporaines*) 9, Vincent Broqua and Jean-Jacques Poucel, eds. (Presses Universitaires du Nouveau Monde, 2012)
"The Maddening of Connections," *Armed Cell* 3 (spring 2012)
"Wild Captioning," in *Qui Parle*, vol. 20, no. 1 (fall/winter 2011)
"The Dream Department," in *English Language Notes* 47.1, special issue on "Experimental Literary Education," spring/summer 2009
"Ko govori" (Who Is Speaking?), in *Pro Femina* 46–50, Belgrade, 2009 (in Serbian)
"The Function of Criticism" (collaboratively written with 11 graduate students), in *Rooms Outlast Us* 1, spring 2009
Interview in *Zoland Poetry: An Annual of Poems, Translations & Interviews*, spring 2007
Interview in *Cal Literary Arts Magazine*, spring 2007
"Cyan," in *Cabinet* 20, January 2006
"Continuing Against Closure," in *Salt: An International Journal of Poetry and Poetics*, v. 14 (published in Australia, UK, and U.S., 2003)
"Figuring Out: 'continual conceptual rebellion' in the writings of Leslie Scalapino and in Werner Herzog's "Kaspar Hauser," in *Kiosk* 1 (2002)
"Reason," in *Shark* 1, 1998, Emilie Clark and Lytle Shaw, eds.
"La Faustienne," in *Poetics Journal* 10, 1998
"Interview" (with Leslie Scalapino and Laura Hinton), in *Private Arts* 10, spring 1996
"a mouthful of lawn," *Freemantle Arts Review*, vol. 10, no. 1 (Perth, Western Australia), August–September 1995

"Note" in *Sojourner*, vol. 19, no. 6 (February 1994)

Interview with Alison Georgeson, *Southern Review* (Australia), vol. 27, no. 3, September 1994

"The Person and Description," *Poetics Journal* 9, 1991

Interview by Tyrus Miller, *Paper Air*, vol. 4, no. 2, 1989

Poetics Journal 8, "Strangeness," 1989

Revista Canaria de Estudos Ingleses 18, "Strangeness" and "Two Stein Talks," April 1989

"Aesthetic Tendency and the Politics of Poetry," in *Social Text* 19/20, fall 1988 (with Barrett Watten, Carla Harryman, Bob Perelman, Steve Benson, Ron Silliman)

Interview by Andrew Schelling, *Jimmy's and Lucy's House of K* 6, May 1986

"Two Talks on Gertrude Stein," in *Temblor* 3, spring 1986

"Language & Paradise," in *Line* 6 (Simon Fraser University, Vancouver, BC, Canada), fall 1985

"The Rejection of Closure," in *Poetics Journal* 4, 1984

"An American Opener," in *Poetics Journal* 1, 1982

"If Written is Writing" in *L=A=N=G=U=A=G=E*, 1979

critical writing in journals and anthologies in other languages:

"Materials" ("Materialni"), translated by E. Suslovoy; *Translit 13: Shkola Yazika* (Saint Petersburg, Russia, 2013)

ProFemina 46–50, "Ko Govori" ("Who Is Speaking?") (Belgrade, Serbia, 2008)

"The Rejection of Closure," in *Gradina* 2–3, 1991 (Nish, Yugoslavia; in Serbian)

Artes 2, 1990, "Strangeness" (in Swedish)

Stilistika i Poetika (in Russian), selections from "Strangeness," Moscow State Institute of Foreign Languages, 1989

Delo, vol. 35, no. 8, "Introduction for *Change*" (Belgrade, Yugoslavia, 1989)

journal publication of translations by LH from other languages (partial list):

(Except where noted, all translations are from Russian.)

Lingo, spring/summer 1993

Grand Street 40, 1992

Pequod 31, 1991

screens and tasted parallels 2, 1991

Bastard Review 3/4, summer 1990

Five Fingers Review 8/9, 1990

Paper Air, vol. 4, no. 2, 1989

Michigan Quarterly Review, vol. xxviii, no. 4, fall 1989

Zyzzyva, 1988

Everyday Life 2, fall 1988

Avec 1, fall 1988

New American Writing 4, fall 1988
Sulfur 19, summer 1987
Ironwood 30, winter 1987
Bomb, fall 1986
Sulfur 14, 1985
Poetics Journal 4, 1984, essay from French

exhibition catalogues:

Away at Home, curator's introduction to exhibition catalogue of new works by German photographer Heike Liss (CUE Art Foundation, spring 2006)

contributions to CDs:

Text for "Poetry and Playing," CD by British avant-garde guitarist Derek Bailey (2003)

work in other media:

Two mixed media drawings, in "Poetry and its Arts: Bay Area Interactions 1954–2004," group exhibition at the California Historical Society (San Francisco), curated by The Poetry Center (SF State University), on exhibit December 2004–April 2005

Two mixed media drawings, in "Poetry Plastique," group exhibition, Marianne Boesky Gallery (New York), February 2001

"The Traveler and the Hill and the Hill," two-person exhibition, Museo Nazionale dell' Architettura, Ferrara (Italy), May–June, 2000

"Letters Not About Love," feature film directed by Jacki Ochs with script based on correspondence between Lyn Hejinian and Arkadii Dragomoshchenko (premier, South by Southwest Film Festival, First Prize Documentary, 1998)

"Que Tran," music and poetry (a collaboration with John Zorn); on CD (*New Traditions in Far East Asian Bar Band Music*), Electra/Nonesuch 1997

"The Eye of Enduring," painting and poetry (a collaboration with Diane Andrews Hall); exhibition at Sherrill Haines Gallery, San Francisco, 1995

Tuumba Press:
A Bibliography

1 Lyn Hejinian, *A Thought Is the Bride of What Thinking* (August 1976)

2 Susan Howe, *The Western Borders* (September 1976)

3 Jeremy Lipp, *Sections from Defiled by Water* (October 1976)

4 Kenneth Irby, *Archipelago* (November 1976)

5 Dick Higgins, *Cat Alley* (December 1976)

6 Kathleen Fraser, *Magritte Series* (January 1977)

7 Barry Eisenberg, *Bones' Fire* (February 1977)

8 T.R. Uthco, *Beyond the Edge* (March 1977)

9 David Wilk, *For You/For Sure* (April 1977)

10 John Woodall, *Recipe* (May 1977)

11 Barbara Baracks, *No Sleep* (September 1977)

12 Clayton Eshleman, *The Gospel of Celine Arnauld* (November 1977)

13 Paul Kahn, *January* (January 1978)

14 Richard Kostelanetz, *Foreshortenings and Other Stories* (March 1978)

15 Lyn Hejinian, *Gesualdo* (May 1978)

16 Tom Mandel, *EncY* (July 1978)

17 Ron Silliman, *Sitting Up, Standing, Taking Steps* (September 1978)

18 Bruce Andrews, *Praxis* (November 1978)

19 Bob Perelman, *a.k.a.* (January 1979)

20 Charles Bernstein, *Senses of Responsibility* (March 1979)

21 Barrett Watten, *Plasma / Paralleles / "X"* (May 1979)

22 Rae Armantrout, *The Invention of Hunger* (July 1979)

23 Carla Harryman, *Percentage* (September 1979)

24 Ray DiPalma, *Observatory Gardens* (November 1979)

25 Larry Eigner, *Flat and Round* (January 1980)

26 Kit Robinson, *Tribute to Nervous* (March 1980)

27 Robert Grenier, *Oakland* (May 1980)

28 Alice Notley, *Doctor Williams' Heiresses* (July 1980)

29 Curtis Faville, *Wittgenstein's Door* (September 1980)

30 Michael Palmer, *Alogon* (November 1980)

31 Ted Greenwald, *Smile* (January 1981)

32 Steve Benson, *The Busses* (March 1981)

33 Alan Bernheimer, *State Lounge* (May 1981)

34 David Bromige, *P-E-A-C-E* (July 1981)
35 John Mason, *Fade to Prompt* (September 1981)
36 Stephen Rodefer, *Plane Debris* (November 1981)
37 P. Inman, *Ocker* (January 1982)
38 Barrett Watten, *Complete Thought* (March 1982)
39 Carla Harryman, *Property* (May 1982)
40 Clark Coolidge, *Research* (July 1982)
41 Kit Robinson, *Riddle Road* (September 1982)
42 Larry Price, *Proof* (November 1982)
43 Jean Day, *Linear C* (January 1983)
44 Lynne Dreyer, *Step Work* (March 1983)
45 Peter Seaton, *Crisis Intervention* (June 1983)
46 Ron Silliman, *ABC* (October 1983)
47 David Melnick, *Men in Aida* (December 1983)
48 Fanny Howe, *For Erato: The Meaning of Life* (April 1984)
49 Bob Perelman, *To the Reader* (June 1984)
50 Lyn Hejinian, *The Guard* (September 1984)

Anne Tardos, *Uxudo* (a joint publication of Tuumba Press and O Books; 1999)
Leslie Scalapino writing as Dee Goda, *Orchid Jetsam* (2001)
Jack Collom, *Red Car Goes By: Selected Poems 1955–2000* (2001)
Lyn Hejinian, *Slowly* (2002)
Lyn Hejinian, *The Beginner* (2002)
Jalal Toufic, *Distracted* (2003)
Nathaniel Dorsky, *Devotional Cinema* (2003, 2005)
Bill Berkson and Bernadette Mayer, *What's Your Idea of a Good Time?* (2006)

The Atelos Publishing Project: A Bibliogrpahy

ed. Lyn Hejinian and Travis Ortiz, founded 1995

1 Jean Day, *The Literal World*
    ISBN 1891190-01-6
2 Barrett Watten, *Bad History*
    ISBN 978-1891190025
3. Rae Armantrout, *True*
    ISBN 1891190-03-2
4. Pamela Lu, *Pamela: A Novel*
    ISBN 1891190-04-0
5. Lytle Shaw, *Cable Factory 20*
    ISBN 1891190-05-9
6. Leslie Scalapino, *R-hu*
    ISBN 1891190-06-7
7. Hung Q. Tu, *Verisimilitude*
    ISBN 1891190-07-5
8. Clark Coolidge, *Alien Tatters*
    ISBN 1891190-08-3
9. Jalal Toufic, *Forthcoming*
    ISBN 1891190-09-1
10. Carla Harryman, *Gardener of Stars*
    ISBN 1-891190-10-5
11. M. Mara-Ann, *Lighthouse*
    ISBN 1-891190-11-3
12. Kathy Lou Schultz, *Some Vague Wife*
    ISBN 1-891190-12-1
13. Kit Robinson, *The Crave*
    ISBN 1-891190-13-X
14. Brian Kim Stefans, *Fashionable Noise*
    ISBN 978-1-891190-14-8
15. Rodrigo Toscano, *Platform*
    ISBN 1-891190-15-6
16. Fanny Howe, *Tis of Thee*
    ISBN 1-891190-16-4

17. Lohren Green, *Poetical Dictionary*
    ISBN 1-891190-17-2
18. Tan Lin, *Blipsoak01*
    ISBN 1-891190-18-0
19. Ted Greenwald, *The Up and Up*
    ISBN 1-891190-19-9
20. Murray Edmond, *Noh Business*
    ISBN 1-891190-20-2
21. Steve Benson, *Open Clothes*
    ISBN 1-891190-21-0
22. Taylor Brady, *Occupational Treatment*
    ISBN 1-891190-22-9
23. Ed Roberson, *City Eclogue*
    ISBN 1-891190-23-7
24. Laura Moriarty, *Ultravioleta*
    ISBN 1-891190-24-5
25. Jocelyn Saidenberg, *Negativity*
    ISBN 1-891190-25-3
26. Juliana Spahr, *The Transformation*
    ISBN 1-891190-26-1
27. Tom Mandel, *To the Cognoscenti*
    ISBN 1-891190-27-X
28. Craig Dworkin, *Parse*
    ISBN 978-1-891190-28-8
29. Edwin Torres, *The PoPedology of an Ambient Language*
    ISBN 978-1-891190-29-2
30. Patrick Durgin and Jen Hofer, *The Route*
    ISBN 978-1-891190-30-8
31. Renee Gladman, *To After That (TOAF)*
    ISBN 978-1-891190-31-5
32. Erik J.M. Schneider, *Last Ditch*
    ISBN 978-1-891190-32-2
33. Tyrone Williams, *Howell*
    ISBN 978-1-891190-33-9
34. Mikhail Epstein, *PreDictionary*
    ISBN 978-1-891190-34-6
35. Brent Cunningham, *Journey to the Sun*
    ISBN 978-1-891190-35-3

Acknowledgments

"Rules and Restraints in Women's Experimental Writing" by Carla Harryman originally appeared in *We Who Love to Be Astonished*, ed. Laura Hinton and Cynthia Hogue (Tuscaloosa, University of Alabama Press, 2002).

"from The Book of a Thousand Eyes" by Lyn Hejinian is excerpted from *The Book of a Thousand Eyes* (Richmond, California: Omnidawn Publishing, 2012).

"On Solitude and Writing: A Memoir of Working with Lyn Hejinian" by Katy Lederer appeared in *Women Poets on Mentorship: Efforts and Affectations* ed, Arielle Greenberg and Rachel Zucker (Iowa City: University of Iowa Press, 2008).

"Numerousness and Its Discontents: George Oppen and Lyn Hejinian" by Peter Nicholls was first published in *Humanities Review*, 9.1 (Spring 2011).

"Face/" by Lisa Robertson appeared in a slightly different form in *R's Boat* (Berekely: University of California Press, 2010).

"Thinking and Being/Conversion in the Language of *Happily* & *A Border Comedy*" by Leslie Scalapino was first published in *How Phenomena Appear to Unfold* (Brooklyn: Litmus Press, 2011).

"Something I'm Dying to Tell You, Lyn" by Jalal Toufic originally appeared in *Two or Three Things I'm Dying to Tell You* (Sausalito, CA: The Post-Apollo Press, 2005).

"A Form of Lingering" by Rosmarie Waldrop appeared in *Splitting Image* (Tenerife: Zasterle, 2005).

"Between bibetgekess and 'but …': Lyn Hejinian's *The Book of a Thousand Eyes*" by Tim Wood originally appeared online at *Jacket 2*.

Contributors

Rae Armantrout's latest collection, *Itself,* was published by Wesleyan in February, 2015. Her book *Versed* won the Pulitzer Prize for Poetry in 2010. Her work has appeared in many anthologies, including *Postmodern America Poetry: A Norton Anthology* (2013), *The Best of the Best American Poetry* (2013), and *The Open Door: 100 Poems, 100 Years of Poetry Magazine* (2012). She is professor emeritus at UC San Diego.

Carla Billitteri teaches poetry, poetics, and critical theory at the University of Maine at Orono, where she is also a member of the editorial collective of The National Poetry Foundation. She is the author of the critical study *Language and the Renewal of Society in Walt Whitman, Laura (Riding) Jackson, and Charles Olson* (Palgrave, 2009) and of numerous essays on English- and Italian-language poetry that have appeared in *Arizona Quarterly, Gravesiana, How2, The Journal of Modern Literature, Paideuma, Textual Practice,* and *The Worcester Review.* She is also active as a translator of contemporary Italian poetry, with work in *The FSG Book of Twentieth-Century Italian Poetry, Aufgabe, Boundary2, How2, Fascicle,* and the *Atlanta Review.* An edition of her translations from Alda Merini's aphorisms (*i am a furious little bee*) was published by Hooke Press in 2008. Her translation of Maria Attanasio's poetry (*Amnesia of the Movement of the Clouds* & *Of Red and Black Verse*) was published by Litmus Press in 2014.

Jack Collom is a poet, essayist, and creative writing pedagogue. His most recent collection of poems, *Second Nature* (Instance Press, 2012), was awarded the 2013 Colorado Book Award for Poetry. His major collection, *Red Car Goes By: Selected Poems 1955–2000,* was published by Tuumba Press in 2001. Other volumes include *Cold Instant, Little Grand Island, Arguing with Something Plato Said, 8-Ball,* and *Entering the City.* His work has been published in countless magazines and anthologies in the United States and abroad. His essays on teaching and anthologies of children's poetry appear in *Moving Windows* and *Poetry Everywhere.* He has produced two CDs of original work performed in collaboration with musician/composer Ken Bernstein and been awarded two NEA fellowships. He received his M.A. in English from the University of Colorado and teaches courses in eco-literature and outreach teacher-training.

Jean Day has published seven books of poetry, including *Enthusiasm: Odes & Otium* (Adventures in Poetry) and the chapbook *Daydream (The Eponym)* (Belladonna). Recent poems from her current project, *Late Human*, appear in *Sal Mimeo, Dreamboat, The Claudius App*, and a chapbook from O'Clock Press called *Early Bird*.

Patrick Durgin is the author of *PQRS* and, with Jen Hofer, *The Route*. Other critical essays appear in *Contemporary Women's Writing, Jacket2, Journal of Modern Literature, Postmodern Culture*, and elsewhere. He also edited *Hannah Weiner's Open House* and *The Early and Clairvoyant Journals of Hannah Weiner*. As of summer 2013, he is writing a book-length essay that consists of a pirate audio tour of encyclopedic art museums, which ought to be accessible to those with the proper GPS coordinates, i.e., as a virtual stack of leaflets retrieved on the street outside the gallery.

Kate Fagan is a poet, editor, and musician who lectures in Literary Studies at the University of Western Sydney. Her latest book, *First Light* (Giramondo 2012), was shortlisted for both the NSW Premier's Awards for Poetry and the Age Book of the Year Award. She is a former editor of *How2* journal and a well-known songwriter whose album *Diamond Wheel* won the National Film and Sound Archive Award for Best Folk Album. Her doctoral thesis was called "'Constantly I Write This Happily' / Encountering Lyn Hejinian."

Carla Harryman is the author of seventeen books, including *W—/M—* (2013), *Adorno's Noise* (2008), *Gardener of Stars* (2001), and *Animal Instincts: Prose, Plays, Essays* (1989). Her collaborative works include the multi-authored work *The Grand Piano: An Experiment in Autobiography: San Francisco, 1975–1980* and *The Wide Road* (with Lyn Hejinian). *Open Box* (with Jon Raskin), a CD of music and text performances, was released on the Tzadik label in 2012. Her Poets Theater, interdisciplinary, and bi-lingual performances have been presented nationally and internationally. She is the editor of two critical volumes: *Non/Narrative*, a special issue of the *Journal of Narrative Theory*, and *Lust for Life: On the Writings of Kathy Acker* (with Avital Ronell and Amy Shoulder). She serves on the faculty of the Department of English Language and Literature at Eastern Michigan University.

Lyn Hejinian is a poet, essayist, teacher, and translator. Her most recent published book of poetry is her compendium of "night works" titled *The Book of a Thousand Eyes* (Omnidawn, 2012). Other books include *Saga/Circus*

(Omnidawn, 2008), *A Border Comedy* (Granary Books, 2001), *Slowly* and *The Beginner* (both published by Tuumba Press, 2002), and *The Fatalist* (Omnidawn, 2003). The University of California Press published a collection of her essays entitled *The Language of Inquiry* in 2000. Hejinian is also actively involved in collaboratively created works, the most recent examples of which include a major collection of poems by Hejinian and Jack Collom titled *Situations, Sings* (Adventures in Poetry, 2008) and the erotic picaresque novella *The Wide Road* (Belladonna, 2011) that Hejinian co-authored with Carla Harryman. Other collaborative projects include *The Eye of Enduring*, undertaken with the painter Diane Andrews Hall and exhibited in 1996; a composition entitled *Quê Trân*, with music by John Zorn and text by Hejinian; two mixed media books (*The Traveler and the Hill and the Hill* and *The Lake*) created with the painter Emilie Clark; the award-winning experimental documentary film *Letters Not About Love*, directed by Jacki Ochs; and *The Grand Piano: An Experiment in Collective Autobiography*, co-written with nine other poets. Translations of her work have been published in Denmark, France, Spain, Japan, Italy, Russia, Sweden, China, Serbia, Holland, and Finland. She is the recipient of a Writing Fellowship from the California Arts Council, a grant from the Poetry Fund, and a Translation Fellowship (for her Russian translations) from the National Endowment for the Arts; she received an Award for Independent Literature from the Soviet literary organization "Poetic Function" in Leningrad in 1989. She has traveled and lectured extensively in Russia, as well as Europe, and *Description* (1990) and *Xenia* (1994), two volumes of her translations from the work of the late Russian poet Arkadii Dragomoshchenko, were published by Sun and Moon Press. Since 1976, Hejinian has been the editor of Tuumba Press, and, from 1981 to 1998, she was the co-editor (with Barrett Watten) of *Poetics Journal*. She is also the co-director (with Travis Ortiz) of Atelos, a literary project commissioning and publishing cross-genre work by poets. She teaches in the English Department at the University of California, Berkeley, and is a founding member of the UC-Berkeley Solidarity Alliance, an activist coalition of union representatives, workers, staff, students, and faculty against the privatization of the University of California.

Jen Hofer is a Los Angeles–based poet, translator, social justice interpreter, teacher, knitter, book-maker, public letter-writer, urban cyclist, and co-founder with John Pluecker of the language justice and literary experimentation collaborative Antena (www.antenaantena.org) and the local language justice advocacy group Antena Los Ángeles (www.antenalosangeles.org). Her essays, translations, and poetry are available from numerous small presses, including Action Books, Atelos, belladonna, Counterpath Press, Kenning Editions, Insert Press,

Les Figues Press, Litmus Press, LRL Textile Editions, NewLights Press, Palm Press, Subpress, Ugly Duckling Presse, and in various DIY/DIT incarnations. Her visual-textual work can be found online at *Alligatorzine*, *Public Access*, and *Spiral Orb*, and in Exhibit Hall 1 at the Center for Land Use Interpretation's Wendover site. She teaches poetics, translation, and bookmaking at CalArts and at Otis College.

Kevin Killian is a novelist, poet, editor, playwright, critic, and art writer based in San Francisco. His most recent books are *Spreadeagle*, a novel; an artist's book with his poems and collages by Swiss-born, NYC-based sculptor Ugo Rondinone; and *Tagged*, a collection of Killian's intimate portraits of poets, artists, musicians, and filmmakers, naked, or nearly so, edited by Darin Klein and with an introduction by Rob Halpern. His next book will be *Wet Paint*, a dramatic pageant on the life of artist Jay DeFeo, from Barry Schwabsky's Lost Soul Editions.

Katy Lederer is the author of the poetry collections *Winter Sex* (Verse Press, 2002) and *The Heaven-Sent Leaf* (BOA Editions, 2008), as well as the memoir *Poker Face: A Girlhood Among Gamblers* (Crown, 2003). She serves as a Poetry Editor of Fence Magazine and is on the advisory boards of Fence Magazine/ Fence Books, The Poetry Project at St. Mark's Church, and the Millay Colony for the Arts. She lives in Brooklyn, New York.

Pamela Lu is the author of the books *Ambient Parking Lot* (Kenning Editions, 2011) and *Pamela: A Novel* (Atelos, 1999), as well as the chapbook *The Private Listener* (Corollary Press, 2006). Her writing also appears in the anthologies *Bay Poetics* and *Biting the Error* and has been published in periodicals such as *1913*, *Antennae*, *Call*, *Chain*, *Chicago Review*, *Fascicle*, *Harper's*, *Mirage*, *Poetics Journal*, and *Tinfish*. She grew up in Southern California and now lives and works in the San Francisco Bay Area.

Laura Moriarty was born in St. Paul, Minnesota, and grew up in Cape Cod, Massachusetts, Sacto, California, and other places. She is an Aries with Virgo rising and a Libra moon. Her most recent books are *The Fugitive Notebook* (Couch Press, 2014), *Who That Divines* (Nightboat Books, 2014), *A Tonalist* (Nightboat Books, 2010), *A Semblance: Selected and New Poems, 1975–2007* (Omnidawn, 2007), and the novel *Ultravioleta* (Atelos, 2006). She is Deputy Director of Small Press Distribution and is attending (and, when possible, helping out at) the Bay Area Public School at the Omni Commons.

Peter Nicholls is Henry James Professor and Professor of English at New York University. His publications include *Ezra Pound: Politics, Economics and Writing*, *Modernisms: A Literary Guide, George Oppen and the Fate of Modernism*, and many articles and essays on literature and theory. He has recently edited *On Bathos* with Sara Crangle and is currently U.S. associate editor of *Textual Practice*.

Tom Raworth was born in London in 1938. Since 1966, he has published more than forty books and pamphlets of poetry, prose, and translations. His graphic work has been shown in Europe, the United States, and South Africa, and he has given readings of his poems worldwide: most recently in China and Mexico. His most recent books are *As When: A Selection*, edited by Miles Champion (Carcanet, 2015), *Structure from Motion* (Edge Books, 2015), and *XIV Liners* (Sancho Panza Press, 2014). In 2007, in Italy, he was awarded the Antonio Delfini Prize for Lifetime Achievement—although he is not yet dead, but living in Brighton.

Lisa Robertson's most recent book is *Cinema of the Present* (Coach House, 2014). *Lisa Robertson's Magenta Soul Whip* was named one of *The New York Times* 100 Notable Books of 2010. Her other books include *Debbie: An Epic*, *The Men, The Weather, Occasional Work and Seven Walks from the Office for Soft Architecture, Nilling*, and *R's Boat*. Born in Toronto, she lived in Vancouver for many years and has held residencies and visiting positions at Cambridge University, Princeton University, UC Berkeley, American University of Paris, and the California College of the Arts. She now lives in France and works as a tutor at Piet Zwart Institute in Rotterdam and as a freelance art writer.

Kit Robinson is the author of *Determination* (Cuneiform, 2010), *The Messianic Trees: Selected Poems, 1976–2003* (Adventures in Poetry, 2009), and twenty other books of poetry. He has written two books in collaboration with Ted Greenwald, *A Mammal of Style* (Roof, 2013) and *Takeaway* (c_L, 2013), and is a co-author of *The Grand Piano: An Experiment in Collective Autobiography: San Francisco, 1975–1980* (Mode A, 2006–2010). Robinson lives in the Bay Area, works as a freelance writer, and plays *tres* guitar in the Afro-Cuban dance band Bahía Son.

Leslie Scalapino (1944–2010) is the author of thirty books of poetry, prose, inter-genre fiction, plays, and essays. She taught writing for nearly twenty-five years at various institutions around the country and was the publisher of O Books, which she founded in 1986. Her expanded and revised essay collection *How Phenomena Appear to Unfold* appeared from Litmus Press in 2011. *The*

Dihedrons Gazelle-Dihedrals Zoom (The Post-Apollo Press), *Flow—Winged Crocodile & A Pair / Actions Are Erased/Appear* (Chax Press), *The Animal is in the World Like Water in Water* (Granary Books), and *Floats Horse-Floats or Horse Flows* (Starcherone Books) were all released in 2010.

Gerhard Schultz was born in Birch Run, Michigan, in 1982. He studied composition at the University of Michigan and holds an M.F.A. in Experimental Sound Practices from CalArts. As a research scholar at the University of Art in Berlin (UdK), he founded the label Care Of Editions, which develops innovative distribution models for releasing music and installations. His own music is released under the Juniper Foam moniker. He lives and works in Berlin.

Ron Silliman has written and edited over thirty books and has had his poetry and criticism translated into twelve languages. He has worked as a political activist, editor, and market analyst. Among his honors, Silliman was a 2012 Kelly Writers House Fellow at the University of Pennsylvania and the 2010 recipient of the Levinson Prize from the Poetry Foundation. His sculpture poetry (*Bury Neon*) is permanently on display in the transit centre of Bury, Lancashire, and he has a plaque in the walk dedicated to poetry in his home town of Berkeley, although he now lives in Chester County, Pennsylvania.

Rod Smith's most recent book is *Touché* (Wave, 2015). He is also the author of *What's the Deal* (Song Cave), *Deed* (U. Iowa), *The Good House* (Spectacular Books), *Protective Immediacy* (Roof), and several others. Smith edits the journal *Aerial*, publishes Edge Books, and manages Bridge Street Books in Washington, D.C. He edited the *Selected Letters of Robert Creeley* with Peter Baker and Kaplan Harris. Smith has taught creative writing and cultural theory at the Corcoran College of Art + Design, George Mason University, the Iowa Writers' Workshop, and Towson University. He currently teaches at the Maryland Institute College of Art in Baltimore.

Anne Tardos is a poet, visual artist, and composer. She is the author of several books of poetry and multimedia performance works, including her 1992 composition *Among Men*. Her recent books include *The Dik-dik's Solitude* (Granary Books, 2003), *I Am You* (Salt Publishing, 2008), and *Both Poems* (Roof, 2011). She is also the editor of Jackson Mac Low's *Thing of Beauty* (University of California Press, 2008), and *154 Forties* (Counterpath Press, 2012). Tardos was a 2009 Fellow in Poetry from the New York Foundation for the Arts. Tardos lives in New York with her husband, Michael Byron.

Jalal Toufic is a thinker and a mortal to death. He was born in 1962 in Beirut or Baghdad and died before dying in 1989 in Evanston, Illinois. Many of his books, most of which were published by Forthcoming Books, are available for download as PDF files at his website: http://www.jalaltoufic.com. He was most recently a participant in the Sharjah Biennial 11, the 9th Shanghai Biennale, Documenta 13, Art in the Auditorium III (Whitechapel Gallery …), Six Lines of Flight (San Francisco Museum of Modern Art), and Meeting Points 6 (Beirut Art Center and Argos). In 2011, he was a guest of the Artists-in-Berlin Program of the DAAD.

Rosmarie Waldrop was born in Germany and has lived in the United States since 1958. The author and translator of dozens of books of poetry, fiction, and criticism, she is the co-founder and co-publisher of Burning Deck Press. Waldrop's many honors include being named a Chevalier des Arts et des Lettres, fellowships from the NEA and the Fund for Poetry, and the Lila Wallace–Reader's Digest Writers' Award. In 2006, she was elected to the American Academy of Arts and Sciences.

Barrett Watten teaches at Wayne State University in Detroit. His major collections include *Frame, Progress/Under Erasure, Bad History, The Constructivist Moment: From Material Text to Cultural Poetics*, and the ten-volume collaboration with ten authors including Hejinian, *The Grand Piano: An Experiment in Collective Autobiography*. Hejinian and Watten edited *Poetics Journal*, as well as the recent Wesleyan University Press volume *A Guide to Poetics Journal: Writing in the Expanded Field, 1982–1998*.

Tim Wood is the author of the book of poems *Otherwise Known as Home* (BlazeVOX, 2010) and co-editor of *The Hip Hop Reader* (Longman, 2008). His critical work can be found at *ActionYes.org* and *Jacket2.org*, as well as in *Convolution* and *Leviathan*; his poetry reviews can be found at the *Colorado Review, The Iowa Review*, and the *Boston Review*. He has recently been a visiting Fulbright scholar at the University of Tübingen in Germany and is currently an associate professor of English at SUNY Nassau Community College in Garden City, New York.

EDGE BOOKS

AERIAL MAGAZINE

(EDITED BY ROD SMITH)

Literature published by Aerial/Edge is available through Small Press Distribution (www.spdbooks. org; 1-800-869-7553; orders@spdbooks.org) or from the publisher at P.O. Box 25642, Georgetown Station, Washington, D.C. 20027. When ordering from Aerial/Edge directly, add $2.00 postage for individual titles. Two or more titles postpaid. For more information or to order online, please visit our Web site at www.aerialedge.com.